International Environmental Law and Policy Series

Negotiating International Regimes: Lessons Learned from the United Nations Conference on Environment and Development (UNCED)

Series General Editor

Stanley P. Johnson

Advisory Editor

Günther Handl

Other titles in the series

The Environment Policy of the European Communities, S.P. Johnson and G. Corcelle
(ISBN 1–85333–225–9)
Transferring Hazardous Technologies and Substances, G. Handl and R.E. Lutz
(ISBN 0–86010–704–3)
Understanding US and European Environmental Law: A Practitioner's Guide, T.T. Smith and P. Kromarek
(ISBN 1–85333–305–0)
Air Pollution Control in the European Community: Implementation of the EC Directives in the Twelve Member States, G. Bennett (ed.)
(ISBN 1–85333–567–3)
International Responsibility for Environmental Harm, F. Francioni and T. Scovazzi (eds.)
(ISBN 1–85333–579–7)
International Law and Global Climate Change, R. Churchill and D. Freestone (eds.)
(ISBN 1–85333–629–7)
Environment Protection and International Law, W. Lang, H. Neuhold and K. Zemanek (eds.)
(ISBN 1–85333–225–9)
The Environment Policy of the European Communities, S.P. Johnson and G. Corcelle
(ISBN 1–85333–611–4)
International Legal Problems of the Environmental Protection of the Baltic Sea, M. Fitzmaurice
(ISBN 0–7923–1402–6)
The Antarctic Environment and International Law, J. Verhoeven, P. Sands, M. Bruce (eds.)
(ISBN 1–85333–630–0)
Basic Documents of International Environmental Law, H. Hohnmann (ed.)
(ISBN 1–85333–628–9)
The Earth Summit: The United Nations Conference on Environment and Development (UNCED), S.P. Johnson
(ISBN 1–85333–784–6)
Environment Pollution Control: An Introduction to Principles and Practice of Administration, J. McLoughlin, E.G. Bellinger
(ISBN 1–85333–577–0)
Amazonia and Siberia: Legal Aspects of the Preservation of the Environment and Development in the Last Open Spacers, M. Bothe, T. Kurzidem and C. Schmidt (eds.)
(ISBN 1–85333–903–2)
Civil Liability for Transfrontier Pollution, G. Betlem (ISBN 1–85333–951–2)
Pollution Insurance: International Survey of Coverages and Exclusions, W. Pfennigstorf (ed.)
(ISBN 1–85333–941–5)
The Environment after Rio: International Law and Economics, L. Campiglio, L. Pineschi, D. Siniscalco, T. Treves (eds.) (ISBN 1–85333–949–0)
European Environmental Law, J.R. Salter (ISBN 1–85966–050–9, Looseleaf)
Environmental Liability and Privatization in Central and Eastern Europe, G. Goldenman *et al.* (eds.) (ISBN 1–85966–094–0)

(order by ISBN or title)

International Environmental Law and Policy Series

Negotiating International Regimes: Lessons Learned from the United Nations Conference on Environment and Development (UNCED)

Edited by

Bertram I. Spector, Gunnar Sjöstedt
and I. William Zartman

A Publication of the
Processes of International Negotiation (PIN) Project
International Institute for Applied Systems Analysis
Laxenburg, Austria

Graham & Trotman / Martinus Nijhoff
Members of the Kluwer Academic Publishers Group
LONDON/DORDRECHT/BOSTON

Graham & Trotman Limited
Sterling House
66 Wilton Road
London SW1V 1DB
UK

Kluwer Academic Publishing Group
101 Phillip Drive
Assinippi Park
Norwell, MA 02061
USA

First published 1994

British Library Cataloguing in Publication Data

A catalogue record for this book is available from the British Library

ISBN 1–85966–077–0
Series ISBN 1–85333–275–5

Library of Congress Cataloging-in-Publication Data

Negotiating international regimes: lessons learned from the United Nations Conference on Environment and Development (UNCED)/Bertram I. Spector, Gunnar Sjöstedt and I. William Zartman, editors.
p. cm. – (International environmental law and policy series)
"A publication of the Processes of International Negotiation (PIN) Project, International Institute for Applied Systems Analysis, Laxenburg, Austria."
Includes index.
ISBN 1–85966–077–0
1. Environmental policy – International cooperation. 2. Environmental protection – International cooperation. 3. Economic development – Environmental aspects. 4. United Nations Conference on Environment and Development (1992: Rio de Janeiro, Brazil) I. Spector, Bertram I. (Bertram Irwin), 1949– II. Sjöstedt, Gunnar. III. Zartman, I. William. IV. Processes of International Negotiation Project. V. United Nations Conference on Environment and Development (1992: Rio de Janeiro, Brazil) VI. Series.
GE170.N44 1994 94–8974
363.7′0526–dc20 CIP

Typeset in 10/11 pt Times by EXPO Holdings, Malaysia
Printed and bound in Great Britain by Hartnolls Ltd, Bodnin, Cornwall

Contents

Preface

What is special about the outcome of the United Nations Conference on Environment and Development (UNCED) is that it was not an outcome at all, but the beginning of a new process. Scholars of negotiation usually conceive of the outcome of negotiation as an agreement, a solution, a formula that is acceptable to all and resolves the initiating problem in some way. The outcome is a singular and conclusive achievement of a successful process; it is, as implied by the term, the finale of the process of joint problem solving and decision making.

UNCED was targeted at – and, in fact, realized – a different type of conclusion. Its outcome was a process that will continue on as a dynamic construct that frames and governs future discussions, debates, and negotiations on the many aspects of sustainable development, a constellation of issues recognized as critical for the economic and environmental well-being of humanity. That process we call an international regime, and it embodies the norms, principles, rules, and procedures by which negotiation on sustainable development will continue. The Rio Declaration and Agenda 21, two of the major documents generated by UNCED, are testaments to the sustained nature of the regime they help to form.

Are negotiations to build regimes different from negotiations that have a fixed endpoint? Does this process of negotiation have special characteristics and respond differently to internal and external stimuli? Certainly, a regime-building negotiation can, by its very nature, operate with a significantly elevated level of ambiguity; partial agreements or broad formulas without the necessary details are acceptable outcomes because additional negotiations to iron out these deficiencies are already programmed. As well, regime-building negotiations require the parties to be futurists. They must be prepared to take some giant leaps of faith concerning how the problem area might evolve, how the problem can be framed to account for obvious and nonobvious policy linkages, and how the international community is likely to want to address these issues beyond the lifetime of the personalities participating in the current negotiations. Such negotiations require foresight, creativity, and flexibility by the participants; the formulas that are concluded must contain these same traits. Many other attributes distinguish regime-building negotiations; they are the subject of this book.

Outwardly, the process of UNCED did not appear that unusual. The Preparatory Committee (PrepCom) meetings often consisted of the standard fare of general national position statements, rhetoric addressing the pet issues of each sovereign party to the negotiation, and a minimum of true dialogue and negotiation among the parties. However, our observation of this process made it apparent at the same time that something visionary was occurring: that even if this process was only partially successful, something new and necessary would emerge. We decided to organize a book – starting with our own research on environmental negotiations and the UNCED process, and then involving others who were already studying or involved first-hand in the process – to understand and explain the negotiation process of building international environmental regimes. Although another process exactly like UNCED will probably not happen again for a very long time, UNCED spawned sub-regimes – in desertification, biodiversity, forestry, and other areas – where the lessons learned from the umbrella negotiations could be applied meaningfully. Our goal was to incorporate an assessment of the major building blocks of the UNCED negotiation – the structure, the process, and the participants – and produce an analysis that would be useful from a conceptual perspective, as well as a practical one. The last section of the book seeks to challenge the scholar by distinguishing this type of negotiation from other types, and to challenge the practitioner by offering concrete recommendations for future application.

This manuscript is a project of the Processes of International Negotiation (PIN) Project at the International Institute for Applied Systems Analysis (IIASA) in Laxenburg, Austria. At the time we began this effort, Dr. Spector was the leader of the Project and Drs. Sjöstedt and Zartman were members of the PIN Project Steering Committee.[1] We are appreciative of our many IIASA colleagues with whom we collaborated and shared ideas on the issues and processes of UNCED, in particular Roderick Shaw, Sture Öberg, Paul Weaver, and Gilberto Gallopin. We also thank Peter de Janosi, the director of IIASA, for his generous support of our efforts over the years. We were fortunate to have the dedicated and thoughtful support of Anna Korula, who gathered and analyzed much of the early data on the UNCED process, and Ulli Neudeck, who cared for the administrative functions of the study and put the manuscript into its final form.

Ultimately, we are indebted to all of the diplomats, members of the UNCED secretariat, and representatives of nongovernmental organizations who were extremely helpful, forthright in their views, and willing to spend much time in interviews to explain the process to us. Specifically, we are grateful to Maurice Strong and Nitin Desai for granting us easy access both to the meetings and to their staff during even the most frenetic moments of the negotiations. Our understanding of the process would not have been possible without their openness and support.

Bertram Spector
Gunnar Sjöstedt
I. William Zartman

[1]Other members of the PIN Steering Committee are Guy Olivier Faure, Victor A. Kremenyuk, Winfried Lang, and Jeffrey Z. Rubin.

Contributors

Lance Antrim is a consultant to the Secretariat for the Intergovernmental Negotiating Committee for a Framework Convention on Drought and Desertification (INCD). During the preparations for UNCED, he observed the negotiations as a guest of the Chairman. At the Third United Nations Conference on the Law of the Sea in 1982, Mr. Antrim was a deputy U.S. representative. He has also served as director of the Project on Multilateral Negotiations at the American Academy of Diplomacy.

Oscar A. Avalle is an Argentine career diplomat presently posted to his country's mission to the United Nations in New York where he participates in intergovernmental negotiations concerning economic and environmental issues. He is an Assistant Professor of International Relations at the Catholic University of Argentina and has written several articles about multilateral environmental negotiations.

Sonja Boehmer-Christiansen is a researcher at the Science Policy Research Unit of the Environment Programme at the University of Sussex in Brighton, UK. She was educated in Australia and Germany. Her main field is Economic Policy and Polities with an emphasis on the Role of Science in it. She is the author of *Acid Politics*.

Pamela S. Chasek holds a doctorate from the Paul H. Nitze School of Advanced International Studies of the Johns Hopkins University. Her research has focussed on evaluating the process of international environmental negotiations within the United Nations system. She participated in the United Nations Conference on Environment and Development (UNCED) and its preparatory process where she co-produced the *Earth Summit Bulletin*.

Ann Doherty is currently working for an international nongovernmental organization (NGO). In 1992, she participated in the Young Scientists' Summer Program at the International Institute for Applied Systems Analysis in Laxenburg, Austria where she conducted a study of the dynamics of NGOs within the UNCED negotiation process.

Tommy Thong-Bee Koh is currently the Director of the Institute of Policy Studies at the National University of Singapore, a member of the Faculty of Law there, and Ambassador-at-large for Singapore. He was the President of the Third United Nations Conference on the Law of the Sea, Chairman of the Preparatory Committee of the United Nations Conference on Environment and Development, and Chair of the Main Committee of UNCED in Rio de Janeiro. Ambassador Koh is currently a member of the UN Secretary-General's Advisory Committee on Sustainable Development.

Julia Marton-Lefèvre has been with the International Council of Scientific Unions since 1978, beginning as Assistant Executive Secretary. She has been in the position of Executive Director since 1991. Previously she was Program Specialist with the UNESCO-UNEP Environmental Education Program at UNESCO Headquaters in Paris. She also has taught at the University of Songhkla in Thailand and has been a Research Associate in the Graduate Program of Urban, Social and Environmental Policy at Tufts University in the US. Publications include the co-editing of several books dealing with international science policy and biological sciences; and honorary positions include membership in a number of international boards such as the China Council for International Cooperation on Environment and Development, Earthwatch, Europe and the Centre for Our Common Future.

Hugo Maria Schally a lawyer trained at the University of Graz, Austria and Diplomatic Academy in Vienna. He has been a member of the Austrian Foreign Service since 1987. Since 1991 he has served as a Counsellor at the Permanent Mission of Austria to the United Nations in Geneva, where he is in charge of all matters relating to the environment. He has been closely involved with the preparatory process for UNCED and international negotiations for the conclusion of the Conventions for the Protection of Biological Diversity and Climate Change, both as a member of the Austrian delegations and as a participant in the domestic decision making processes. He continues to be closely involved with a variety of international environmental negotiations such as on the Montreal Protocol on the Control of Substances which Deplete the Ozone Layer, the Basel Convention on the Control of Transboundary Movements of Hazardous Wastes, and negotiations for further substantive protocols with the Geneva Convention on Long Range Transboundary Air Pollution.

Gunnar Sjöstedt is senior research fellow at the Swedish Institute of International Affairs and associate processor of political science at the University of Stockholm. His research work is concerned with processes of international cooperation and consultations in which negotiations represent an important element. He has studied the OECD as a communication system and the external role of the European Community and is currently working on a project dealing with the transformation of the international trade regime incorporated in GATT and its external relations. Among his latest publications are *International Environmental Negotiation* (1993) and *International Environment on Process, Issues and Contexts* (1993).

Bertram I. Spector is the Director of the Center for Negotiation Analysis in Potomac, Maryland (USA) and Fellow of the Foreign Policy Institute of the Johns Hopkins University School of Advanced International Studies. He is currently investigating the post-agreement negotiation process for international environmental issues to uncover ways to improve pre-agreement negotiation mechanisms. He has published several journal articles and book contributions on this and related subjects. He has advised the UNCED secretariat, the UN Economic Commission for Europe, the UN Institute for Training and Research, and the Global Environment Facility on negotiation and decision-making issues. Prior to his current positions, Dr. Spector was the Leader of the Processes of International Negotiation (PIN) Project at the International Institute for Applied Systems Analysis, Laxenburg, Austria.

Lawrence Susskind is Professor and Director of the Environmental Policy Group at the Massachusetts Institute of Technology and Director of the MIT-Harvard Public

Disputes Program. He is also Coordinator of the International Environmental Negotiation Network secretariat and author of *Breaking the Impasse* (1987) and *Environmental Diplomacy* (1993).

Amanda Wolf is a Lecturer in the Public Policy Group, Victoria University of Wellington, New Zealand. She has degrees in Philosophy from Boston College and public management from the University of Maryland and is a candidate for the interdisciplinary Ph.D. in policy studies at the University of Maryland. In recent years, she has analyzed food policy, environmental negotiations, and the Global Environment Facility for the International Food Policy Research Institute and WWF-International. As a summer scholar at the International Institute for Applied Systems Analysis, she investigated issue linkages in the process of UNCED negotiations and the role of fairness in environmental negotiations. Her current research focuses on the interplay of knowledge, bargaining interests, and fairness in international conservation and pollution negotiations.

I. William Zartman is Jacob Blaustein Professor of Conflict Resolution and International Organization at the Nitze School of Advanced International Studies (SAIS) of the Johns Hopkins University. He is author of *The Practical Negotiator* (with M. Berman, 1982) and *Ripe for Resolution* (1989), and editor and coauthor of *The 50% Solution* (1983), *The Negotiation Process* (1978), and *Positive Sum* (1987), among other books. He is organizer of the Washington Interest in Negotiations (WIN) Group and has been a distinguished fellow of the United States Institute of Peace.

To Bo Kjellén, Tommy Koh and Maurice Strong, for negotiating a sustainable development regime.

Abbreviations

ACP	African, Caribbean and Pacific Group
CITES	Convention on International Trade in Endangered Species
DAC	Development Assistance Committee
ECE	UN Economic Commission for Europe
ECOSOC	UN Economic and Social Council
EEC	European Economic Community
ESCAP	Economic and Social Commission for Asia and the Pacific
FAO	UN Food and Agriculture Organization
GATT	General Agreement on Tariffs and Trade
IAEA	International Atomic Energy Agency
ICAO	International Civil Aviation Organization
ICSU	International Council of Scientific Unions
IFAD	International Fund for Agricultural Development
ILO	International Labor Organization
IMO	International Maritime Organization
INC	Intergovernmental Negotiating Committee
ITTA	International Tropical Timber Agreement
ITTO	International Tropical Timber Organization
IUCN	International Union for the Conservation of Nature and Natural Resources
OECD	Organization for Economic Cooperation and Development
TFAP	Tropical Forestry Action Plan
UNCED	United Nations Conference on Environment and Development
UNCHS	United Nations Commission on Human Settlements
UNCSTD	United Nations Centre for Science and Technology for Development
UNCTAD	United Nations Conference on Trade and Development
UNDP	United Nations Development Programme
UNEP	United Nations Environment Programme
UNESCO	United Nations Educational, Scientific and Cultural Organization
UNFPA	United Nations Population Fund
UNICEF	United Nations Children's Fund
UNIDO	United Nations Industrial Development Organization
UNSO	United Nations Sudano-Sahelian Office
WFP	World Food Programme
WHO	World Health Organization
WIPO	World Intellectual Property Organization
WMO	World Meteorological Organization
WRI	World Resources Institute
WWF	Worldwide Fund for Nature/World Wildlife Fund

Part I

The Structure of Analysis

1

The Dynamics of Regime-building Negotiations

Gunnar Sjöstedt, Bertram I. Spector, and I. William Zartman

Cooperation among nations is taking place increasingly within the context of international regimes. These regimes codify rules, norms, and regulations; establish expectations; and manage the governance of formal and informal agreements to integrate cross-national action to achieve common goals on targeted issues. To varying degrees, depending on the issue area, regimes provide the necessary principles, structures, institutions, procedures, and standards that guide national behaviors, policy development, and coordinative strategies.[1]

Regimes are formulations within which international cooperation and coordination can be nurtured through mutually understood definitions of a problem and appropriate strategies to combat it, and common perceptions of fairness and acceptable procedures on how further disputes in the problem domain should be resolved equitably. Regimes are not limited to governing only legally binding conventions; they can be the organizing concepts for softer, nonbinding agreements that embody cross-national intentions on particular issues.

Regimes are not new constructs. They exist in the areas of security (for example, on the issue of nuclear nonproliferation), trade (for example, via the General Agreement on Tariffs and Trade), human rights (for example, on the treatment of prisoners of war), and the environment (for example, concerning acid rain in Europe). However, regimes have taken on new and important functions recently in the environmental field where international diplomats have found it useful to approach these transboundary problems in a partial and incremental fashion. International environmental agreements are not generally hammered out at the negotiating table at a single blow. Many are the product of the convention–protocol approach, in which broad, often vaguely worded, statements of principles are established, followed by multiple agreements that elaborate on the details. Thus, a continuous negotiation process is established that must be implemented, managed, adjusted, and sustained by some mechanism, which in many cases are regimes. During the formative and operative stages of agreement implementation, regime mechanisms are needed to foster a sense of cohesiveness, common purpose, and continuity among a set of nations that have agreed to abide by common objectives and standards.

[1]See Krasner (1983) and Young (1989) for detailed discussions of international regimes.

Negotiating International Regimes: Lessons Learned from the United Nations Conference on Environment and Development (G. Sjöstedt, *et al.*, eds.; 1-85966-077-0; © IIASA; pub. Graham & Trotman, 1994; printed in Great Britain), pp. 3–19.

Almost every sector of international environmental concern is governed by one or more regimes – conservation and living resources, marine environment, marine living resources, transboundary freshwaters, land resources, hazardous and toxic substances, nuclear safety, and the work environment. The innovation of the United Nations Conference on Environment and Development (UNCED) was to suggest that all of these sectors should be subsumed under a large regime umbrella that recognizes explicitly the linkages among these environmental sectors, as well as the linkages between these sectors and economic concerns. Of the products developed by UNCED in this regard, the Rio Charter, which espouses agreed principles on the environment and development, and Agenda 21, a global action plan that establishes desired standards, goals, and targets, provide the foundation for such a regime umbrella that takes a very broad view of the problem area. The Commission on Sustainable Development proposed by UNCED and established by the General Assembly is the structural entity charged with monitoring the regime.

Regimes are created and operated primarily through the mechanism of negotiation. Parties that subscribe to the regime meet, monitor progress toward achieving the assigned goals, issue warnings to free-riders, and attempt to enforce compliance within their means. They address the binding and nonbinding agreements that serve as the founding principles of the regime, revise them as scientific evidence, feedback, and political interest demand, and resolve new problems or disputes as they arise. The balancing of demands and concessions among the subscribing nations to arrive at a solution that is deemed fair and equitable by the parties is the typical mode of operation and governance. Formal votes are rarely taken in such multilateral fora; consensus derived from formal and informal negotiations is the chosen mechanism for reaching joint decisions.

Regimes are not only mechanisms that encourage the use of negotiation to govern agreements and resolve disputes that arise in their implementation, they are also born of negotiation. To establish a regime, nations must indicate the desire to coordinate action, demonstrate sustained political will, and engage in the tradeoff of values. Although nations that seek to develop a regime in a particular area may share the desire to cooperate, the formative negotiations can succeed or falter on many very contentious issues: how will the problem area and solution set be defined to the mutual satisfaction of all; what extent of monitoring will be acceptable; how should decision making and dispute resolution within the regime be handled; are all parties considered to be equal within the regime in terms of their rights and privileges; how will free-riders be dealt with; will continued scientific research be sponsored; will financial and technological support be offered to less-developed participants and to what extent; should nongovernmental organizations play a role and, if so, what type; how will the agreed standards, norms, rules, and procedures of the regime be enforced; and, most importantly, how much intrusion into national sovereignty will be tolerated? Moreover, different formulas for regime architecture must be negotiated: is it to be based on a legally binding convention or a soft law understanding; and is the regime to be institutionalized with a formal, sitting commission or secretariat, or is to have only occasional meetings of the parties and experts? These are only some of the difficult and complex questions that must be negotiated.

The outcome of regime formation negotiations must be well crafted in order to be sustainable. Regimes must be constructed to manage relationships between signing parties over extended periods of time. That means they must be organic and malleable, capable of dynamic change in response to new scientific findings, or the feedback of compliant behavior. At the same time, regimes must be able to manage international cooperation within what are often ambiguous ranges or constraints given the nonbinding nature of the founding principles.

THE UNCED NEGOTIATIONS

The 1992 United Nations Conference on the Environment and Development represents the analytical point of departure of this study. However, the ambition of this project goes beyond mere description of this important event and the preparatory work preceding it. It analyzes the UNCED process as a prime example of how international regimes are negotiated. It points to conclusions drawn to facilitate the further negotiation of environmental regimes that are likely to follow in the wake of UNCED. UNCED succeeded in formulating an umbrella regime in the field of sustainable development that will continue into the future and spawn sub-regimes in particular environmental sectors and cross-sectoral policy areas. In many areas, UNCED merely marked out areas in which it is vital that serious negotiations get under way as soon as possible, such as for instance in the case of deforestation and desertification. In several areas in which relative success was proclaimed at Rio, continued negotiation is still regarded as a necessity by most parties. Here belong several of the key topics of UNCED, such as climate change, biological diversity, technological transfer, and financial assistance. These negotiations will undoubtedly yield new sub-regimes or strengthen existing regime mechanisms.

Continuity of the process begun at Rio was by deliberate design. One purpose of UNCED was to expand upon the goals and programs of action that originated at the Conference on the Environment in Stockholm in 1972. Agenda 21, a very special outcome of the UNCED process, represents a blueprint for a plan to modify, extend, and more effectively coordinate on-going treaty-regulated processes of cooperation in the area of environmental problems at the regional and global level. Implementation procedures represent an important element of this process of coordination, requiring the appropriate technological, financial, and institutional structures to support it, especially within the UN system. Needless to say, the future implementation process related to the ambitious plan of action represented by Agenda 21 cannot be accomplished merely with existing approaches, organizations, and coordinative mechanisms. Complex collective decisions will have to be taken at the international level to ensure the effective implementation of the outcome of the Rio meeting.

Still another task of UNCED was to stimulate and support negotiations in new areas made more complex by introducing their cross-sectoral nature, notably climate change, deforestation, biodiversity, and economic development. The major theme of UNCED was the conception of sustainable development. However, many of the issues that fall under this broad heading became stalemated as a result of political sensitivities between North and South, pressures to assign responsibility for past environmental destruction, financial funding shortfalls, and intellectual property rights disputes over technology transfers. Thus, the process begun at UNCED will require continued negotiations with respect both to backlog issues *and* to matters that have been dealt with relatively successfully.

If various aspects of UNCED continue to be negotiated after the 1992 Rio meeting, it is a safe bet that the practitioner will find these negotiations to be a cumbersome process. Many of the backlog issues were warehoused because they were politically sensitive, as well as technically complex to deal with. In some cases, for instance the issue of deforestation, it was totally impossible to get negotiations on matters of substance off the ground. It was even difficult to undertake discussions about some general principles concerning forests and deforestation. In those areas where agreements were attained, the success was often the result of the fact that sensitive topics had been circumvented altogether or handled with the help of partial or unsatisfactory compromises. In many cases, technical complexities related to physical linkages across issues were avoided in the UNCED negotiations.

Given these difficulties experienced in the UNCED process, what are the useful lessons that can be learned? It has often been pointed out that UNCED represents a unique chain of events, a very special kind of negotiation process that is not likely to be repeated in the near future. Certainly, any negotiation or international event can be viewed as unique, but each shares some common characteristics as well with other activities. Regime-building negotiations on particular sustainable development issues will invariably encounter similar actors, positions, interests, complexities, and sensitivities. Learning of the successes and pitfalls from the UNCED negotiations can only serve to enhance the opportunities for effective negotiations in these future regime-building situations.

Very simply, analytical conclusions drawn from studying the UNCED negotiations can assist in future regime-building negotiations in at least two ways – learning from the problems and learning from the successes. Many of the problem areas in the UNCED negotiations were backlogged or left partially unresolved. Once can learn in hindsight from what went wrong in the UNCED negotiations and contemplate ways to circumvent pitfalls and seemingly unresolvable sticking-points under similar circumstances. One of the successes of UNCED, on the other hand, was its regime-building process. UNCED was not itself intended to produce legally binding treaties related to particular environmental issue areas. Such convention texts were developed in parallel fora and only signed at UNCED. UNCED's objective was to develop a mandate and basic set of guidelines for international governance and continued negotiations on the intersection of environmental and developmental issues. It was to be only a way-station, but one that establishes the path, structure, and principles – the regime – to guide subsequent agreements in a process of global integration. How this occurred, who participated and was influential, and how they interacted to produce the negotiated outcomes of Agenda 21, the Earth Charter, and the Commission on Sustainable Development is analyzed in the following chapters to support more effective negotiations that formulate new regimes.

CHARACTERISTICS OF REGIME-BUILDING NEGOTIATIONS

In its heyday in the 1960s, the study of regional integration was plagued by an ambiguity in its very name. Integration as an outcome was continually confused with integration as a process. The process of integrating frequently led to results short of integration and aroused counterpressures at the same time, pushing away from an integrated outcome; yet that process was assumed to be composed of steps toward a goal that, in specific realities, was never reached. Regime-building, a looser reincarnation of integration, suffers from the same debilities, although because of the looser nature of the subject, many regimes can be said to have been created, including environmental regimes. The dynamics of regime-building result from a number of separate and often contradictory processes.

Part of the ambiguity can be brought under control by recognizing the role of negotiation in regime-building. Specific encounters from time to time mark the formalization of the evolving regime, and therefore characteristics of the negotiation process, and particularly of the process of multilateral negotiations, govern the building of regimes. That gives some form to the amorphous notion of regime creation as integration, but it also raises further assumptions about the regime-building process that reflect its complicated dynamics.

It must be assumed that the process of regime-building is, at least at the hands of some of the parties, a purposive exercise heading toward the establishment of rules, regulations, and expectations governing the given issue area (Krasner, 1983). It should also be assumed that some parties are interested in preventing regime formation or at least limiting the attainment of the goal of others, and that, concomitantly if not identically, progress toward regime formation arouses a counterprocess of limiting regime effects. Finally, it can be assumed that any momentary process of regime-building has its own interfactional dynamic, in which the outcome will lie somewhere between the extreme positions, although not necessarily in the middle (as is sometimes assumed). These three sources of dynamics need to be kept in mind and will be referred to subsequently when necessary in the discussion, but are also implicit and subjacent even when not directly mentioned.

PROCESSES

It will first be important to lay out the characteristics of multilateral negotiations to understand the basic process of regime-building (Zartman, 1994). Within the standard definition of negotiation as the process by which conflicting positions are combined to form a common decision (Zartman and Berman, 1982: 1), there are six characteristics that define the multilateral version of the process.[2] Multilateral negotiations do not have the characteristic dynamics that the two-party structure imposes on bilateral negotiations; instead, their essential nature is one of managing complexity to produce an outcome. These six defining characteristics all point to salient ways of managing aspects of complexity.

Most obviously, multilateral means *multiparty* negotiations, with multifaceted interests in each party. UNCED, in particular, was characterized by the representation of over 170 sovereign states, dozens of intergovernmental organizations, and nearly 1500 nongovernmental organizations, each with overlapping and diverse interests and stakes on the various issues. A second defining characteristic is the *multi-issue* nature of the negotiations. Multiple issues provide the means as well as the subject of agreement, since they allow for the tradeoffs that provide the network for a single outcome. They also allow for texture in the negotiations, since not

[2]This list is necessarily similar to, but importantly different from, Oran Young's in "The Politics of International Regime Formation," XXXXIII, *International Organization*, 3:359–66 (Summer 1989). His "multiple actors" is of course the same. "Consensus" replaces "unanimity" as being more accurate; "coalition" and "variable values, parties and roles" replace "transnational alliances" and "shifting involvements" as being more specific. Young's "integrative bargaining" seems to mistake an optimal search for a basic characteristic. Both "uncertainty" and "(selective) problems and approaches" are interesting features, but do not appear to be defining characteristics.

all the many parties have the same intensity of interest on any issue, any more than they have the same substantive interest. This allows Homans's Maxim – "The more items at stake can be divided into goods valued more by one party (or parties) than they cost to the other(s) and goods valued more to the other party (or parties) than they cost to the first, the greater the chances of successful outcome" (Homans, 1961: 62) – to be played out to the fullest, and Homans's Maxim is the key to any negotiation.

The recognition of multiple cross-sectoral issue linkages was one of the unique innovations of UNCED, as well as the source of its many inherent problems. The General Assembly resolution establishing UNCED acknowledged not only the physical linkages across issues, but also the policy linkages that must be addressed by the international community if the problems of environment and development are to be confronted effectively. At the same time, while it is useful to acknowledge the interrelationships between issues at a high level, the scientific community is still uncertain as to the physical linkages surrounding global warming, for instance, and policy makers are not yet quite sure of the appropriate policy linkages – the tradeoffs that should be made – to create the balance necessary for sustainable development (see Shaw, Gallopin, Weaver, and Öberg, 1991, for a systems approach to answering these questions). As a result, much effort was exerted at UNCED merely to define the network of issue clusters in an impressionistic fashion, benefiting only from partial answers available from scientists and policy makers.

As a result of the first two characteristics, multilateral negotiations are characterized by *coalition.* Coalition among many parties is often noted to be the major analytical characteristic, but its applicability to many other issues as well, in order to reduce their complexity and make them manageable, is not usually recognized. Packaging, linkages and tradeoffs – the basic devices of the negotiation process – are all ways of making coalitions among issues, interests, and positions.

Many of the institutionalized coalitions were ever-present forces on the conference floor – the EC and the Group of 77, for example. In addition, though, newly formed, nontraditional, special-interest groupings also emerged – small island states, mountain states, economies in transition, for example. The intensive networking conducted by NGOs also generated many coalitions outside of the traditional governmental form. These alignments were driven more by the motives of common economic and ecological interests than by common geographic location, as in the traditional Second Committee groupings of the General Assembly. These coalitions helped to simplify the public proceedings of the negotiation. However, much time was devoted in coalition caucuses during the PrepCom meetings, as well as at the Rio Conference itself, to intra-coalitional bargaining – to deal with disputes among coalition members, iron out common positions and strategies, and respond to alternative coalition demands and proposals.

Multilateral agreement is by *consensus*, a decision rule in which, essentially, abstention is an affirmative rather than a negative vote. Multilateral agreements are arrived at by consensus when a coalition formed by a significant but unspecified number of parties is in favor and the rest do not oppose. Parties not in agreement can abstain without blocking the outcome, and parties opposing can be left out as long as their number does not become significant. Strategies of incremental participation and agreement then become possible (Zartman, 1987, ch. 10). At the same time, the significant number requirement means that lowest common denominator (LCD) agreements without teeth are a residual possibility.

No voting ever occurred at UNCED or at the PrepCom sessions. Rather, the procedure for agreement was consensus. Certainly, there were abstentions, but generally they were not allowed by the Bureau to block approval if the majority was generally in favor of a proposal. Given the mission of UNCED to establish nonbinding guidelines and mandates for future negotiations that *would* produce binding agreements, obtaining consensus was not an unreasonable goal. It was commonly understood that under a future sustainable development regime, many of the same issues would be debated and negotiated again, so that partial disagreement was acceptable and agreements reached by consensus at UNCED were not irrevocable.

The fifth defining characteristic is the *multirole* nature of the negotiations. Roles are divided initially into leaders and followers, but then additionally into other positions such as defenders of single issues, general orchestrators, and others. Without such role diversity, the issue and party complexities could not be combined in an agreeable outcome. Playing on all levels of interaction, parties not only work to shape the values attached to various issues, but also to manipulate the other parties and their roles in order to come to an agreement. They must do so because, if they choose to ignore these possibilities, others will make use of them, forcing the other parties to play on these levels in response. It is again the immense complexity of having to deal with many parties, issues, and roles that makes such multiple variability the price of winning an agreement, thus further increasing the characteristic complexity.

Leaders on some issues at UNCED were followers on others. Individual delegates often were asked to take on the responsibilities of leading working groups in negotiating specific issues, thus neutralizing sometimes powerful personalities. Moreover, NGO representatives were placed on the official delegations of several countries, thus bridging the gap between official and special interest stakeholders, requiring these agents to represent both narrow and broad constituencies.

Finally, multilateral negotiations – particularly for building regimes – are matters of *rule-making* rather than the redistribution of tangible goods. Neither of the basic characteristics of division and exchange are frequently present in multilateral negotiations; instead, the main goal is to establish procedures that harmonize national legislation or establish rules that can be applied by and to states (Winham and Kizer, 1991), and that only secondarily govern substantive outcomes. This does not mean that tangible goods are not thereby affected, but it does mean that effect is uncertain, long range, and universal. It does mean that the importance of the formula is enhanced, since the adoption of a rule depends more on a convincing justification or a notion of justice than on exchanged concessions in detail.

Rule-making has two dimensions – diachronic and synchronic – that reflect the three simultaneous processes. The particular outcome represents the results of the moment in a synchronic process, but it is also a stage in the battle over the evolution of the regime. Regimes are temporary, evolving, and continuously expandable and perfectible rather than being overarching and deductive as an optimal formula should be in a negotiated agreement. They are often built up inductively, in an incremental process, in which many parts are put together by trial and error into a momentary, unstable resting place, preparatory to further movement. For those who are trying to move the process forward, instability can be a creative characteristic of negotiations; the temporary formula should be so constructed that it calls for its own improvement and moves the process along – or, like the Sinai disengagement agreements of 1974–5, so that it "falls forward" as a temporary solution that, constructively, cannot last in its momentary form. However, for opponents, that same instability is an opportunity to renegotiate later for a looser agreement.

The diachronic process of incremental formulation for multilateral regimes takes place over an extended period. The formulating negotiations are preceded by preparatory and partial negotiations, as well as other events. Often the incremental process begins bilaterally and even nongovernmentally, and the main round serves to collect and coordinate these diverse efforts around a coherent formula. The initial or salient negotiation lays out the basic formula and the subsequent negotiations fill in and revise the details. Negotiations move from "whether" in the main round to "when," "what," and "how" in later meetings.

This incrementalism involves both steps in regime construction and resistance, and momentary midpoints among the parties, interests, and roles at the particular negotiation encounter. Definitions are often avoided in favor of lists of covered activities, which are only later joined under a definitional umbrella. Areas of attention are identified and cobbled together to form the scope of the agreement. A package is constructed out of either a core coalition of key interests or a diverse coalition of disparate interests; then the agreement is expanded, to the extent possible, either to extend the coverage or fill in the holes. Commitments are outlined and then strengthened, and resistance against them weakened. Environmental negotiations have characteristically begun with statements of intent, codes of conduct, or differential obligations, exceptions, and reservations, which are then gradually turned into binding obligations; private watch groups monitoring behavior replace signatories' engagements or international organizational constraints, until new norms have been introduced far enough to constitute informal international law.

UNCED did not yield rules *per se*, but a framework setting the stage for continuous rule-making negotiations. The global action plan, Agenda 21, for example, inventories goals, targets, alternative strategies, and conditions that should be considered in future talks across all of the sectors and cross-sectoral issues related to sustainable development. These elements are likely to be the components of eventual treaty provisions that specify rules, constraints, and procedures that must be complied with for effective implementation.

The process of expanding the scope of the momentary agreement is a particularly good illustration of the dual synchronic and diachronic nature of regime-building. Procedural tradeoffs are used to construct the unstable agreement, and their elements then become the ingredients for its expansion toward a more stable regime. Tradeoffs are the essence of formula-building and of negotiation in general; they provide the means of creating a positive sum agreement, both by constituting elements evaluated differently by the parties and by incorporating additional sidepayments to enlarge the pie (Nash, 1950; Homans, 1961). In the regime-building process, the potential items for tradeoffs are as ill-defined as the issues themselves, and are differentiated in time as well as nature and size. Time-related payoffs are unusually difficult to compare and equate, not only because discount rates fluctuate wildly, but also because delayed payments can change in value or even be evaded (Sebenius, 1991). However, by the same token, they do lend themselves well to diachronically evolving agreements.

Three types of rule-making tradeoffs are available. One is the exception: agreement to a regulatory situation is often obtained at the price of claiming exceptions at the end of the agreement. In this way, a principle is established, but its effectiveness is weakened. Later, the incipient regime can be consolidated by negotiating away the exceptions, presumably against other tradeoffs in new circumstances. A second tradeoff exchanges breadth for depth in regulation. Many are the cases where a regime began with a relatively strict coverage of a relatively small number of items, often implemented through a small number of steep steps, and later expanded the scope of the coverage. The opposite approach is a relatively broad coverage through loose restrictions or gentle steps. The first can lead to incoherence and imperceptible results, whereas the second invites generalized resistance and tends to "fall backward," to less rather than more extensive effectiveness.

The third type of tradeoff is the reverse of the first, trading restrictions for inducements, which are then tapered off as compliance proceeds on its own and becomes it own inducement. Many environmental negotiations have turned to compensation as a way of establishing tradeoffs across the North–South divide. Indeed, the entire structure of UNCED is based on such a massive tradeoff designed to bridge the North–South gap between environment and development. Compensation can provide an immediate transfer of resources, but has an air of bribery; it must be so structured that individual parties are not able to enjoy its benefits as a public good while opting out of its obligations.

ACTOR DYNAMICS

There is no prescribed model or method to this process, although there are strategies that the parties use to play. There is a procedural sequence, which gives a certain order to the parties' efforts at finding a formula: philosophical or plenary thoughts, sectoral interest-related positions, horsetrading resolutions. In the process of being more or less active in multilateral negotiations, parties select from a limited list of roles that differ in nature. They can Drive, Conduct, Defend, Brake, or Cruise (Sjöstedt, 1992). Drivers try to organize the participation to produce an agreement that is consonant with their interests. Conductors also seek to produce an agreement, but from a neutral position, with no interest axe of their own to grind. Defenders are single-issue participants, concerned more with incorporating a particular measure or position in the agreement than with the overall success of the negotiations. Brakers are the opposing or modifying resistance, brought into action by the progress being made on either the broad regime or on specific issue items. Cruisers are filler, with no strong interests of their own and so available to act as followers. Two other marginal strategies are left, that of exit, through individual exceptions and derogations, and that of compensation, through a trade of exceptions for inducements and side payments. All of these roles are available, to be used by various parties at various times, although the adoption of certain roles – driver or conductor, for example – colors the ability to shift to another later on.

These roles aggregate into the two types of goals – the building of a partial and eventually minimum winning (or blocking) coalition, and the building of a universal coalition or consensus. Coalitions can be based on transnational or international cooperation. The transnational cooperation of scientists, technologists, and business is one type of coalition that can be built as a basis for an environmental bargain, but it is generally not enough. It is merely the grouping that constitutes one side of the negotiations, and it must then use its pluralistic resources – knowledge, skill, and money – to either raise the consciousness or strike an interest deal with political leaders accountable to constituent groups. This strategy clearly appears to be the equivalent of the incrementally aggregating process already noted on the issue side.

The other type of coalition building is international, among – rather than across – states. In this, the political leaders are the motor, with science, technology, and business as their advisory groups. The building blocs of such coalitions are frequently regional identity groups, but may also be caucusing groups based on issue-related common interests. Strategies are drawn from the three classic baskets labeled Coalesce, Cut Up, and Confront. Groups seek either to aggregate other groups and parties into a growing winning coalition, or to divide opposing groups into smaller parts so as to absorb or merely to weaken them, or to work out a deal with them.

This second strategy can be termed one of leadership or orchestration for the building of consensus. As opposed to the acephalic conglomerating strategies of coalition, orchestration strategies depend on a designated conductor or leader who agglomerates parties into a consensual process. Each party pursues its own interests and is brought to play its own score in the right way to bring a harmonious result. The conductor could be a sovereign with his own interest-related agenda, but above all interested in obtaining a generally satisfactory agreement. However, the multilateral conference nature of the negotiations weigh in favor of a disinterested leader to provide some order to the proceedings. Thus, many environmental conferences give a prominent role to a secretary general, conference chair, secretariat, or other organizing agency. States rarely aspire to this role, for many reasons: often, no state is powerful enough to be hegemonic, interests are usually defensive and partial rather than global, and every potential leader is above all a regional and interest group player and so is tainted. In this situation, the procedural conductor is actually welcome, since he allows the state-parties to pursue their own interests more effectively and to facilitate agreement.

Several other dynamics are important in describing actor behavior in large multilateral regime-building negotiations such as UNCED. The first dimension embraces the wide variety of entities that participate. The traditional actors in international negotiations are, of course, the nations themselves, who embody the interests of governments and are usually the exclusive agents invited to the table to conduct bargaining. At UNCED, and in any projected negotiations conducted under the umbrella of sustainable development for the foreseeable future, North–South differences will likely play a prominent role. This was certainly the single most important division characterizing interstate relations at UNCED. The industrialized states, with their emphasis on the environment, their ownership of the technology and resources needed to achieve environmental and developmental goals, and their domination of the UNCED agenda, were in a much more powerful position than the developing countries. In part, through an analysis of how the relative power of these two camps was actually exercised, we can attempt to understand the negotiation process and outcome of UNCED. Beyond the central position of the national actors, pivotal roles were played at UNCED and in the prenegotiation phase by two types of nontraditional actors: intergovernmental organizations (IGOs) and nongovernmental organizations (NGOs). The IGOs played relatively neutral, though extremely important, information provider roles, feeding studies, analysis, and data into the UNCED process primarily through the UNCED secretariat. The NGOs mirrored the division between North and South and, in their own way, attempted to influence the primary state actors. Most NGOs were advocates of a singular position, but an important segment of NGOs represented the international and national scientific communities, offering scientific information and analysis focused on particular technical issues.

Another characteristic relates to how actors organize themselves internally. Traditionally, delegations at international negotiations represent and are members of the foreign ministry of their country. Given the cross-sectoral nature of so many issues at UNCED, this approach was infeasible if truly knowledgeable delegates were to be appointed. National delegations from countries with sufficient resources were composed of officials from various relevant ministries and departments: foreign affairs, finance, environment, development and trade, etc. As well, several delegations included small numbers of NGO representatives as official members, representing important interests within their national populations. As a result, the internal composition of official negotiation actors often epitomized the multifaceted interests of a wide range of domestic stakeholders – both in and out of government. Another important feature of internal organization is coordination between the negotiation delegation and the home office. At UNCED, many delegations were on a "loose string" with limited instructions and broad latitude; others were under much tighter control. When very limited support was available from home, as was the case for many developing countries, internal organization and activities on behalf of their national interests were often a matter of discovery. Many of these national delegates were themselves learning about the issues – their scientific as well as policy implications – in real time and creating formulations of their national interests on these issues for the first time at the negotiation sessions. These internal opportunities and constraints played a major role in facilitating and inhibiting the progress of the negotiations.

PROCESS DYNAMICS

This book addresses how each of these characteristics influenced the regime-building negotiations of UNCED. Generating a common political willingness to first come to the table and then continue negotiating is the additional catalytic element that must be injected into the equation. This willingness or *flexibility* is a dimension that cuts across all of these descriptive attributes and is common to most successful negotiations. Flexibility is the attitudinal and/or behavioral shift from rigidity and toughness toward conciliation and agreement. It is characterized by a willingness to adjust perceptions of the problem, issues, and solutions, which in turn frees parties to modify their behavior to achieve agreement (see Druckman, 1992, for a review of the literature related to flexibility).

Flexibility in negotiation may be viewed as a necessary condition for the convergence of widely divergent interests to occur, but conceptually we are hard pressed to pinpoint what flexibility is, how it came about, and what its implications are. Yet these are among the central dynamics of the process itself! There are *inputs* into the negotiation process (new information about the issue or new stakeholders entering the fray or new tactics introduced by another party, for example) that can influence a willingness to review the issues and one's interests concerning those issues. These stimulants of cognitive adjustment can yield increased flexibility or stubbornness, which in turn yield *outputs*, ultimately of agreement, partial agreement, or stalemate. The transformation process from input to output – from initial and distant positions to modified and more closely situated converged positions – is the process of flexibility that is important to examine, but eludes most negotiation analysis. Practitioners often can identify turning points in specific negotiation cases, but find it difficult to put their finger on *why* formerly conflicting parties adjusted their perceptions and exhibited a willingness to agree at that point in time. Researchers (Druckman, 1986, and Druckman, Husbands and Johnston, 1991) have examined the concept of turning points in negotiations as well, and conclude that they occur in response to signals from other participating actors that their bargaining behavior has changed, or is about to change. Others (Cross, 1978) hypothesize that flexibility is a manifestation of a continual learning process in negotiation. Adaptation in attitude and behavior is a response to persistent observation, monitoring of other parties, the introduction of new information, and changes in the ambient surroundings of the talks. However, these efforts still beg the question of *why* there was a change at a specific point in time toward either agreement or deadlock. The stimulants of the flexibility process remain vague and secretive, despite their clear importance in explaining the negotiation process.

Conceptual headway can be made in understanding negotiation flexibility by focusing on two negotiation dynamics – *issue and interest development*. Both are the product of flexibility, and both experience iterative adjustment by all parties to the negotiation based on cognitive reassessments – in successful negotiations yielding consensual issue definition and coalitions based on common interests. Reframing the issues that divide parties and adjusting national interests so that they better satisfy international goals are major steps away from confrontation and toward integrative, cooperative problem solving (Rothman, 1991). By mapping these dynamics, we can understand and evaluate the process by which negotiators and policy makers undergo adjustment regarding issues and interests *cognitively* – in terms of their understanding of the issues; *perceptually* – in terms of assessments of their own and other actors' positions, interests, and strategies; and *evaluatively* – in terms of their beliefs of fair formulas for agreement.

Several factors stimulate this cognitive, perceptual, and value flexibility (see Figure 1.1). These factors operate primarily within the context of the internal policy making system of each national actor. As the parties to a conflict gradually adjust their understanding of complex issues under dispute, through the interjection of *new information* from other negotiators as well as from sources external to the negotiation, their definitions and framing of the problem may transition to new understandings. Another important stimulus of issue and interest reframing is the gradual clarification of national policy objectives, spurred on by *domestic public and intragovernmental debate.* As a nation's values and preferences concerning a particular issue mature and clarify, its changed perspectives on those issues may cause a redefinition that rationalizes the issue in line with the newly adjusted interests. Certainly, the use of *power and persuasive tactics* by other parties to the negotiation can influence the way national interests are stated and issues are framed. In the best of circumstances, these factors can produce a consensual understanding of issues and interests, thereby enabling a shared search for solutions to proceed among the negotiating parties.

A possible outcome of this common learning experience due to the evolution of issue and interest understanding is the development of a common sense of fairness concerning possible solutions. (See Albin, 1992, for a review of different conceptions of fairness in negotiation.) Formulas perceived as fair by all parties are achievable as consensual knowledge about the issues develop and interests converge.

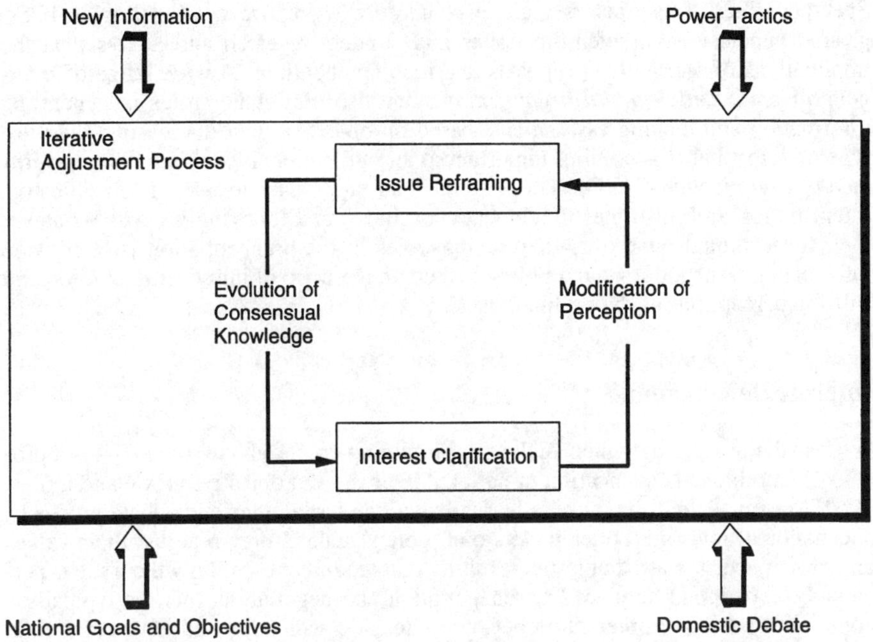

Figure 1.1 The Iterative Dynamics of Issue Reframing and Interest Clarification

Issue Development

The process of prenegotiation, in large part, is the process of issue redefinition and reframing. In UNCED, the complexity of issue linkages caused issue reframing to extend into the negotiation phase as well. As actors redefine issues, with the input of new information, there is the possibility that multiple conflicting definitions of these issues will eventually converge, leading to a common understanding and consensual knowledge. Given the emergence of consensual knowledge in an issue area, viable and acceptable formulas for solution are more likely.

Conflict often arises over issues that are perceived and defined differently by actors who are stakeholders on those issues – those who have something to gain or lose in settling the dispute. Initially, the way an issue is perceived and defined is largely determined by broad national objectives and the state of issue knowledge by national policy makers. As the subject of much international negotiation today focuses on complicated and interlinked multi-issue problems involving the interaction of complex social, scientific, technological, and economic factors, issue definition is becoming extremely information-dependent and difficult, especially for developing countries who do not have the resources to expend on extensive data gathering and analysis.

This fact has given rise to the heightened role played by several third party actors who are not principals in the negotiation themselves; however, they have become critical adjuncts to the process of issue definition and redefinition (Sjöstedt and

Spector, 1992). These actors include *conference secretariats*, who provide background papers on the scientific issues and conduct research and analysis on the implications of alternative proposals and recommendations. A wide range of *intergovernmental and regional organizations* can also play major roles in generating information and making assessments based on objective data. Increasingly, a third type of actor that is becoming important at an international level is the *nongovernmental organization* (NGO). These NGOs can take many forms – from objective scientific research institutes to advocacy, business, and lobbying groups. Whatever their form, though, one of their principal roles in the prenegotiation is to provide information to negotiators and policy makers in the hope of influencing opinion and shifting perceptions of the problem itself.

Interest Development

What is the process by which such issue reframing comes about? In part, it is a process of incremental clarification of national interests and objectives (Iklé and Leites, 1962; Spector, 1983). As more is learned about an issue, domestic debate proceeds, and national goals are better understood, policy makers may readjust their values and preferences toward that issue, resulting in a modification of how the issue is perceived, scoped, and defined. In prenegotiation and negotiation, there is typically a continuous push–pull interaction between interest clarification and issue reframing. Interests are formed and modified based upon new information and a clarification of national objectives. Issues are reframed and redefined as national interests change, in turn refreshing the consensual knowledge about these issues.

This iterative process occurs on two levels. Internally, within pluralistic negotiation actors, each stakeholder is continually attempting to reformulate the way issues are represented and understood, so that their particular interests are best served. This definition and clarification process also occurs on a multilateral level among negotiating parties that are jointly seeking a way of accommodating their mutual interests. Issue and interest clarification and adjustment are major dynamics addressed by the various authors in this book. We seek to track, understand, and evaluate how and why negotiators and policy makers change their minds concerning their definitions and preferences on issues under debate and what the implications of such changes are.

ORGANIZATION OF THIS BOOK

One striking feature of UNCED was its vast agenda. It covered virtually the whole range of environmental issues and confronted complicated cross-sectoral issues, such as financial support to developing countries, transfer of technology, and trade and development as well. By design and out of necessity, UNCED steered clear of dealing with any of these issues comprehensively. Rather, these substantive issues were conceived of as an integrated part of a large system of many on-going negotiations, most of which are likely to continue in the future. This important element of the structure and system of the UNCED negotiations is described in Chapter 2.

We turn from the structure of the analysis to the process of negotiation itself in Part II, beginning with an impartial eyewitness account of what happened in the prenegotiation and negotiation phases (Chapter 3). The study continues by focusing on two analyses of the UNCED negotiation process: one focused on issue definition and linkages, and the other on interest adjustment. An important element of UNCED was the nature of problem solving and collective learning about the substance of issues that is usually associated with the prenegotiation stage of international bargaining. In particular, issue definition and clarification was an important element of the UNCED process. In several areas, a stable issue formation was not concluded before the Rio meeting, but continues within the context of negotiations that will proceed into the future. Several of the main problems confronting negotiators at UNCED were not clarified sufficiently in a scientific sense or early enough in the process. One example is the physical linkage between several of the major issues like those between climate change and, for example, deforestation, biological diversity, and oceans. These physical – or real world – couplings across issues were largely avoided, but must reemerge in future negotiations for solutions to be developed. The reality of these physical issue linkages have to be considered in global negotiations on environment and development because of their mutual interdependence. Therefore, useful lessons for the future may be drawn from examining issue dynamics, linkages, and issue redefinition (see Chapter 4).

The UNCED process was in many ways a direct continuation, not only of earlier negotiations on particular environmental problem areas, but also of the protracted North–South struggle about the ruling regimes for international economic cooperation. As seen in this perspective, the UNCED process recalls the grand debates of the 1970s in the UN system, especially in UNCTAD, on a New International Economic Order. This continuity from the past is due to the ambition of UNCED to link the global problems of environment and development. Many observers feared that this strategy would inevitably revive the North–South ideological trench war that proved to be so destructive earlier. Therefore, it is not surprising that North–South contentions did, indeed, have a great impact on the UNCED negotiations. Several of the key issues on the UNCED agenda were elements in the traditional North–South dialogue – or confrontation. Here notably belong the cross-sectoral issues of transfer of technology and financial resources from the North to the South that increasingly dominated negotiations over Agenda 21. However, the North–South conflict was clearly also a typical feature of the negotiations over the pure environmental issues. A recurrent claim of developing countries was that they should be treated preferentially in comparison to industrialized countries; Third World countries should retain the right to prioritize their own developmental needs where these conflicted with the environmental policy measures discussed in UNCED.

Notwithstanding these highly significant differences between developed and developing countries, the North–South confrontation was not as dysfunctional as it had been in the 1970s. One explanation is the new pattern of cooperation and coalition-building involving developing countries that emerged at UNCED. The Group of 77 certainly remained a key actor in the process. In line with General Assembly norms, all endgame negotiations were conducted on the basis of draft texts offered by the Group of 77. However, many of the more significant developing countries were not satisfied to have their own national interests defended by the larger coalition. These states either performed individually or became partners in smaller coalitions created to defend a limited set of interests. Illustrative examples are the coalition of countries with highly fragile mountain ecosystems on their territories and the coalition of low-lying island states. The negotiations progressed as national and coalitional interests changed from their initial positions and drew closer together. This process of interest adjustment on issues and the coalition-building that results from common-interest groupings of nations is an area in which significant lessons can be drawn for the future (see Chapter 5).

While Chapters 4 and 5 analyze issue formation and interest adjustment in UNCED at a macro level, Chapter 6 addresses these same process factors, but employs a quite different approach. This is a case study representing a micro perspective. It traces how a particular constellation of linked issues were dealt with. An objective of this chapter is to highlight negotiation problems related to the kind of complexity typical of the UNCED process – that represented by issue linkages. Chapter 6 offers an evaluation of the extent to which the UNCED process was able to cope with a package of highly important physical linkages that were not *a priori* acknowledged at the political level, but one that is very likely to resurface in the future regime negotiations.

Part III of the book reflects the Actor Perspective – how the key participants in UNCED behaved in the process. Chapters 7 and 8 pertain to the most important type of participant in the UNCED process: the nation state. They address the problem of how nations function to perform effectively as unitary actors. One consequence of issue complexity typical for the UNCED agenda is the need for extensive intragovernmental negotiation. This feature of the negotiation process is by no means exceptional for UNCED. It is, in fact, quite normal that agendas of complex international negotiations in issue areas like the environment or, say, economic affairs and trade, impact on the responsibilities of two or more ministries or central agencies. Still, the need for intragovernmental coordination was of a particular concern in the UNCED process. One reason was the sheer number of issues that was unusually large, even by UN standards. More importantly, new couplings across issues were made at UNCED that had not been dealt with in earlier negotiations. This was notably the case with themes related to the new concept of "sustainable development" and particularly the cross-sectoral issues. Accordingly, in these areas experience from earlier intragovernmental consultation and negotiation was comparatively weak. The linkage between environmental and trade issues is one case in point. Thus, intragovernmental coordination is one area in which useful lessons for future negotiations can be developed (see Chapters 7 and 8).

Chapters 9 and 10 relate to the function of negotiation leadership, which can be performed by several types of actors at the national, intergovernmental, or international levels. An important negotiation problem highlighted in the UNCED process, with ramifications for the future, is that of effective leadership. In many processes of complex multilateral negotiations before UNCED, a successful outcome was dependent on Great Power leadership. For instance, the bilateral relationship between the United States and the EC has given clear and authoritative guidance to several rounds of trade negotiations in GATT. In UNCED, this sort of Great Power leadership was largely lacking, particularly in the early stages of the negotiation process when issues were framed and the agenda set. In this phase of the UNCED process, negotiations were almost entirely dependent on the input supplied by the UNCED secretariat and the Bureau, including the chairman of the PrepCom as well as the chairmen of the working groups. In the preparation of future regime-building negotiations on environment and development, it is an essential analytical task to evaluate the opportunities and limits of leadership.

A rapidly growing literature on international regime-building highlights the decisive role of the scientific community in the creation of conventions concerning the protection of the environment. However, the scientific community seemingly did not make as significant a contribution to the UNCED process as required. In fact, many scientists were frustrated by the relatively modest achievements made in UNCED. Chapters 11 and 12 offer an assessment of the efficacy of scientific attempts to influence UNCED and climate change negotiations that should be useful in considering enhancements to their role in future regime-building negotiations.

Opinion-building has always represented a significant element in policy making at the national level, as well as the international level, concerning environmental matters. Sometimes, public opinion has enhanced negotiations on international environmental problems by stimulating national agencies in the various countries concerned to take constructive decisions. However, public opinion intervention in a negotiation process is not always helpful. For instance, the involvement of public interest groups in environmental negotiations has sometimes prevented the quiet and secretive diplomacy necessary for constructive solutions. One case in point was the negotiations for the Basel Convention concerning the handling of hazardous waste. Therefore, the role of nongovernmental organizations (NGOs) may become a critical factor in future negotiations on environment and development (see Chapter 13). From this point of view, the performance of NGOs in the UNCED process is significant. NGOs attained greater access to the UNCED process as compared to earlier conferences or negotiations in the UN context. This was by no means a certain outcome given the protracted discussions during the first PrepCom sessions concerning the status of NGOs. The roles played by NGOs in the UNCED process and the kind of contributions made by them are elucidated and analyzed systematically to draw insights for future negotiations.

Part IV relates to the outcome and lessons learned from the UNCED process. Chapter 14 gives an account and an assessment of the concrete results achieved in the UNCED process in terms of building a new environmental regime. Partial successes and shortcomings are also evaluated and recommendations to improve future practice are offered. Finally, Chapter 15 offers an important perspective to support future regime-building negotiations on sustainable development issues. Lessons learned from UNCED are deduced to improve actor strategies and negotiation processes in upcoming negotiations. Institutionalization of techniques to manage complexity and help build consensus to govern regimes effectively are described as a new type of procedural outcome that should be addressed early in the regime-building negotiations themselves. Ultimately, regimes evolve and adjust through a reflexive process of sustained negotiations. This continual process of transformation to maintain effectiveness and support of international commitments is a challenge that existing regimes and future regime-building negotiations must face. The experience and lessons of UNCED are sure to be of assistance to practitioners and analysts alike.

2

The Negotiating System of Environment and Development

Pamela Chasek

This chapter puts UNCED into the context of a larger system of international negotiations on environment and development-related issues. Since the 1972 Stockholm Conference on the Human Environment, there has been a growing number of international negotiations, conferences, and agencies to deal with environmental issues. Concomitantly, as the economic conditions in many developing countries worsened, organizations and agencies were formed and conferences were held to generate solutions to development-related problems. The growing interaction among these fora is an indicator of the formation and development of a *negotiating system*.

A negotiating system is composed typically of specialized intergovernmental and transnational structures and processes, involving state and non-state actors, that are capable of handling at least some collective tasks in an *ex ante* coordinated manner. Such systems are characterized by the fact that they never become static. They evolve continuously in response to their own inner dynamics as well as to changes in the political, economic, and social environments (Kremenyuk, 1991; Rittberger, 1983; Young, 1989). Such systems do not represent necessarily comprehensive or institutionalized processes that incorporate talks among countries on *all* disputable and controversial issues. Nor does such a system simply consist of the sum total of national governments and their dyadic interactions.

A multilayered system of international negotiation is characterized by: (1) an identifiable political agenda filled with a host of issues in which a variable number of state and non-state actors have a stake, and which they cannot, and do not want to, handle by themselves; (2) more or less durable multiparty networks of coordination through which state – and, to some extent, non-state – actors deal collectively with one or more of these issues; and (3) collectively chosen policies of regulation, distribution or redistribution in an issue-area, the implementation of which is again sustained through such networks (Rittberger, 1983). The major actors in such systems are national governments, intergovernmental organizations, agencies established by national governments, and nongovernmental organizations. Binding the system together is a body of agreements and arrangements ranging from unofficial expressions of national interest to firm treaty commitments under international law (Caldwell, 1990:95). While such negotiation systems can certainly operate within

Negotiating International Regimes: Lessons Learned from the United Nations Conference on Environmental and Development (G. Sjöstedt, *et al.*, eds.; 1-85966-077-0; © IIASA; pub. Graham & Trotman, 1994; printed in Great Britain), pp. 21–41.

the context of international regimes, they do not necessarily imply that the participants share common principles and norms of behavior; they have only agreed to continue negotiating over such issues.

In 1989, when the UN General Assembly adopted Resolution 44/228 establishing UNCED (see Appendix A), one of its goals was to evaluate the state of the system of environmental and development negotiations. The Resolution asked the conference to: "examine the state of the environment and changes that have occurred since the United Nations Conference on the Human Environment ... taking into account the actions taken by all countries and intergovernmental organizations to protect and enhance the environment." It also said that the conference should: "recommend measures to be taken at the national and international levels to protect and enhance the environment, taking into account the specific needs of developing countries... with special emphasis on incorporating environmental concerns in the economic and social development process..." (UNGA, 1989).

In effect, the conference was to determine the extent of cohesiveness between the treatment of environmental and development issues in the negotiating system and then recommend the means to strengthen this system.

This chapter examines UNCED as the focal point of a negotiating system, evaluating the degree of coordination across different negotiations, conferences, and treaties, and determining how these elements contributed to one of the conference's major products: Agenda 21. Agenda 21 is a 750-page detailed blueprint for action to be taken by governments, agencies, UN organizations, and independent sectors in all major areas affecting the relationship between environment and economic development (see Appendix C). Looking at UNCED as the core of the larger system, this chapter describes the two essentially independent sub-systems of environment and development negotiations at the outset of the UNCED preparatory process and how they contributed to the PrepCom's negotiations. The next section describes the output of UNCED – the recommendations within Agenda 21 for initiating new negotiation processes and institutions that will have an impact on changing the system. Finally, both UNCED and the overall system are analyzed as to the impacts they had on each other and the significance of this relationship for the future of the negotiating system.

UNCED INPUTS

As part of the preparatory process, the UNCED secretariat and the PrepCom examined the components of the existing international system of environment and development negotiations before preparing Agenda 21. To manage the complicated list of issues set out in Resolution 44/228, the PrepCom divided environmental issues into eight groups: atmosphere, land resources, forests, biodiversity, biotechnology, oceans, wastes, and freshwater resources. The issues related to the underlying patterns of development that cause stress on the environment – such as poverty, unsustainable consumption patterns, demographic pressures, trade, and investment – were examined separately. While this method proved to be a practical way of dealing with such a long and complex agenda, the sectoral division of issues made it difficult to assess the system as a whole.

The negotiations, treaties, and conferences described in the following section and portrayed graphically in Figures 2.1 and 2.2 do not include every linkage in

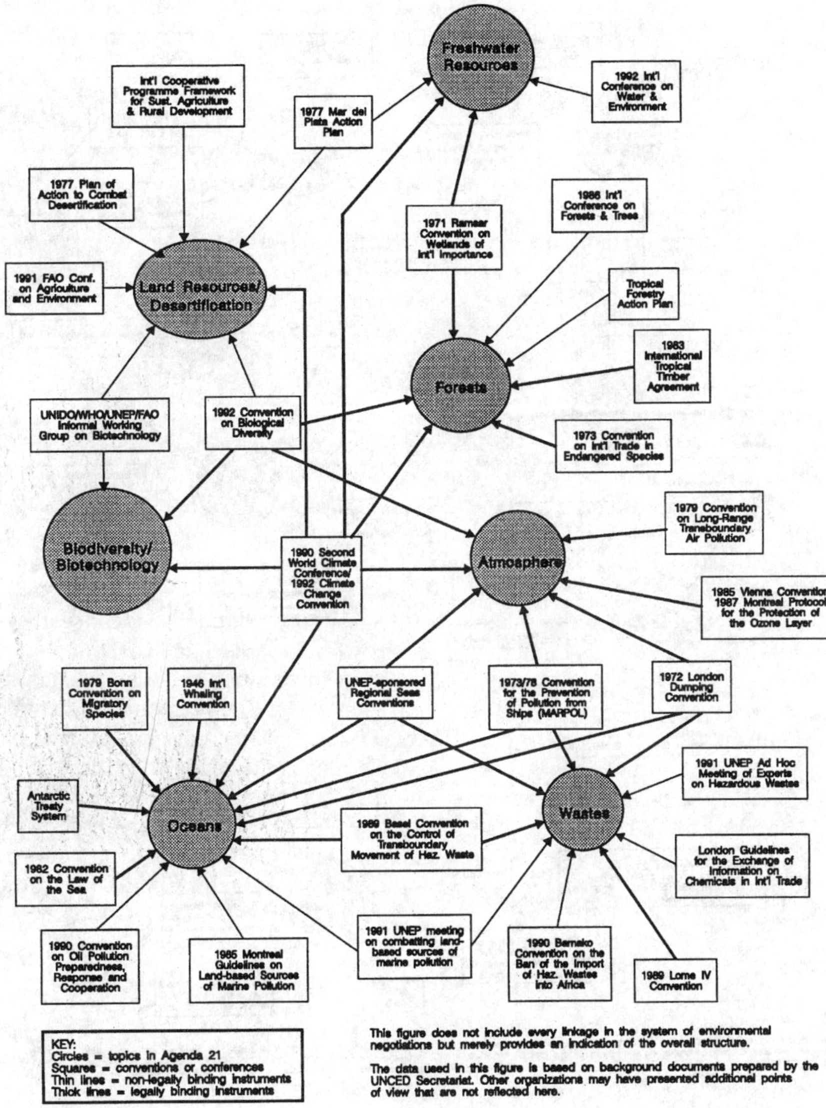

Figure 2.1 The System of Environmental Negotiations

the systems of environment and development negotiations, but merely provide an indication of the overall structure of the system. The components of each system's structure are based on those cited in background documents prepared by the UNCED secretariat during the preparatory process. Other negotiations and organizations may have contributed to the system, but as they were not cited directly in

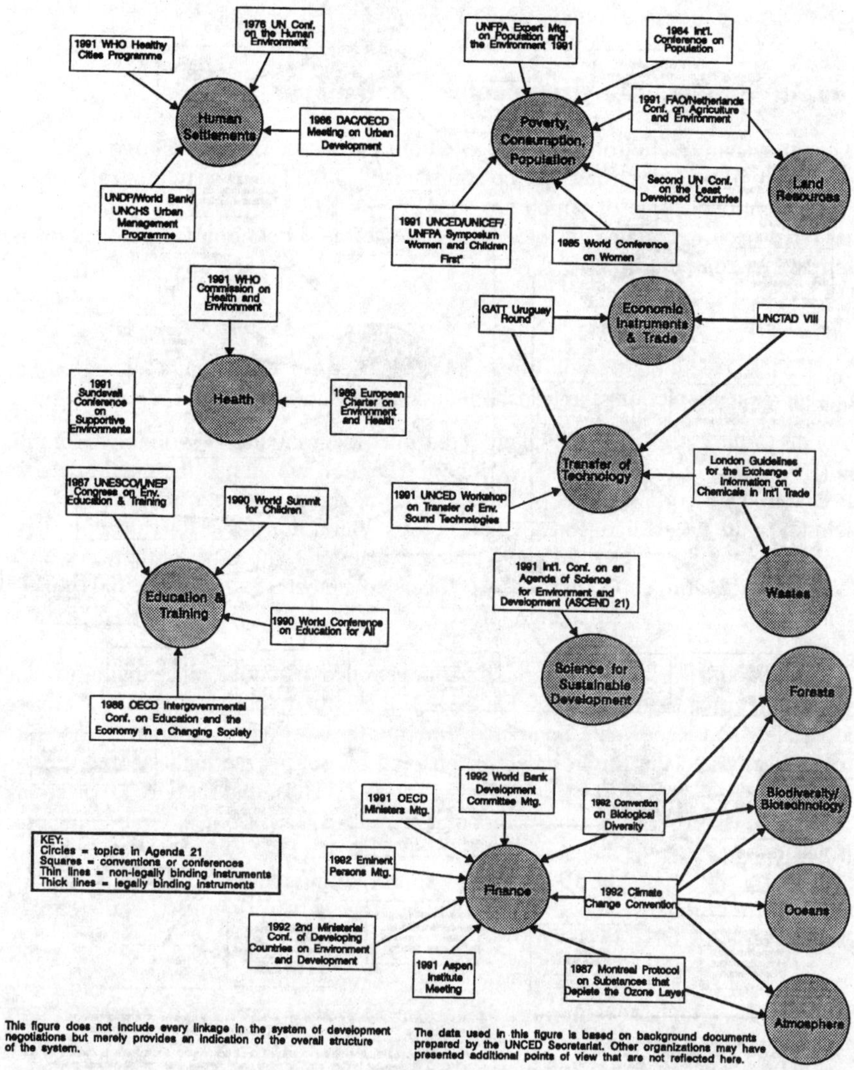

Figure 2.2 System of Developmental Negotiations

the background documents, they are not reflected here. In addition to the contributions from ongoing negotiations, UN agencies, intergovernmental organizations, nongovernmental organizations and conferences described below, the PrepCom also took into account the recommendations from the regional meetings that were held to discuss the issues on the UNCED agenda.[1]

The Sub-System of Environmental Negotiations

The sub-system of environmental negotiations is characterized by a large number of cross-sectoral linkages. Many of the components of the sub-system are legally binding conventions, some of which are supplemented by protocols and amendments, that have been negotiated in the 20 years since the Stockholm Conference on the Human Environment in 1972.

Atmosphere

The UNCED negotiations on atmosphere focused on three major areas: climate change, ozone depletion, and transboundary air pollution.

Climate Change On climate change, the Intergovernmental Negotiating Committee (INC) for a Framework Convention on Climate Change had the greatest impact on UNCED. In certain respects, the UNCED negotiations on a number of issues, including climate change, forests, and oceans, could not move forward until these parallel negotiations were complete. UNCED also took into account the work of the Second World Climate Conference (October/November 1990) and the Intergovernmental Panel on Climate Change (IPCC), which published its First Assessment in August 1990.

A number of regional and international conferences also took place that influenced the UNCED preparatory process. On the UN level, these included: the UN Committee on New and Renewable Sources of Energy; the May 1991 Helsinki Symposium on Electricity and the Environment, sponsored by the International Atomic Energy Agency (IAEA), the World Health Organization (WHO), and the UN Environment Programme (UNEP). Other international activities that contributed to the PrepCom's discussions on climate change included the 1991 Asian Energy Institute's 11 Country Climate Costing Study, the 1991 OECD-sponsored International Conference on Coal and the Environment, and the Sustainable Energy Development Conference in Copenhagen (A/CONF.151/PC/60).

Protection of the Ozone Layer The Vienna Convention for the Protection of the Ozone Layer, which was initially signed in March 1985, created the framework for international cooperation on measures to protect the ozone layer. Within this framework came the Montreal Protocol on Substances that Deplete the Ozone Layer, which was signed in September 1987 and went into force in January 1989. The Protocol was amended and strengthened at the Second Meeting of the Parties (London – June 1990). The Vienna Convention/Montreal Protocol regime is one of the strongest international regimes aimed at protecting the global environment. Its

[1] These meetings included the UN Economic Commission for Europe's Conference (Bergen, Norway – May 1990); UN Economic Commission for Latin America and the Caribbean's Conference (Mexico City – March 1991); the UN Economic and Social Commission for Asia and the Pacific's Ministerial-Level Conference (Bangkok – October 1990) and the Meeting of Senior Officials on Environment and Development (Bangkok – February 1991); the African Regional Preparatory Conference for UNCED (Cairo – July 1991); and the West Asian Regional Preparatory Conference for UNCED (Cairo – September 1991).

strength and acceptance within the international community enabled the PrepCom to reach agreement on this issue with comparatively little difficulty.

Transboundary Air Pollution Two types of international instruments used to regulate air pollution influenced the UNCED negotiations: agreements for transboundary air pollution control and technical standards to control emissions from different sources. Among the regional conventions is the 1979 Convention on Long-range Transboundary Air Pollution (in force since 1983), elaborated and administered within the framework of the UN Economic Commission for Europe (ECE), and geographically limited to Europe and North America. The convention has been supplemented by a series of protocols on joint long-term financing of the Cooperative Programme for Monitoring and Evaluation of the Long-range Transmission of Air Pollutants in Europe, EMEP (in force since 1988); the reduction of sulphur emissions or their transboundary fluxes by at least 30 percent (in force since 1987); and the control of emissions of nitrogen oxides or their transboundary fluxes (in force since 1991). During the course of the UNCED negotiations, additional protocols were under consideration.

Other legally binding agreements for transboundary air pollution abatement have been concluded within the sub-regional framework of the European Community and on a bilateral basis between neighboring countries in Europe (e.g., Finland–USSR in 1989) and North America (Mexico–United States in 1987, Canada–United States in 1991). In addition, several of the UNEP-sponsored regional agreements for marine environment protection include among their objectives the abatement of "land-based" air pollution.

In terms of sectoral regulation, international technical standards for the control of specific emission sources have existed in the automobile sector since 1970. Aircraft engine emissions have been monitored since 1981 by the Council of the International Civil Aviation Organization (ICAO). For air pollution from ships, the Marine Environment Protection Committee of the International Maritime Organization (IMO) established a working group in 1990 to determine target loads and strategies for the reduction of ship-based air pollutants to be laid down in a new annex to the 1973/1978 MARPOL Convention for the Prevention of Pollution from Ships. As regards air pollution from waste incineration at sea, the Parties to the 1972 London Convention on the Prevention of Marine Pollution by Dumping of Wastes and Other Matter decided in 1990 to terminate all marine incineration of liquid noxious wastes by the end of 1991 (A/CONF.151/PC/59).

Forests

During the last two decades, the world has witnessed a significant increase in concern for and action on forests. On the international level, the International Tropical Timber Organization (ITTO) was established by the 1983 International Tropical Timber Agreement (ITTA), under the auspices of the UN Conference on Trade and Development (UNCTAD), and was the only existing international agreement on tropical forests prior to UNCED. The Food and Agriculture Organization (FAO), together with the World Bank, the UN Development Programme (UNDP) and the World Resources Institute (WRI), launched the Tropical Forestry Action Plan (TFAP) in June 1985. The Plan provides a framework for actions at national, regional, and global levels on tropical forestry. The FAO Committee on Forestry, at its 10th session in September 1990, recommended to increase the efficiency of the

TFAP, particularly through strengthening national capabilities. The FAO Council at its November 1990 session endorsed the concept of an international instrument on the conservation and development of forests, which became a major part of the UNCED negotiations (A/CONF.151/PC/27). Other international initiatives included the launching of the International Conference on Forests and Trees ("Silva") organized by the French government in February 1986, and the Ministerial Conference for the Protection of Forests in Europe (Strasbourg – December 1990) (A/CONF.151/PC/64).

Cross-sectorally, in the context of the 1990 Second World Climate Conference, the Ministers declared that they recognized that forests and forest products play a key social and economic role in many nations and communities. They also noted that the conservation of the world's forests in their role as reservoirs of carbon is of considerable importance for global climate stability, keeping in mind the important role of forests in the conservation of biological diversity and the protection of soil stability and the hydrological system (A/CONF.151/PC/27). The PrepCom took into consideration input from related conventions, including the 1971 Ramsar Convention on Wetlands and the 1973 Convention on International Trade of Endangered Species (A/CONF.151/PC/64).

Land Resources

On the subject of land resources, the UNCED negotiations covered four major topics: integrated management of land resources, combating desertification and drought, sustainable mountain development, and sustainable agriculture and rural development. In spite of a general lack of international attention and the paucity of international negotiation on these issues, several institutions and initiatives have addressed land resources.

Desertification The major international instrument guiding efforts to combat desertification has been the 1977 United Nations Plan of Action to Combat Desertification. Despite this plan, desertification remains unabated; more land is desertified now than it was in 1977 and a larger population is affected. Within the UN system, UNEP and the FAO are the lead agencies working on desertification matters. Other organizations working on combating desertification include the International Fund for Agricultural Development (IFAD), the United Nations Educational, Scientific, and Cultural Organization (UNESCO), and the United Nations Sudano-Sahelian Office (UNSO) (A/CONF.151/PC/62).

Integrated Land Management There are no international agreements that specifically address integrated land management. Organizations concerned with the management of land and natural resources for development include: the FAO, IFAD, UNEP, UNESCO, the World Food Programme (WFP), WHO, specifically its Environmental Health Programme, and the World Meteorological Organization (WMO). Other agencies within the UN system, such as UNDP and the World Bank, are concerned with various aspects of land resources management for development purposes, focusing on agriculture, fisheries, forestry, and other related issues (A/CONF.151/PC/24).

Sustainable Agriculture Options for action on sustainable agriculture and rural development were contained in the proposed International Cooperative Programme Framework for Sustainable Agriculture and Rural Development prepared by FAO.

The program is based on the Den Bosch Declaration and Agenda for Action for Sustainable Agriculture and Rural Development agreed at the FAO/Netherlands Conference on Agriculture and the Environment in April 1991(A/CONF.151/PC/42/ Add.2).

As regards water use for sustainable agriculture, a global interagency program framework was also developed in 1990 at the FAO Conference on Agriculture and Environment as a follow-up of the 1977 Mar del Plata Action Plan, which deals with the relevant aspects of controlling water-logging, salinity, and drainage in irrigated and rain-fed agriculture. Finally, sustainable agriculture also encompasses both conservation and use of biological diversity for agriculture. Diverse elements regarding this program framework have been developed and implemented by FAO in close consultation and cooperation with other institutions concerned with biodiversity, including UNEP, UNESCO, WRI, the International Union for the Conservation of Nature and Natural Resources (IUCN), the Ramsar Convention on Wetlands of International Importance, and the INC for a Framework Convention on Biodiversity (A/CONF.151/PC/26).

Mountains There are no international treaties that specifically address sustainable development of mountain ecosystems. Although some UN agencies, including the World Bank, IFAD, and UNESCO contributed information to the UNCED discussions on this topic, the majority of the information came from NGOs such as the IUCN, the International Mountain Society (IMS), Woodland Mountain Institutes (WMI), and the International Center for Integrated Mountain Development (A/CONF. 151/PC/100/Add.18).

Biodiversity

The major input to the negotiations on biological diversity from outside the UNCED PrepCom came from the parallel negotiations in the INC for a convention on biodiversity. The INC resulted from UNEP's establishment of an ad hoc Working Group of Experts on Biological Diversity in 1988 to begin discussing the need to conserve biological resources. Following three sessions of this ad hoc working group, UNEP convened the first meeting of the ad hoc Working Group of Legal and Technical Experts in November 1990. After two sessions that resulted in the drafting of a convention, UNEP formed the INC in 1991 to further elaborate and adopt a Convention on Biological Diversity.

During the UNCED negotiations, there was also discussion of key scientific and technical linkages between biodiversity, and forests, climate change, biotechnology, and oceans (A/CONF.151/PC/66). Assistance and advice were also received from UNEP, FAO, UNESCO, UNDP, IUCN, WRI, WWF and the International Union of Biological Science (A/CONF.151/PC/28).

Biotechnology

In spite of the close linkages between biodiversity and biotechnology, these topics were negotiated separately by the UNCED PrepCom, on the insistence of several developed countries. Although there are no existing international legal instruments on biotechnology, nor were there any international negotiations underway, there are a number of fora in which biotechnology is being addressed. During the course of the negotiations for the Convention on Biological Diversity, the topic of biotechnology was discussed. At the third session of the ad hoc Working Group of Experts on Biological Diversity (Geneva – July 1990), the meeting decided that biotechnology elements demanded further examination. A Sub-Working Group on Biotechnology met in Nairobi in November 1990 and recommended a number of issues that should be considered in the preparation of a biotechnology component in the biodiversity convention. These recommendations were also examined by UNCED.

Recommendations from the UN Industrial Development Organization/WHO/UNEP/FAO Informal Working Group on Safety in Biotechnology, which was established in 1985, were also examined by the UNCED PrepCom. Other WHO projects on biotechnology include biosafety guidelines for workers engaged in the production of vaccines and a training program on biotechnology safety (A/CONF.151/PC/29).

Oceans

Since the late 1950s, the international community has steadily developed a system of international institutions and legal instruments to cope with problems affecting the oceans. At the global level, the 1982 UN Convention on the Law of the Sea comprehensively covers all marine issues, including protection of the marine environment and its living resources. The 1972 Convention on the Prevention of Marine Pollution by Dumping of Wastes and Other Matter (London Convention) has been progressively adapted to take account of the need to prohibit or restrict dumping of toxic substances and wastes and to promote comprehensive waste reduction and management policies. The 1973 International Convention on the Prevention of Pollution from Ships, as modified in 1978 (MARPOL), addresses ship-source pollution. The 1990 Convention on Oil Pollution Preparedness, Response, and Cooperation is the most recent agreement addressing oil pollution. The 1989 Basel Convention on the Control of Transboundary Movements of Hazardous Wastes and their Disposal also addresses the maritime transport and disposal of wastes. Work is underway to harmonize the Basel Convention with the London Convention, MARPOL, and other IMO conventions and codes, and to develop a liability regime.

On the issue of land-based sources of marine pollution, the primary instrument has been the 1985 Montreal Guidelines. In conjunction with the UNCED negotiations, UNEP began an evaluation of these guidelines as well as an outline of strategy options or actions to reduce the effects of land-based sources of pollution and other activities threatening marine and coastal resources. Canada, in cooperation with the UNCED secretariat, UNEP, the International Oceanographic Commission, and the UN Office for Ocean Affairs and the Law of the Sea, hosted an Intergovernmental Meeting of Experts on Land-based Sources of Marine Pollution (Halifax, Nova Scotia – May 1991). This was followed by a UNEP-sponsored meeting of government-designated experts to formulate a draft strategy for the reduction of the degradation of the marine environment from land-based sources of pollution and activities in coastal areas (Nairobi – December 1991).

On the issue of living marine resources, UNCED examined conventions that deal with or otherwise encompass the protection of marine species, particularly the 1946 International Convention for the Regulation of Whaling and the 1979 Bonn Convention on migratory species. The work of other organizations, such as the Inter-American Tropical Tuna Commission and the Agreement on Small Cetaceans in the

Baltic and North Sea under the Bonn Convention, in the conservation, management, and study of cetaceans and other marine mammals was also consulted.

The UNCED PrepCom also looked at instruments covering the polar regions. In the Arctic, there is only the 1973 Oslo Agreement on Conservation of Polar Bears. Within the Antarctic Treaty system, a protocol was adopted in October 1991 that consolidates and strengthens the measures for environmental protection adopted under the Treaty and extends them to all Antarctic activities, while also subjecting mineral development to at least a 50-year prohibition.

At the regional level, the system of UNEP Regional Seas conventions addresses a wide range of issues. The seven conventions cover the Mediterranean, Kuwait Action Plan Region, Wider Caribbean, West and Central Africa, Eastern Africa, Red Sea and Gulf of Aden, South Pacific, and South-East Pacific. They are supplemented by a total of 19 protocols: two on ocean dumping, three on land-based sources of marine pollution, one on offshore industrial activities, eight on emergency response to pollution incidents, one on radioactive pollution, and four on protected areas and species.

There are also five oceans conventions in the European region: the Oslo Convention on ocean dumping, the Paris Convention on land-based sources (extended by amendment to encompass atmospheric sources), and the Bonn Agreements on the North Sea, all of which reach into the North Atlantic; the Helsinki Convention, dealing with all sources of marine pollution, which covers the Baltic Sea; and the 1991 Convention on Environmental Impact Assessment in a Transboundary Context (A/CONF.151/PC/69).

Freshwater Resources

The primary input into the Agenda 21 chapter on freshwater resources was the International Conference on Water and the Environment (Dublin, Ireland – January 1992). The conference addressed critical freshwater issues and acted as the formal entry for those issues into UNCED. The conference was the first major UN-sponsored water conference since the 1977 United Nations Water Conference and the resulting Mar del Plata Action Plan.

There were several conferences and meetings that led into and contributed toward the synthesis of opinion at the Dublin Conference. Foremost among these were the Symposium on a Strategy for Water Resources Capacity Building (Delft – June 1991); Water Quality Assessment and Management (Bratislava – August 1991); ESCAP Meeting on Water Resources Planning (Bangkok – October 1991); informal consultation on integrated water management for developing countries (Copenhagen – November 1991); and ASCEND 21 (an ICSU conference on scientific aspects of environment and development, Vienna – November 1991) (A/CONF.151/PC/73).

Other international water-quality monitoring and management programs that contributed to Agenda 21 were the Global Water Quality Monitoring Programme, the UNEP Environmentally Sound Management of Inland Waters, the FAO regional inland fishery bodies, and the Convention on Wetlands of International Importance Especially as Waterfowl Habitat (Ramsar Convention).

The PrepCom also looked at negotiations and institutions on a number of other issues related to freshwater resources, including the Second World Climate Conference, and the INC for a Framework Convention on Climate Change.

Wastes

UNCED's treatment of wastes resulted in the elaboration of four chapters of Agenda 21: hazardous wastes; radioactive wastes; solid wastes and sewage-related issues; and toxic chemicals.

Hazardous Wastes A number of steps have been taken with the aim of reducing transboundary movements of hazardous wastes. Some of these are the Basel Convention on the Control of Transboundary Movements of Hazardous Wastes and their Disposal (1989); the Bamako Convention on the Ban of the Import into Africa and the Control of Transboundary Movement of Hazardous Wastes within Africa (1991); the Convention on the Prevention of Marine Pollution by Dumping of Wastes and Other Matter (London Convention, 1972) and the 1989 Lomé IV Convention between the EC and the African, Caribbean, and Pacific Group (ACP).

Other events that also contributed to the formulation of the Agenda 21 chapter on hazardous wastes included the December 1991 UNEP-sponsored Ad Hoc Meeting of Government-designated Experts in Nairobi to discuss international strategy and develop an action program, including technical guidelines for the environmentally sound management of hazardous wastes. The Seventh Ordinary Meeting of the Contracting Parties to the Convention for the Protection of the Mediterranean Sea against Pollution and its related protocols (Cairo – October 1991) discussed a draft protocol for the prevention of pollution of the Mediterranean Sea by transboundary movements of hazardous wastes and their disposal (A/CONF.151/PC/88).

Toxic Chemicals Although no legally-binding international convention exists on the subject of toxic chemicals, there is activity on a number of different fronts that contributed to UNCED. The 1989 London Guidelines for the Exchange of Information on Chemicals in International Trade was designed to assist governments in the process of increasing chemical safety through the exchange of information on chemicals in international trade. The FAO has maintained a substantial program on agrochemicals, providing assistance to its member countries on their safe and efficient use. Guiding principles, policies, and procedures are covered in the International Code of Conduct on the Distribution and Use of Pesticides that was adopted unanimously by member governments, the pesticide industry, and international and environmental organizations in 1985. The International Labor Organization's (ILO) Convention (No. 170) and Recommendation (No. 177) on safety in the use of chemicals at work adopted by the 1990 International Labour Conference, provide a universal basis for national- and enterprise-level action. Outside the UN system, OECD expanded its work in this field in 1978 and created a special program on the control of chemicals under a Management Committee reporting to the Council (A/CONF.151/PC/35).

Radioactive Wastes A Code of Practice on the International Transboundary Movement of Radioactive Waste was adopted at the International Atomic Energy Agency's (IAEA) General Conference in September 1990. This code of practice, in conjunction with relevant provisions from the Basel Convention and the London Convention, formed the basis of the negotiations on the environmentally sound management of radioactive wastes within UNCED (A/CONF.151/PC/100/Add.4).

Solid Wastes Although there are no international treaties on the management of solid waste, there are a number of important initiatives that contributed information to the PrepCom's negotiations on this chapter of Agenda 21. These include: the UNDP/World Bank Water Supply and Sanitation project; the Urban Management and Environment component of the joint UNDP/World Bank/UNCHS Urban Management Programme; UNICEF's Urban Basic Services Programme; and other programs coordinated by UNEP, WHO, FAO, and UNCHS, among others (A/CONF.151/PC/76).

The Sub-System of Development Negotiations

Unlike environmental concerns, most development issues have not been the subject of formalized international treaties and conventions reached through negotiation. They have been discussed primarily in international or regional conferences, by the relevant UN agencies or at national or local levels. The output of these debates typically has been reports, declarations, and nonbinding recommendations. Unlike the sub-system of environmental negotiations, there are very few cross-sectoral structural linkages within the sub-system of development negotiations, making it less cohesive (see Figure 2.2).

Human Settlements

The UN first dealt with the issue of human settlements in its 1976 Conference on Human Settlements. Among other things, this conference resulted in the creation of the UN Commission on Human Settlements (UNCHS). At its 1991 session, held in Harare, Zimbabwe, UNCHS endorsed a report entitled, "People, Settlements, Environment and Development," which had previously been adopted at an intergovernmental meeting (The Hague – November 1990). The report sets out the role of human settlements in the context of sustainable development and formed the basis of what was to become the Agenda 21 chapter on human settlements. Other initiatives on human settlements that were examined by the PrepCom included the UNDP/World Bank/UNCHS Urban Management Programme, the WHO's Healthy Cities Programme, and the Development Assistance Committee (DAC)/OECD 1986 meeting on Urban Development (A/CONF.151/PC/43).

Poverty, Consumption, Population

In developing the Agenda 21 chapters on "Combating Poverty," "Changing Consumption Patterns," and "Demographic Dynamics and Sustainability," the UNCED secretariat enlisted the assistance of a number of UN agencies including the FAO, ILO, UN Population Fund (UNFPA), IFAD, and UNDP. The PrepCom also took into consideration declarations and statements from the report of the International Conference on Population (Mexico City – August 1984); the report of the World Conference to Review and Appraise the Achievements of the United Nations Decade for Women (Nairobi – July 1985); the International Development Strategy for the Fourth UN Development Decade; the Declaration of the 18th Special Session of the General Assembly; the Second UN Conference on the Least Developed Countries, and UNFPA's Expert Meeting on Population and Environment (New York – March 1991). UNCED also co-sponsored with the UN Children's Fund (UNICEF) and UNFPA a symposium on "Women and Children First." Finally, in one of the few overt linkages between environment and development within the aegis of the conference, the PrepCom also looked at the recommendations from the 1991 FAO/ Netherlands Conference on Agriculture and the Environment on raising labor productivity and incomes in agriculture.

Environmental Health

Although there are no legally binding international agreements on health and the environment, there were a number of conferences that contributed to the UNCED negotiations. For example, the Ministers of the Environment and of Health of the member states of the European Region of WHO adopted the European Charter on Environment and Health, which covers agreed-upon principles and strategies. The Sundsvall Conference on Supportive Environments, held in June 1991, identified practical ways to create physical, social, and economic environments supportive of health and compatible with sustainable development, and to build bridges between sectors for practical problem solutions. The major UN agency involved in the preparation of the Agenda 21 text was the WHO Commission on Health and Environment (A/CONF.151/PC/54).

Science for Sustainable Development

Many of the recommendations on science for Agenda 21 came from the ICSU's International Conference on an Agenda of Science for Environment and Development (ASCEND 21) (November 1991 – Vienna) (see Chapter 10). In addition, UNCED collaborated with a number of UN and related agencies including UNESCO, the UN Center for Science and Technology for Development (UNCSTD), the World Bank, FAO, WHO, UNEP, WMO, and UNESCO (A/CONF.151/PC/52).

Transfer of Technology

The debate on this chapter of Agenda 21 was one of the most polarized between North and South during the PrepCom's negotiations. Despite the fact that UNCED sponsored a workshop on the Transfer of Environmentally Sound Technologies in 1991 aimed at easing these tensions, it was to little avail. The PrepCom did take into account parts of the 1989 London Guidelines for the Exchange of Information on Chemicals in International Trade that addressed intellectual property rights. Other UN and related agencies that contributed to the secretariat's working party on this issue were UNCTAD, the UNCSTD, the UN Centre on Transnational Corporations, UNESCO, UNEP, UNDP, UNIDO, the World Intellectual Property Organization (WIPO), the World Bank, and the General Agreement on Tariffs and Trade (GATT) (A/CONF.151/PC/53).

Education

The recommendations from a number of conferences on education contributed to the negotiations on "Promoting Education, Public Awareness and Training." These included the UNESCO/UNEP Congress on Environmental Education and Training (Moscow – August 1987); the OECD Intergovernmental Conference on Education and the Economy in a Changing Society (Paris – March 1988); the World Conference on Education for All, convened by UNDP, UNESCO, UNICEF, and the World

Bank (Jomtien, Thailand – March 1990); and the UNICEF World Summit for Children (New York – September 1990) (A/CONF.151/PC/55).

Economic and Trade Issues

The negotiations on the chapter of Agenda 21 dealing with "International Cooperation to Accelerate Sustainable Development in Developing Countries and Related Domestic Policies" dealt primarily with the issues of trade and debt. In the negotiations on trade and the environment, the principal area of concern related to agricultural commodities was market access, a matter that is under negotiation in the Uruguay Round of GATT. The UNCED negotiations reflected the impact of the GATT negotiations on such issues as agricultural protectionism in developed countries. In the broader field of commodities in general, the major difficulty faced by developing countries has been the sharp fluctuations in prices leading to great instability in export earnings. This question has been under discussion for a long time and an Integrated Programme for Commodities, with a focus on stabilization of earnings, was discussed within the framework of UNCTAD. The Cartagena Commitment signed at UNCTAD VIII became a major input into the text of Agenda 21.

Financial Resources and Mechanisms

The area of financial resources and mechanisms, which dealt with the funding of Agenda 21 implementation, was, due to its nature, the most cross-sectoral of issues considered by UNCED. A number of different negotiations, conferences, and meetings contributed to the UNCED negotiations on this topic. The PrepCom examined reports prepared for the UNEP Governing Council on the costs to developing countries for implementing the Montreal Protocol, a costing exercise of measures adopted to limit possible climate changes (A/CONF.151/PC/23), a study prepared for UNEP's Ad Hoc Working Group of Experts on Biological Diversity on estimated costs of conserving biodiversity, and a recent study by the World Institute for Development Economic Research of the United Nations University that examined the issue from the perspective of the needs of developing countries (A/CONF.151/PC/51).

Meetings held during the course of the UNCED negotiations that influenced the outcome included: the Aspen Institute Working Group on International Environment and Development Policy (July 1991); the Meeting of OECD Ministers of Environment and Development (Paris – December 1991); the annual High-level Meeting of the members of the DAC, joined by the World Bank, the International Monetary Fund (IMF) and UNDP (December 1991); the "Eminent Persons" Meeting on Financing Global Environment and Development" hosted by Former Japanese Prime Minister Noboru Takeshita (Tokyo – April 1992); the IMF and World Bank Development Committee meeting (April 1992); the GEF Participants' Meeting (May 1992); and the Second Ministerial Conference of Developing Countries on Environment and Development (Kuala Lumpur, Malaysia – April 1992).

UNCED OUTPUTS

UNCED based its negotiations on an examination of these existing structures and the effectiveness of the system, and then proposed a series of strategies and action plans for strengthening and improving the future coherence and coordination of the system. The preparatory process and the Conference examined the pieces of the system and discussed means of improving existing institutions and treaties and, where there was a need, for generating new ones. The governments then negotiated specific recommendations for action that became Agenda 21. Some of these recommendations were aimed at strengthening and unifying the overall system; it is these recommendations that formed the output of the UNCED process.

In general, Agenda 21 proposed two important types of mechanisms: (1) the strengthening of existing institutions and the establishment of new ones, and (2) the negotiation of new treaties that take into account the need for integrating environment and development (see Figure 2.3). It is through these mechanisms that the future of the system will be determined.

Institutional Arrangements

To facilitate institutional coordination, enhance international cooperation, and examine the progress of the implementation of Agenda 21 at the national, regional, and international levels, UNCED recommended the establishment of a high-level Commission on Sustainable Development that would report to the UN Economic and Social Council (ECOSOC). Chapter 38 of Agenda 21, ("International Institutional Arrangements") elaborates further:

> The Commission should provide for active involvement of organs, programmes and organizations of the United Nations system, international financial institutions and other relevant intergovernmental organizations, and encourage the participation of non-governmental organizations, including industry and the business and scientific communities.

Among the proposed functions of the Commission on Sustainable Development are several that are aimed at strengthening and integrating the international negotiating system. Agenda 21 specifically states that the Commission should:

> monitor progress in the implementation of Agenda 21 and activities related to the integration of environmental and developmental goals throughout the United Nations system through analysis and evaluation of reports from all relevant organs, organizations, programmes and institutions of the United Nations system dealing with various issues of environment and development, including those related to finance.

From an institutional perspective, the major outputs from UNCED to the international system are the creation of this Commission and the pledge to work to further integrate environment and development within the decision-making apparatus of the UN system.

International Negotiations and Conferences

In Chapter 39 of Agenda 21 ("International Legal Instruments and Mechanisms"), the Conference agreed that there is a need for:

(1) the further development of international law on sustainable development, giving special attention to the delicate balance between environmental and developmental concerns;
(2) clarification and strengthening of the relationship between existing international instruments or agreements in the field of environment and relevant social

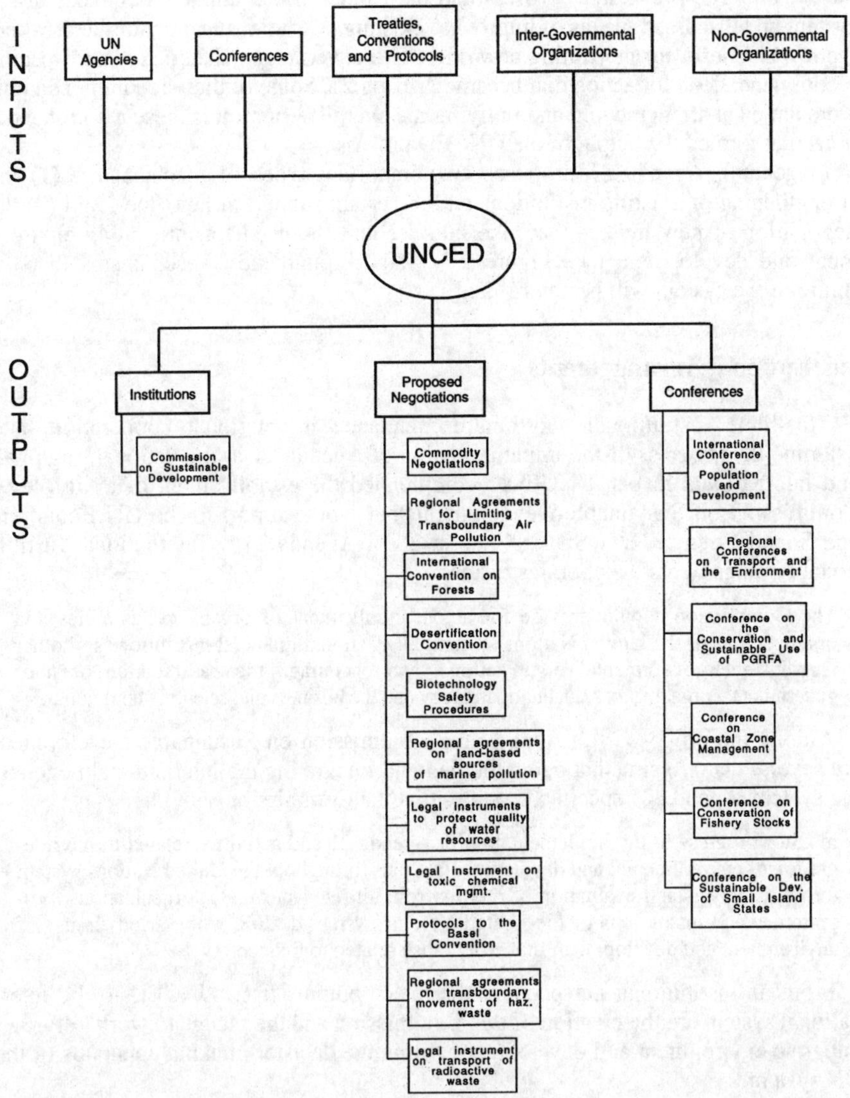

The data used in this figure is from the text of Agenda 21.

Figure 2.3 UNCED as Part of Negotiating System

and economic agreements or instruments, taking into account the special needs of developing countries;

(3) the participation in and the contribution of all countries, including the developing countries, to treaty-making in the field of international law on sustainable development.

With this in mind, UNCED recommended the negotiation of a number of new international or regional conventions and protocols that would further the integration of environment and development in the international system. Not all of these proposed negotiations or conferences will result in the elaboration of legally binding instruments, yet they should all contribute to the overall system.

Proposed Negotiations

Among the future negotiations proposed by Agenda 21 is the recommendation that governments pursue substantive negotiations between producers and consumers "with a view to achieving viable and more efficient international agreements that take into account market trends, or arrangements, as well as study groups. In this regard, particular attention should be paid to the agreements on cocoa, coffee, sugar and tropical timber" (Chapter 2).

On the issue of transboundary air pollution, Agenda 21 encourages the "establishment of new and the implementation of existing regional agreements for limiting transboundary air pollution" (Chapter 9).

For strengthening the sub-system on combating deforestation, one of the objectives is:

> to consider the need for and the feasibility of all kinds of appropriate internationally agreed arrangements to promote international cooperation on forest management, conservation and sustainable development of all types of forests including afforestation, reforestation, and rehabilitation (Chapter 11).

Agenda 21 also calls for:

> strengthening the coordination and improving the capacity and ability of intergovernmental organizations such as FAO, ITTO, UNEP and UNESCO to provide technical support for the management, conservation and sustainable development of forests, including support for the negotiation of the International Tropical Timber Agreement of 1983, due in 1992/93 (Chapter 11).

On the issue of combating desertification, UNCED agreed to request the UN General Assembly to establish "an intergovernmental negotiating committee for the elaboration of an international convention to combat desertification, in those countries experiencing serious drought and/or desertification, particularly in Africa, with a view to finalizing such a convention by June1994." This is one of the more specific recommendations to emerge from UNCED (Chapter 12).

To strengthen the sub-system of negotiated agreements on biotechnology, Agenda 21 calls on governments, relevant international and regional organizations, the private sector, and nongovernmental organizations to "compile, update and develop compatible safety procedures into a framework of internationally agreed principles as a basis for guidelines to be applied on safety in biotechnology, including consideration of the need for and feasibility of an international agreement" (Chapter 16).

On oceans, Agenda 21 recommends that states, with the support of the relevant international organizations, should initiate and promote the development of new regional agreements aimed at the prevention, reduction, and control of degradation of the marine environment from land-based activities (Chapter 17). For freshwater resources, Agenda 21 recommends the development of national and international legal instruments that may be required to protect the quality of water resources particularly for:

(i) Monitoring and control of pollution and its effects in national and transboundary waters;
(ii) Control of long-range atmospheric transport of pollutants;
(iii) Control of accidental and/or deliberate spills in national and/or transboundary water bodies;
(iv) Environmental impact assessment (Chapter 18).

To improve the management of toxic chemicals, Chapter 19 of Agenda 21 recommends that governments and relevant international organizations, with the cooperation of industry, should implement the Prior Informed Consent procedures as soon as possible and, in the light of experience gained, invite relevant international organizations, such as UNEP, GATT, FAO, WHO, and others, in their respective area of competence, to consider working expeditiously toward the conclusion of legally-binding instruments.

On the environmentally sound management of hazardous wastes, Chapter 20 of Agenda 21 urges the ratification of "the Basel Convention on the Control of Transboundary Movements of Hazardous Wastes and their Disposal and the expeditious elaboration of related protocols, such as the protocol on liability and compensation, mechanisms and guidelines to facilitate the implementation of the Basel Convention." Similarly, the delegates urged "ratification and full implementation by the countries concerned of the Bamako Convention on the Ban on the Import into Africa and the Control of Transboundary Movement of Hazardous Wastes within Africa and the expeditious elaboration of a protocol on liability and compensation." The delegates also recommended that governments "formulate, where appropriate, regional agreements such as the Bamako Convention regulating the transboundary movement of hazardous wastes."

Finally, on radioactive waste, UNCED called for states to

> implement the Code of Practice on the Transboundary Movements of Radioactive Waste and, under the auspices of IAEA, in cooperation with relevant international organizations dealing with different modes of transport, keep the question of such movements under active review, including the desirability of concluding a legally binding instrument (Chapter 22).

Proposed Conferences

In addition to proposing these future negotiations, UNCED recommended the convening of international conferences that could add to the body of soft law that constitutes part of the system. One of these is the International Conference on Population and Development to be held in 1994. UNCED recommended that "governments formulate integrated national policies for environment and development, taking into account demographic trends and factors" and to report on the status of implementation to the conference (Chapter 5). Although the scheduling of this conference took place prior to UNCED, it will provide one of the first post-Rio opportunities to deal with the issues of population, development, and environment in a single forum.

On the issues of energy and atmosphere, UNCED called on governments and the private sector to "study, within the framework of the United Nations and its regional economic commissions, the feasibility of convening regional conferences on transport and the environment" (Chapter 9).

To strengthen the sub-system of negotiations on sustainable agriculture, UNCED did not call for any new negotiations, but recommended that the appropriate UN agencies and regional organizations promote, for 1994, the Fourth International Technical Conference on the Conservation and Sustainable Use of Plant Genetic Resources for Food and Sustainable Agriculture (PGRFA), which is to adopt the first state of the world report and the first global plan of action on the conservation and sustainable use of PGRFA (Chapter 14).

Agenda 21 contains three recommendations for conferences on oceans-related issues. On integrated coastal zone management, delegates agreed that "States should cooperate ... in the preparation of national guidelines for integrated coastal zone management and development, drawing on existing experience. A global conference to exchange experience in the field could be held before 1994."

On the issue of sustainable use and conservation of marine living resources of the high seas, Agenda 21 states that nations should negotiate, where appropriate, international agreements for the effective management and conservation of fishery stocks. UNCED also recommended that "States, should convene, as soon as possible, an intergovernmental conference under United Nations auspices ... with a view to promoting effective implementation of the provisions of the United Nations Convention on the Law of the Sea on straddling fish stocks and highly migratory fish stocks. ..."

Finally, on the sustainable development of small islands, Agenda 21 recommends that:

> Small island developing States, with the support, as appropriate, of international organizations ... should develop and strengthen inter-island, regional and interregional cooperation and information exchange, including periodic regional and global meetings on sustainable development of small island developing States with the first global conference on the sustainable development of small island developing States, to be held in 1993 (Chapter 17).

CONCLUSIONS

Negotiating systems consist of two basic parts: the elements of the system and the relationships between those elements. With regard to the system of environment and development negotiations, the elements include: on-going negotiations, treaties, conferences, UN agencies, intergovernmental organizations, treaty secretariats, governments, and nongovernmental organizations. The relationships between these elements include: coordination, implementation, interdependence, and delegation of responsibilities. Focusing on these relational aspects, one can easily see the many problems challenging UNCED followup.

There was an absence of coordination and communication within the system at the start of the UNCED negotiating process. This lack of coordination between governments, intergovernmental organizations, UN agencies and secretariats for different treaties had a definite impact on the results of UNCED. From the start, UNCED accentuated the fact that there were two negotiating sub-systems (environment and development) rather than a single integrated system (sustainable development) by treating environment and development issues on a sectoral basis. Although the treatment of cross-sectoral development issues was supposed to improve coordination between the two sub-systems, the structure of the PrepCom's working groups only formalized the distance between environment and development. For example, the Agenda 21 draft chapters on environmental issues were discussed in Working Groups I and II beginning at PrepCom III, whereas draft chapters on development issues (poverty, education, health, etc.) were not ready until PrepCom IV. Very few of these development issues were taken into consideration during the negotiation of the environmental chapters.

The system was also characterized by an overall lack of effective implementation of international treaties on environmental issues. Although most treaties include monitoring and/or reporting mechanisms, treaty signatories did not always follow through with implementation. This makes it difficult to determine the effect that legally-binding agreements have actually had. The UNCED process accentuated this major shortcoming in the system, while suffering from limited feedback on treaty effectiveness.

Although there was a significant amount of acknowledged issue interdependence within the environment sub-system (for example, the Climate Change Convention negotiations affected negotiations and institutions that dealt with atmospheric issues, oceans, biodiversity, desertification, forests, and freshwater resources) and recognition of the mutual effects of economic development on environment issues and vice versa, the system had very few institutional mechanisms set up to address this interdependence. In most existing environmental treaties, not only is there little mention of the economic development issues that are often the underlying causes of environmental degradation, but there is often little attempt to relate provisions of existing treaties.

As indicated in the earlier discussion, many agencies and secretariats have responsibilities to act on behalf of environmental and developmental programs. Although there is some overlap (for example, UNEP and WMO both working on climate change), there is little coordination and sharing of responsibilities. Governments certainly bear the brunt of responsibility for cleaning up the environment and promoting economic development. Yet, within the system, the majority of institutional responsibility is placed on the IGOs, UN agencies, and secretariats. As well, NGOs have served traditionally as the watchdogs to ensure that existing treaties are implemented and that ongoing negotiations result in the strongest treaties possible.

Overall, when the UNCED preparatory process began, the system was structured such that there were, in effect, two systems – one on environment, and another incomplete system on development. There was little coordination and communication within or between the systems; implementation mechanisms were not well defined or well carried out; issue interdependence existed, but was not always reflected in other elements of the system; and responsibilities were shared between governments and the other actors in the system, with no one taking full responsibility.

The conference and its follow-up mechanisms will likely have a major impact on transforming this system. Although it is too soon to tell how the overall structure of the system may change, some initial observations can be made.

There was unprecedented cooperation and coordination between the elements of both sub-systems during the UNCED preparatory process. The cooperative efforts that began with UNCED may be able to live on in the new institution created by UNCED, the Commission on Sustainable Development, thus increasing overall coordination between elements within the system.

It is too soon to tell if UNCED will have any effect on improving implementation of agreements within the system. However, it is expected that the Commission may be able to play a role in monitoring and, possibly, improving implementation. How effective that role will be depends on the degree of increased commitment from governments.

UNCED may have set the stage for an overall strengthening of issue interdependence. Although UNCED was the first major conference to look seriously at both environment and development, the issues were still treated in more of a sectoral than a cross-sectoral manner. Furthermore, as seen by UNCED's outputs, the recommendations for future conferences and negotiations are still sectoral, although issues of particular importance to developing countries will be incorporated more explicitly.

The creation of the Commission on Sustainable Development may allow for improved and more coordinated delegation of responsibilities within the system. The Commission could become a new focal point for the system, so that agencies, IGOs, NGOs, governments, and secretariats can all receive assignments and report back to this coordinating body.

By its nature, a negotiating system is fluid. The changing nature of the issues under negotiation, the regimes that have been established to address these issues, and the interrelationship between both issues and regimes, ensures that the system will be continually evolving. The UNCED negotiating process has cleared the path for a stronger and more effective unified system on environment and development negotiations. The structure of the system is in place. It is now up to the actors in the system to make it work.

Part II

A Process Perspective

3

The Story of the UNCED Process

Pamela Chasek

In June 1992, the largest UN conference in history took place in Rio de Janeiro. Not only was UNCED the first global gathering of heads of state or government on environment and development, it drew delegates from over 175 countries, representatives from numerous intergovernmental organizations and UN agencies, more than 1400 accredited nongovernmental organizations, and thousands of journalists. Although much attention was focused on UNCED – or the "Earth Summit" as it was popularly known – the conference was not a single event. Rather, it was the culmination of more than two years of preparation. The negotiations of the Preparatory Committee (PrepCom) and the Main Committee of the conference were only part of the numerous activities that contributed to the Earth Summit. While the PrepCom negotiated the form and content of the plan of action ("Agenda 21" – see Appendix C), the statement of rights and duties (alternatively the "Earth Charter" or the "Rio Declaration on Environment and Development" – see Appendix B), and the statement of principles for the management, conservation, and sustainable development of forests, Intergovernmental Negotiating Committees simultaneously negotiated conventions on climate change and on conserving biological diversity for signature at UNCED. Numerous regional and technical conferences contributed findings and recommendations to the negotiating process. Nongovernmental organizations, too, held an extensive series of activities in preparation for UNCED and the Global Forum, which was conducted in parallel with UNCED. Despite the importance of these numerous parallel events, this chapter focuses solely on the official UNCED negotiations.

THE ORIGINS OF UNCED

The origins of UNCED can be traced back to the first global conference on the environment, the United Nations Conference on the Human Environment, which was held in Stockholm in 1972. The Stockholm Conference produced a set of principles for ecologically sound management of the planet, put environmental issues on the world's agenda, and led to the creation of the UN Environment Programme (UNEP). In the years that followed, however, little was done in practical terms to integrate the

Negotiating International Regimes: Lessons Learned from the United Nations Conference on Environment and Development (G. Sjöstedt, *et al.*, eds.; 1-85966-077-0; © IIASA; pub. Graham & Trotman, 1994; printed in Great Britain), pp. 45–61.

environmental dimension or the idea of sustainability into policies and plans for economic development (UNDPI, 1992).

In 1983 the UN called upon the Secretary-General to convene a World Commission on Environment and Development. In 1987, this Commission, chaired by Norwegian Prime Minister Gro Harlem Brundtland, produced a report, *Our Common Future*, that served as a guide for the structuring of a global approach to what was called "sustainable development." The landmark report documented the need for sustainable development in both industrialized and developing countries, called on the UN General Assembly to "transform this report into a UN Programme of Action on Sustainable Development," and recommended that "an international Conference could be convened to review progress made and promote follow-up arrangements that will be needed over time to set benchmarks and to maintain human progress within the guidelines of human needs and natural laws" (WCED, 1987:343).

Building on the Brundtland Commission report, a number of industrialized nations began to push for a world conference to address environmental matters on a comprehensive and global scale. The rising interest coincided with the approach of the 20th anniversary of the Stockholm Conference. The UN General Assembly first considered the matter of a global environmental conference in 1988, but some countries expressed concern about the feasibility and cost of a global conference with a broad agenda. Many developing countries were concerned that the conference would have a strong environmental (Northern) bias and would not sufficiently address their development concerns. It was not until 22 December 1989, after a long and often difficult debate between industrialized and developing countries, that the UN General Assembly adopted Resolution 44/228 (see Appendix A) calling for a global conference that "should elaborate strategies and measures to halt and reverse the effects of environmental degradation in the context of increased national and international efforts to promote sustainable and environmentally sound development in all countries" (UNGA, 1989).

The resolution was created by compromise and consensus, so its goals are broadly enunciated and encompass the broad array of interests of the participating countries. While it was clear that both environment and development would be essential elements of the conference, there were protracted negotiations over the precise terms of reference. When possible, the negotiators included specific language in the resolution, but when disputes could not be resolved, the negotiators often used ambiguous language or national statements of interpretation to postpone the resolution of contentious issues in the hope that the differences would be resolved by the conference's PrepCom (Antrim and Chasek, 1992).

The breadth of these goals added to the already complicated process of multilateral negotiation. The list of tasks assigned to the conference included over two dozen specific items, ranging from review of past policies and actions to the development of new strategies for national, regional, and global action (Antrim, 1991). Thus, the multiplicity of actors, combined with the multiplicity of issues and only two and a half years to prepare for the conference, which was to be held in June 1992, created a difficult task for both the PrepCom and the secretariat. Within these limits it became necessary to be creative and effective in the preparatory negotiations to ensure that the conference would fulfill its goals.

THE PREPARATORY COMMITTEE (PREPCOM)

Organizational Session: 5–16 March 1990, New York

UN Resolution 44/228 established the Preparatory Committee for UNCED, which "shall be open to all States Members of the United Nations or members of the specialized agencies, with the participation of observers, in accordance with the established practice of the General Assembly" (UNGA, 1989). The UNCED PrepCom met for its organizational session in New York from 5–16 March 1990. The matters addressed were generally procedural in nature, but the decisions had important implications for later negotiations.

Ambassador Tommy T.B. Koh of Singapore was elected chairman of the PrepCom; Ahmed Djoghlaf of Algeria as rapporteur; and 39 vice chairmen were elected to form the Bureau of the PrepCom. UN Secretary-General Javier Perez de Cuellar had appointed Maurice Strong as Secretary-General for the conference earlier in the month. Both Koh and Strong came to UNCED with a wealth of experience: Koh was president of the UN Conference on the Law of the Sea in 1981 and 1982, and Strong served as Secretary-General of the 1972 UN Conference on the Human Environment. The unwieldy size of the bureau was due, in part, to the arithmetic involved in maintaining appropriate geographic distribution in line with UN operating practices (Antrim and Chasek, 1992).

In preparation for this session, the secretariat for the session (drawn from the UN secretariat, since the secretariat for the conference had not yet been established) prepared a plan for the organization of the PrepCom. The plan called for organizing work in three substantive committees addressing global, regional, and national issues, with a fourth committee to be established to address cross-cutting legal and institutional issues. The delegates at the organizational session, however, did not accept the secretariat plan, and, after extensive negotiations that were driven largely by the positions of the developing countries, they agreed to organize their work in two working groups that between them would take responsibility for the specific items identified in Resolution 44/228 (Antrim, 1991). The mandate of the first group included protection of the atmosphere; protection and management of land resources; conservation of biological diversity; and environmentally sound biotechnology. The second group's mandate included protection of the oceans, seas, and coastal areas; protection of the quality and supply of freshwater resources; and environmentally sound management of wastes.

A decision on convening a group on legal and institutional issues was postponed for later discussion. The PrepCom also decided that the basic issue of integration of environment and development and a series of related issues that cut across each of the individual agenda items, e.g., access to and transfer of environmentally sound technology, financial resources requirements, economic instruments, and institutional arrangements, would be considered on an issue-by-issue basis, and then more comprehensively by the PrepCom itself.

An agenda for the first substantive session of the PrepCom structured around the two working groups was accepted in the late hours of the session. In fact, Koh kept the PrepCom in session all night until the delegates had reached a compromise agreement (Antrim, 1991). This strategy of Koh's was to be repeated throughout the preparatory process.

A decision was also taken to establish a Voluntary Fund for the purpose of supporting participation by developing countries, in particular the least-developed countries, in the preparatory process. The secretariat was asked to prepare suggested guidelines for preparation of National Reports and to recommend arrangements for the participation of nongovernmental organizations (Assuncao, 1990).

PrepCom I: 6–31 August 1990, Nairobi

The first substantive session of the PrepCom (PrepCom I) was held in Nairobi in August 1990. This location was selected for both political and substantive reasons. Nairobi is the only developing country site of the headquarters of a UN organization, the UN Environment Programme. Failure to utilize this site during the UNCED preparations would cast doubt on the commitment to address the interests of developing countries. Substantively, it was hoped that convening a session at the site of UNEP could increase the participation of diplomats and technical experts skilled in international environmental diplomacy and encourage a more collaborative atmosphere than anticipated from sessions based in New York or Geneva where North–South divisions often dominate negotiations (Antrim and Chasek, 1992).

Early in the session, the secretariat presented a proposal for the structure of the work to be prepared for UNCED. This structure comprised a declaration of principles for environment and development, Agenda 21 – a plan of action for the twenty-first century, and the signing of international conventions related to UNCED. The PrepCom accepted this general structure to guide its work. The PrepCom also elected Ambassadors Bo Kjellén (Sweden) and Bukar Shaib (Nigeria) as chairs of Working Groups I and II, respectively.

The first week was dominated by opening speeches by heads of delegation, followed by a debate on NGO participation. UN Resolution 44/228 directed that NGOs in consultative status with the Economic and Social Council (CONGOs) be able to participate in the work of UNCED. The secretariat took this to include the deliberations of the PrepCom and, in accordance with this understanding, prepared a draft decision that would formally define the role of NGOs (Antrim, 1991). Unexpectedly, the NGO issue dominated the discussions of the PrepCom for nearly a week. Some delegations inferred that NGOs without consultative status were deliberately excluded. Other delegations, specifically Tunisia and Mauritania, objected to the participation of any NGOs. Finally, after nearly a week of unanticipated debate, the PrepCom agreed that for PrepCom I only, any NGO could attend working group sessions and ask for permission to speak. The decision of a policy for NGO participation in future sessions of the PrepCom was left to the General Assembly (May 1990).

The remaining two weeks of the session were devoted primarily to the two working groups, which attempted to define their interests and needs for information and to draft requests for reports to be prepared by the secretariat. The processes by which the working groups conducted their work combined both formal and informal procedures. Each agenda item was introduced for discussion in a formal session of the working group. National delegations, groups of countries, intergovernmental organizations (IGOs), and NGOs were all invited to make statements and comments. After the formal sessions, the groups convened again in informal sessions for a more open and interactive discussion. These discussions guided the chairmen of the two groups in the preparation of a series of conference room papers and draft decision documents that eventually led to a set of decisions that were adopted by consensus of the groups (Antrim, 1992).

The creation of the working group on legal and institutional issues was again postponed. Opposition came mostly from the Group of 77 developing countries (G-77), who on the whole saw this as a working group focused on "northern interests" (Schally interview, 1992). African countries, particularly Kenya, saw the agenda item on institutional arrangements as a thinly veiled plot to move the UNEP headquarters out of Nairobi. Finally, members of the G-77 believed that the small size of their delegations meant that they could participate in no more than two simultaneous working group sessions. So, as a result, Working Group III's establishment was postponed until PrepCom II.

PrepCom II: 18 March–5 April 1991, Geneva

Much of the second substantive session was devoted to the two working groups, continuing the work of the Nairobi session in gathering information to support the development of recommendations. During the intersessional period, the secretariat began the process of convening working parties of experts to prepare background reports on the various substantive issues to be addressed by the PrepCom. The working parties included representatives from UN agencies and other intergovernmental organizations, research institutions and experts, and NGOs and interest groups. A special effort was made to ensure that experts and institutions from developing countries were well represented. By PrepCom II, working parties had been constituted for the following areas: atmosphere issues; land and agriculture; forestry; biodiversity; biotechnology; oceans; toxic chemicals and hazardous wastes. In the case of freshwater issues, the inter-secretariat group preparing for the 1992 Conference on Water and the Environment acted as the coordinating group (Desai, 1991). According to UNCED Deputy Secretary-General Nitin Desai, the secretariat wanted to "work consciously to ensure that what went before the countries reflected a certain consensus in the UN system" (Desai, 1992).

At PrepCom II, the working groups were supposed to discuss the first set of background reports prepared by the secretariat. These reports, however, were not available in time to allow sufficient examination and review by many governments before the session, so additional time had to be spent reviewing the documents and, even then, some countries were unable to engage in substantive negotiations since they had not received instructions from their ministries. This limited prior access to conference documents foreshadowed a similar, but more severe, documentation problem in the third session of the PrepCom (Antrim, 1992).

Working Group I

Among the topics considered by Working Group I, chaired by Ambassador Kjellén, the issue that gave rise to the most protracted discussion was forests. While a number of countries felt that early action should be taken to start negotiations on an international agreement on this subject, others considered that the various options needed further clarification before final decisions were taken. An ad hoc sub-group was formed to discuss the whole subject, and ultimately a request was made to the secretariat to provide more information at PrepCom III, so that Working Group I would "be in a position to examine all steps towards and options for a global consensus on the management, conservation and development of all types of forests" (UNCED, 1991). The group also decided that UNCED would negotiate a non-binding set of principles on forests for signature in Rio, rather than an international forest convention, as originally suggested by the United States.

Working Group I also discussed the other items on its agenda, although much less time was devoted to these subjects. On the subjects of atmosphere and biodiversity, Working Group I asked the secretariat to work closely with the secretariats of the Intergovernmental Negotiating Committees (INCs) for conventions on these topics and to provide additional information at PrepCom III. The secretariat was also asked to prepare additional background reports on biotechnology and soil loss.

Working Group II

Among the topics considered by Working Group II was the environmentally sound management of wastes. Discussion on solid wastes and sewage-related issues centered on ways of diminishing the creation of these wastes through changes in lifestyles and consumption patterns. Discussion on hazardous wastes focused on the "need to help developing countries strengthen their financial and technical capacities, their institutions and personnel, *inter alia*, through appropriate training, for the management of their domestically produced hazardous wastes" (UNCED, 1991). Working Group II requested that the secretariat provide additional information on these issues, as well as on toxic chemicals.

Another key topic before Working Group II was oceans. This working group asked the secretariat to present a comprehensive report at PrepCom III, and to elaborate the potential areas for action proposed in the present report. The main focus of the discussion of freshwater resources was on the International Conference on Water and the Environment to be held in Dublin in January 1992 and the UNCED input to it.

Working Group III

During the first week of the PrepCom, consultations were held to discuss and agree upon the scope of Working Group III's mandate (Goree, 1991). Agreement was finally reached that Working Group III would prepare a statement of environment and development principles to govern the conduct of nations and people toward each other and the Earth, which UNCED Secretary-General Maurice Strong had started to call the "Earth Charter," evaluate existing instruments in the field of international environment law, and examine institutional arrangements required for the effective implementation of the conclusions of the conference in the UN system (UNCED, 1991). The PrepCom also appointed Ambassador Bedrich Moldan (Czechoslovakia) as the chair of Working Group III. The initial meetings of Working Group III, which were held during the last week of the PrepCom, were devoted to a general exchange of views and the adoption of the agenda for PrepCom III.

Plenary

Although the Plenary had met several times early in this session to approve the mandate of Working Group III and to formulate policy for NGO accreditation and participation in the UNCED preparatory process, the Plenary did not formally open until the beginning of the third week. During the first week, the PrepCom approved a process whereby the UNCED secretariat would recommend certain NGOs for accreditation, and then the Plenary would either authorize or deny such accreditation within 24 hours. The accredited organizations would then be allowed to speak and address the different sessions of the PrepCom and would be allowed to attend the Rio Conference. Although NGOs welcomed the solution to this issue that had plagued the PrepCom since Nairobi, many expressed frustration over the fact that the first set of NGOs were not approved until the end of the first week, and thus could not speak in the formal sessions until the second week. Many more NGOs were not approved until later in the session, effectively barring them from participating in the sessions through most, if not all, of the PrepCom (Goree, 1991).

During the third week of the PrepCom, the Plenary discussed the cross-sectoral issues under its mandate. Discussion focused on two conference documents that had been prepared by the secretariat, "Poverty and Environmental Degradation" and "Environment and Development." According to one NGO observer, "The Plenary was poorly attended and fairly boring, even by PrepCom standards. The PrepCom was in a strange transition: moving from issues to actions but no one had bold conceptual frameworks to put on the table at this early date" (Goree, 1991). When PrepCom II came to a close, the one thing that was clear was that the secretariat had a lot of work to do during the short intersessional period before PrepCom III.

PrepCom III: 12 August–4 September 1991, Geneva

As PrepCom III opened in Geneva, UNCED Secretary-General Maurice Strong said that the major objective of this session was to move from discussion of complex issues to looking at measures to be taken. Working Groups I and II, in fact, were ready to commence negotiations on the substantive issues, but Working Group III and the Plenary had barely begun to analyze and discuss the issues under their mandate. Thus, other objectives for the session included: beginning substantive discussions in Working Group III; the initiation of discussion in the Plenary on cross-cutting issues, including human settlements, financial resources, poverty, sustainability, health and education, transfer of technology, and a wide range of economic issues; and formation of a contact group to negotiate a statement of forest principles.

PrepCom III was initially organized so that Working Groups I and II would meet for the first two weeks, Working Group III would meet during the second and third weeks, and the Plenary would meet during the third and fourth weeks. After the first week, however, it quickly became apparent that there was too much material to cover in each of the working groups during the limited time available. As a result, Working Groups I and II ended up meeting throughout the PrepCom and the Plenary barely made a dent in the substantive discussions of cross-cutting issues. Though the process was well organized at the surface, it quickly ran into problems. The enormity of the agendas of each working group forced the institution of evening sessions and, often, several informal negotiating sessions had to be held simultaneously, in spite of the protests of small delegations from developing countries.

Each of the working groups and the Plenary followed the same procedure as in previous PrepComs: formal discussion on each issue, followed by informal negotiating sessions. For the most part, negotiations were based on the secretariat-produced draft "Options for Agenda 21." In the informal sessions, there were no assigned seats, often no interpreters and, at times, no NGOs or IGOs were allowed to observe the proceedings. After the conclusion of these informal sessions, the working group convened once again in a formal session to approve decision documents on each topic to be forwarded to the Plenary for final approval.

More NGOs attended PrepCom III and made statements than at previous sessions. At certain points, PrepCom Chair Tommy Koh and the chairs of the working groups requested that NGOs give joint statements, since so many wanted to speak and time was of the essence. By this session it was apparent that NGOs were participating in the UNCED process for three major reasons: to influence the official process, to network with other NGOs, and to push their own agendas. Those NGOs that were trying to influence the official process were not always effective because of their lack of understanding of UN conference diplomacy, failure to make statements that contributed concrete recommendations to the text under negotiation (most NGO statements were general statements of principle or ideology) and, in many cases, the inability of delegates to respond to NGO lobbying efforts and change their positions without approval from their capitals (see Chapter 12 for more analysis of NGO participation).

Working Group I[1]

The focus of the Working Group I negotiations was secretariat Document PC/42 "Options for Agenda 21." Of the issues on the agenda, progress was only made in the negotiations on atmosphere and forests. In the discussions on atmospheric issues, the discussions focused on energy in relation to its influence on the atmosphere. Transboundary air pollution and ozone issues were largely ignored because of the preponderance of energy expertise in the secretariat. The negotiators once again stressed that UNCED should not duplicate, preempt, or prejudge the outcome of the parallel climate change negotiations. By the end of the PrepCom, Working Group I had succeeded in reaching consensus on less than half of the secretariat draft.

As a result of the decision at PrepCom II to negotiate a statement on forest principles rather than a convention, a contact group was formed out of Working Group I that worked for ten days negotiating a consolidated document under the chairmanship of Ambassador Charles Liburd (Guyana). By the conclusion of the session, much of the text remained "bracketed" (still under negotiation) for further discussion at PrepCom IV. Due to time constraints, discussion on the Agenda 21 options for combating deforestation was postponed until PrepCom IV.

Owing to the amount of time spent on atmosphere and forests, little time was available to deal with the remaining subjects on Working Group I's agenda. On the subject of land resources, formal discussion was held on three areas of concern: protection and management of fragile ecosystems; an integrated approach to planning and management of land resources; and sustainable agriculture and rural development. Agreement was also reached to include a new Agenda 21 chapter on mountains. Specific Agenda 21 proposals on combating desertification and drought remained poorly developed, in part because the documents were not translated into all six UN working languages until the second week of the PrepCom. In response to African delegations' concerns that desertification had not been dealt with adequately, the chair proposed that desertification be the first item on the agenda at PrepCom IV.

[1]The summaries of the activities at PrepCom III are excerpted from J. Bernstein, P. Chasek, and L. Goree, "PrepCom III: A Compilation of the Four Weekly Synopses" (document posted on Econet in the electronic conference en.unced.news), 9 September 1991.

Working Group I agreed not to impinge on the parallel INC negotiations on a biodiversity convention. Thus, discussion on biodiversity focused on issues of access to genetic resources and technology, financial resources, and the relationship between biodiversity and biotechnology. On the related issue of biotechnology, discussions revealed two major rifts. One was between the majority of delegations, which were concerned about the risks of genetically altered organisms, and the United States, which considered those risks to be exaggerated. The second rift was between developing countries who wanted to consider biotechnology and biodiversity issues together and those who did not want to establish this linkage.

Working Group II

The focus of Working Group II's negotiations was also Document PC/42, "Options for Agenda 21." Although progress was made in the negotiations on oceans and coastal management, a number of contentious issues remained, including: protection of whales and small cetaceans (dolphins and porpoises) and the role of the International Whaling Commission; the inclusion of Antarctica in the chapter; land-based sources of marine pollution; and the relationship between UNCED and the 1982 UN Convention on the Law of the Sea.

The discussions on wastes were divided into four groups: transboundary movement of hazardous wastes; management of radioactive wastes; environmentally sound management of toxic chemicals; and solid waste and sewage. After much negotiation in informal sessions, a number of proposed Agenda 21 items remained bracketed. Working Group II was unable to reach agreement on the need to include a separate chapter in Agenda 21 on radioactive wastes, largely due to US opposition.

The key issues in the discussions on freshwater were the elaboration of implementation mechanisms, groundwater, research and development, inland fisheries and aquaculture, and the participation of women and indigenous people. As in the previous PrepComs, negotiation was postponed until after the Dublin Conference on Freshwater Resources in January 1992.

Working Group III

This working group on legal and institutional issues held its first substantive sessions at PrepCom III. Discussions were focused on definition of issues and the background documents prepared by the secretariat, but very little real negotiation took place. On the subject of evaluation of environmental instruments, delegates reached consensus on a list of existing agreements for the secretariat to review and criteria for their evaluation. The PrepCom requested the secretariat to compile background information on these agreements before the next session. In the general discussion on institutional matters, issues raised included: the need for greater coordination among existing organizations, the possibility of a strengthened UNEP or UN Economic and Social Council (ECOSOC) to coordinate environmental matters throughout the UN system, and whether or not to create new institutions.

No substantive negotiations took place on the statement of general rights and principles. Delegates spent much time arguing over the name: should the statement on general rights and principles be called the "Earth Charter," as proposed by Strong, or should it be called the Rio Declaration on Environment and Development, as proposed by the G-77. Another procedural dispute focused on which text should form the basis for negotiations, as the secretariat, Peru, Canada, and the G-77 all submitted drafts. By the end of the session it was agreed that a compilation of all the drafts would be prepared by the secretariat.

Plenary

The Plenary held initial discussions on cross-sectoral issues, including: human settlements; financial resources; poverty, sustainability, health and education; transfer of technology; and economic issues. A discussion was also held on the structure of Agenda 21. The formal sessions were composed essentially of comments on the secretariat's background documents. No substantive textual negotiations took place, although some of the informal discussions did make progress toward identifying options for Agenda 21. Initial informal discussions on financial resources and technology transfer revealed serious North–South deadlocks on a number of fundamental issues.

PrepCom IV: 2 March–4 April 1992, New York

As PrepCom IV began in New York, most issues had still not been negotiated. Since insufficient time was allocated at PrepCom III for substantive negotiation, all unresolved matters were deferred to PrepCom IV's already overtaxed agenda. Thus, as the session opened, delegates had before them 750 pages of text, in various stages of negotiation, that formed Agenda 21; an "Earth Charter" compilation text of over 136 paragraphs; a partially negotiated statement on forest principles; and impending deadlock on financial resources and technology transfer. With five weeks of difficult negotiations ahead of them, government delegates not only faced an enormous agenda, but also the real possibility that little or no progress could be achieved on the more contentious issues.

PrepCom IV was the first session devoted entirely to negotiation. Formal sessions of the working groups and the Plenary were kept to a minimum. Although only two informal sessions were held at any given time (keeping to the G-77 two-meeting rule), most of the actual negotiation took place in the small contact groups that met behind closed doors with limited interpretation and translation facilities. In the waning days of PrepCom IV, there were often five or more different contact groups meeting at any given time. Evening sessions also became a reality during the third week of the session.

Another difference between PrepCom IV and the previous sessions was the delegates themselves. In many cases, the technical experts who had participated in the earlier PrepComs were supplemented or replaced by political strategists. In addition, there was a preponderance of UN General Assembly Second Committee delegates as the meeting took place in New York. Many of those delegates who had not attended previous PrepComs brought with them both an absence of history of the negotiations (which both helped and slowed down the process) as well as a knack for Second Committee procedural and political wrangling. As a result, this session was marked by increased politicization.

PrepCom IV was also characterized by NGO frustration. Due to the paucity of formal sessions of the Plenary and working groups, there was little opportunity for NGOs to make formal statements. Furthermore, since most of the informal sessions were closed to NGOs, it was difficult to follow the negotiations, influence the process, and lobby delegates.

Thus, there was an overall change of climate as PrepCom IV progressed. Time was running out and the procedures that had dominated the first three PrepComs – the two-meeting rule, the deferment of difficult issues to the next session, and constant procedural debates – were replaced by a more pragmatic, yet frenetic, approach. With the possibility of failure looming in front of the delegates, round-the-clock meetings and creative problem solving became the norm rather than the exception.

Working Group I[2]

Discussions in Working Group I ran the gamut from productive to acrimonious. The negotiations were based, for the most part, on the secretariat's draft chapters for Agenda 21. Negotiations on the chapters on integrated management of land resources, sustainable mountain development, and promoting sustainable agriculture development were comparatively noncontroversial and dispensed with easily. That was not the case, however, with the remaining items on the agenda. The negotiations on desertification stalled over an African request for the preparation and adoption of an international convention to combat desertification. This initiative met resistance from developed countries and could not be resolved by the end of the session.

Protection of the atmosphere was not discussed by Working Group I until the fourth week. The debate reflected the impasses in the negotiations for a climate change convention that were due to resume after the conclusion of PrepCom IV. The United States refused to accept targets and timetables for reduction of carbon dioxide emissions and the Arab Group refused to accept text on energy efficiency and conservation. Similarly, the discussions on biodiversity were also held hostage to the incomplete negotiations for a convention on biodiversity. On the related issue of biotechnology, progress was impeded by a dispute between the EC and the United States on the need for international regulation of biotechnology.

Negotiations on the chapter of Agenda 21 on deforestation began rather inauspiciously when Malaysia, on behalf of the G-77, introduced five new program areas and tabled 256 textual changes. Despite a difficult beginning, the final text was not only agreed upon, but was considered to be quite comprehensive. Unfortunately, the negotiations on the statement of forest principles were not so easy. Despite the high expectations that negotiations on the forest principles document would move quickly, the debate turned into one of the most contentious series of negotiations in New York. Negotiations on many of the principles were linked to the outcomes of other ongoing UNCED negotiations (i.e., trade, Earth Charter, biodiversity, climate). So, in many cases, progress could not be made until those issues had been resolved. Many delegates were frustrated at the end of the session. Even though they were negotiating until 2:00 or 3:00 in the morning, they could not make any progress (Zentilli, 1992).

Working Group II

The Agenda 21 chapter on oceans was the longest and one of the most complex. The secretariat draft, which formed the basis for negotiations, had 152 paragraphs and

[2]The summaries of the activities at PrepCom IV are excerpted from J. Bernstein, P. Chasek, and L. Goree, "A Summary of the Proceedings of the Fourth Session of the UNCED Preparatory Committee," *Earth Summit Bulletin*, Vol. 1, No. 27, 20 April 1992.

did not even include text for two of the seven program areas. Six contact groups were established on oceans alone. The most contentious issues were in the program areas on marine living resources, including overfishing of straddling and highly migratory fish stocks, and conservation of marine mammals, especially whales. The contact group on marine environmental protection spent a great deal of time integrating into the document the recommendations made by the intergovernmental meeting of experts on land-based sources of marine pollution, held in Nairobi in December, 1991. By the end of PrepCom IV, much to the amazement of observers, there was agreement in all areas except straddling fish stocks.

Issues of concern in the chapter on freshwater resources initially included potential environmental problems caused by construction of dams and water channelization; transboundary rivers and freshwater resources; impacts of climate change; and the incorporation of the recommendations of the Dublin Conference on Water and the Environment. The contact group was able to resolve most issues, although negotiations on the introduction, including reference to the Dublin Conference, never took place because of lack of time.

As much progress was made in the negotiations on waste at PrepCom III, discussion on the four chapters on waste and toxic chemicals focused on the bracketed text. Agreement was finally reached on inclusion of the chapter on radioactive waste, and by the end of the session only two major issues were left unresolved: military disposal of hazardous wastes and disposal of radioactive wastes in or near the marine environment.

Working Group III

Most of the time allotted to Working Group III was spent on the Earth Charter/Rio Declaration. The often tortuous process got off to a poor start when Working Group III rejected the chair's proposed working method. After a week of debate over procedure and the choice of negotiating text, PrepCom Chair Tommy Koh stepped in and mediated a compromise allowing negotiation to begin on the G-77 draft text, without prejudice to other submissions. General discussion on the proposed principles and concepts lasted for over two weeks, before a contact group was established to actually begin drafting the final text. Negotiations broke down when an attempt was made by the co-chairs of the contact group to streamline the text. With only two days to go in the session, Koh took over, established a new drafting committee consisting of eight G-77 delegates and eight OECD delegates, and worked for two days until agreement was reached on a final text of the Rio Declaration on Environment and Development. The draft contained 27 norms for state and interstate behavior, many of which have never been universally accepted before. Much to the surprise of the entire PrepCom, the Declaration was the only totally unbracketed text to go to Rio, largely because Koh borrowed heavily on his great reservoir of personal and political capital. Many delegates were not pleased with either the final text or the manner in which it had been negotiated (that is, limited number of participants and consensus forced by time pressure and the chair). Had it not been for Koh's insistence, the late hour, and a very fast gavel, debate would have been protracted during the final session of the PrepCom and the fragile consensus would have been lost.

Owing to the amount of time spent on the Rio Declaration, negotiation on the other issues in Working Group III got off to a late start. The main focus of debate in the institutions chapter of Agenda 21 was the creation of a new institution, the Commission on Sustainable Development to monitor implementation of Agenda 21. Other unresolved issues related to the actual role of NGOs within the UN system generally, and within UNCED implementation specifically, dispute settlement and national reporting.

Conflict arose in the negotiations on the chapter on international agreements and instruments. Most of the divisions were on North–South lines, with the G-77 opposed to inclusion of language saying that states should ensure compliance with international agreements, the need for new regulatory regimes to deal with areas where adequate measures are lacking, such as nuclear safety, and further study of alternative dispute prevention and settlement techniques. The paragraph calling for the prevention of deliberate large-scale environmental destruction was heavily debated. The G-77 insisted that the paragraph should only apply in times of war, whereas the Northern countries insisted that it apply in both war and peacetime. What was originally expected to be a relatively noncontroversial debate, evolved into one of the more heated and acrimonious exchanges.

Plenary

PrepCom IV was the first time that negotiations took place on the large number of cross-sectoral issues under the Plenary's mandate. In some cases, such as in the chapters on the integration of environment and development in decision making, human settlements, information for decision making, science for sustainable development, capacity-building, and education, negotiations progressed smoothly. In other areas, debate was more protracted.

The negotiations on international economic issues were plagued with many of the same problems that characterized the Uruguay Round of the GATT and the eighth round of the UN Conference on Trade and Development (UNCTAD VIII). The contentious issues included agricultural protectionism, the use of subsidies, and the need for mutually supportive environmental and trade policies.

The chapters on poverty, consumption patterns, and demographic dynamics were not as difficult as expected, although the United States objected to any text that explicitly called for changing consumption patterns. The negotiations on the health chapter led to a heated debate on contraception and family planning, which was not resolved until the final hours of the session.

The negotiations on the chapters addressing the need to involve all social groups in the effective implementation of all program areas of Agenda 21 were among those most closely watched by NGOs. The secretariat draft was divided into nine parts to include the role of women; youth; indigenous peoples; nongovernmental organizations; local authorities; trade unions; business and industry; the scientific and technological community; and farmers. Before this document was even addressed by the Plenary, the coordinator held consultations between representatives of the major groups and key government delegates to exchange ideas and proposals and help governments understand the positions of these major groups and possibly to propose text on their behalf.

The most difficult negotiations were those held on technology transfer and finance. Discussions on technology transfer began on the second day of PrepCom IV, and lasted until the last Plenary session. The contact group finally emerged with a comparatively clean document. There was no agreement on the terminology "technology cooperation" as opposed to "technology transfer." A number of paragraphs, including amendments requested by Saudi Arabia on "environmentally [safe and] sound technology," remained bracketed – as did paragraphs on the terms of transfer and protection of intellectual property rights.

Financial resources was given top priority at PrepCom IV and negotiations lasted throughout the session. Disagreement quickly emerged over the use of a G-77 draft text as the negotiating text; the need for new and additional resources to finance Agenda 21 implementation; and the use of the Global Environment Facility (GEF) as a mechanism for funding Agenda 21. After several weeks of discussion the negotiations stalled. When the coordinator, Ambassador John Bell (Canada), was unable to make further progress, PrepCom Chair Tommy Koh stepped in and asked Mexican Ambassador Andrés Rozental to coordinate a new round of talks. This was conducted at the Mexican mission and was limited to a select number of representatives from industrialized and developing countries. When it finally appeared as if progress was being made, another impasse was reached between the EC proposals and the G-77 expectations (especially on the GEF), and talks again broke down on the eve of the last day of the PrepCom.

Although PrepCom IV was neither an unmitigated disaster nor an overwhelming success, in actual fact progress was indeed achieved – close to 85 percent of Agenda 21 was in some state of agreement. It was, however, the remaining 15 percent that was deeply problematic, as the most difficult issues remained to be resolved at Rio. And so, what was expected to be a two-week massive photo opportunity in Rio was quickly transformed into a critical negotiating session (Bernstein, Chasek, and Goree, 1992a).

THE CONFERENCE: 3–14 JUNE 1992, RIO DE JANEIRO

Although the PrepCom had finished its work in April, the final two months leading up to Rio were filled with numerous meetings that contributed to the UNCED negotiating process. The INC for a Framework Convention on Climate Change reached agreement at the end of its fifth session in New York on 9 May, although many countries and NGOs expressed dissatisfaction with the outcome. The INC for a Convention on Biological Diversity also completed its negotiations during its final session in Nairobi, which concluded on 19 May.

On the issue of financial resources, numerous meetings were held, allowing the dialogue on finance to continue despite the deadlock at the end of PrepCom IV. Former Japanese Prime Minister Noboru Takeshita hosted the "Eminent Persons' Meeting on Financing Global Environment and Development" in Tokyo in mid-April. The IMF and World Bank Development Committee met in late April, providing a forum for finance ministers to discuss the "interaction between environment and development policies and the preparations for UNCED" (Bernstein, Chasek, and Goree, 1992e). The GEF participants meeting took place in early May to discuss the future of the GEF and UNCED participants' concerns with it. Finance was also discussed at the OECD Ministers' meeting and the EC Environment and Development Ministers' Meeting, both held in May. Finally, financing Agenda 21 was the center of discussion as ministers from 55 developing countries met in late April in Kuala Lumpur, Malaysia, for the Second Ministerial Conference of Developing Countries on Environment and Development (UNDPI, 1992). Then, as May drew to a close, all eyes turned to Rio.

UNCED formally opened on 3 June after two days of pre-conference consultations, during which the conference officers were elected, the rules of procedure approved, and the agenda agreed upon. The conference itself was divided into two main bodies: the Plenary and its subsidiary body, the Main Committee. The Plenary, under President Fernando Collor de Mello of Brazil, was the forum for the general debate, which consisted of country statements delivered at the Ministerial level. The series of 204 statements lasted from 3–11 June. On 12 June, the Summit portion of the conference began, and for two days heads of state and government addressed the world for seven minutes each.

By contrast, the Main Committee was the site of the actual political negotiations – in essence, a PrepCom V. Not only were many of the negotiators the same as in the PrepCom, but the conference elected Ambassador Tommy Koh to chair the Committee. The mandate of the Main Committee was to finalize the products of UNCED: Agenda 21, the Statement on Forest Principles, and the Rio Declaration on Environment and Development. Those areas in need of substantive negotiations were forwarded to contact groups established by Koh and his Bureau. The eight contact groups were: atmosphere, biodiversity/biotechnology, institutions, legal instruments, finance, technology transfer, freshwater resources, and forests (including both the Statement on Forest Principles and the Agenda 21 chapter on forests). Other outstanding or bracketed text was negotiated by the Committee. In most cases, Koh asked the PrepCom coordinator for the specific issue to hold informal consultations. On some issues, like the proposed desertification convention, Koh conducted the consultations himself. During seven days of intense negotiation, the mood oscillated dramatically from issue to issue and day to day. The entrance of ministers and other high-ranking politicians into the negotiations alternatively improved the pace, as they were able to make the necessary decisions, and impaired the process, as they were often unaware of the history of the issue within the UNCED context. When the Main Committee ran out of its allotted time at 6:00 a.m. on Thursday, 11 June, three issues still had not been resolved: forests, finance, and atmosphere. These issues were forwarded to the Plenary for further negotiations at the Ministerial level where, at the eleventh hour, agreement was finally reached (Bernstein, Chasek, and Goree, 1992d).

The Ministerial consultations on forests, coordinated by Klaus Töpfer, German Minister for the Environment, Nature Conservation, and Nuclear Safety, were able to make progress where the Main Committee could not. The Main Committee's contact group on forests had grown too large. At the Ministerial level, the participants had the possibility of getting involved and making decisions on issues that could not be dealt with at the Ambassadorial level. There was no other level to which the Ministers could refer the discussions to (interview with B. Zentilli, UNCED Secretariat, July 1992). After a marathon five-hour session that concluded at 3:00 a.m. on 12 June, 18 countries, represented by no less than 11 ministers, finally agreed to a package proposed by Töpfer (Bernstein, Chasek, and Goree, 1992d). This package, which included compromise language for all outstanding issues in the forest principles statement, was approved unanimously when presented to the Plenary, although many believed the Statement to be weak or ineffectual. Regardless, these principles constitute "the first global consensus on forests," and affirm the importance of forest management and conservation for sustainable development.

Final discussions on financial resources lasted until 13 June. The issues that could not be resolved by the Main Committee included: conditionality and the GEF, IDA replenishment levels, debt relief, and the UN target of 0.7 percent of GNP for ODA by the year 2000. This last issue proved to be the most divisive, as the G-77 insisted that the provision of new and additional resources from the developed countries was necessary to ensure the G-77's support for the rest of Agenda 21. The developed countries were quite split on the issue: some countries, such as France and the Nordics, had already reached the target; other countries (such as Great Britain and Germany) that had pledged to meet the target did not think they were able to; and still others, like the United States, had never committed to anything. The failure of the EC to reach a unified position on this issue only served to prolong the debate. A final compromise that accommodated these disparate positions stated that countries would *reaffirm* their commitments to reach the UN target of 0.7 percent of GNP for ODA and augment their aid programs in order to reach that target *as soon as possible*. This compromise did not have the targets nor the timetable that the G-77 had wanted, but was the most the industrialized countries were willing to agree to.

Next to discussions on finance, the atmosphere negotiations proved to be the most difficult and protracted at UNCED. On the insistence of the Arab Group, PrepCom IV was forced to transmit a completely bracketed chapter to Rio. The Arab Group maintained that the chapter was not only duplicative of the work of the climate change negotiations, but that it placed an over-emphasis on energy efficiency and conservation. In contact group discussions, many Northern countries fought hard for the retention of the reference to new and renewable energy sources throughout the text and called into question Saudi Arabia's true motives for wanting to delete these references.

Another contentious matter pertained to the phrase "safe and" in the context of energy sources. Most countries had requested the deletion of that phrase on the basis that it connoted an anti-nuclear bias. By contrast, Saudi Arabia insisted adamantly that the phrase be retained. The chair of the contact group, Ambassador Kjellén, with the assistance of the Brazilians, was able to resolve both outstanding matters late on 13 June. Although the Saudis accepted the compromise text at the final Plenary on 14 June, they formally placed on record their government's reservations with the atmosphere chapter. Since Agenda 21 is not a legally binding instrument, but instead a statement of policy, the Saudis' formal reservations to the chapter had no substantive implications (Bernstein, Chasek, and Goree, 1992e).

CONCLUSIONS

As UNCED came to a close on Sunday morning, 14 June, the common theme of the closing statements was that Rio was only a beginning and that much more work needed to be done. The high expectations that had marked the early stages of the UNCED negotiating process was replaced by a realization that two and a half years of negotiation alone was not sufficient. What did emerge was a sense of satisfaction that agreement was reached. For two weeks in June, the world was focused on Rio and the issues of environment and development, making it the most publicized and the largest conference in UN history.

Was UNCED a success? This question will most likely be debated long into the future, but the answer depends on what one's goal and expectations were for the conference. For the most part, the success of UNCED can only be evaluated in the future, when the results of this negotiation and educational process will be seen.

Negotiators worked hard and long on reaching consensus on several new instruments of international law – both hard law, such as the Conventions on Climate Change and Biological Diversity, which were opened for signature in Rio, and soft law, such as the nonlegally-binding Agenda 21, Rio Declaration, and the statement on forest principles. Although consensus diplomacy often results in a great deal of frustration as well as "lowest common denominator" agreements that lack the teeth advocates want, it did offer a forum in which governments could discuss the interrelated issues of environment and development for the first time.

The conference also resulted in the creation of new institutional mechanisms to allocate costs and benefits of resource use and conservation more fairly. A new institution, the Commission on Sustainable Development, was created to act as a coordinating body within the UN system to monitor the implementation of Agenda 21. UN procedures were opened so that NGOs could actively participate – both in the formulation of policy and in its future implementation. Although many would argue that the Commission on Sustainable Development will be another moribund UN institution and that NGO participation was too limited, it is still a step in the right direction.

There are, however, some immediate lessons that can be learned from the UNCED negotiating process. For example, perhaps the biggest problem in the UNCED negotiations was the size of the agenda and the limited amount of negotiating time available. UN Resolution 44/228 opened a Pandora's box of environment and development issues to be dealt with by the UNCED PrepCom. With just over two years to prepare, less than two years of substantive sessions, and, in some cases, less than five weeks of serious negotiation, it was a difficult task from the start. The fact that any agreement came out of this process is quite an accomplishment.

What precedents UNCED will set remain to be seen. UNCED marks the beginning of a new era of international cooperation on environmental protection and environmentally sound development. UNCED has created a new global agenda on sustainable development. What its legacy will be is largely in the hands of the governments, intergovernmental organizations, nongovernmental organizations, and individuals from all areas of society who must continue to ensure that the future is an environmentally sound one. As Maurice Strong said in his closing statement:

> There has been, of course, some weakening of [Agenda 21] in the process, but it still stands as the most comprehensive, the most far-reaching and, if implemented, the most effective programme of international action ever sanctioned by the international community. It is not a final and complete action programme, and was not intended to be, but one which must continue to evolve.

4

Issue Clarification and the Role of Consensual Knowledge in the UNCED Process

Gunnar Sjöstedt

INTRODUCTION

The overall aim of this chapter is to assess how issues were introduced into UNCED, and particularly how they were framed and developed during the negotiations. Lessons learned in this regard will become useful to consider in future negotiations extending the work concluded at the Rio Conference. Such a continuation will, no doubt, become necessary. The UNCED process represented but a moderate success. The objectives established for UNCED at the outset were only partly attained, although the accomplishments of UNCED were by no means negligible (see Chapter 13). Two important treaties, on climate change and biological diversity, were opened for signature at the Meeting of Heads of State or Government in Rio de Janeiro. Although the Rio Declaration did not attain the formal status of an "Earth Charter," it does contain a number of fundamental principles and guidelines for future international cooperation on the environment and development. One hundred and seventy nations formally participating in the UNCED process accepted specific understandings – for instance, the formal acknowledgment of the fundamental principle that "the polluter pays." The idea was also endorsed that in the future, environmental considerations should be more fully integrated into governmental decision making (*Financial Times*, 29 July 1992).

However, in spite of its undeniable accomplishments, the Rio Conference was in some respects more of a beginning than the termination of a process of international decision making. Several of the agreements attained in the process, for instance that concerning climate change, are likely to be of only an intermediate duration. In order to become effective, commitments incorporated in these treaties (for example, promised reductions of industrial emissions) will have to be considerably strengthened to have a real impact on the environmental problem to which they pertain. Negotiations on a number of highly salient environmental problem areas – for instance, deforestation and desertification – hardly got off the ground in UNCED. Some of the ideas discussed in UNCED will have to be considerably specified to become negotiable from a political point of view. One example is the

Negotiating International Regimes: Lessons Learned from the United Nations Conference on Environment and Development (G. Sjöstedt, *et al.*, eds.; 1-85966-077-0; © IIASA; pub. Graham & Trotman, 1994; printed in Great Britain), pp. 63–86.

notion that changed lifestyles in industrialized countries represent one of the most effective strategies to cope with serious environmental problems. Many formal and informal stipulations of the UNCED agreements must become clarified and further developed before they can become transformed into meaningful policy action.

There are good reasons to search for improved methods to facilitate continued environmental negotiations emerging from the UNCED process. One important task is, for instance, to look for constructive ways of dealing with sticking points and conflicts of interest that could not be properly solved in the UNCED process (see Chapter 5). However, *issue clarification* and the creation of *consensual knowledge* in the UNCED process are the key concepts addressed in this chapter. These notions refer to how the UNCED agenda was created, established, and developed to make issues negotiable. This was partly a conventional diplomatic exercise at the negotiation table, and partly a collective learning process. The exchange of concessions and the recurrent drama of the endgame have tended to attract the attention of analysts more than agenda-setting and issue clarification. However, these elements of the negotiation have a strategic significance, particularly for the parties able to significantly influence these stages of the process. These conditions can be expected to further enhance the importance of prenegotiation and agenda-setting.

The way issues are defined and understood does not only influence the process – that is, the political struggle in the negotiation. Ultimately, issue definitions also condition *the effectiveness* of agreements reached in the negotiations – to what extent a treaty contributes to solving the problem to which it pertains (Underdal, 1992). Sometimes a tradeoff has to be made between an easy agreement and an effective agreement. In order to become acceptable on the negotiation table, solutions may have to be deliberately simplified. In other cases, some aspects of the problem area will have to become emphasized out of proportion to new importance in order to attract the interest of a sufficient number of negotiation parties. This kind of simplification, or even manipulation, of issues may have a negative effect on the problem solving that the agreement in question is meant to produce. For example, key elements of the problem may have been "defined away." Still, issue simplification may under some conditions not only be acceptable, but also desirable, as it may be a *sine qua non* for an agreement in a situation where non-agreement is prohibitively costly. For instance, non-agreement may sometimes endanger achievements made in earlier negotiations. A major premise of the present chapter is that while alternative understandings of issues may be diffuse or difficult to identify, they may have important consequences for negotiation outcomes. Understanding the methods and processes of issue clarification may thus facilitate negotiation and regime effectiveness in the future.

The more complex the issues are, the more important agenda-setting and issue clarification are likely to be compared to other elements of the negotiation process. A focus on agenda-setting and issue clarification in the UNCED setting is particularly warranted. The agenda confronting negotiating parties in the UNCED process was extraordinarily large. Many issues were highly complex from a technical point of view – for instance, climate change or the relationships between biological diversity, biotechnology, and intellectual property rights. Existing knowledge on many of the issues was comparatively scarce and undeveloped. While agenda-setting and issue clarification represented crucial stages of the

UNCED process, it had a number of significant characteristics. These particular attributes may indicate useful lessons for the future, things that should either be avoided or repeated.

ISSUE FORMATION AND CLARIFICATION: THE ROLE OF CONSENSUAL KNOWLEDGE

A Key Concept: Consensual Knowledge

In theoretical analyses focusing on negotiations *per se*, the issues on the agenda are in reality often considered to be "given," especially in works inspired by game theory (Luce and Raiffa, 1957; Rapoport, 1964). Note that game theory is no exceptional case; most process-oriented analyses of negotiations take the disputed issues for granted (Cross, 1983). It is usually only studies with a descriptive orientation that are concerned with the substance of issues (Winham, 1986). However, as highlighted by a growing literature on prenegotiation, agenda-setting often represents a critical stage (Stein, 1989). However, descriptions of agenda-setting do not usually focus on the dynamics of the issues as such.

The conventional understanding of "agenda-setting" conveys the image of a selection process in which parties jointly agree on the topics they are willing to negotiate on, such as climate change, oceans, or forestry, to mention but a few examples from the UNCED process (Druckman, 1977). In the standard analysis, these topics are assumed to exist and have a clear meaning before the negotiation begins. Once the agenda has been established, the analyst may conceive of the issues included in it as a set of given conditions for the negotiation. Often this perspective on the issues may be fully warranted. In many cases the stakes of a certain negotiation issue are obvious and do not need to be clarified and explained to negotiators.[1] An example of such recurrent negotiations are talks concerning fish catches in a certain sea area. However, even in such straightforward cases, the issues "on the table" may require some clarification. For example, determination of the quotas of fish catches may require a common understanding between parties of conservation needs. Such analytical requirements, however, are comparatively easy to satisfy when, as in the example of fish catches, issues and stakes are simple and have been dealt with in earlier rounds of negotiations.

However, issues often need to be further developed and clarified after the formal establishment of the agenda. This is likely to happen when, as in the case of the UNCED process, the agenda contains a multitude of relatively new and technically complex issues. When parties meet at the negotiation table to deal with such complex issues, they are likely to need more and better information about them than they initially possess. For this purpose, a general description of the problem area concerned is not sufficient. The problem dimensions that will be moved to the forefront at the negotiation table will have to be highlighted in the information gathered. Issue definitions, and related negotiation problems, will have to be expressed in terms that help make them negotiable. For instance, the concepts used should integrate, or

[1]The *stake* is the dimension, or set of dimensions, of an issue that represents the main bone of contention dealt with in the negotiation or in any other form of conflict resolution (Mansbach and Vasquez, 1981).

connect, the language of problem assessment with that of problem solving. The base of information and knowledge built up collectively to service and support negotiations will have to be consensual. To negotiate on a certain issue the parties involved will have to share a common understanding about it. In multilateral negotiations on complex issues, this objective is usually difficult to attain. Knowledge and information is likely to be asymmetrically distributed. Information requirements are likely to differ among nations as well. Industrialized nations are generally much better informed about environmental problems than the average developing country. However, in order to begin to negotiate in earnest, parties will have to share a common understanding with respect to the issues on the agenda. The more complex the issues are from a technical point of view, the more elaborate methods are needed to create and establish such a *consensual knowledge*.

Consensual knowledge is an aggregate of cognitions that reflects what relevant actors *know* about the problem(s) concerned, rather than their interests or attitudes towards them.[2] Knowledge is considered to be consensual when it reflects what the quasi-totality of the actors involved in a negotiation acknowledge as valid cognitions. There is likely to be a significant correspondence between the consensual knowledge developed in a negotiation system and the mainstream scientific, "objective" discernment of the same matters. One reason is that as a main supplier of critical information, the scientific community is in a good position to influence issue clarification. Another explanation is that in order to function effectively in a negotiation, the cognitive understanding of the problem area needs to be anchored in a scientifically recognized or authorized body of knowledge and interpretation.

Consensual knowledge is not a static body of cognitive elements. It may change during the negotiation, hopefully in such a way that the issues on the agenda become increasingly clarified and specified. It cannot, however, be taken for granted that the efforts to create a consensual knowledge will be successful. Consensual knowledge may be at different stages of development at any given point of time. It represents a kind of political agreement between parties concerned. Like other accords, this agreement may be the result of a political struggle. There may be a confrontation between two or more bodies of knowledge competing for supremacy. Recall, for example, the struggle between the North and the South concerning a New International Economic Order (NIEO) during the 1970s in UNCTAD and other UN institutions. The demands of the Group of 77 were linked to the thinking of the "dependency" school, looking at the world economy from a new perspective that was partly inspired by Marxism (Bhagwati, 1977). The case of NIEO illustrates that the creation of consensual knowledge may become a heavily politicized process and develop into an ideological struggle. In this encounter, one of the contending bodies of knowledge may become a winner and prevail. The other possibility is that consensus is *not* achieved, and no common understanding of the issues on the agenda is attained. In this case, the probability for an agreement is low.

A number of critical attributes of consensual knowledge are discernible.[3] One is the *extent of acceptance* of consensual knowledge above a certain critical threshold. In order to function in the negotiations, the body of cognitions representing an

[2]The concept of "consensual knowledge" is closely related to the theoretical analysis of "epistemic communities" (Haas, 1991).

[3]In principle, it should be possible to estimate most of these attributes fairly precisely with quantitative measures. For the present analytical purposes, it is however satisfactory to make a fairly general assessment.

emerging consensual knowledge cannot be too strongly opposed. For analytical purposes, it is sufficient to establish the rule of thumb that a body of knowledge is consensual if it is not outspokenly opposed by any significant party or coalition.

A second attribute of consensual knowledge is its *contents identity*, which is related to the academic discipline or disciplines from which it originates. For instance, trade theory gives a clear contents identity to the well-established consensual knowledge pertaining to the GATT system.

The *language code* reflects the kind of vocabulary that is used when the consensual knowledge is formulated. For instance, the language code may have been offered by lawyers and thus have a legal dressing, or the vocabulary may have a scientific tone.

A fourth attribute is the *degree of coherence* characterizing consensual knowledge. A body of consensual knowledge consists of a number of factual propositions. The more individual propositions are linked together by acknowledged causal relationships, the higher the degree of coherence of the consensual knowledge. With an increasing degree of coherence, the correspondence between the consensual and the related scientific knowledge is also likely to grow.

Especially when consensual knowledge has little coherence, it is likely not to have any particular *goal-orientation*. With an rising degree of inherent coherence, the likelihood increases that consensual knowledge develops a consistent goal-orientation in either of two directions. Either the knowledge built up will be oriented toward problem analysis or toward problem solving.

A sixth variable describing the character of consensual knowledge may be referred to as *degree of formalization*. The consensual knowledge may develop as an informal understanding of a problem area, which is not codified in any kind of formal texts. For instance, international lawyers may be in perfect agreement about what legal requirements an agreement will have to meet without having this spelled out in any formal document produced as part of the negotiation process. However, consensual knowledge may also be expressed in documents produced in the negotiation process. As demonstrated by GATT, consensual knowledge may even become incorporated into the basic treaty of the organization servicing the negotiation.[4]

Consensual knowledge may fulfill several functions in the negotiation process. Basically, it serves as a *general frame of reference for negotiators*. It offers a taxonomy and elaborate concepts that may be helpful to facilitate communication between negotiating parties. Consensual knowledge may also supply a *code of interpretation* of crucial causal relationships pertaining to the substance of issues under negotiation. Such acknowledged causation may represent important premises for problem solving as well as for the attribution of responsibility or values to negotiating parties.[5] In this regard, when computer models provided a commonly accepted way to specify the traffic patterns of transboundary air pollution flows, the attainment of an agreement was facilitated (Alcamo, Hordijk, and Shaw, 1990). Finally, consensual knowledge may also *indicate*, or even *recommend, a certain solution to the problem* dealt with in the negotiation. It may, for instance, contain an analysis of the causes of the problems negotiated, the logic of which implies a certain solution.

[4]In the case of GATT, the essence of the free trade theory is built into the Preamble of the General Agreement.

[5]One example is the establishment of the transboundary spread of certain pollutants as a prerequisite for the finalizing of the UN–ECE Convention on Long-range Transboundary Air Pollution (1979).

The process through which consensual knowledge is created or modified is referred to as *issue clarification*, which in turn may be broken up into two kinds of sub-processes. One of these is *collective learning;* parties to the negotiation are "educated" about the issues on the agenda by having access to the same background information, analysis, and assessments that are produced and circulated within the context of the negotiation process. The other sub-process is *editing diplomacy*; parties typically sit "at the table" to process a text into an agreement. This typically pertains to the final documents to be produced in the negotiation – the outcome. In a multilateral context, editing diplomacy often characterizes bargaining over details at the end of the process. However, editing diplomacy may also pertain to the definition of the issues in the context of issue clarification. For instance, it is not uncommon that key concepts to be used in the negotiations will have to be established by means of careful bargaining – editing diplomacy. Collective learning and editing diplomacy may develop independently in the negotiation process or they may interact.

The Research Strategy

The objective of this chapter is to clarify what roles issue clarification and the emergence of a consensual knowledge played in the UNCED process. The questions addressed in the chapter are framed in terms of the conceptual framework summarized in Table 4.1. The first research task is to characterize the processes of issue clarification at a fairly high level of generalization. The second research task is to describe the character and functions of consensual knowledge. The third, and last, research task is to draw lessons regarding issue clarification and consensual knowledge for future environmental negotiations.

Table 4.1 A conceptual framework: The process of "Issue Clarification" and the Attributes and Functions of "Consensual Knowledge"

	Consensual knowledge		
FUNCTIONS	Frame of reference	Code of interpretation	Indication of solution
ATTRIBUTES	Extent of acceptance Formalization	Language code Contents identity	Coherence Goal orientation
	Issue Clarification		
SUB-PROCESSES	Collective learning	Editing diplomacy	

PROCESSES OF ISSUE CLARIFICATION IN UNCED: A GENERAL CHARACTERIZATION

The Delimitation of the Issue Clarification Stage

Issue clarification may occur, in principle, any time during a negotiation, even in connection with the endgame. Redefinition of controversial concepts may show, for instance, a way out of an impasse. Still, issue clarification is likely to be most closely associated with agenda-setting, the organization of the negotiation, and the search for formulas to permit nuanced exchanges of concessions. In the case of UNCED, "the distribution game" definitely prevailed at the fourth meeting of the UNCED PrepCom IV in New York, February 1992. During the first part of PrepCom IV, negotiations had no clear direction (see Chapter 3). However, from the beginning of the third week, parties showed a new determination to work out agreements in the many areas in which negotiations had become bogged down.[6] The changed atmosphere in the negotiations manifested itself in the abolishment of a number of procedural rules that had so far guided the negotiations. These changes represented the discontinuation of the UN code of procedure, which had been relied upon before PrepCom IV. For example, the norm that editing diplomacy should be based on papers prepared by the Group of 77 (G-77) was revoked.[7] Likewise, the rule that only two different committee meetings could be conducted at the same time, because most Third World countries did not have sufficient manpower resources in their delegations to negotiate at more than two places at once, was abandoned. These, and a few other, procedural rules were exchanged because they were believed to obstruct effective bargaining.

The change of atmosphere and direction during PrepCom IV was seemingly a reaction to the prospect of a total failure at the Rio Conference in June. The leading nations in the UNCED process were not willing to accept the visible costs of a default, or canceled, "Earth Summit." Therefore, it was necessary to inject a new spirit into the negotiation with the purpose of finding viable agreements regarding the various issues on the UNCED agenda. As time was running out, it became mandatory to use more flexible "rules of the game" than the formal UN procedures. For example, it was indispensable to let particularly resourceful, or especially interested, countries play a leading role when this could be expected to facilitate negotiations, or otherwise move them forward even if the formal prerogatives of G-77 would become compromised. It was also necessary to permit the creation of small, restricted contact groups of "especially interested parties" to handle outstanding, unresolved negotiation problems even if this meant a proliferation of negotiation bodies.

Thus, from PrepCom IV onwards, the UNCED negotiations had the character of editing diplomacy focusing on a given number of texts that should be finalized, preferably before the Rio Conference. Issue clarification and the creation of consensual knowledge was seemingly insignificant from PrepCom IV onwards. Therefore, the premise for the present analysis is that issue clarification in UNCED was essentially terminated during PrepCom III in August 1991.

The General Development of Issue Clarification Activities

The idea for UNCED harkens back to a Swedish proposal from 1986 that a stocktaking UN conference should take place in 1992 to commemorate the 1972 Stockholm Conference on the Human Environment (Palme, 1992). This idea gained the

[6]This assessment is shared by key participants in the UNCED process (interview with Ambassador Bo Kjellén, who chaired Working Group I).

[7]The rationale for this procedural rule, which had been respected in UNCED before PrepCom IV, was that G-77 controlled the majority of the votes in the UN context.

support of a small group of like-minded countries: Canada, the Netherlands, and Norway.[8] Together with Sweden, this constellation of small and middle powers formally introduced the proposal for UNCED in the General Assembly of the UN. This initiative was further underpinned by the Brundtland Report, *Our Common Future* (WCED, 1987:343). The aims of UNCED, as well as the general structure of its agenda, were formally established in a General Assembly resolution (UNGA, 1989, Resolution 44/228).

Resolution 44/228 was the outcome of an inter-state political struggle in which a North–South dimension was clearly discernible (see Appendix A). Negotiation in the General Assembly concerning UNCED was difficult and protracted; it started in 1988, but was not concluded until December the following year. The aim of the preparatory work – prenegotiation – related to UNCED in the General Assembly was to include a detailed agenda and a precise plan of work in the text of the Resolution (see Chapter 3). These efforts were, however, only partly rewarded. Certainly, the General Assembly mandate for UNCED identified the full range of issues of substance that were to be dealt with in the negotiation. It also contained some general guidelines and objectives for the UNCED process leading to the Rio meeting. Furthermore, it acknowledged a few crucial elements of the emerging consensual knowledge related to the upcoming negotiation – for instance, the coupling between environmental problems through the conception of sustainable development (UNGA, 1989). In this respect, the UNCED agenda was clearly inspired by the Brundtland Report.

Still, the UNCED agenda ordained by the General Assembly lacked direction in certain respects. Essentially, it represented an inventory of themes to be negotiated on. The General Assembly had not been able to formulate a concrete plan of action or general strategy for the UNCED process. It remained unclear exactly how many issues were to be understood and approached in the negotiation.

PrepCom's Organizational Session in spring 1990, formally opening the UNCED process, was to some extent concerned with agenda-setting and issue clarification. The contributions made in this respect were, however, mostly of an indirect nature (see Chapter 3). They largely resulted from the completion of the main practical task of the Organizational Session, which was to set up an institutional machinery for the conduct of the UNCED negotiations. Initially, it consisted of a Plenary Meeting and two working groups. A decision was made to set up a negotiation body for legal and institutional matters, but its implementation was deferred to a later stage in the process (A/44/48, para. 56). The election of chairs, vice chairs, rapporteur, and a "Bureau" was also postponed to PrepCom I (A/CONF.151/PC/13, p. 4).

The terms of reference given by the UN General Assembly for the formal negotiation bodies of UNCED implied a certain strategic perspective on the issues put on the agenda. The General Assembly expressed the opinion that the UNCED agenda should be looked upon in a holistic perspective, and that physical issue linkages should be taken into consideration in the negotiations. These aspirations were later repeated during the UNCED process (A/CONF.151/PC/20). However, the General Assembly had not worked out any concrete strategy to attain these objectives. Neither was the Organizational Session devoted to this type of strategic discussion, although some concrete measures were undertaken to plan negotiation work. Some

[8]At this time, the EC had not yet developed a common policy in the area of environmental problems. Hence, the Netherlands cannot be regarded as an agent of the EC for these purposes.

consideration was given to physical linkages between issues when the distribution of work was organized between the Plenary Committee and Working Groups I and II. Working Group I was given responsibility for environmental problems pertaining primarily to the atmosphere and the land surface. Working Group II was allocated water pollution and hazardous waste. The Plenary Committee was given two main functions, the first of which was to supervise the negotiation as a whole and serve as the main decision-making body during the preparatory work. The other function of the Plenary Committee was to process some of the issues that were allocated to neither Working Group I nor II, particularly all the so-called cross-sectoral issues.[9]

It was not until PrepCom I in August 1990 that negotiating parties in the UNCED process became directly concerned with the substance of the issues on the agenda.[10] These talks did not, however, contribute to clarify the issues immediately. At PrepCom I, deliberations at the table were still steered by the frame of reference set up for UNCED by the UN General Assembly (UNGA, 1989). The next step in the process of issue clarification was represented by instructions given by PrepCom to the secretariat to produce documentation on virtually all the issues identified by the General Assembly (A/CONF.151/PC.13). The results of this secretariat work began to be reported to PrepCom II. This documentation was meant to serve three broad purposes. The first was to offer a synoptic background on the problems of substance on the UNCED agenda. The second objective was to describe the work that was going on with respect to particular issues of substance. The third aim was to indicate suitable areas for action on the issue areas concerned (A/CONF.151/PC/14). According to the official opinion of the Secretary General of UNCED, these secretariat documents provided "the basis for the essential transition from the overview of the UN system-wide activities relevant to General Assembly resolution 44/228 and the preliminary discussion of the issues concerned at the first session of the Preparatory Committee to the concrete action proposals which the Preparatory Committee is expected to produce for consideration by the Conference" (Ibid., p. 11).

At PrepCom I, the PrepCom instructed the secretariat to prepare reports concerning the relationship between the environment and development (UNCED, decision 1/25; 1/28). Related studies were also requested concerning the cross-sectoral issues – for instance, technology transfer and financial resources (UNCED, decision 1/29). Also, the notion of Agenda 21 was first introduced at PrepCom I (A/CONF.151/ PC/ 14, P15). The themes introduced at PrepCom I were pursued at PrepCom II in compilations of information and analytical papers that had been prepared by the UNCED secretariat. These secretariat documents served as a basis for discussions between delegations at both PrepComs II and III. In this process, essentially retaining the character of issue clarification, the secretariat continued to produce more information concerning the issues of substance, as well as ordering concepts. For instance, the notion of Agenda 21 grew steadily clearer and was increasingly filled with substance (A/CONF.151/PC/100). Governments and international organizations also provided input information supporting issue clarification. Notably, countries participating in the UNCED process had agreed to develop national reports related to the issues under negotiation. Eventually, most nations produced such

[9]Recall that Working Party III, dealing with institutional and legal matters, did not start functioning until PrepCom II (A/CONF.151/PC/13, p. 5).

[10]Recall that PrepComs I–IV, which followed after the Organizational Session, were the four formal sessions focusing on matters of substance. Hence, PrepCom I was the *second* formal session of the UNCED PrepCom.

national reports, although the bulk of them were sent in at a relatively late stage of the process of issue clarification (UNCED, A/CONF.151/PC/98). Furthermore, the secretariat sent out questionnaires to sound out the views of governments on most of the main environmental issues dealt with in the UNCED process (UNCED, A/CONF.151/PC/ 104–110).[11] These questions and responses were, however, more related to the bargaining stage of "exchange of concessions" that began to influence the character of the UNCED process during PrepComs III and IV.

This overview indicates that issue clarification and related negotiation activities dominated a relatively large portion of the UNCED process. The formal existence of UNCED extended from the beginning of 1990 until late June 1992. Only one-fifth of this time was characterized by a clearcut "distribution game" – the exchange of concessions. These circumstances raise the intriguing question of whether issue clarification in UNCED was unusually protracted or if the distribution game was unproportionally brief or if the first replaced a part of the second.

Typical Properties of Issue Clarification Processes in UNCED

Issue clarification activities in UNCED retain a number of *typical* attributes, some of which may also be *special* for UNCED. The special characteristics distinguish UNCED from other multilateral negotiations. In order to identify and assess typical and special attributes of UNCED, conceived of as a process of negotiation, a standard of comparison is needed. Therefore, cross-references will be made to another process of multilateral negotiation that unfolded more or less parallel to the UNCED process: the Uruguay Round of GATT negotiations. This is an interesting reference case, as issue clarification activities developed quite differently than in UNCED, although the Uruguay Round and the UNCED process had significant similarities too, as seen from a negotiation point of view. Both the Uruguay Round and the UNCED process were multilateral, and involved at least one hundred nations. The same states that participated in UNCED also negotiated in the Uruguay Round. The two processes were concerned with an agenda that was extremely broad, as well as unusually complex. Several issues in UNCED, as well as in GATT, were comparatively unknown to most parties when negotiation began. Both processes were serviced by an international secretariat and were characterized by conference diplomacy. In each case, the negotiation unfolded within the context of an institutional structure and was influenced by a particular organizational culture, that of the UN and GATT respectively. The two negotiations took place at about the same time. When UNCED started, the Uruguay Round was approaching its midterm review, and was still going on when the Rio Conference was concluded.

The comparison with GATT focuses particularly on the treatment of the so-called new trade issues in the Uruguay Round: trade in services, trade-related intellectual rights, and trade-related investments. Like many of the main issues in the UNCED process, these new trade problems required sophisticated analysis and extensive information-gathering to become negotiable.

Recall that the Uruguay Round was initiated in 1983–4 by one of the leading actors – indeed, the strongest nation – in the GATT system, the United States

[11]The issues were protection of the oceans; land resources; forests; protection of the atmosphere; biological diversity; biotechnology; desertification and drought.

(Sjöstedt, 1994).[12] The American proposal for a new GATT Round was initially opposed by many countries, especially by a large coalition of developing countries, including regional powers like Brazil and India. This opposition to another GATT Round especially contested the introduction of the so-called new trade issues on the agenda. These circumstances strongly conditioned how processes of issue clarification unfolded in the Uruguay Round. Earlier, the new trade issues had fallen outside the scope of the GATT regime; they were not even considered to represent trade. Therefore, they required a considerable amount of qualified analysis and information gathering. The creation of the needed consensual knowledge regarding the new trade issues started during the lengthy prenegotiation preceding the Ministerial Meeting in Punta del Este that formally opened the Uruguay Round in 1986. The analytical work of the prenegotiations was to a great extent carried out by national delegations. Leading trading nations like the United States and the EC were particularly active in this respect. The nations initially opposing the negotiation on trade in services and the other new trade issues in the GATT context tried to promote or defend their interests by means of analytical arguments supporting the contention that the new issues were not of a genuine trade character and, hence, fell outside the competence of GATT. The GATT secretariat supplied important information into the process of issue clarification, particularly after the formal opening of the Uruguay Round. However, these contributions of the secretariat had been commissioned by the member states and its work was carefully supervised and closely guided by them. Typical of issue clarification in the GATT negotiations was the strong political struggle, with the help of scarce information and analytical arguments, between leading trading nations.

The present analysis particularly concerns the differences between UNCED and GATT with respect to how the processes of issue clarification were generally organized and functioned. The comparison focuses on a small number of themes, one of which is the *organizational structure* set up to support issue clarification and other negotiation functions. A second topic relates to *the relationship between member governments and the international secretariat* servicing the process. *Communication with other international organizations* (IGOs) was handled somewhat differently in the GATT and UNCED contexts, with likely ramifications for issue clarification. This included governmental as well as nongovernmental organizations.

The Organizational Structure

The organizational machinery set up in the Uruguay Round and UNCED respectively was significantly dissimilar and, consequently, developed differently during the negotiation process. These institutional differences reflect distinct and significant dissimilarities with respect to issue clarification strategies and methods.

One of the first formal decisions taken during the Uruguay Round concerned the negotiation machinery. With respect to trade in goods, a main body was set up, a Trade Negotiations Committee (TNC) (Sjöstedt, 1994). Its tasks were to guide and supervise the unfolding negotiations in all areas, and to take necessary operational decisions at appropriate points of time during the process. Below the Trade Negotiations Committee, 14 different working groups were instituted. For political reasons,

[12]The information about the Uruguay Round needed for a comparison with UNCED has been gathered within the context of a project concerning the transformation of the GATT system at the time of the Uruguay Round.

a separate Negotiations Committee dealing with trade in services was also established.[13] Each of these negotiation groups was given responsibility for a certain delimited problem area, for instance, trade-related intellectual rights, government procurement, or trade in agricultural goods. The negotiation work in the groups was conducted quite autonomously, particularly regarding the analysis and information collection typical for issue clarification. The principal task of the Trade Negotiations Committee was stock-taking and supervision rather than coordination and management of linkages across areas of responsibility. The "issue packages" allocated to each negotiation group in the Uruguay Round were quite broad. For example, one group was responsible for the whole tariff question, which had represented virtually the whole agenda in earlier GATT Rounds.

However, the average issue space given to the individual Negotiation Group was conspicuously narrower in the Uruguay Round than in the UNCED process. Recall, that until PrepCom IV, the UNCED agenda was distributed between only four formal negotiating bodies, the Plenary Committee and Working Groups I–III (of which the last mentioned did not begin operation until PrepCom II). Still, the UNCED process was obliged to deal with an overall agenda that may be considered to have been broader than that of the Uruguay Round. It covered not only the whole range of environmental problems, but also a number of broad cross-sectoral issues linking environmental problems and development concerns.

Occasionally, informal negotiation groups, usually called contact groups, were set up in the UNCED process. Typically, such groups gathered the "most interested" countries in a given issue area to work out an agreement that other, less interested parties could "take or leave." For example, one such grouping was instituted during PrepCom III to deal with the politically complicated issue of additional financial support to enable countries with scarce resources to be able to implement Agenda 21 and other results of the UNCED process. However, in the UNCED process, contact groups and other informal negotiating bodies did not proliferate before PrepCom IV, when issue clarification had ceased to dominate negotiations (see Chapter 3). For instance, at the Rio Conference, remaining negotiation work was distributed between the Plenary, the Main Committee, and eight coordinating groups, each of which was responsible for a certain "package" of issues: the atmosphere, water, forests, biological diversity and biotechnology, environmental law, institutions, the financial issue, and transfer of environmentally sound technology (Swedish UNCED Delegation, 6 August 1992). Thus, in the UNCED process, the expansion of the number of negotiation bodies occurred in the accelerating "distribution game" at PrepCom IV rather than in the earlier stages of the negotiation characterized by issue clarification. It was seemingly bargaining for final agreements rather than information gathering and problem solving related to issue clarification that needed an extensive and flexible network of negotiation bodies. Interestingly, the negotiation process in the Uruguay Round moved in the opposite direction; when the clearcut "distribution game" substituted for issue clarification as the dominant process dimension, the number of negotiation bodies decreased. At the Ministerial Meeting in Brussels in December 1990, which was meant to conclude the Uruguay Round, several of the negotiating groups were fused with one another, with the

[13]Services had to be treated in a special way because one group of developing countries, including Brazil and India, only accepted to negotiate on this issue area if it was kept formally outside the GATT context.

effect that the number of committees diminished considerably. When, in spring 1991, an attempt was made to relaunch the Uruguay Round, negotiations were concentrated on "four tracks" only (Sjöstedt, 1994).

Thus, the layout of organizational structures indicates that the negotiation work in the Uruguay Round was more focused than in the UNCED process during the stage of issue clarification. In each of the four formal negotiation groups operating in the UNCED process before PrepCom IV, the same delegation would deal with a wide range of different issues. As a consequence, the "negotiation vocabulary" that was developed in the negotiation tended to pertain to relatively general aspects of the issues "on the table." In contrast, in the various negotiation groups operating in the Uruguay Round, concepts, as well as the analysis generally, were more penetrating into the substance of issues. Several of the negotiation groups in GATT established a quasi-autonomous consensual knowledge of its own that "outsiders" could not automatically interpret in detail. In UNCED, concepts and consensual knowledge generally were more universally accessible.

The Role of Governments and the UNCED Secretariat

The contribution of the GATT secretariat to the Uruguay Round was, no doubt, important. The secretariat had two main tasks in this respect. First, the secretariat supplied background information deemed to be useful and relevant in the negotiations. Secondly, the secretariat recurrently summarized, and occasionally synthesized, discussions in the various formal negotiation bodies. The assistance of the GATT secretariat was, no doubt, a *sine qua non* for the step-wise successful development of the Uruguay negotiations. Also, the UNCED secretariat made an important contribution to the negotiation process it served. This role was, however, in certain crucial respects different from that performed by the GATT secretariat in the Uruguay Round, as well as in earlier multilateral trade negotiations. The work of the GATT secretariat was consistently and closely monitored by national governments through their delegations. The contributions made by the GATT secretariat represented *responses* to requests made by national delegates in committees and working groups (Sjöstedt, 1994). In contrast, the UNCED secretariat performed an independent and "driving" role in the PrepCom negotiations to such a high degree that it exercised an effective leadership role.

As in the Uruguay Round, or any other international negotiation, decisions taken by national governments gave direction to agenda-setting and issue clarification in UNCED. The UN General Assembly established a frame of reference for these negotiations, identified the topics that UNCED was going to deal with, and set up a goal structure for UNCED. It is fair to say that neither the UNCED process nor its outcome exceeded the limits of this frame of reference. The guiding decisions taken by national governments in the General Assembly were confirmed at the first sitting of the PrepCom, the Organizational Session (UNCED, A/CONF.151/PC.13). When, at this very first meeting with the UNCED PrepCom, Maurice Strong was appointed Secretary General and the UNCED secretariat was, hence, created, this act became an agreement among governments. Thus, the initial stages of the UNCED process and the Uruguay Round had in common that, first, they were closely directed by governments and, secondly, that they anticipated a tightly state-controlled secretariat service. However, in spite of this correspondence, the stage of issue clarification in reality unfolded quite differently in the UNCED and the GATT process, respectively.

One noteworthy difference from UNCED is that in the GATT context, governments continued successfully to influence issue clarification through the process. In the Uruguay Round, issue clarification stood out as a strategically crucial stage of the negotiation process that developed into a political struggle dominated and steered by the interaction between the great powers in this particular issue area, international trade. Key players were the United States, the EC, Japan, and a number of other states with the capacity to have an impact on the development of multilateral trade negotiations. The GATT secretariat was one of the key players in this game, but was not free to take any decisive initiatives. Its mission was entirely to gather or aggregate information in line with government instructions. Thus, in the Uruguay Round, the servicing and subordinate role of the secretariat was unambiguous.

As compared to the Uruguay Round, the roles of national governments and the international secretariat were virtually reversed in the UNCED process. In UNCED, national delegations did *not* make any grand moves to frame the issues on the emerging agenda in the stage of issue clarification before PrepCom IV. Instead, it was the Secretary General and the UNCED secretariat that took the necessary and decisive initiatives. As compared to the situation in the Uruguay Round, leading governments remained strangely passive. It is interesting to note that the secretariat initiatives were not limited to individual issue areas, but related to the UNCED agenda as a whole. Closely interlinked elements of the secretariat initiatives were the notions of Agenda 21 and the Earth Charter. The latter was meant to set up a list of principles and goals for dealing with various global environmental problems. The function of Agenda 21 was to serve as a long-term plan of action coordination on international environmental cooperation, and problem solving in line with the Earth Charter after the termination of the UNCED process. Thus, the Earth Charter as well as Agenda 21 was meant to be part of the outcome of UNCED; an idea that the governments-participants in the UNCED process accepted from the outset. However, Agenda 21 was also given important functions in the UNCED process, and especially with respect to issue clarification. Agenda 21 was from the start conceived of as a three-layer, long-term plan of action with essentially the following anatomy:

First layer: Basis for action: (1) state of environment/state of development; (2) principles of sustainable development; sustainable development goals.

Second layer: Action agenda: (1) programmatic approaches; (2) program of action.

Third layer: Instruments for action: (1) Tools for analysis, management, and action; (2) supporting structures and enabling mechanisms (A/CONF.151/PC.14, Figure 1)

Conceived of in these fundamental terms, Agenda 21 evolved into an operational frame of reference for the negotiations containing objectives as well as a goal-oriented conceptual framework. Consequently, Agenda 21 considerably specified the relatively loose terms of reference that the General Assembly had formulated for UNCED, and gradually made it more concrete as negotiation moved from one PrepCom session to the next. Its most important contribution was that the parameters negotiated on in the many disparate issue areas could generally be expressed in terms of elements of Agenda 21. For instance, the operational objectives in the environmental problem area regarding deforestation were defined in terms of "options for Agenda 21" (UNCED, A/CONF.151/PC.100/Add.16). Thus, the gradual specification and clarification of the structure and elements of Agenda 21 through PrepComs I, II, and III conditioned a more or less parallel clarification of the issues of substance. During the same period, governments consistently abstained from taking significant initiatives with respect to issue clarification. The debate between national delegations at the PrepCom sessions recurrently pertained to issue clarification. The point is, however, that national delegations were content to debate the definition and meaning of issues in terms of the ideas and concepts proposed by the UNCED secretariat.

Recall that formal measures were undertaken to cumulate information systematically about how governments looked at the issues. However, the questionnaires sent out to governments primarily sought to elucidate their interests and positions with regard to a number of selected issues (UNCED, A/CONF.151/PC.104–110). Likewise, for several reasons the national reports submitted to the UNCED process had little to contribute to issue clarification (UNCED, A/CONF.151/PC.98). First of all, country reports were as a rule not available until PrepCom III in August 1991. Secondly, most reports did not elaborate on the issues on the UNCED agenda, but rather described the domestic situation of the country concerned with respect to environmental problems and policy choices.

Although country reports generally did not contribute to issue clarification, in many cases they still had an important role to play when the country concerned determined its national position in the UNCED negotiations. For example, in Chapter 7, Schally explains that the preparation of the Austrian national report facilitated coordination between different Ministries and Central Agencies when Vienna determined its UNCED policy. Furthermore, Schally reports that the preparation of the national report helped the Austrian authorities to become aware of the meaning and significance of the linkages between environment and development. Accordingly, national reports did not serve to supply input into the UNCED processes of collective learning. Rather, they had the opposite function: to disseminate information about the emerging consensual knowledge *from* the UNCED process to national ministries and central agencies.

Communication Between UNCED and Other International Organizations

GATT has always been very restrictive in letting other international organizations take part in its own work, including in the multilateral trade negotiations. However, in the early stages of the Uruguay Round, a number of international governmental organizations were, in fact, invited to participate in the negotiation work. Usually, the invited organization also had responsibilities in an issue area with which the Uruguay Round was concerned, and was therefore asked to inform negotiating parties about its current work. For instance, the negotiation group dealing with trade-related intellectual property rights (TRIPs) had reason to invite the World Intellectual Property Organization (WIPO) to several meetings.

Similarly, a number of international organizations were invited to report to UNCED about their responsibilities and current activities in the areas of environmental or development problems. However, it is striking that the supply of information by international organizations was much broader in UNCED than in GATT. Its impact on the negotiation process was also seemingly more far-reaching, particularly with regard to issue clarification. In fact, the extensive links of communication to UNCED from a great number of international organizations contributes to explain the leadership role that the UNCED secretariat was able to perform during the first sessions of PrepCom when issues were essentially clarified.

At an early stage in the UNCED process, it was decided that a holistic perspective should be retained on the substantial number of environmental and development issues on the agenda (UNCED, A/CONF.151/PC.13). This meant, first, that issues should be addressed simultaneously rather than sequentially; secondly, that issue linkages should be taken into account; thirdly, that cross-sectoral means, related to finance, technology, institutions, or education, should be established in order to link environmental problems to development considerations in terms of concrete political action (UNCED Newsletter, 11 March 1991). This outlook directed the strategy that the UNCED secretariat developed to gather information to consolidate the agenda and to achieve a satisfactory degree of issue clarification. The UNCED secretariat is considered to have had a competent staff and an effective, charismatic leader in Maurice Strong (see Chapter 9). These qualities enabled the UNCED secretariat to produce analytical papers that affected how issues became collectively understood. However, the UNCED secretariat was not resourceful enough to carry out independent studies concerning all critical topics on the agenda. The number of issues was far too large, the substance of issues too complex, and the time available too limited. The staff of the secretariat was quite small. Furthermore, it took some time before the secretariat was working to full capacity, which affected the initial phase of issue clarification. The recruitment of staff was relatively protracted because the Secretary General was careful to find people that he personally found competent and loyal. Because of these circumstances, the UNCED secretariat had to draw extensively on external sources when it gathered and assessed information that could help to clarify the issues on the UNCED agenda and to build up the necessary consensual knowledge for the negotiations.

To receive external contributions, a suitable communication system was needed to find, retrieve, and process the necessary input information and knowledge. For this purpose, a network system of working parties was set up by the UNCED secretariat (UNCED, Newsletter, 11 March 1991). The character of these bodies can be described by the term "issue-specific contact groups." They were issue-specific in the sense that they were given responsibility for a particular package of issues. The dimensions of these aggregates were comparable to the agenda confided to individual negotiation groups in the Uruguay Round; the focus was set on a particular theme. Thus, related to the activities of Working Group I, working parties were set up at an early stage of the negotiations for the following topics: atmosphere issues, land and agriculture, forestry, biodiversity, and biotechnology. Under Working Group II, two new working parties were created to deal with oceans and toxic chemicals and hazardous wastes. Working Group II activities could, furthermore, also be linked to bodies that already existed and functioned parallel to UNCED. One notable example was the inter-secretariat group preparing for the 1992 Conference on Water and the Environment that was linked to the UNCED issue of "freshwater." Another example was the working relations established between the UNCED secretariat and the Dublin Conference on Water and Environment. In this connection, it may be added that Working Group I activities were linked to institutions external to UNCED. Prominent examples were the couplings to the FAO/Netherlands Conference on Sustainable Agriculture, the Intergovernmental Panel on Climate Change, and the Ad Hoc Group on Biodiversity.

These working parties – or contact groups – included a mixture of people from the UNCED secretariat as well as from international organizations, primarily UN institutions or, in a few cases, representatives of on-going negotiation processes (notably on climate change and biological diversity). Spokesmen of nongovernmental organizations and research institutions were also part of these networks. For instance, the International Council of Scientific Unions was selected to represent the scientific community. Working parties did not merely function as fora for discussion. Most of them became closely involved in the UNCED process, especially during the stage of issue clarification. The task of the working parties was to take part directly in the preparation of the secretariat papers that represented the basic input into processes of consultation and negotiation that finalized agenda-setting in UNCED. That is, they specified objectives and issues as well as the terms of reference for the UNCED process (UNCED, Newsletter, 11 March 1991; UNCED, A/CONF.151/PC.14).

Most of the working parties were concerned with problems under the responsibility of Working Groups I and II – to a large extent, "pure" environmental matters. Needs of issue clarification were met in a similar way with regard to the over-arching and cross-sectoral issues allocated to the Plenary Committee in its capacity as a specialized working group. Such a strategy was manifested in the creation of working parties on, for instance, environmental education and technology transfer (UNCED, Newsletter, 11 March 1991). However, the cross-sectoral issues had certain inherent qualities that prevented them from being treated in the same way as the "pure" environmental questions. The latter were usually already on the agenda of some other organization than UNCED when this process started. In these cases, the assignment of the working party concerned was essentially stock-taking and synthesis. The working party reported how the problem area, for example forestry, was understood within the context of international cooperation, what results had already been attained in this work, and what was currently going on in parallel processes of negotiation.

The analytical work concerning the cross-sectoral domain was in many ways more demanding. Regular stock-taking was usually not sufficient owing to the simple fact that the linkages constituting the backbone of the cross-sectoral issues had hitherto not been particularly analyzed. Targeted, and partly innovative, analysis was necessary to clarify the meaning and significance of the many cross-sectoral issues – for instance, the linkages between poverty and environment; economic growth patterns, consumption standards, demographic pressures and environment; and debt, terms of trade, "reverse resource flows," and environmental degradation (UNCED, A/CONF.151/PC.16). These analytical needs required new methods, and ultimately new institutions, to be handled effectively. One approach chosen by the UNCED secretariat to meet these requirements was to set up study groups to analyze the meaning of the various cross-sectoral issues and their significance in different respects. Like the working parties, these study groups assembled representatives from organizations considered to possess the necessary and relevant information. In order to refine the integrative conceptual framework for these studies, the UNCED secretariat organized a project en-titled "Sustainable Development: From Concept to Action." The method typical for this approach was to ask experts, often in their individual capacity, to prepare analytical papers on specific themes. The papers were discussed at a seminar at the UNCED secretariat in order to become synthesized into a concluding report that was eventually assessed at a conference organized in the Netherlands at the end of 1991, at the time when issue clarification processes were being phased down (UNCED, Newsletter, 11 March 1991). This is not the only example of an academic approach to problem solving. Prominent research organizations were engaged to analyze certain problems where the UNCED secretariat did not have all the necessary knowledge. For example, the International Institute for Applied Systems Analysis (IIASA) was commissioned to analyze the physical linkages between, on the one hand, the problem of climate change and, on the other, forestry, food production, and water resources (Shaw, Gallopin, Weaver, and Öberg, 1992). The International Conference on an Agenda of Science for Environment and Development into the 21st Century (ASCEND 21) seemingly made an important contribution to the chapter in Agenda 21 concerning science for sustainable development.

The UNCED secretariat reserved for itself the study of the means to be employed for the implementation of the results of the UNCED process, and especially Agenda 21: institutions, technology, and finance (UNCED, A/CONF.151/PC.15). These issues were of strategic significance as they determined whether Agenda 21 would only be of symbolic significance, or whether it would become an operational program of action. To some extent, cross-sectoral issues like finance or technology transfer were dependent on direct political support rather than on scientific analysis. However, political support was only a necessary condition, and not a sufficient condition, for effective processing of the cross-sectoral issues in UNCED. The cross-sectoral issues had hitherto been dealt with rather superficially in international organizations, including in the UN family. In some of these areas, the UNCED secretariat was obliged to undertake something akin to an academic assessment of the theoretically oriented literature in order to create a viable basis of consensual knowledge. The issue of "costing" is a good example.

"Costing" represented a key element of the studies concerning the implementation of the outcome of UNCED. The idea was that the essential costs required by implementation of a certain program of action should be determined *a priori* so that the necessary financial resources could be secured. It was particularly important to calculate the need for "additional" financial resources that certain nations, notably the developing countries, needed in order to be able to carry out the recommendations stipulated in the Final Acts of the Rio Meeting. However, costing calculations presupposed penetrating analyses that, as a rule, had not been carried out prior to UNCED. Consequently, costing was an extremely demanding task for the UNCED secretariat, which needed external assistance. A revealing case is the report concerning costing with respect to climate change (UNCED, A/CONF.151/PC.23). The terms of reference for the work in this area were derived from the objective of adopting measures to limit possible climate change and mitigate its reverse effects. The approach required a thorough inventory of relevant academic ideas and notions. It was necessary to begin with the choice of a suitable definition of "cost." This concept had been given quite different meanings in recent discussions of the economic consequences of climate change. A rational choice of a definition presupposed a competent assessment of competing theoretical approaches which, in turn, needed a thorough stocktaking and analysis of the literature. In this work, the UNCED secretariat cooperated with seven regional or intergovernmental organizations, 16 nongovernmental organizations, as well as 25 national governments (UNCED, A/CONF.151/PC.23, p. 9). The organizations, as well as the governments concerned, were all logical and competent actors in the area of climate change.[14]

The participation of nongovernmental organizations (NGOs) in the UNCED process was in many ways exceptional. At the time of the Rio Conference, approximately 1400 NGOs were formally associated with the UNCED process (see Chapter 12). Most of these organizations rarely made a contribution to issue clarification in UNCED. Instead, many organizations tried to pursue their own agenda in the UNCED process. For instance, some organizations wanted to come to the Rio Meeting only to get publicity at home or attention in the media. However, a considerable number of NGOs made a contribution to UNCED without being invited to any of the study groups set up by the UNCED secretariat. Such NGOs primarily carried out two types of activities that were somehow related to issue clarification. First, several NGOs were invited to deliver speeches to PrepCom (in the Plenary Committee) on selected themes. Many of these presentations communicated new expertise on particular issues. Secondly, NGOs were also able to give direct support to certain delegations with a limited capability to follow developments in UNCED. One example is a newsletter produced by a small consortium of NGOs, which followed PrepCom proceedings from day to day. The original objective of the newsletter had been to help the community of NGOs keep track of the negotiations, but as time went on it became increasingly used also by national delegations, particularly from the Third World. Thus, it seems that some NGOs contributed to the creation of consensual knowledge by disseminating information and knowledge among the participants of the UNCED process.

THE CHARACTER OF CONSENSUAL KNOWLEDGE

It is a difficult task to make a detailed characterization of a body of consensual knowledge related to a negotiation agenda that is as wide and complex as that of UNCED. The requirements for issue clarification did not only pertain to the contents of individual issues, but also to the overall agenda. Consensual knowledge was needed to understand, and conceptualize, the agenda in a uniform language and to aggregate its various issues into one, single whole. Considering the technical complexity of many issues in combination with the multitude of problems to which they pertained, one might have expected an absence of consensual knowledge in the UNCED context. However, the body of consensual knowledge "conditioning" the UNCED process was quite different. It was highly integrated and expressed in concepts that were understandable and applicable in all negotiation groups. Finally, consensual knowledge was, no doubt, an important prerequisite for the relative ease with which the "distribution

[14]*Governmental organizations*: Commission of the EC, United Nations Economic Commission, Association of Southeast Asian Nations, the World Bank, Asian Development Bank, OECD, International Energy Agency, United Nations Environment Program.

Nongovernmental organizations: Asian Energy Institute (New Delhi), Stockholm Environment Institute, Alliance to Save Energy, Natural Resources Defence Council (Washington DC), Lega Par L'ambiente (Italy), Greenpeace, World Wildlife Fund (Washington DC), Institute for European Environmental Politics, Center for Global Change (Washington DC), Batelle NW Labs (Washington DC), Royal Institute for International Affairs (London), Bariloche Institute (Argentina), Africa Center for Technical Studies (Kenya), Bangladesh Institute for Advanced Studies (UNCED, A/CONF.151/PC.23, p. 9).

game" of the UNCED process could be conducted from PrepCom IV onwards. It is interesting to note that the typical, and partly special, attributes of the UNCED consensual knowledge differed significantly from the consensual knowledge of GATT, which has played an important role in multilateral trade negotiations.[15]

Recall the conceptual framework, summarized in Table 4.1 (p. 68), declaring that one of the basic criteria for the characterization of a body of knowledge, be it consensual or not, is its *contents identity*. This property essentially reflects the academic discipline or disciplines on which consensual knowledge leans directly or indirectly – for instance, physics, biology, or economics. The contents identity of consensual knowledge may represent an important influencing factor in the process of bargaining. For instance, the strength of the GATT regime as a guiding principle for the multilateral trade negotiations is partly conditioned by the close and recognized relationship between the GATT rules and mainstream trade theory.[16] The GATT regime contains norms and principles that give guidance to problem solving as well as decision making in the negotiation process. Thus, the consensual knowledge of a GATT Round contains criteria for what solutions and decisions are "correct" as seen from a rational and knowledge-based perspective.

The character of the consensual knowledge developed in the UNCED process had different qualities. The GATT regime is supported by a single, strong academic theory pertaining to an authoritative discipline: economics. In contrast, the UNCED consensual knowledge was connected to a multitude of academic disciplines, a variety of natural and social sciences explaining the many aspects of the environmental problems on the agenda. The objective to promote economic instruments required a supply of knowledge from several sub-disciplines of economics. The work in Working Group III on institutions and legal matters was dependent on contributions from the profession of international law. The links between consensual and scientific knowledge was considerably weaker in UNCED than in GATT.[17] In UNCED, the scientific component of consensual knowledge was essentially a background factor. The flows of information into the UNCED process concerning the substance of the agenda were, as a rule, not coming from scientific communities directly. The main sources of information were institutions that were part of, or closely associated with, the UN system. These UN bodies share a similar culture that is bureaucratic–organizational rather than scientific– professional.

The characteristics of the UN bureaucratic–organizational culture have colored the UNCED consensual knowledge significantly, notably with regard to *goal-orientation*. Thus, consensual knowledge retains what may be called a *program perspective* on the agenda of UNCED. The frame of reference is not related to problem solving in a scientific sense, but rather represents a program of action. In the case of the UNCED process, this orientation was an important explanation for the functional significance of consensual knowledge. Information accumulation and

[15]Recall that the GATT negotiations, and especially the Uruguay Round, is here used as a reference case, a standard of comparison, when the UNCED process is assessed. However, both the Kennedy Round (1964–7) and the Tokyo Round (1973–9) were guided by essentially the same consensual knowledge as the Uruguay Round.

[16]By mainstream trade theory, I refer to the neo-classical theory of free trade based on the principle of comparative advantage.

[17]Recall that in the multilateral trade negotiations the general principles of free trade were formally codified in the GATT treaty. These principles have been explicitly referred to when the objectives for the GATT Rounds have been established.

analysis regarding "poverty and environmental degradation" has been selected as a case illustrating the significance of the program perspective of the UNCED consensual knowledge.

Regarding the poverty/environment problem, UNCED was ordained by the UN General Assembly to address the issue of "improvement of the living and working environment of the poor in urban slums and rural areas, through the eradication of poverty by, *inter alia* implementing integrated rural and development programs, as well as taking other appropriate measures at all levels necessary to stem the degradation of the environment" (UNGA, Res. 44/228). In order to clarify this cross-sectoral issue, the secretariat organized an analytical work process outside the UNCED negotiation machinery, the results of which were duly reported to the PrepCom in a series of documents. The basic problem of substance evoked in this analysis was clearly relevant for the academic agenda: the causal relationship between poverty and environmental degradation. In the UNCED process, this meant a focus on three sets of "independent variables": (1) "the macro-economic context within which development is taking place, (2) demographic developments, and (3) access to means of livelihood and sustenance" (A/CONF. 151/PC/15). This outlook was strongly conditioned by the Fourth United Nations Development Decade, a kind of super, multi-agency program within the UN system. Thus, for clarification of the key concept of poverty, UNCED relied on reports prepared by the World Bank (World Development Report, 1990) and the UN Development Program (Human Development Report, 1990). Other suppliers of information at this stage were, for instance, the International Fund for Agricultural Development and the Swedish International Development Agency, which offered the preliminary results of a study on poverty, environment, and development. As the UNCED study unfolded, a number of themes were increasingly incorporated. Many of these new sub-issues were clarified by an international institution that had on-going activities in the area concerned: (1) Anti-poverty programs related to resource/management issues – World Bank; (2) the relationship between agricultural productivity and environment – FAO; (3) employment and sustainable development – ILO; (4) health, poverty, and environment – WHO; (5) demographic developments, poverty, and environment – UNDEP; and (6) the impact of environmental stress on children – UNICEF (A/CONF.151/PC/.15, p.13).

All these assessments, concerning highly dissimilar subjects, were expressed in a program language that was basically the same for the various UN agencies contributing to the assessment. The same program language was easily understood at the receiving end – among national delegations. These were dominated by diplomats-generalists, many of whom were professionally familiar with the UN system. Under these conditions, the program format of the unfolding consensual knowledge contributed to strengthening its *coherence* for at least two reasons (see Table 4.1 on p. 68). First, the program approach as such helped negotiating parties to have the same focus on the problems concerned. Secondly, the program format in its UN linguistic dressing represented a familiar, common frame of reference for the UNCED negotiators.

The integrating impact on the agenda achieved by the general program orientation of the UNCED consensual knowledge was strongly reinforced by Agenda 21. Particularly, it significantly facilitated issue clarification in the UNCED process. Agenda 21 constituted a central, elaborate, as well as *formalized*, core element of the UNCED consensual knowledge. It served as a frame of reference as well as a *code of interpretation* in the negotiation process, a set of criteria that could serve effectively to coordinate negotiation efforts in different issue areas. The basis for this correlation was the inherent logic of the program character and the operational goal-orientation of Agenda 21. Thus, when the idea of Agenda 21 was acknowledged at an early stage of the UNCED process, this corresponded to the acceptance of a set of elaborate criteria for the guidance of the UNCED negotiations. These guidelines functioned well within the context of individual environmental or development issue areas where negotiations concerned commitments with regard to particular chapters of Agenda 21. Also, most of the cross-sectoral issues, representing different types of political linkages between environment and development, manifested themselves as chapters of Agenda 21 – for example, additional financial resources, technology transfer, etc.[18]

What may be called physical or real world issue linkages were also nominally on the UNCED agenda according to the mandate given by the UN General Assembly. However, in reality, physical linkages across several environmental issue areas were not seriously evoked in the negotiations. Some studies were carried out to elucidate issue linkages (see Shaw, Gallopin, Weaver, and Öberg, 1992). The results of these analyses were communicated to the UNCED process, although not really considered by delegations. One reason was that physical linkages were not part of Agenda 21 explicitly and, hence, was not expressed in a language that made these issues negotiable.

CONCLUSIONS: LESSONS FOR THE FUTURE

Our assessment leads to the conclusion that both *issue clarification* and *consensual knowledge* in the UNCED negotiations were comparatively instrumental and effective. A comparison with the reference case, the Uruguay Round in GATT, is suggestive. Although the agenda of UNCED was even more extensive and complex than that of the Uruguay Round, the time needed for agenda-setting and issue clarification was considerably shorter. Thus, as compared to the Uruguay Round, UNCED was clearly a success story rather than a failure.[19] It seems that *one* positive driver of this outcome was the consensual knowledge that was established in the UNCED process before the bargaining about final agreements began in earnest at PrepCom IV. Therefore, the UNCED process offers a number of useful lessons for future environmental negotiations with respect to the methods of issue clarification as well as to the functions of consensual knowledge, once it has been established.

Positive Attributes of Consensual Knowledge

The consensual knowledge established for the purposes of the UNCED negotiations had a number of positive critical qualities as seen from the point of view of the practi-

[18]Agenda 21 contained chapters concerning groups of environmental problems relating the atmosphere, the land, forests, mountains, agriculture, and biological diversity. Cross-sectoral issues represented a second category of issues that, in addition to technology transfer and financial resources, included economic relations, poverty, consumption patterns (lifestyles), population, health, living conditions, and environmental and development considerations in decision making.

[19]At the time of writing, the Uruguay Round had not yet been completed. However, the conclusion of the Uruguay Round at the end of 1993 was (Sjöstedt 1994) more than two years overdue, and hence represents a failure in this sense.

cal negotiator. The most important attribute of the consensual knowledge was evidently its capacity to give operative guidance to negotiators, to indicate feasible solutions to negotiation problems (see Table 4.1 on p. 68). These operative objectives began to be established at an early stage of the negotiation thanks to the acceptance of the notion of Agenda 21, already at PrepCom I. Agenda 21 also represented a useful code of interpretation, functioning as a criterion for the selection of information servicing as input into the processes building consensual knowledge. The discriminatory edge of this criterion of selection evidently contributed to limit the volume of documents containing the UNCED consensual knowledge. This mass of information was by no means insignificant. Many developing countries complained that they had great difficulties in taking part, and of assessing all the official information provided for the various sessions of the PrepCom. Praise was duly given to the secretariat for its competence and its impressive capacity to produce substantive documents quickly. However, considering the great number of issues, and their complexity, the quantity of documents delegates had to deal with to be active in the process was comparatively small and manageable. Furthermore, conceived of as a frame of reference for negotiators, consensual knowledge was relatively easily accessible and understandable. Although a large element of the consensual knowledge, particularly related to the environmental problems on the UNCED agenda, had a scientific contents identity, it still retained a language code that was quite familiar to the average negotiator "at the table." Thus, the UNCED consensual knowledge was not expressed in a scientific language, but rather an administrative–organizational language typical for the UN system. Recall that most of the delegates to the UNCED meetings had experience with the UN in Geneva or New York, or some specialized agency elsewhere. Also, note that this proportion further increased from PrepCom III to IV when UNCED moved to the UN Headquarters in New York.

Positive Attributes of Issue Clarification

The positive attributes of the UNCED consensual knowledge was to a great extent deliberately designed by the processes of issue clarification. Therefore, an important lesson of UNCED relates to the properties of the process of issue clarification that conditioned this favorable outcome.

One explanation of the limited time required for issue clarification in UNCED was its predominant character of stock-taking within the system of UN agencies. Little new original information was generated within the context of the UNCED process. This is a significant difference from the Uruguay Round, in which new knowledge had to be created concerning the so-called new trade issues, especially trade in services. At the same time, it has to be stressed that the UNCED consensual knowledge conceived of as an encompassing cognitive platform did not exist before the UNCED negotiations got under way.

Thus, one significant lesson for future negotiations on the environment and development concerns the conditions under which separate bodies of knowledge and information pertaining to different international organizations are to be combined into an effectively functioning consensual knowledge. It is doubtful that this integration could have been achieved by means of the regular, permanent mechanisms and procedures for coordination of organizational activities within the UN system. The coordination of information-gathering and analysis was directed and administered by a competent organization, the UNCED secretariat, using an effective ad hoc and partly informal organization for this purpose: the system of multi-agency study groups. Coordination work was subordinated to a widely visible plan of action particularly manifested in Agenda 21. Finally, the suppliers of information (UN agencies), the coordinators (the UNCED secretariat), as well as the final users of the consensual knowledge, were familiar with the administrative–organizational UN language in which it was essentially expressed.

Negative Lessons Regarding Issue Clarification and Consensual Knowledge

In many ways the experience gained in the UNCED process with regard to issue clarification methods and procedures is so positive that one might want to repeat them in a possible future comprehensive overview of the outcome of the 1992 Rio Conference. One strategy might, for instance, be to transform the Rio Declaration into a stronger Earth Charter, to review and update Agenda 21 and to establish a new temporary UNCED structure with an ad hoc secretariat to administer this process. However, before the prospect of a repeated UNCED process is contemplated, its weaknesses have also to be spelled out and considered.

With special regard to issue clarification, the flaws of the UNCED process largely correspond to factors that condition its positive attributes. Negotiations in UNCED were largely conducted in terms of Agenda 21, which was evidently a condition for the relative success of this process as it actually evolved during the meetings of PrepCom and at the Rio Conference. This meant that negotiations in UNCED itself did *not* concern concrete policy measures, and state obligations in particular environmental issue areas like climate change or biological diversity. Although the results of the negotiations over these issues were integrated into the UNCED process at the Rio meeting, the bargaining as such took place elsewhere. There are indications that these external negotiations were disturbed rather than supported by the discussions over the same topics in UNCED. The general character of the consensual knowledge seemingly did not permit a sufficiently strong focus on either the matters of substance or on the legal dressing of the various clauses of an agreement.

At the same time, consensual knowledge was also insufficient to attain the desired holistic perspective on the ecological and development problems on the agenda. The trick of Agenda 21 was that it advocated a comprehensive global outlook at the same time as it compartmentalized the working schedule into smaller pieces – the various chapters of Agenda 21 – that were manageable at the negotiation table. Key cross-sectoral issues like finance or technology transfer were in reality delimited single topics with which negotiators working in the UN system were quite familiar. These issues had been covered by various UN agencies and conferences for many decades. In contrast, the UNCED process proved quite incapable of handling new issue linkages, because of the existing anatomy of consensual knowledge. If in future negotiations it will be necessary to address the physical linkages between problem areas like climate change, ozone depletion, deforestation, desertification, and biological diversity, another kind of approach to issue clarification than that represented by Agenda 21 will have to be designed.

5

The Search for Flexibility on Financial Issues at UNCED: An Analysis of Preference Adjustment

Bertram I. Spector

The negotiations that preceded the 1992 United Nations Conference on Environment and Development (UNCED) focused on a complex set of multi-sectoral issues that cross-cut national and coalitional interests and objectives. For agreements to emerge, it was necessary to search for and achieve compromises on highly contentious subjects at the nexus of these issue linkages. There were many successes or partial successes, as attested to by the leaders of the process (see Ambassador Koh's account in Chapter 10) and the mutually acceptable texts that were cobbled together using a tedious "editing diplomacy" process. The search sometimes yielded stalemates because the sheer number and complexity of issues overpowered the ability of national delegations to traverse the bargaining space. Moreover, delegations did not always have the authority to truly negotiate from initial positions and effectively explore that space for compromise options.

At various stages in the prenegotiation and negotiation processes, impasses materialized on probably the most pugnacious of all issues, that of financial resources. Essentially, the deadlock revolved around the questions of "how much?" and "how distributed?" Besides the generally pervasive rift in interests and objectives between North and South, the debate was concerned with the propensity of industrialized nations to pledge large economic and technological assistance packages and commit themselves to confronting global and regional environmental problems. Conducted in the midst of these UNCED negotiations, the analysis presented in this chapter seeks to understand where the opportunities for compromise lay on these difficult issues, what concessions were needed, and the extent of concessions required to reach successful agreement. Analytically, the chapter explores the *flexibility* of negotiating actors in difficult situations – their willingness to modify their positions to reach an accord.

Conducting a systematic analysis of negotiations while they are still in progress is a tenuous exercise. First, critical information to conduct the analysis may not be available or may be difficult to access while negotiations are still under way. Issues may not be fully defined, and interests and positions may not be established; even if they are, actors in the process may not view it as advantageous to disclose their

Negotiating International Regimes: Lessons Learned from the United Nations Conference on Environment and Development (G. Sjöstedt, *et al.*, eds.; 1-85966-077-0; © IIASA; pub. Graham & Trotman, 1994; printed in Great Britain), pp. 87–103.

preferences prematurely or through third parties. Secondly, negotiations are dynamic processes; an analysis conducted in midstream cannot, by definition, provide a complete understanding of the effectiveness of persuasive strategies or tactics in reaching agreement, for example. Overall, a process that is still active is difficult to treat analytically until it has reached a stable resting state.

At the same time, one way for negotiation research to have real utility for practice is to apply its conceptual and analytical frameworks to processes that are still in progress.[1] Because of the problems identified above in obtaining information for systematic analyses, a contingency approach for negotiations-in-progress is proposed. The results of such an approach will be of interest to researchers, and likely to be usable by practitioners in a realistic way. In a contingency analysis, users can ask "what if" questions that relate to future circumstances and the conclusions can be stated in an "if then" format. The analysis of ten is based on historically meaningful or hypothesized scenarios and explicitly stated assumptions. While complete information about the negotiation is obviously not available, such an analysis uses what is known to date about the structure of the issues, positions, interests, and so on. Practitioners can employ the results to test their own assumptions about the effectiveness of a possible strategy, the reactions of other parties to the use of a new tactic, or the likely negotiated outcome of a new proposal. Contingency analyses can provide practitioners with a common information structure and approach to diagnosing the negotiation situation and planning new strategies in the prenegotiation period. Such analyses can also identify and examine opportunities for compromise on contentious issues.[2]

This chapter has several objectives. First, and most generally, we want to understand more about the dynamics of cognitive interest adjustment that lead to compromise in negotiation. Can it be characterized as a mechanistic tit-for-tat concession-making process? Or is it primarily a learning process in which preferences are modified as new information and arguments persuade of the need for change? Secondly, we are interested in assessing the role of interest adjustment within the process of negotiating new environmental regimes. Are particular interests especially prominent in the development of new regimes? Are these at the center of controversy in the negotiation, or on the sidelines? We focus here on rule-making concerning the design of financial resource mechanisms and processes. Finally, we seek to demonstrate the practical utility of a certain analytical methodology to support negotiations while still in progress. Related research was performed during the prenegotiation phase to support planning and diagnosis activities of the secretariat and the conference leadership of UNCED (Spector, 1991). The current study was conducted with these same end users in mind.

INTERESTS, PREFERENCES, AND LEARNING

Chapter 1 referred to the interactive relationship between issue and interest clarification during the course of the prenegotiation and negotiation periods. Adjustment in

[1]Another is to apply lessons learned from past cases and analyses to current negotiations. See Sjöstedt (1993), for example, in the area of international environmental negotiations.

[2]See Spector (1993c) for a survey of analytic techniques that can be of use to negotiation practitioners, primarily in the prenegotiation phase.

one is intertwined with change in the other, and is stimulated by the behavioral inputs of domestic and international negotiation, the introduction of new information, and the clarification of national goals and objectives. As issues and interests change, opportunities for tradeoffs become possible and convergence on a mutually acceptable formula is feasible. On the other hand, issue and interest modification can lead to a hardening of positions or, worse still, a radical divergence of the parties away from any possible joint solution. The factors responsible for pushing the negotiation process one way or the other are not well understood, but this is the subject of much continuing research (see Kremenyuk, 1991).

The process of interest modification is not a mechanistic tit-for-tat interplay, but rather a learning experience in which negotiators frame and reframe issues and interests based on domestic and international influences. It is a learning experience within a joint problem-solving context, one in which the parties have agreed on the common objective of seeking an agreement together.

Interests and Preferences

Interests and preferences, the key concepts in our framework, are used here interchangeably. These terms identify the desires, concerns, and aspirations of a negotiating party in the context of the particular negotiation in question (Fisher, Ury, and Patton, 1991; Burton, 1990). They constitute the attitudes that motivate behavior in the negotiating environment toward agreement or stalemate. Burton refers to the concept of *values* to specify the longstanding, stable, and relatively invariant goals and objectives of a nation or society. Interests and preferences, on the other hand, refer to the more transient attitudes that are at the basis of decision making in particular negotiations. Considered policy decisions are often made in relation to a set of hierarchically ordered criteria that represent the interests and preferences of the decision makers in that particular situation. These criteria, in effect, operationalize the values of society in relation to the issues being negotiated. In many cases, these values can be operationalized in different ways, and that is where the idea of interest and preference modification comes into play. Interests and preferences also can refer to the more specific desires or concerns of a negotiating party toward various proposals and formulae. Adjustment and tuning of negotiator attraction to alternate sets of decision criteria or specific formulae is the phenomenon we are particularly interested in understanding and explaining.

Essentially, interests and preferences are negotiable (Burton, 1990). They can be influenced by information, power, and persuasion, the essential media of negotiation. When commitments to initial positions become unstuck, it is usually because the initial preferences of the negotiating parties have been influenced, resulting in a reprioritization of the negotiator's affection for alternative solutions. If interests and preferences can be adjusted, they can serve as the stimulus or pretext for parties to engage in logrolling to generate mutually acceptable formulae.

Issue-Interest Cycle

Adjustment of interests and preferences is intimately intertwined with the process of issue definition and clarification (see Chapter 4). Issues are defined, framed, and reframed in terms of national interests. Negotiators and policy makers think of issues in terms of their concerns, desires, and goals. Many negotiation problems relate to multiple interests; especially conflicting interests must be considered in combination to facilitate a coherent understanding and formulation of the issues at hand. If these interests change over time, issue definition may undergo a transformation as well.

What causes interests and preferences to change? Internal factors within a negotiation actor, as well as external factors, play important roles. Internally, a national government may change, revamping the broad principles and values by which national goals and objectives are established. Certain catalytic events may occur, such as the Chernobyl accident or a natural disaster, that serve to drastically reorient national interests on an issue. As well, domestic negotiations among stakeholders – in government bureaucracy, business, nongovernmental organizations (NGOs), and the public – can influence the motives of international negotiators and policy makers. External factors that influence national interests and preferences are primarily focused on the international negotiation process itself. Other negotiation actors, international organizations, and NGOs can present effective arguments, use persuasive tactics, and offer attracting or repelling incentives and tradeoffs to reorient preferences on an issue. New information, especially in scientific and technological areas, can be a potent force in changing preferences toward an issue. Obtaining such data is a particular problem for developing countries, which are often highly dependent for information on industrialized nations.

This issue-interest cycle can be viewed as a learning process. Actors adapt their attitudes and behavior in reaction to new situations and inputs from others. In a multilateral negotiation environment, the potential for both positive and negative stimuli, urging and discouraging change, are likely to be great. The actors' response to these stimuli, through adjustments to preferences and reframing of issues, will determine whether or not logrolling will become a productive activity in the negotiation situation.

APPROACH

Methodology

A decision analytic model can be employed as a simplifying vehicle to represent and structure national interests, preferences toward possible negotiated solutions, and opportunities for interest adjustment. In particular, a Multi-Attribute Value (MAV) analysis model is applied in this study to operationalize the analysis of interest dynamics in the prenegotiation process (Spector, 1993b). This modeling approach is capable of tracking change in the values and preferences of national policy makers toward particular issues and sub-issues under debate in negotiations, providing an explanation as to why interests have changed and highlighting compromise options that may represent achievable outcomes due to the adjustment of actor interests.

Decision analysis is a normative technique that seeks to prescribe appropriate courses of action that coincide with decision maker values and preferences. Central to all decision analysis models are personal preferences or interests. MAV models, in particular, provide an analytical structure to trade off decision objectives across alternate decision options given these preferences or interests, resulting in a prioritization of options. It requires the modeling of a decision maker's preference structure by specifying evaluation criteria that are weighted in terms of their relative importance in making the decision. The range of decision options are then rated against each criterion, and calculations are performed that yield a prioritization of options.

This modeling approach has been employed by several negotiation researchers to provide both practical advice for negotiation teams involved in on-going talks, and an explanation of historical negotiations for research and analytical purposes. Spector (1993a) demonstrated the use of MAV models to understand and explain the adjustment of national and coalition preferences in two multilateral negotiations, the Uruguay Round of GATT and the Single European Act of the EC. MAV models also have been applied prescriptively to assist in prenegotiation strategy development concerning US military bases in the Philippines (1978), the Panama Canal (1974), and international oil tanker standards (1978) (Raiffa, 1982; Ulvila and Snider, 1980; Ulvila, 1990). MAV models typically evaluate the decision calculus of each negotiating party independently. In this study, however, models of each key nation or coalition are compared directly to facilitate a multiparty analysis that features the interdependence of negotiator preferences.

The development and exercise of a MAV model to evaluate prenegotiation interest dynamics is conducted in several steps (Spector, 1993a and 1993b). A separate model must be structured for each actor and each issue being analyzed. A *criterion structure* is developed that models the range of national interests for all interested parties concerning the issue under debate. The range of possible negotiated outcomes is specified and arrayed in an *outcome structure*. Data is gathered to estimate the extent to which each possible outcome satisfies each of the interests in the criterion structure (the *outcome ratings*). For each national or coalition entity, the relative importance of each criterion is assessed (the *criterion weighting*). The model is then exercised by performing calculations for each national or coalition entity, yielding a prioritization of alternative negotiated outcomes for each entity. Comparisons across entities can be assessed to evaluate the extent of convergence or divergence on the various possible outcomes.

Most importantly, the dynamics of preference adjustment are analyzed through *sensitivity analysis*. Prominent outcomes that are identified in the model's exercise –that is, those outcomes that are most preferred by the key national or coalition entities – are used as the basis for the analysis. The objective is to evaluate the extent to which each principal actor must adjust its interests and preferences to be able to accept these prominent outcomes. To do this analytically, the initial weighted preferences on each prominent outcome, interest-by-interest, are compared to the maximum possible preference each actor can have (that is, equal to a weighted preference score of 100). The difference between these two values is defined as the *weighted deficiency*, the distance between the actor's initial preference for the outcome and its *undisputed* acceptance of that solution. This score represents the degree to which the actor's preferences must change from its going-in position to reach total endorsement of the outcome option. Because this sensitivity analysis is calculated on an interest-by-interest basis, it is possible to specify which interests must be adjusted more than others by each actor in order for a prominent outcome to be acceptable.

The application of this type of analytical approach to a prenegotiation that is still in progress introduces many risks. Issues and interests are not fully defined. Coalitions among national entities may be only in a formative stage. Strategies and tactics used by negotiators to influence other actors may not be formulated yet; certainly, their effectiveness is not determinable. Only some proposals envisioning potential outcomes or formulas for agreement have been generated. The researcher's ability to collect useful objective or subjective data within this context is difficult, to say the least.

However, if it is possible to identify the emerging issues and sub-issues, recognize the going-in positions, uncover the national interests, and array the existing proposals during the prenegotiation phase of an international debate, the researcher may be able to provide the practical negotiator with valuable insights. In the case of the UNCED prenegotiation, it was possible at the end of the last PrepCom meeting in April 1992 to specify the issues and sub-issues that were being debated, and the ways in which these issues were understood and framed by the negotiators at that time. It was also possible to define the preliminary range of alternative proposals for each of these issues and sub-issues. It is certainly much more difficult to specify national interests or preferences concerning these issues. However, through the debates that were conducted, public statements made, interviews performed, and national reports submitted to the conference, estimates of the initial going-in interests and preferences of nations and coalitions could be interpolated. As a result, interest profiles were developed for prominent nations or coalitions, estimating their internal decision-making priorities. Using these profiles, the MAV model could be applied and sensitivity analyses conducted to test various contingencies: What if actors stand firm on certain issues? Is a convergence of interests possible that results in integrative win–win solutions? How much must each party give up of its key demands?

Simulating negotiator interest profiles with MAV models offers practical end-users with a decision support system that can diagnose prenegotiation opportunities and pitfalls. Practitioners can assess how much flexibility is required to achieve reasonable compromise agreements, and if agreement can be reached at all. Different paths toward bridging the gaps between contending parties can be explored ahead of time to facilitate the ones likely to be most effective.

Context

An innovative feature of UNCED was its recognition of linkages among environmental issues (for example, between deforestation and climate change), and between environmental and other issues (for example, with development and international trade). Ideally, these linkages would figure significantly in the search for solutions: to solve a multidimensional problem requires that the entire system of issue relationships be accounted for in prior planning. Linkages between issues offer negotiators potentially novel tradeoffs with which to construct deals: balancing environmental constraints with development benefits, for example.

UNCED addressed issue linkages in two negotiated documents: the Rio Declaration, which states global principles and objectives, and Agenda 21, an action plan identifying specific goals, targets, and implementation programs. It is within Agenda 21 that several cross-sectoral issues, most prominently, financial resources and technology transfer, are featured. These cross-sectoral issues, as their name implies, are jointly linked to both environmental and developmental issues; for example, extensive financial resources must be mobilized to implement anti-pollution technologies, as well as to foster new industrialization programs.

In this chapter, two critical issues within the financial resources area are examined – developing a viable funding mechanism and agreeing on acceptable funding levels – in which tradeoffs were required to bridge gaps between the positions of the key coalitions. The first issue concerns the mechanism to fund future sustainable development projects that fall under the Agenda 21 umbrella. The debate focused primarily on the appropriateness of the Global Environment Facility (GEF) proposed by the industrialized countries and the Green Fund proposed by the developing countries. The GEF is currently a jointly managed pilot program of the UN Environment Programme, the UN Development Programme, and the World Bank to provide grants for investment and technical assistance to developing nations for environmentally sound development projects that benefit global environmental problems. It has come under extensive criticism from developing countries because of its structure, scope, and governance rules, which tend to limit the voice of these nations in how funds are distributed, and place limiting conditions on the use of funds that are granted. From their perspective, developing countries are treated as second-class citizens. The aim of the Green Fund and other similar conceptions put forth by several developing countries – China, Argentina, and Brazil, in particular – is to address technology transfer issues, national capacity building, and environment–development problems not already covered by specific international agreements. The goal is to deal explicitly with issues of specific concern to developing countries. Thus, contributions are compulsory, preferential conditions are provided to the recipient nations, and parity in the governance of the fund is provided to both donors and recipients.

The second issue deals with the target levels of funding that should be established to yield meaningful progress on sustainable development programs. Currently, the mean level of funding for all overseas development assistance from the OECD countries amounts to 0.35 percent of the GNP. The UN has established 0.7 percent as the goal by the end of the century. Given the economic downturn currently being experienced by most countries, this doubling of assistance is viewed by many as unlikely in the near term. At the same time, the UNCED secretariat has estimated that the average annual cost for implementing all of the Agenda 21 programs is US$ 125 billion from 1993 to 2000. The principal question being debated is how industrialized countries should reallocate savings in defense spending and current expenditures devoted to implementing environmental programs at home to benefit global environmental problems.

At the end of PrepCom IV, in April 1992, several proposals were on the table for each of these two issues. They are presented in Table 5.1.

The principal criteria upon which policy decisions were made by the key UNCED participants (nations and coalitions) on these issues were identified based upon a reading of national statements made at the PrepComs. These represent the critical factors that are considered in the domestic policy-making process. Table 5.2 lists the criteria and their ranges of values that were used in the analysis. As shown below, each negotiation actor prioritizes these criteria differently, but each one takes these criteria into account to some degree. (See Appendix 5.1 on p. 103 for the importance of the weights accorded to each criterion for the actors analyzed in this study.)

Three of the key actors in the UNCED talks have been modeled – the United States (US), the European Community (EC), and the Group of 77 (G-77). They represent the range of interests and preferences across the two financial issues under analysis, the US and G-77 often being at either extreme and the EC often somewhere in the middle.

Table 5.1 Proposals for Funding Mechanism and Funding Level

Issue: Developing a viable funding mechanism

- Existing GEF Alone: Establish the Global Environment Facility as the sole mechanism for granting and coordinating financial support
- Modified GEF: Use a modified Global Environment Facility that incorporates greater participation by developing countries and adjusts the governance rules by which financial support is granted
- GEF plus Other Funds: Use the Global Environment Facility as one of several available and accepted funding mechanisms
- Green Fund Alone: Establish the Green Fund as the sole mechanism for granting and coordinating financial support

Issue: Agreeing on acceptable funding levels

- Existing Levels: Employ existing levels of overseas development assistance (ODA) with no additional funding
- Additional Funding, but Unspecified: Agree to additional funding above current ODA levels, but leave the target level ambiguous
- Additional Funding, but Conditional: Agree to additional funding above current ODA levels, but indicate that such funding will be subject to certain, mainly economic, conditions
- Additional Funding, but Variable: Agree to an overall target for additional funding above current ODA levels, but each nation is allowed to specify its own targeted level
- Additional Funding Set at 0.5% of GNP: Agree to an overall target for additional funding of 0.5% of GNP by the year 2000
- Additional Funding Set at 0.7% of GNP: Agree to an overall target for additional funding of 0.7% of GNP by the year 2000

Estimates of actor preferences for each criterion (the actors' prioritized interest profiles), as well as proposal ratings against the criteria (how well each proposal satisfies each criterion), were generated in this study by expert coding of statements and proposals made by the actors. In particular, the compilation of national/coalitional perspectives on these issues prepared by the UNCED secretariat in Document A/CONF.151/PC/102, "Institutional Proposals," proved to be very helpful. While the MAV model requires precise integer values to perform calculations, such precision is not appropriate in measuring such preferences and ratings. As a result, these items were coded into a simple five-point scale, from very high to very low, and then transformed into numerical values.[3]

[3]The numerical scale (0–100) was divided into equal quintiles. Verbal ratings were assigned the mean value within each quintile. An intercoder reliability test was performed to assess the reliability of data coding. Employing Spearman correlations to compare coding similarity, two independent coders using the same source materials had a .52 and .67 correlation with the author's coding over a total of 145 different value judgments.

Table 5.2 Criteria for National/Coalitional Policy Decisions

Locus of Power: Where does control over the agreement reside?

RANGE: National sovereignty
International control

Responsibility: Where does responsibility lie for resolving the issues?

RANGE: Main responsibility (primary responsibility for past environmental degradation rests with industrialized countries who must bear the burdens of resolving the problem now)
Partnership (resolution of current and future environmental problems must be considered a mutual responsibility of all nations acting in partnership and cooperation, without recourse to blame)

Scientific Basis for Action: What are the scientific triggers compelling action?

RANGE: Precaution (anticipation of possible future environmental degradation motivates preventative action now)
Await certainty (act only when scientific findings of future environmental degradation are more certain)

Funding Conditions: What are the conditions under which developing countries can receive additional funding to deal with environment-development problems?

RANGE: Conditionality (conditions must be placed on granting additional financial resources)
Preferential treatment (concessions are made in granting additional financial resources to facilitate the resolution of the problems)

Amount of Funding Required: Are additional financial resources required to deal effectively with environment-development problems?

RANGE: Additionality (additional financial resources – beyond current levels – are required)
Existing efficiencies (current levels of development aid should be used more efficiently before additional resources are considered)

RESULTS

The results of the MAV analysis and sensitivity tests are presented in this section in graphical format to facilitate comparisons. The quantitative model results are presented in Appendix 5.1 on p.103.[4]

Developing a Viable Funding Mechanism

Figure 5.1 presents the results of the MAV analysis comparing actor preferences on funding mechanism proposals. As one might suspect, the two extreme proposals – to establish *only* a GEF or *only* a Green Fund – are favored in the extreme by the US and the G-77, respectively. The compromise path to agreement falls somewhere in between. Of the two compromise options in our analysis, the "GEF plus other

[4]The MAV models developed in this study were structured and analyzed utilizing a PC-based decision analysis software package developed by James Huttinger of Booz, Allen, and Hamilton Inc., Bethesda, Maryland.

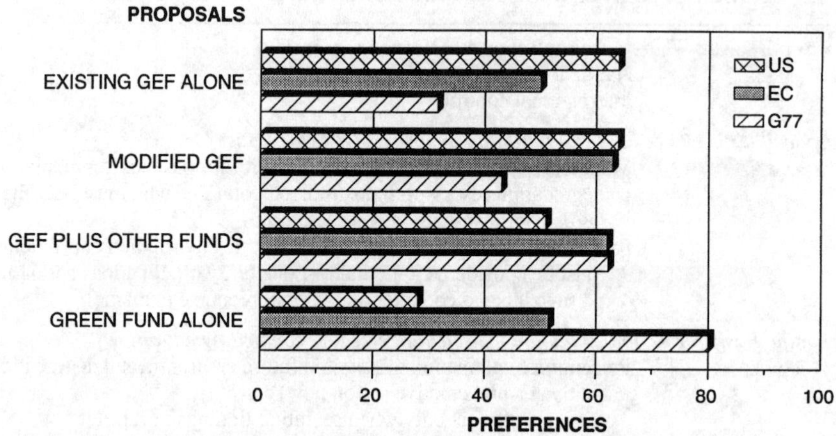

Figure 5.1 Preferences for Funding Mechanism Proposals (US, EC, and G77)

funds" proposal more closely approximates the preferences of both the US and G-77 than the "Modified GEF" proposal.

What will it take to achieve the former compromise solution? As discussed earlier in the chapter, compromise will take place when there are significant preference changes from initial (and often rigid) positions, and these preference adjustments must be such that the preference space between conflicting parties is narrowed. The extent of adjustment required of each actor, as one might expect, is not equally distributed; the demand for preference modification may be highly asymmetrical. The model provides results on the relative degree of change needed by each actor to facilitate each compromise proposal. The results for the "GEF plus other funds" proposal indicate that the largest burden for change rests with the US (38 percent), with the EC and G-77 together bearing a somewhat lower, but equal, burden (31 percent to each) to modify their preferences.

Figure 5.2 describes which preferences must indeed be adjusted to achieve the "GEF plus other funds" compromise based on a sensitivity analysis. The clearest conclusion that can be drawn from this figure is that each actor has a very different preference profile that influences its ability to compromise. Each actor must be motivated to modify different preferences to different degrees. Looking at the US, by far the biggest adjustment needs to be made in its demand for scientific certainty. The US and the GEF have pursued a relatively conservative approach to environmental action – to resist preventative action and await greater scientific certainty before committing to action. The high priority placed by the US on awaiting certainty must be deflated, along with demands for greater efficiency in the use of current funds and the placing of restrictive conditions on granting funds.

The G-77 must modify a very different set of preferences in order to reach a compromise stance. It must concede somewhat on its demands for preferential treatment and its strong stance on national sovereignty. The G-77 must also back down to a

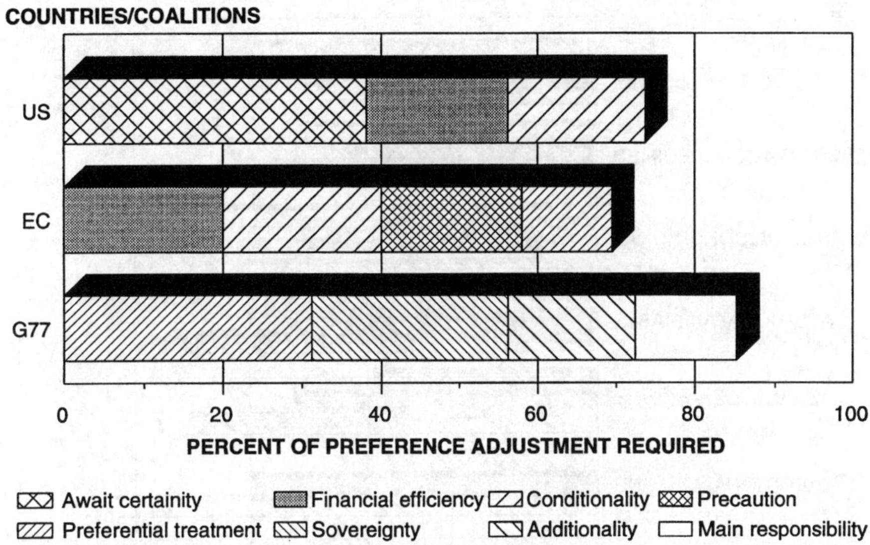

Figure 5.2 Preference Adjustment Required to Achieve "GEF Plus Other Funds" Compromise

degree on its demands for additional funds, and the placing of blame and responsibility for current global environmental problems on the industrialized countries.

The EC, for its part, must modify a different mix of preferences to reach compromise. Moving toward the G-77 perspective, the EC must back down a bit on pressing for financial efficiencies before new funds are allocated, and must constrain its demands for placing conditions on granting new funds for environmental solutions. At the same time, the EC's preferences must move a little toward the US perspective by reducing its demands for preventative, anticipatory action and for preferential treatment for developing countries.

Agreeing on Acceptable Funding Levels

Figure 5.3 presents actor preferences for the six proposals on acceptable funding levels. Preferences across all proposals are extremely diverse, save one, "Additional Funding but Unspecified Target." All three actors share a common preference for this proposal. But, as with the funding mechanism issue area, underlying this commonality are very different reasons and criteria. The data suggest that this proposal appears to be a true compromise, requiring almost equivalent preference adjustments by each of the three actors.

Based on a sensitivity analysis, such a compromise requires that the US modify its preferences to await certainty, seek international partnership, and press for conditionality (see Figure 5.4). The G-77, on the other hand, must be more flexible in its demands for preferential treatment, additionality of funds, national sovereignty, and

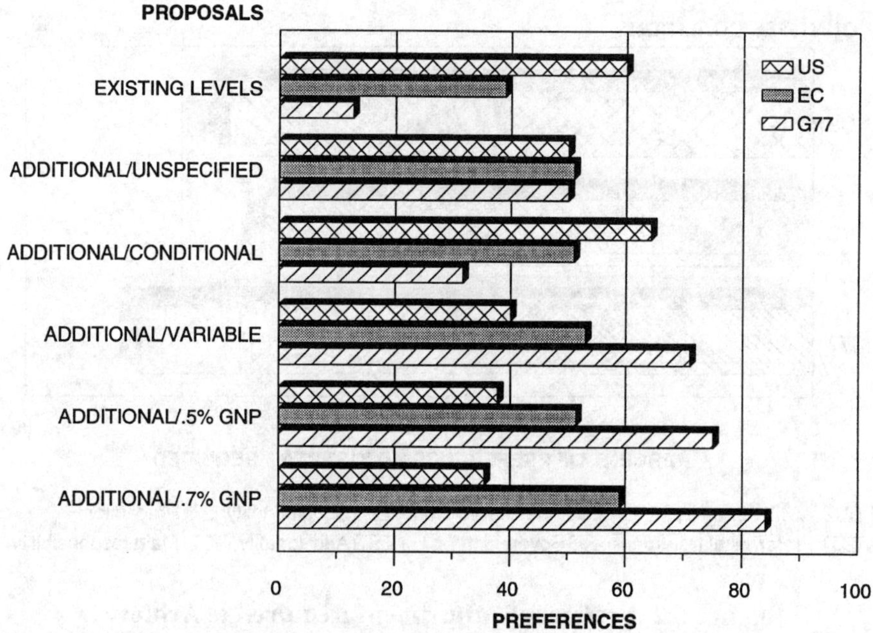

Figure 5.3 Preferences for Funding Level Proposals (US, EC, and G77)

main responsibility blame. The EC must reduce its stance on precaution, while at the same time reducing its demands for international partnership and conditionality.

In contrast with this "Additional but Unspecified" proposal, the "Additional but Variable Target" proposal yielded a greater divergence of interests by the three actors, as indicated in Figure 5.3, being much more favored by the G-77 than by the US. To achieve this alternative compromise, much more movement is required by the US than the G-77, as their overall interests would imply. To make this alternative proposal a realistic compromise, the degree of change in preferences demanded of the US would have to be double that required of the G-77 (44 percent versus 22 percent)! The nature of those changes for the G-77 mirror the changes indicated above for the "Additional but Unspecified" proposal. The changes required of the US are somewhat different though, with the extra demand for changing its firm stance on financial efficiency.

DISCUSSION

Contingency Analysis and the UNCED Outcome

This analysis examined several potential scenarios, comparing assumed preferences with salient compromise formulas. How far were these postulated scenarios and

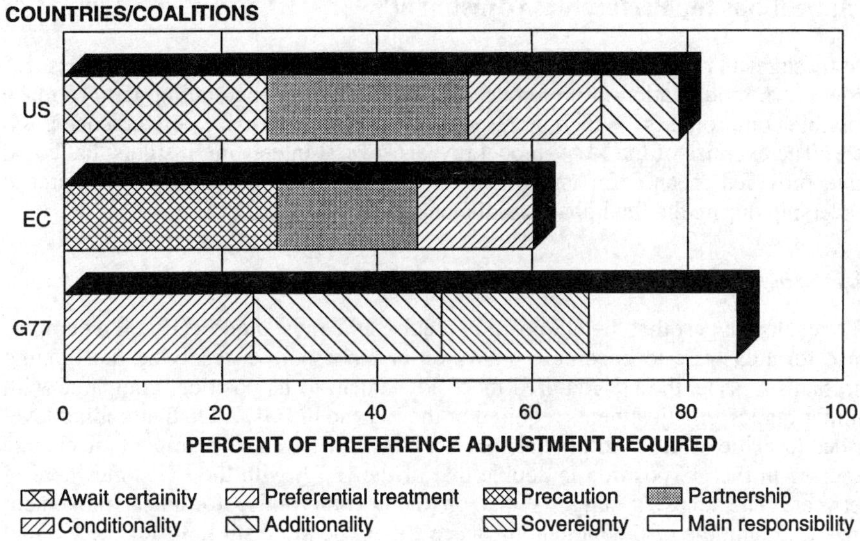

Figure 5.4 Preference Adjustment Required to Achieve "Additional but Unspecified Funding" Compromise

their implied conclusions from the real outcomes achieved at UNCED? The ultimate compromise at UNCED concerning funding mechanisms was a modified GEF, one that allows for greater developing country participation and reduced conditionality constraints. According to our analysis, this proposal was much more preferred by the US and EC than by the G-77. However, the G-77 apparently was willing to reorder its preferences and trade many of its demands to secure the highly desired nonconditionality clause (*Earth Summit Bulletin,* 11 June 1992).

Concerning funding levels, the final compromise at UNCED was an affirmation of developed country commitments to the target of 0.7 percent of GNP by the year 2000, the most preferred G-77 option. An important feature of this compromise, and what made it indeed a compromise, was the looseness of the commitment: developed countries only pledged their intent to reach this target by 2000 if possible, or beyond that time if necessary. Thus, the negotiated result is a direct merger of the "Additional funding at 0.7% of GNP" and the "Additional funding, but unspecified" proposals. This formula cleverly reduced the need for the key parties to modify their preferences: the G-77 could certainly accept the 0.7 percent goal, while the "unspecified" time limit was highly attractive to the US and EC.

Overall, had the UNCED negotiators exercised the hypothesized scenario described in this analysis during the planning stages of the conference, they might not have guessed the ultimate agreement; they would not have been far off, though. Certainly, they could have used the analytical technique in the "what if" mode to examine alternative scenarios and compromise outcomes.

Implications for Preference Adjustment

Do these results suggest that compromises are possible on these contentious issues? How much modification in preference is needed by each negotiating party to reach possible compromises? Which preferences must change to make convergence possible? The exercise of the MAV model reveals several interesting insights that could have provided meaningful and practical information to the UNCED conference leadership during the final phases of the negotiation process.

Degree of Modification

The results suggest that the US position required the most modification if a compromise formula were to become a reality on either issue. On resolving the funding mechanism issue, the US required more adjustment to its position, compared with similar but lesser adjustments required of the EC and the G-77. On the funding level issue, to achieve the "Additional, but Variable" proposal, the amount of change required in the US position is double that of the G-77, with the EC somewhere in between. The analysis suggests that on these compromise formulas, movement toward the middle of the bargaining space should be more stressful for the US and less stressful for the G-77.

Only for the "Additional but Unspecified" compromise is the amount of change required by all three parties relatively equivalent. Using an equality measure of justice in negotiation, perhaps this last proposal can be considered the most fair, since the degree of change needed from each is about the same. But is this a reasonable conclusion? The initial stance taken by the US on many financial sub-issues in the UNCED process was extreme. The US could be seen as practicing an endgame strategy of stating extreme positions and remaining firm until the final stage of the negotiation in Rio, thereby trying to convince others that the only way to reach compromise solutions was to modify their positions toward that of the US. The widespread outlook on the US position of intransigence at the Rio Conference concerning financial as well as biodiversity issues led to an increasing ostracism and isolation of the US, even from its usual allies.

Type of Modification

The results also point to the significant national interests in which flexibility is required for the compromise formulas to be viable. Sensitivity analyses of the model indicate the particular interests on which preference adjustment is needed by each party for each compromise. These results offer insight into the convergence process that must ensue. The set of preference adjustments required of all parties, when viewed all together, suggest the precarious balance of tradeoffs needed to achieve the compromise outcomes.

The US must give way on some of its key interests and demands in the negotiation – in particular, the demand to wait for increased scientific certainty before negotiating further on key issues such as climate change, the demand for increased efficiency in the use of current development aid, and the rejection of direct blame for past environmental degradation. For its part, the G-77 must give way on some of its principal demands, that of obtaining preferential treatment and concessions on future financial and technological assistance, and seeking additional financial resources for new sustainable development projects beyond current development aid levels. The EC, a coalition in the middle, must move increasingly away from the US camp, principally giving way on its demands for increased efficiencies in the use of existing aid packages and demands for conditionality in the provision of new financial aid. At the same time, the EC must also back off from its demands for precautionary action on environmental issues, moving it away from an importantly held G-77 interest. Flexibility on these interests, according to the analysis, will yield the circumstances within which compromise formulas can be successfully achieved.

CONCLUSIONS

What insights can the practical negotiator participating in future environmental regime-building talks draw from this analysis? First, it is important for practitioners to assess the size of the bargaining space and the distance that must be bridged among the parties to solve the problem. This evaluation involves reviewing the range of proposals on the table and the degree to which each negotiating party indicates a preference for these proposals. The purpose of this review is to determine where there are possibilities for finding compromise outcomes. Secondly, practitioners can go a step further in their review of proposals and preferences by assessing their own and the others' national interests. In so doing, negotiators and their staffs can evaluate opportunities that yield possible tradeoffs. Practitioners need to evaluate possibilities for change in their own interests with regard to the negotiation issues, and anticipate possible changes that other parties might be willing to make. This will result in a comparative assessment of firm commitments to certain bargaining positions and the degree of flexibility available in the negotiation environment. Ultimately, such an assessment will identify where there is a willingness to generate compromise, and how far each party must modify their position to achieve compromise outcomes.

The UNCED test case demonstrated in this chapter suggests that this methodological approach can be meaningful in a post hoc analysis to understand and explain flexibility and compromise in historical negotiations. Equally important, the technique can also provide important insight to support planning and analysis by negotiators and their staffs prior to and during the course of negotiations – as a practical decision support tool. It can help to structure the bargaining space and compare the preferences of the various parties toward the proposals on the table. The technique can be viewed as an accounting device that simplifies and structures several important aspects of complex negotiation situations.

The analytical results clearly highlighted which of the competing proposals matched closest to a multidimensional framework of actor preferences. Then, by focusing on the most likely compromise proposals – where the gaps in preference were not that great – the analysis offered a picture of the extent of mutual movement – or flexibility – required of all parties to achieve the compromise; the amount of flexibility required of each party was not always allocated equitably. Finally, and perhaps most importantly, the analysis provided insight into the "makings" of compromise solutions – the often implicit changes to interests and preferences that must be made to bridge the initial gap between actors. By decomposing the preferences that must change for a compromise to be struck, the catalysts of negotiating flexibility are at least partially revealed.

This analytical technique may be especially useful for practitioners in deadlocked negotiations. The detailed analysis of alternate proposals by means of assessing interests, contrasting priorities, and disaggregating preferences can help to identify opportunities that can overcome impasses. The methodology provides a vehicle for understanding the spread between preferences that can result in impasse and the dynamics of bridging some of those gaps between parties. Case analyses of stalemated negotiations using this technique would provide guidance for researchers interested in designing such a practical decision support tool. Applications to other negotiations already under way – such as in the area of forestry, climate change, and the sulfur dioxide protocol renegotiation in Europe – could also be instructive in refining such a practical support method.

Conceptually, additional related research would be useful to understand what causes preferences to change – what stimulates preference adjustment. The MAV methodology indicates how much change is required and the types of modifications needed to reach compromise agreements, but not how such intentions to be flexible are initiated or can be incited. Analytically, the MAV model, as we have used it, provides two snapshots in time, comparing the going-in position to a potential compromise position. With so few data points, it is difficult to assess the actual learning and adaptation accomplished by the negotiating parties in achieving agreements. Further study of these concepts is needed to provide researchers and practitioners alike with a clearer idea of how the process of convergence in negotiation operates.

Finally, how does an assessment of preference adjustment help us to better understand the process of negotiating regimes? The analysis of financial resource issues is a classic case of negotiations over rule-making, a necessary and central feature of regime-building discussed in Chapter 1. The issues of establishing funding targets and structures within which parties can comfortably operate are straightforward examples of the need to set general principles and norms for a new regime. As such, though, the UNCED negotiations over financial issues do not appear atypical. The dynamics of preference transformation that facilitate the ultimate achievement of compromise does not seem much different in concept or practice from the dynamics one might observe in other complex multilateral negotiations *not* dealing with regime-building.

What does appear unique to these rule-making negotiations, especially through the special lens of our multi-attribute analysis, is the formulaic structure that frames the effective compromises. Regime-building that is multi-partied and multi-issued is also multi-interested, implying that the outcome must appeal in a multi-faceted way. The package that is acceptable must satisfy the unique combination of prioritized preferences that characterize each actor's interest profile. And while malleable in many cases, these interest profiles most always stabilize around a multidimensional set of preferences that each actor, in his or her own way, identifies as reflecting a "fair" solution. After all, the negotiations concerning rule-making ultimately spell out the proposed process and structure for sustained interaction within a regime after the initiating negotiations are completed. Finding the acceptable balance among these multi-interest profiles across actors is the difficult task of learning and problem solving with which professional negotiators are faced.

Acknowledgments

The author wishes to express his thanks to Gunnar Sjöstedt and Amanda Wolf for their many useful comments during the early stages of this study. As well, the kind assistance of Pamela Chasek and Ann Doherty is gratefully acknowledged.

APPENDIX 5.1: MODELING DATA AND RESULTS

The following tables present the quantitative input and results of the MAV models.

Normalized Criterion Weights for Both Issues

Criteria	*United States*	*European Community*	*Group of 77*
Locus of power	9	8	21
Historical responsibility	18	16	21
Scientific basis for action	27	29	7
Funding conditions	18	24	26
Amount of funding	27	24	26

Funding Mechanism Issue: Aggregate Preferences Calculated by the model

Aggregate preferences: model results	*GEF as is only*	*Modified GEF*	*GEF plus other funds*	*Green Fund only*
United States	64.0	64.3	51.2	27.7
European Community	49.9	62.5	62.0	52.3
Group of 77	30.7	42.7	62.3	79.7

Funding Level Issue: Aggregate Preferences Calculated by the model

Aggregate preferences: model results	*No change in existing levels of aid*	*Additional funding/ uncertain levels*	*Additional funding/ conditions applied*	*Additional funding/ variable levels per country*	*Target of 0.5% GNP for ODA by 2000*	*Target of 0.7% GNP for ODA by 2000*
United States	60.1	50.2	63.7	40.0	38.2	36.0
European Community	39.4	50.9	51.2	53.2	52.1	58.8
Group of 77	12.7	50.1	32.2	71.1	75.1	83.9

6

Food Security, Environment, and Development: A Case Analysis of Process Dynamics

Amanda Wolf

The UNCED negotiations addressed separate issues, such as desertification and toxic wastes, even though the overall mandate was to forge a consensus on international policy to address environmental problems at the *interface* between human development and physical realities. Some cross-sectoral issues that arose, notably technology transfer and financial assistance, tended to reinforce traditional ways of thinking in UN agencies, rather than paving the way for a new and possibly more productive packaging of the issues. This structural characteristic, together with the structure set up by the PrepComs, the process of clarifying issues on the agenda (see Chapter 4), and the process of preference adjustment (see Chapter 5), created the parameters for new international environmental regimes. Throughout the process of developing these new regimes, negotiators were ultimately concerned with creating and preserving the well-being of present and future generations.

The interface between environment and development is really the main subject of concern in the emerging regimes. Concrete human interactions with the physical environment gave the negotiations their motivating force. For instance, in the short to medium term, the pollution of inland water resources, desertification, or toxic pollution may have dramatic consequences for food production in poverty-stricken regions. In the longer term, climate change may have severe effects, undermining the conditions for stable and productive agriculture in the same or other regions. Similar examples could be sketched out to show how the issue areas on UNCED's agenda relate to the provision of energy, of effective transportation of goods and services, and even the provision of a modest level of aesthetic or cultural services. In short, food security, energy security, mobility, and nonutility services are some of the prime reasons why people care about the condition of the environment.

Before the issue agendas were finalized, the secretariat commissioned some analyses of the environment-development linkages (see, for example, Shaw *et al.*, 1991). However, the sheer complexity and insufficient knowledge of causal relationships worked against broader attention to feasible tradeoffs across issue areas. Rather, negotiators focused on narrower and simpler issues, through which they nevertheless kept a focus on the implications for the well-being of their constituencies.

Negotiating International Regimes: Lessons Learned from the United Nations Conference on Environment and Development (G. Sjöstedt, *et al.*, eds.; 1-85966-077-0; © IIASA; pub. Graham & Trotman, 1994; printed in Great Britain), pp. 105–119.

It will be years before any plausible assessment can be made of the new UNCED regimes in terms of addressing the basic mandate and meeting countries' interests. As the post-UNCED regimes are further fleshed out, evaluative approaches will be useful to consider periodically the validity of interlinked rules and institutional systems. Such approaches would seek to understand the multidimensional character of each problem area managed by the regimes.

This chapter is designed as an initial attempt at that broader assessment. Of all the underlying concerns at the interface of environment and development, one of the most basic is an assured access to food. Food security epitomizes the collective objective of UNCED. UNCED did not expand upon exactly what specific duties and requirements this underlying objective establishes. Yet, by examining food security, it is possible to illustrate the general nature of linkages in the negotiation setting.

FOOD SECURITY AND UNCED

The interconnection of environmental deterioration and development needs with food security is evident across the entire spectrum of the negotiating "compartments" of UNCED. Table 6.1 makes clear how the treatment of any of UNCED's issue areas was bound to have implications for food security. The remainder of the chapter examines the various ways in which food security was implicitly linked into the negotiation process.

ISSUE CLARIFICATION: LEVELS OF LINKAGES

Figure 6.1 presents schematically the overall linkage context. In developing plans of action to effectively address the linkages of issues with other issues (lateral links), negotiators take account of relevant political and ethical principles, including, for example, compensation for past damage and equitable access to financial and technical assistance. Ideally, these plans of action, as set out in Agenda 21, will be translated into very precise policies, largely expressed in economic and technical terms, and implemented in thousands of different contexts. The consequences of such policies, against the background of the "natural" environment, will in turn be translated into the concrete effects on people's well-being.

Figure 6.1 makes the distinction between the *existence* of an environmental problem and its *policy implications*. For instance, it is a simple matter to state that there are relationships between CO_2 emissions, climate change, and shifting agricultural productivity (at the bottom level). But what do these relationships imply for India or for Finland? That will depend in part on policy decisions (at the second level) that affect trade and technology transfer. What policies or negotiated decisions will be favored? That may well depend on how one issue area links to another (at the top level). Many more questions could be raised. Importantly, although scientific studies have greatly advanced understanding of many linkages, a number of important linkages are not "scientific" or "technical" at all. For example, there are ethical linkages that will shape regime decisions. A typical case involves the linkages drawn between past emissions of greenhouse gases and responsibility for future climate change mitigation efforts. Another type of linkage is drawn explicitly by individuals or organizations to encourage the joint consideration of the linked elements –

Table 6.1 Linkages between UNCED Environmental Areas and Food Security

	Food Security
Atmosphere	Climate change leading to drought; poleward advance of the monsoon rainfall; other precipitation and temperature impacts on crops and biota production; air-borne pollutants; UV radiation; reduced soil moisture; acid deposition on perennials; climate change leading to sea flooding impact on productive wetlands and decrease in agricultural land; species loss due to climate effects; change in habitat; ozone effects on biota.
Land, Agriculture	Changing energy and other input requirements due to degradation; desertification; population and activity distribution pressures on land; clearing forests for crops; coastal erosion and siltation; destruction of nesting grounds; agrichemical pollution of productive resources; competition for water use; biota as a source of germplasm for genetic engineering; increased demand pressures; migration and labor considerations.
Forests	Degradation of productivity after deforestation; land-use conflicts; decreased protection and habitat conditions for wildlife; decreased availability of fuel for food preparation; decreased soil protection (leading to decreased fertility as well as increased runoff into rivers); changes in the hydrological balance of the drainage basin.
Oceans	Source of food.
Freshwater	Limiting factor in agricultural food production; contamination effects on crops; salinity; stability; possible increase in water-borne infectious diseases to livestock and humans; decreased quality or quantity of drinking or cooking water; habitat for fish.
Biodiversity	Loss of species; loss of soil organisms.
Biotechnology	Food production with specialized species; new varieties; release of modified organisms; increased forest production; maintenance of gene pool; substitution for traditional species.
Toxics and wastes	Land and water contamination of food chain; accidents; pollution in coastal zones; effects on biodiversity; persistent effects on health; elimination of land for alternative uses; eutrophication from sewage.

Note: Some factors may have both positive and negative consequences. For example, biotechnology can improve food production intensity, but may increase the risk of a local disaster, such as an entire crop failing simultaneously through a pest explosion.

Sources: UNCED PrepCom (1991), various documents, and Intergovernmental Panel on Climate Change (1990).

UNCED's agenda-setting is the best example. All of these different types of linkages influence policy decisions and the course of negotiations.

With the rise into predominance at UNCED of the sustainable development paradigm, a separate approach to each environmental and developmental component of food security is no longer tenable.

Food security is mentioned in various places in UNCED documents. Most notably, it is one of the principles of sustainable development (UNCED PrepCom, A/CONF.151/42 para. 11, vi). Food security is an "issue constellation,"

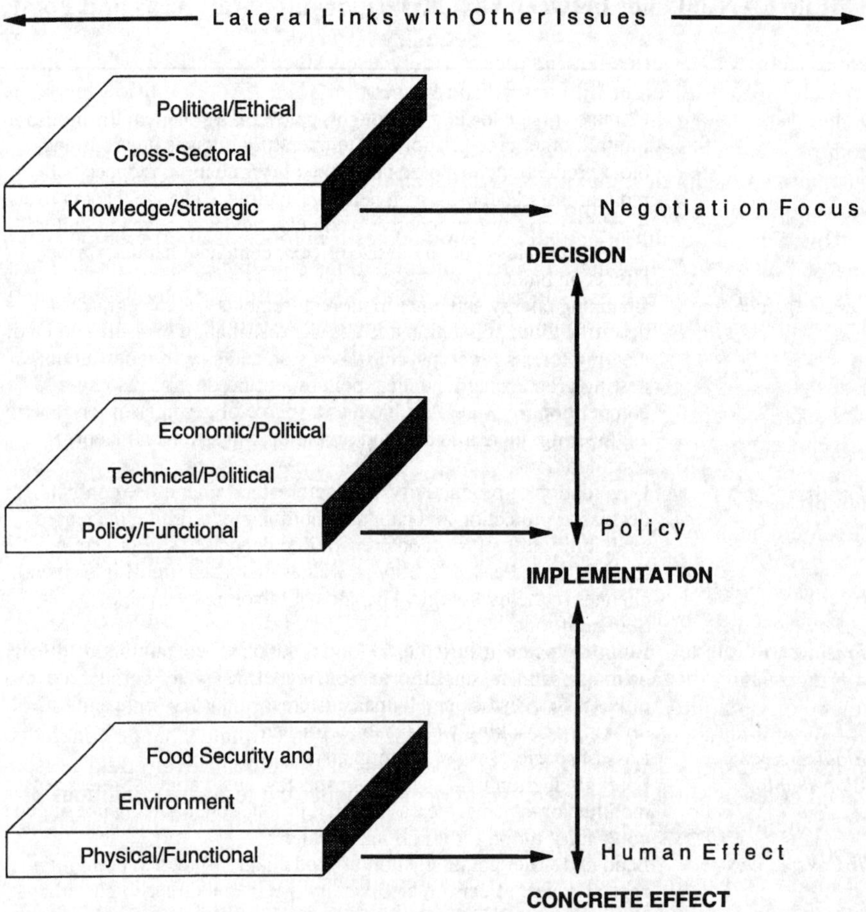

Figure 6.1 Levels of Linkage

bringing in many of the interlinkages implicit in the "sociopolitical" and "biogeochemical" spheres. Ideally, then, the negotiators might have treated food security (and energy security, etc.) explicitly in this broad frame. However, the sheer technical complexity of coping with the issue linkages under such an integrating notion as food security was a serious impediment. Knowledge about the causal relationships was only beginning to be sketched in. Just as importantly, explicit attention to food security would have made it impossible to avoid treating many sensitive issues, notably population and agricultural policies. The result could well have been a complete stalemate in Rio. Instead, serious problem solving seemed to imply breaking the problems into smaller pieces. This is exactly what was done at UNCED. In the process, the larger context got pushed out of view, but presumably not out of mind.

THE MEANING OF FOOD SECURITY

Food security is a term that has been widely used since the early 1970s, but has typically meant different things to different people.[1] The FAO definition has been generally accepted since the mid-1980s: "Ensure that all people at all times have both physical and economic access to the basic food they need. Ensure production of adequate food supplies; maximize stability in the flow of supplies; secure access to the supplies on the part of those who need them" (FAO, 1987).

This general definition actually accommodates a number of interpretations. In a negotiation context (in which different interpretations can emerge as different interests and policy stances), five separable elements of the definition may be discerned. These are: (1) the composition and nutritional adequacy of food to sustain an active life; (2) "who" is secure in terms of food availability – a country, a household, a person, particularly the poor; (3) "security" – the assurance of access to food as needed, which is really the heart of the concept – expressed as physical supply-based assurance, effective real income demand-based assurance, or both; (4) intertemporal elements – whether food insecurity is transitory or chronic and whether consumption levels are sustainable as population expands; and (5) linkages with the developmental and political needs of the country (that is, with "national" security more broadly), and of the individual, such as guarantees of the right to work for reasonable wages.[2]

Food security problems may arise in a number of ways. First, supply may fall short. Variations in production and world price, both of which can cause domestic shortages, have been substantial and are increasing. Weather is by far the largest source of variability, but civil strife, shortages of critical inputs, and misguided policy may all play a part. The Intergovernmental Panel on Climate Change concluded in its well-respected report that food production at the global level could be sustained at levels sufficient to meet world demand under the test case conditions of a CO_2 doubling scenario, but that the cost of achieving this remained unclear (IPCC, 1990).

Supply is also affected by price. Price variability is much higher in the world markets than in the domestic markets of most countries. Agriculture and trade policies, especially in the developed countries, and price policies that protect consumers, especially in the developing countries, insulate producers and consumers from supply shocks. The insulation forces adjustment on to a thin world market, magnifying the price effect of small global production shocks, and further reduces the ability of poor countries to rely on world markets for food security. Sensitivity to price thus becomes a crucial component of food security adjustments. Secondly, the demand component adds to the food security problem. Populations are expanding faster than agricultural productivity in many countries. One study, for example, examined 104

[1] Much of the material in this section is drawn from Wolf (1990).

[2] The various issues have been highlighted in the following works defining food security: (1): Valdes and Konandreas (1981), pp. 28–9; Garcia (1981), p. 127; Bread for the World (1989), p. 2; Huddleston *et al.* (1984), p. 3; FAO (1987). (2): Adams (1983), p. 550; Koester and Valdes (1984), p. 431; Lappe and Collins (1978), p. 154; von Braun (1988), p. 1083; and FAO (1987). (3): Hathaway (1981); Brown *et al.* (1984), p. 185; World Bank (1986); Advisory Panel (1987), p. 3. (4): FAO (1987); Adams (1983), p. 550; von Braun (1988), p. 1083; Valdes and Konandreas (1981), p. 38; (5): Huddleston *et al.* (1984), p. 3; Koester and Valdes (1984), p. 431; Lappé and Collins (1978), p. 154; Lele and Chandler (1981), p. 102; Bread for the World (1987).

developing countries for 1961–83 and found that although only 16 of these countries had negative food production growth rates, 65 had negative per capita production growth rates (Ezekiel, 1989). If per capita income is also increasing, food demand will grow even faster. Fluctuations in non-food production and prices can lead to decreased real incomes, and thus decrease the ability to purchase adequate food.

Although all of the components of food security are important to the concept of sustainable development, it is likely that the national level is most relevant for the UNCED regimes. Countries may be particularly concerned about the decisions of other countries and of the international community.

Finally, economic efficiency is inadequate as the sole criterion of sustainable food security. The ultimate objective must also include reliability. This translates into the *right* of all people to be free from hunger.[3]

DEFINITION OF ECONOMIC DEVELOPMENT AND SUSTAINABILITY

Despite the difficult, and perhaps intractable, philosophical concerns raised by a discussion of rights, as in the right to be free from hunger, the notion is central to the concept of economic *development*. Development, in contrast with growth, carries much more of an individualistic sense. No longer is growth alone taken automatically to be a good thing, nor only in economic terms. According to the most widely used definition, sustainable development "meets the needs of the present without compromising the ability of the future generations to meet their own needs" (WCED, 1987:43). This definition was echoed throughout UNCED.

The notion of *needs* in the WCED/UNCED definition of sustainable development is, of course, an expandable concept. Many commentators have recognized that human needs are more than just subsistence requirements. The UNDP, for example, has addressed this in its Human Development Report (UNDP, 1991). Here human development is again framed in terms of rights; it is defined as the "process of enlarging people's choices." It incorporates basic needs (health, nutrition) with social needs (education, participation, and opportunities).

Exactly how "needs" may evolve as development progresses is not well understood. Two points seem evident, however. First, all the characteristics of needs apply to *individuals*, but are aggregated into a national frame. The way this happens is not necessarily directly related to individual needs, or even predictable. Secondly, changes in needs, as politically defined, may occur over a different time frame than do changes in the causes of those needs. Nevertheless, it is such needs, however defined, that national representatives purport to represent at the international negotiating table. When the issues are environmental, the social and economic aspects of development needs must be integrated into the new dimension of interest.

[3]See, for example, the Food and Agriculture Organization *Den Bosch Declaration* (1991), as reported in UNCED PrepCom A/CONF.151/PC/61.

FOOD SECURITY LINKAGES

One way of organizing linkages is to classify them as physical (the biogeochemical sphere), functional (causal relationships that include human behaviors, usually expressed in political or economic terms), or strategic (linkages "forced" intentionally, principally by agenda-setting in negotiation) (Sjöstedt, 1991). Because this analysis takes an illustrative "slice" of an overall environment-development relationship through various levels of linkages, it is useful to distinguish the linkages according to: (1) *concrete physical/functional*, in which food security at the most basic level is examined as an environmental/human interface; (2) *policy/functional*, which may be subdivided into (a) economic–technical linkages and (b) economic–political linkages; and (3) *negotiation knowledge/strategic* – that is, broadly actor-mediated ways of creating meaningful linkages.[4] There are two subdivisions here: (a) ethical/political linkages and (b) the UNCED cross-sectoral linkages.[5]

Concrete Physical/Functional Linkages

The basic food security identity says that production plus imports, plus any food still in storage from the previous period, must equal consumption plus food put in storage for later use. Combining the storage terms (net carryover), gives:

$$\text{Production} + \text{Net Imports} + \text{Net Carryover} \equiv \text{Consumption}$$

To judge whether or not a food-secure condition exists, the frame of consideration must first be specified. Is it food security for the individual, household, region, nation, or world? Or is it food security throughout the year, across the years, for future generations? Then each term in the identity may be assessed. Factors affecting each term include:

Production

Production has two basic components, yield and land area (or water area) harvested.[6] Changes in either can affect the production of food. Environmental factors and macroeconomic policy relating to factor costs, terms of trade, availability of credit, etc., can also influence the choice of crops and levels of production. For food security, it is helpful to look at the micro levels of particular crops, regions, or seasons, since significant differences can be noticed at these levels of disaggregation.

[4]This category clearly has an overlap with the functional categories, but the knowledge dimension as it interacts with the "world out there" is extremely important in negotiation. In the UNCED PrepCom process, information collection, management, and dissemination were strongly highlighted.

[5]Refer back to Figure 6.1 on p. 108 for an overview diagram of these levels of linkages.

[6]A secondary component of production is the processing of food. Further refining of raw produce before it is marketed or consumed, or the production of livestock, add another layer to the considerations delineated here, but do not substantially affect the analysis.

Net Imports

This term concerns debt and the economics of the trade situation, credit possibilities, foreign exchange earnings, managerial capacity for appropriate decision making, environmental impacts in other countries, laws in other countries, and the political considerations of trade.

Net Carryovers

This term considers the stocks of food supplies that are held between periods, by households, governments, and traders. Factors that can affect storage are related to management and infrastructure finance and information and forecasting.

Consumption

Access to food, either because the consumer has produced the food or has adequate exchange entitlement, determines consumption (Sen, 1990). Other important factors are: macroeconomic policies that influence access; consumer information regarding health and nutrition practices; degree of health (lack of weakness and illness); technology and finance to get food to people under normal and emergency circumstances; labor, migration, or other conditions that influence the distribution of people relative to where the food is; population growth rates relative to the rates of change in food availability; and cultural factors and taste that relate to the ability to adjust consumption under changing conditions.

The food security identity is expanded in Figure 6.2. Many, but not all, of the influential factors are shown. Different countries will place differing emphasis on the various food security factors. For example, a country that has an important fishery may put more emphasis on conservation policies, and be more concerned about legal and institutional factors regulating the use of the common ocean resources. Another country may agree that oceans are of important common concern, but if it does not itself support an ocean fishery, the country may maintain that oceans are of very low priority for international negotiated action. To take a final example, a country that is very poor will tend to place lesser value on problems that may arise in the future than will a rich country. This has implications, for instance, on food storage policies, which in turn may be affected by external economic or environmental shocks.

Similarly, information and perceptions differ. Parties will view different sections of the figure as more or less important regardless of how well the linkages seem to be factually known, and will make different judgments regarding the relative importance of what is known, and the implications for policy. For example, one country may believe that stability of import supplies requires commodity agreements, whereas another might believe that food security may be best assured only in a free-market regime. In raising these sorts of issues, the linkages are extending to the next higher level – that of policy determination.

Economic/Political and Economic/Technical Linkages

The linkages at the next level are embedded in the physical/functional linkages noted in Figure 6.2. However, the lens is focused on policy decision making. This is

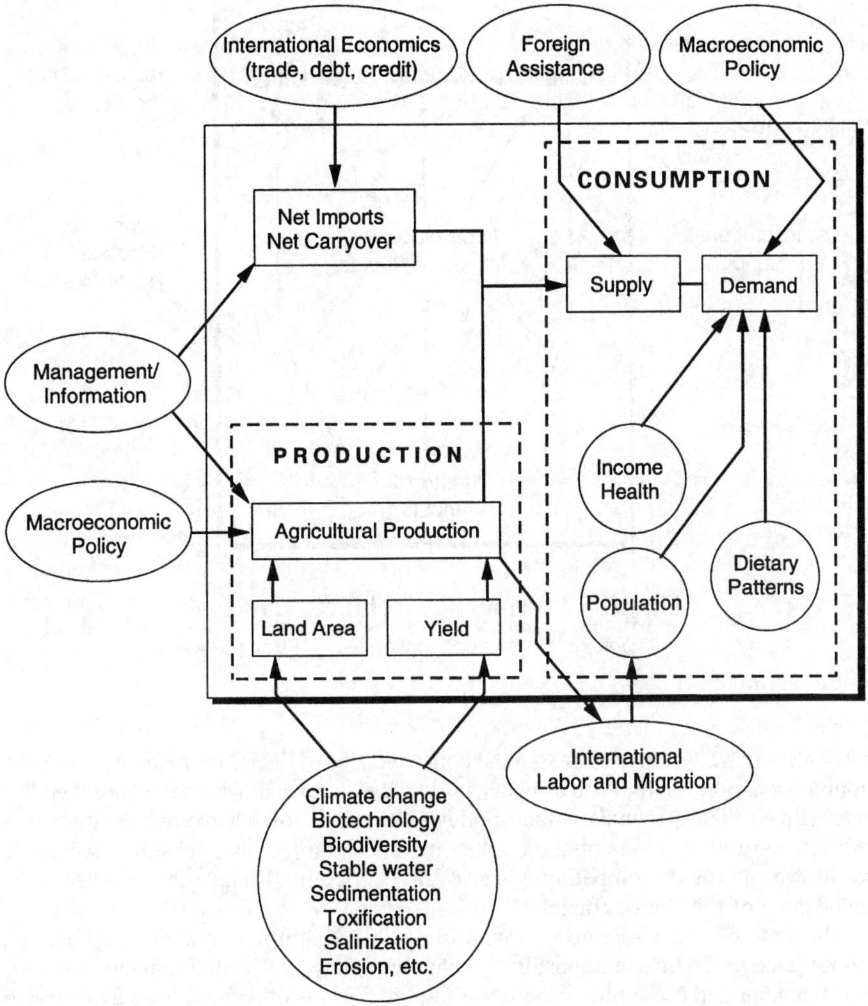

Figure 6.2 Food Security, Environment and Development

Source: IIASA/EDP (1991), modified by author.

the level at which the physical concerns for production and adequate food supply are translated into proposals for the coordinated implementation of activities aimed toward the objective of sustainable development.

Referring to Figure 6.2, the economic/political linkages are most prominent in the consumption, trade, and storage segments, while the economic/technical factors dominate the production linkages. Second-level linkages show the interactions between decisions and outcomes, given certain external conditions. For a given country, the "world out there" consists not only of the physical environment beyond

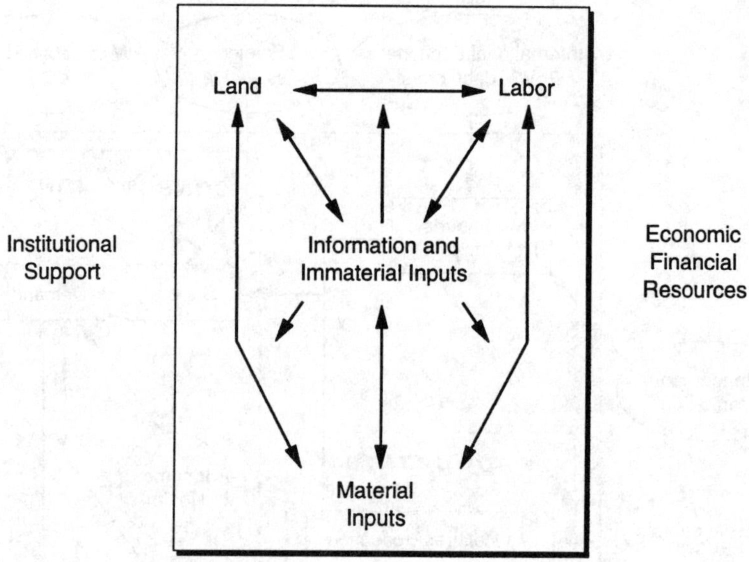

Figure 6.3 Economic/Technical Linkages

Source: Internal frame; Goodwin (1991), p. 94.

its control (e.g., weather), but also the consequences of decisions made by others. A country sets policies to try to affect change in the manner in which the "out there" is internalized. Thus, it makes trade policy in the light of what others' influence – products and volume – is on the market; it may set agricultural subsidies according to the way it values competing goals of, say, agricultural-industrial terms of trade and degree of food self-sufficiency.

The first of the two figures that follow is the simpler, but helps show the importance of the interrelationship of technology transfer, institutional mechanisms, and financial and economic resources. Flows and kinds of technologies available to a country influence a country's prospects in the world – that is, its opportunities for growth and development. Moreover, technology transfer, economic instruments and financial aspects, and institutional considerations are the three most important of the cross-sectoral issues as defined by the UNCED PrepCom. They are all elements of technical policy coordination. The model shows the move from classical economics (a land/labor tradeoff) through the neoclassical period (the addition of technology) to the "modern" emphasis on immaterial technologies that are information/human capital intensive.

The economic/political linkages that are important for food security concern the relative degrees of interaction of government policies with the components of the food security identity that are mediated by economic considerations. These policies encompass those that influence trade, pricing, the structure of the economy, labor and migration conditions, perceived and actual inequities in the distribution of economic goods, policies influencing the relative desirability of factor combinations

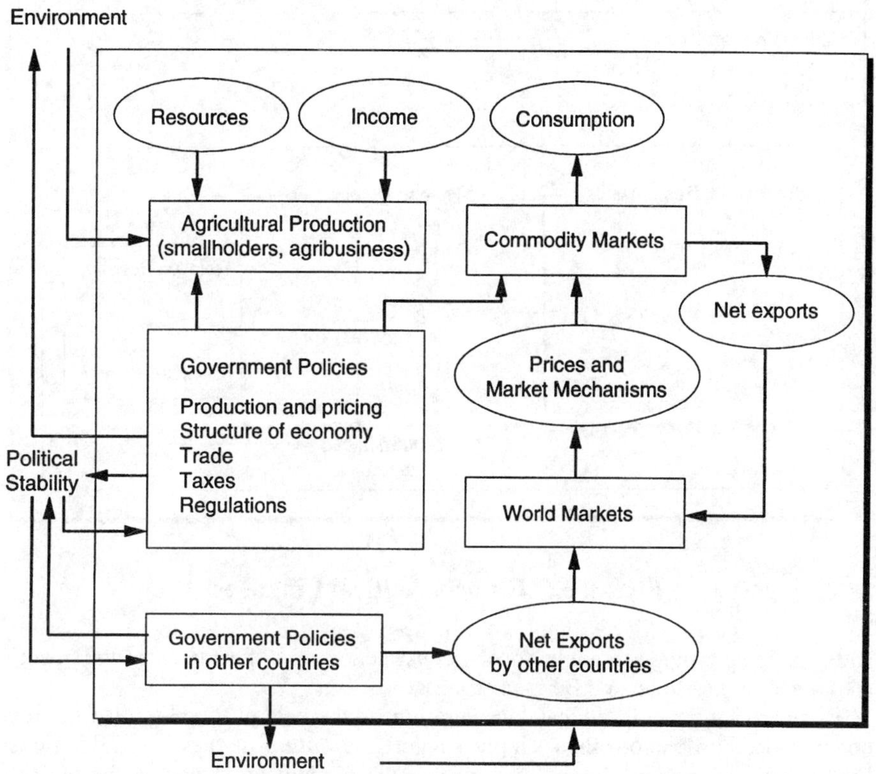

Figure 6.4 Economic/Political Linkages

Source: Adapted from Parikh (1990), p. 116.

in production, and many others of a similar type. Figure 6.4 shows the linkages of one country in a world context. Environmental conditions and political stability are shown as contextual factors. The bottom portion of the figure shows the external effects of other governments on the focal country. Environment and political stability both affect the internal linkages by setting limits on actions that can feasibly or effectively be undertaken.

Ethical/Political and UNCED Cross-Sectoral Linkages

At the third level of linkages, perceptions of problems have important foundations in cultural and social structures, and in the institutions, laws, and norms that have evolved within these structures. This "knowledge history" shapes more than perceptions, however. It influences motivations to act or in specific ways. The cultural/social structures that have preconditioned perceptions are also evolving, and giving rise to new notions of justice and fairness, needs and desires, which can influence problem and solution boundaries. In the process of negotiation, knowledge

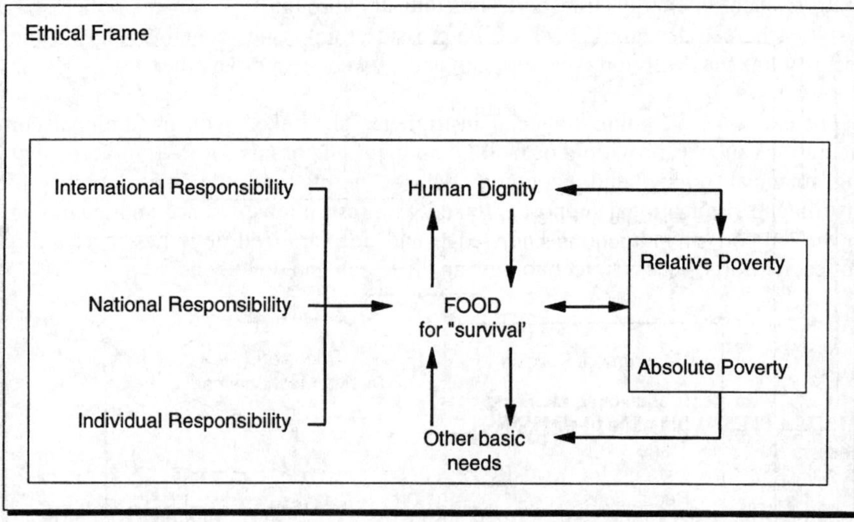

Figure 6.5 Ethical/Political Linkages

and principles provide referents for the construction of a "formula" for the negotiated outcome (Zartman and Berman, 1982).

There are a number of ethical considerations in the field of food security and it is not intended to do more than simply suggest the *nature* of these considerations. Figure 6.5 is therefore simply a rough and impressionistic sketch of the ethical/political domain. The surrounding environment is an "ethical frame," perhaps a dominant theory, such as the United States' emphasis on individual human rights or perhaps a tradition-bound pattern of responsibilities that is religiously, not legally, grounded. This frame implies what should be the division of responsibility for ensuring food to the hungry. Depending upon the allocation of responsibility, certain supporting policies are required. For this reason, the figure is labeled "ethical/political." The negotiation formula provides the thematic overview of responsibilities, which are then built into the specific policies. Finally, the specific policies lead to concrete impacts on people.

The last set of linkages are the cross-sectoral linkages among UNCED problem areas. These linkages were purposefully made in the agenda-setting process. UNCED has specified these as: (1) economic/financial resources; (2) technology transfer; (3) legal instruments; (4) institutional considerations; (5) poverty and urban settlements; (6) supporting measures (education); and (7) science. Cross-sectoral implies both that the issues are common to more than one sector and that they connect sectors. From this it follows that consideration of these issues needs to be cross-disciplinary and multiple-resource oriented. For example, economic and financial aspects link with all the others in terms of resources to carry out the scientific and educational tasks, or to undertake technological research, or to institute an anti-poverty plan that reduces environmentally stressful impacts. The resources themselves are a combination of differently trained personnel and different sources and types of financial resources. The *sectoral* concerns of agriculture link with other sectors, such as energy, transport, and industry through government policies and resultant human decisions. Each of the cross-sectoral issues contains relevant food security linkages within its own domain and between it and the others.

For example, economic/financial instruments are linked with institutional considerations such as providing or facilitating loans and grants for food imports, making financial policy, and economic data gathering and the use of economic instruments. Educational support is linked with institutions, science and technology in the support of indigenous knowledge and decentralized activities, agricultural outreach efforts, access to technology, and research and development.

LINKAGES AND INTERESTS

Together, the set of linkages described above (as well as those linkages that have not been listed) give definition and detail to the "conceptual space" for food security in UNCED. Within this space are the concerns and interests of parties attempting to incorporate both global goals and substantive action responses into an acceptable plan. These interests have two levels. First, "country goals" of a *fundamental* ideological/normative sort underlie issue definitions for each country. Secondly, there are the *particular* preferences of each country for various proposed outcomes. For example, some countries maintain that the right to a healthy environment exists and is a basic human right; a particular preference might be that a per capita criterion be used in allocative decisions.

In UNCED negotiations, as already noted, the focus was on the particulars. The UNCED secretariat summarized the task facing delegates to the conference as one of discovering a detailed and particularized solution to a multiple challenge:

> [How] to achieve the appropriate mixture of regulatory and market mechanisms, how to free social creativity, how to satisfy the need for economic development while protecting the resource base, and how to balance the requirements for social equity with both individual and communal needs (UNCED PrepCom A/CONF.151/PC/63, paragraph 14).

Negotiations, which are joint problem-solving exercises, tackle exactly such challenges of finding balances among a number of objectives. Parties arrive on the scene with different definitions of the problems and the work to be done. As the work gets under way, negotiators assess the quality of proposed outcome "packages" according to the interests that they *appear* to satisfy. Over time, there may be several types of movement: parties change their definitions of the problems (along any number of dimensions); new solutions may emerge that better match the definitions of parties; and aspects of the negotiations themselves may enhance the process of convergence. Throughout the process, the parties are comparing the developments against a background of *interests*.

UN regional economic councils submitted public reports as part of the preparation process for UNCED. These reports stated how environment and development problems and their interfaces were viewed from these regions. The highlights are discussed briefly below. These statements of objectives provided an initial way to infer interests about food security in UNCED.

The Bergen Declaration (ECE, 1990) emphasized the precautionary principle, the need to "integrate environmental considerations with economic and sectoral planning policies," and the importance of balancing the use of economic instruments with regulatory measures. There was also an emphasis on cost/benefit analysis to determine the merits of "anticipatory and adaptive strategies." Among the important environmental needs, pollution control was labeled the single most important need in a synthesis paper prepared from a number of national reports (ECE, 1991).

The Final Declaration of the Ministerial Conference on Environment and Development for Asia and the Pacific (ESCAP, 1990) emphasized an integrated approach, together with the precautionary principle. The statements further revealed that this group saw the major cause of environmental degradation as the "unsustainable pattern of production and consumption," but also cited the importance of both population growth and distribution and of poverty. They further stated that environmentally sound and sustainable development was primarily an economic issue, and that states have sovereign rights to exploit their resources, provided they do not cause damage (ESCAP, 1991).

The Tlatelolco Platform, and supporting information from the Economic and Social Council for Latin America and the Caribbean (ECLAC, 1991), highlighted the principle of equity in changing production patterns and called for a dynamic balance in the use of all forms of capital: human and cultural, natural, financial, and institutional. International competition and increasing trade, greater integration across sectors and levels of the economy, and intraregional cooperation were essential ingredients. Similar to ESCAP, ECLAC called for principles of environment-development integration and the "harmonious occupation of national territory." Development depends on exploitation and marketing of natural resources, according to this view, and thus the developing countries must be able to realize the benefits of natural resources. This view implies the necessity for conservation efforts, but also the need for trade and other practices to ensure that the value these resources represent is not siphoned off by other (perhaps wealthier) countries.

Some indications of African concerns were found in a report of the 1989 meeting of the Organization of African Unity (OAU).[7] Four such issues brought out were: (1) the need to prevent and reverse desertification; (2) the need to manage demographic change and pressure; (3) the requirement of self-sufficiency and food security; and (4) the need to maintain species and ecosystems.

Much of the information in the regional reports expressed "preferences" as well as "facts." Clearly, though, interests diverged. The five ranges shown below are the dimensions along which specific proposals were arrayed:

(1) the degree of *market freedom* (in contrast with regulation/protectionism) in called-for actions;
(2) the degree of international *control* (in contrast with national control or the primacy of national sovereignty) in determining actions;
(3) the degree to which legal measures would be *binding laws* (in contrast to "soft" laws);

[7] As reported in the *Brundtland Bulletin* (1990), Issue 9/10.

(4) the degree to which *scientific uncertainty* would be tolerated and how flexible policies would be to accommodate change; and
(5) the degree to which *development* would be emphasized (in contrast with environment).

Agenda 21 is the result of interest-based bargaining applied to each of the UNCED issue areas. The food security impacts will flow from the implementation of Agenda 21 and further evolution of the UNCED regime.

CONCLUSION

Food security issue/interest interactions motivated a joint and dynamic process of defining the salience of an issue and formulating judgments about possible policy responses to address the problems. These judgments were grounded in the traditions of ethics and political philosophy, but manifested themselves as preferences along a continuum of policies. Over the course of the negotiation, a number of changes occurred. Among them were changes in "objective" knowledge about the problem; in judgments about the importance of this change in knowledge; in the relative importance of the change within a given knowledge base, because of changes in preference determination; and in the formation and actions of coalitions in the day-to-day play of the negotiations. Over the course of implementation, further changes will occur.

Using the issue of food security, a number of interrelated linkages were illustrated in this chapter. As negotiators went about the particular efforts to draft the Rio Declaration and Agenda 21, among the most critical factors influencing the process were the *perceptions* of these linkages against a background of fundamental interests: perceptions and knowledge of the problem and its scientific characteristics; degree of risk aversity; preconditions, precedents, and history; political factors and tradeoffs outside the immediate decision context; competing objectives and counterproductive feedback effects; financial and managerial capacity; and finally, aspirations, values, and beliefs. As the figures make clear, these factors were underlying the direct environmental discussions that were the particular negotiation focus.

Part III

An Actor Perspective

7

Problems and Opportunities in Intragovernmental Coordination: A Northern Perspective

Hugo Maria Schally

Now that UNCED and other related international negotiating fora, like the Intergovernmental Negotiating Committees for Climate Change and the Protection of Biological Diversity, are over, one can say that the task was one of managing unprecedented complexity. The characteristics of the negotiating process leading up to the Stockholm Conference on the Human Environment in 1972 are all the more evident in UNCED. There it was said that what had happened at the negotiating table was just the visible tip of the iceberg; a whole mountain of arduous preparatory labor was the necessary prerequisite for final success (Sohn, 1973). At UNCED, the number of actors involved at international, regional, and national levels far outpaced the earlier conference and brings into sharp relief the question of how actor dynamics fashioned the process and outcome of UNCED. A book that was published by the Center for our Common Future to review the national responses to the Brundtland Report underlines that in building regimes, all actors "must forge new partnerships among groups that do not normally listen to each other, forcing a dialogue on the changes needed" (Starke, 1990). This small sentence points to the governmental actors, as well as the nongovernmental ones, in the process. The lessons learned from analyzing their interaction during UNCED can certainly be applied in the domestic area for improvements in legislation, implementation, integration of policies, and the involvement of the public.

This chapter focuses on the intragovernmental negotiating process in industrialized countries from the perspective of a participant. The subject will be treated mainly in the light of the national preparatory process for UNCED and the actual conduct of negotiations from Austria's experience, but with a view to finding similarities to such processes in other industrialized countries. Most of the documentation on intragovernmental coordination and on domestic bargaining and negotiations is not declassified and not freely available. Thus, this analysis is based on first-hand experience. It is also a investigation into the way industrialized countries approached the process. Developing countries' approaches to the negotiating process were doubtless similar in many ways, but given differences in available

Negotiating International Regimes: Lessons Learned from the United Nations Conference on Environment and Development (G. Sjöstedt, *et al.*, eds.; 1-85966-077-0; © IIASA; pub. Graham & Trotman, 1994; printed in Great Britain), pp. 123–133.

resources and administrative and political structures, one would expect that intragovernmental coordination would vary widely.

For most industrialized countries, the actors involved are the same: government ministries and agencies at national, regional, and local (federal provinces or states) levels, business, organizations representing special interest groups such as trade unions, chambers of industries, and other NGOs. Western European countries had one additional layer of coordination – the quasi-intragovernmental coordination process within the EC. The Commission of the EC participated in all the negotiations, and even negotiated as an independent actor in areas where authorized (mainly trade-related issues).

Three underlying questions guide the description and analysis of the preparation and coordination processes:

(1) Did the responses from different layers of government diverge significantly during the preparation?
(2) Was there a growing awareness of the needs and opportunities of regime-building throughout the process?
(3) Was there a redefinition of the concept of "national interest" or "national position"?

The process leading up to Rio was unparalleled both in its complexity and the short time allotted to it. The UN-GA Resolution 44/228 of 21 December 1989, which gave the mandate for the beginning of the preparatory process, left only 2 years for it to be completed. Given the sheer number of topics that were to be dealt with during the conference, the time would have been short even if there had been only one set of negotiations to be conducted. As it turned out, there were a number of other parallel negotiations in the environmental field that were conducted simultaneously, with an increasing intensity toward the end. There were, for example, regional preparation meetings (EC-regional meeting on sustainable development, Bergen, Norway, May 1990), negotiations for Conventions on Climate Change and for the Protection of Biological Diversity, and participants' meetings for the Global Environment Facility. All this added up to a frenetic pace of meetings that went on almost continuously until the very end of the UNCED preparatory period. It stressed the capacity of many national administrations to cope with such a heavy schedule. A growing number of actors from various national agencies and government institutions had to participate in several of these fora. Two main difficulties emerged. Either they had to follow all negotiations almost continuously without having time to consult and co-ordinate at home, or the job was distributed to different groups of negotiators who ran the risk of losing touch with each other. In either case, the process led to a considerable concentration of personnel resources, placing great strain on the capability of smaller states to participate effectively.

THE AUSTRIAN EXAMPLE

The Austrian response to the UNCED challenge has to be understood against the backdrop of historic and geographic facts. As the introduction of the Austrian National Report for UNCED (1992) points out, "Austria is part of the central European interior" and its foreign policy and interests are targeted accordingly. In line with its neighbors, Austria was under the impression at the beginning of the

UNCED process, influenced by the media and political discussions, that UNCED was going to be a pure Stockholm II, a misconception that was to be proved wrong as economic development issues insisted upon by the South became more and more prominent in relation to environmental issues during the preparatory negotiations.

Organization and Participation

Due to historical and logistical reasons, two ministries plus the Federal Chancellory were involved in the UNCED preparations from the very beginning. The Ministry for Foreign Affairs was the traditional government organization concerned with international cooperation and it played a key role in the whole preparatory process. The Ministry for the Environment, Youth, and Family Affairs, on the other hand, which came into being as a direct result of the Stockholm conference and is the ministry that deals directly with the UN Environment Programme (UNEP), was also highly interested in the follow-up conference to Stockholm. The third main player was the Federal Chancellory, partly because it retains the national competence for bilateral development cooperation, but also because the Federal Chancellor commissioned an independent contribution to the process: "International Environment Charter, The Austrian Contribution to the International Environment Charter" (1990). Initially, the preparatory process for UNCED was conducted in a number of fora where different but interrelated topics were discussed. The industrialized countries participated, for example, in the meeting resulting in the Declaration of The Hague, March 1989; OECD Ministerials of May 1989; the UN-ECE Conference in Bergen, May 1990; the UN-ECE Espoo Ministerial Declaration, February 1991; and the World Bank meetings to set up the Global Environment Facility, November 1990. Many of these sessions were attended by ministers and/or representatives of different ministries. This obviously did not help to focus the national response to the upcoming UNCED conference, as different ministries had separate interests, and different priorities and approaches.

As the institutionalized preparatory process within the UN system followed the traditional path of setting up a conference structure (that is, installation of working groups, election of officers, setting up of a secretariat) without going into substance until later, it was primarily the representatives of the environment and foreign affairs ministries that were involved at the initial phase. A national response to the substantive matters was rather slow in being formulated. Neither the public nor the administration and interest groups really grasped the complexity of the matter at this early stage. It was not until after the first session of the PrepCom was held in Nairobi from 6 to 31 August 1990 that the scene was set for intensified work on national coordination and national responses to the challenge now presented.

By the end of 1990, elaboration of national reports began to gain some urgency. Focusing and structuring the response to the UNCED process and the preparation of concrete answers to key questions on a national level was largely influenced by the need to develop a national report. The report served as a useful early reminder to several national institutions that it was necessary to deal with a stunning variety of interconnected issues in the preparation of UNCED. In the preparation for the second PrepCom in Geneva (April 1991), when the breadth of the agenda became apparent, various segments of the administration became distinctly aware that UNCED would touch their designated area of competence. As the issues and objectives of the conference began to be spelled out more clearly, it dawned upon more and more of the participants involved that it was necessary to formulate a coherent response and to integrate approaches in order to present a single national position in the negotiating process. Thus, at the beginning of 1991, a national coordinating structure was established, the so-called "Nationale UNCED Kommission zur Koordinierung der österreichischen Vorbereitung" ("National Commission for the Coordination of the Austrian Preparations for UNCED"). Looking at the topics listed in Resolution 44/228, a list that was still to change and grow in the course of the negotiations, one quickly becomes aware that virtually all aspects of human activities as they relate to the environment are covered, from climate change to human health, from human shelter to international trade, from desertification to the development of international environmental law. During the PrepCom negotiations, an attempt was made to draw up an organization chart relating specific tasks to responsible organizations of the UN system. The results show clearly that a comprehensive approach on the international level would have to involve all sectors of the UN family, as well as other international organizations. Accordingly, a sound national preparation had to involve the totality of national administrative agencies.

The Commission met for the first time in February 1991. Focal points in each ministry were designated to collect and distribute information relating to the UNCED process, hoping that horizontal communication within ministries would thereby be improved. The initial idea for Austria's national report was to base it on the Austrian contribution to the World Commission on Environment and Development (Brundtland Report); a first concept was presented in spring 1991. That concept gave a fairly good indication of the priority interest and action areas from the Austrian perspective. It was, however, too narrowly focused, and some important issues contained in the proposed agenda were not adequately covered. It was also evident that effective coordination required the establishment of a smaller group to guide the work of the report. A steering group was designated to coordinate the coordinators. It was composed of representatives of the Federal Chancellory, and the Federal Ministries for Foreign Affairs; Environment, Youth, and Family Affairs; Science and Research; Finance; and Economic Affairs. In the course of the preparatory process, it appeared that even that structure was too large and cumbersome to coordinate the process efficiently. A yet more informal group, composed of representatives of three ministries, prepared and implemented most of the substantial work. These included representatives from the Ministries for Foreign Affairs, and Environment, Youth, and Family Affairs, and the Federal Chancellory, the units that contributed financially to the process. The final packaging and editing of the texts supplied by the various parts of the administration were entrusted to consultants in the end. Thus, the national process of managing complexity involved an ever-wider range of consultations coordinated by a nested series of smaller groups.

The National Commission met 88 times before UNCED, roughly every two months. Information was received both through the Permanent Missions at the UN in New York and Geneva, and through the institutional channels of other ministries, and circulated through the Steering Committee to all the participants. The sheer mass of documentation and the fact that most people concerned had little or no multilateral experience presented the coordinators with a considerable problem. UN documents were difficult to tackle in any case, and it was not always possible for the concerned ministries to evaluate the contents of all documents. Some participants also encountered language problems.

Patterns of behavior and contribution were influenced based on personal involvement, the interest of certain members of negotiating groups, and influences from the political scene, which made themselves felt more strongly as the conference drew nearer. Some ministries, which logically should have been more closely involved in the negotiations on certain issues, took a deliberate decision to abstain. These decisions were often explainable in the context of domestic political considerations, though they may have had little to do with the UNCED process itself.

The Commission included wide participation, involving not only all federal ministries, but the Bundesländer (the federal provinces) and the independent sectors (environmental and development NGOs, the Trade Union Federation, the Federal Chamber of Commerce, the Industrialists Assembly, the Austrian Agriculture Chambers, and the Chamber of Austrian Workers Assembly). This participation was chosen to extract the distinct contributions of all groups to the National Report. The deliberations of the National Commission were such that in the end several participating groups from the independent sector actually won the right to be represented in the report with a separate and distinct contribution. The integration of NGOs into the Commission was a delicate process, involving partners that were very suspicious of each other at the beginning. Differing from the traditional special interest groups, such as the Trade Union Federation or the Federal Chamber for Commerce, which are very much integrated into the normal national decision-making process, the NGOs, both environmental and developmental, were very suspicious of their involvement at first, and at times felt excluded from the real process. It is important to explain this difference clearly in order to understand the dynamics of the coordination process in Austria. The Austrian concept of Social Partnership until recently allowed special interest groups to participate in the elaboration of national positions, but not NGOs in the narrow sense of the word – that is, grassroot organizations like Greenpeace. These NGOs were confronted for the first time with the chance to make positive contributions to the elaboration of national positions and were faced with the same dilemma as others: how to deal with and process large amounts of information. Their critical appraisal was voiced in the National Report:

> The financing of economic interest groups (social partnership) is particularly safeguarded as a special feature of Austrian society by legal regulations. Although their tasks have changed greatly since the war, the make up of the social partnership has remained untouched. Nature conservancy and environmental protection as a counterbalance to socio -economic interests is not supported even though this is doubtless among the most important tasks today (p. 100).

NGOs felt partly excluded from the UNCED preparation process, but, as with other participants, they were handicapped by the fact that they did not participate in the negotiating process throughout the preparatory phase, and therefore did not evaluate the negotiating progress appropriately at times. Contributions by NGOs came late and were not always well coordinated, although they did from the very beginning receive all the official documentation. There was certainly a lack of clear understanding from their side concerning the dynamics of the negotiating process. As was to be seen at the conference itself, the potential contribution of NGOs could have been greater in particular fields where they possessed special expertise, such as for example on youth, indigenous people, primary producers, human health, decision making, or science for sustainable development. Their overall impact on the work of the delegation in Rio, however, was positive and valuable, and they contributed very constructively.

Selection of NGOs for participation in the preparatory process was based on their competence in the field and relevance of action. The three NGO representatives chosen for the Austrian delegation at Rio represented three distinct aspects of the NGO spectrum, one coming from an environmental, one from a developmental, and one from a special interest group (Global 2000, Austrian Information Service for Development Cooperation, and the Society for Endangered People, respectively). It was left to the NGO community to decide on the individual representatives; the national administration accepted the decision of the NGOs. This involvement led to an important mutual learning process, where the proponents of open diplomacy – the NGOs – and the more traditional negotiators from the bureaucratic structures began to learn from each other. Their strengths – public diplomacy on the NGO side and traditional international bargaining on the government side – were largely complementary; mutual respect and understanding emerged as the conference proceeded.

Position Taking

UNCED dealt with issues that transcend narrow definitions of national interest and that clash with strong tendencies to defend national sovereignty. Issues such as desertification, forests, and freshwater, for example, cannot be solved without a view toward mutual cooperation and interdependence. Initially, Austria's preparations and position taking were based on national interests that were closely defined in terms of Austria's political and economic positions. However, when it came to some of the key environmental issues that dominated the conference, a vital Austrian national interest could not be defined; in fact, being a small, landlocked country made a global interdependent view of issues, such as climate change, forests, and nuclear waste, most prominent.

The criteria to develop a national position was simple, providing a sharp edge to cut through the complexity of issues. The question asked was, "Will a certain development or decision of the conference have financial or economic repercussions?" If certain proposals involved financial consequences, different ministries jockeyed for control of the issue. Typical were differences between the Ministries of Finance, Technical Cooperation, and Environment about possible financial mechanisms, where supporters of the Bretton Woods institutions would oppose those favoring a solution more directly within the UN system. Many issues were brought to the attention of the coordinating committee by the public at large, NGOs, and public political debate. One significant example was the debate over tropical rainforests that kept growing in importance throughout the preparatory phase, and influenced national positions on the forest issue as well as trade, climate change, and agriculture. Many diverging forces (NGOs, special interest groups, different ministries) engaged in heavy political infighting over the issue. Ultimately, a resolution and new legislation on tropical timber were passed by the Austrian parliament just before UNCED, prompting an UNCED initiative by the Austrian government: the "Fonds für die Förderung der aufrechterhaltbaren Nutzung des tropischen Regenwaldes" (Tropical Forest Initiative), which provides 200 million Austrian schillings for projects that contribute to the sustainable use of tropical forests. This unusual approach to position taking was a direct consequence of strong public interest and political action in connection with the particular issue of tropical forests.

In the beginning, the conference raised little public interest. The ideas put forward were initially met with little or no resistance. This changed, however, as the external political and economic framework altered over the period of the preparatory process. Early, the economic situation was widely perceived to be stable and on the upswing; there was a high propensity for change. By the time concrete action plans were developed, the economic indicators had turned downward and the readiness for radical change dwindled among many sectors both in the government and the private sector.

The Negotiation

Intragovernmental coordination was further complicated by the complex structure of the proposed conference itself. On the one hand, the high level Earth Summit called for participation by heads of state and governments. On the other hand, the ministers of environment were to play a substantial role during the conference. At the same time, substantial political preparation was to be done by the traditional apparatus of the foreign ministries. This was a clear recipe for misunderstandings among ministries, as there is a very practical, and political, difference between involvement in internal coordination, outward representation, and designated competence. There were several Austrian ministries that chose not to be represented in the negotiation process, although concerned with some of the sensitive issues. This led to changing leadership patterns during the negotiation process causing some loss of clarity over time. The strength of leadership emanating externally from the Foreign Ministry, and internally from the Ministry of Environment and Federal Chancellory, varied over the course of negotiations, yielding some coordination and coherence problems in the delegation.

The reasons for and consequences of stronger or weaker involvement by ministries varied from case to case. It usually stemmed from a combination of factors such as different priorities, availability of qualified personnel to attend the meetings, tactical considerations, and a perceived lack of importance of the issues on the political agenda. Three important ministries were particularly underrepresented, namely the Ministries for Economic Affairs, Agriculture and Forestry, and Finance (at least in the initial stages).

The composition of the delegations at the various PrepComs, and finally at the conference, indicates both the interest and influence on the process of various ministries, as well as changing interest over time (see Table 7.1).

Table 7.1 shows that it was mainly a few ministries that were involved from the very beginning and that carried the brunt of the actual negotiating work. Their dominating role was further amplified as the preparatory process continued. As the subject of negotiation became more complex, the issues were not only discussed on the basis of existing documentation, but with a view to merging the collective institutional memory into a coherent and permanent negotiating team. This proved difficult, since only one delegate participated in all rounds of negotiation, three participated from PrepCom I (Nairobi) to UNCED, four from PrepCom II (in Geneva) to UNCED, seven from PrepCom III (Geneva) to UNCED, and eight from PrepCom IV to UNCED. The composition of the delegations at the third and fourth

Table 7.1 The Composition of the Austrian delegation

Organization Meeting (New York)	Foreign Affairs	2
	Environment	1
PrepCom I (Nairobi)	Foreign Affairs	4
	Environment	2
PrepCom II (Geneva)	Foreign Affairs	5
	Environment	3
PrepCom III (Geneva)	Foreign Affairs	4
	Environment	4
	Federal Chancellory	1
	Finance	1
PrepCom IV (New York)	Foreign Affairs	4
	Environment	4
	Federal Chancellory	2
	Finance	1
	Economic Affairs	1
UNCED (Rio de Janeiro)	Head of Delegation: *Bundeskanzler* (Federal Chancellor) and, in his absence, the Minister for Environment, Youth and Family	
	Foreign Affairs	6
	Environment	4
	Federal Chancellory	5
	Finance	2
	Health and Consumer Protection	1
	NGOs	3
	Federal Provinces	2
	Special Interest Groups	6

PrepComs clearly showed that there are limits to a small country coping fully with a major negotiating process like UNCED. Out of a delegation of 39 at UNCED (including clerical staff and security), less than half (13) were actual negotiators. This was not sufficient to cover the work of conferences and meetings that split up in many simultaneous working groups.

The peculiarities and characteristics of the Austrian preparatory process and its specific intragovernmental problems and challenges have, of course, to be seen in the light of it being a smaller industrialized country. Participants in the domestic coordination and the negotiation proper were largely identical, thereby increasing coherence on the one side, but also creating a big risk by spreading everything too thinly; one person dropping out at a particular point would have jeopardized the whole preparation. This was simply because of a lack of people available within the public service capable of actively participating in such a multilateral negotiating exercise. The language problem was only one stumbling block. The Austrian delegation had to rely on the people available to cover those negotiating groups that where considered to be of special importance. Unlike some other countries, Austria could not fall back for support on any regional or political group - like, for instance, the EC and Nordic group could. It could not rely on an automatic flow of information, institutional support, or even representation in negotiating groups that come with membership in a group. Substitutes like the "Central European Initiative" did not offer a workable alternative. Its membership (Austria, Hungary, Italy, Poland, and Yugoslavia) at the time was only loosely cooperative, and because of the rapidly emerging conflict in Yugoslavia, it could not generate a coherent approach.

The development of the Austrian negotiating position on several issues that were high on its agenda emerged along different lines. These processes of position development and coalition formation demonstrate the various ways in which agencies and ministries became involved in the larger negotiation process.

International Legal Instruments

Austria traditionally has had a strong commitment to the legalization of international relations. At UNCED, the Austrian Minister for Foreign Affairs launched the idea of developing enhanced mechanisms for the prevention and resolution of environmental disputes. In the preparatory phase of the conference, Austria worked through the Central European Initiative to introduce specific text on dispute resolution into Agenda 21 as well as the Rio Declaration. This was undertaken and negotiated primarily by delegates representing the Office of the Legal Counsel of the Foreign Affairs ministry. However, as indicated above, the Central European Initiative did not prove to be a practical instrument for joint efforts. In general, the former socialist countries did not have very experienced negotiators on their delegations and they each were pursuing other goals and priorities independently. Italy, for its part, was often hindered in working congruently with the other partners in the Initiative because of its strong participation in EC position taking.

The environmental dispute resolution text ran into some opposition from developing countries and was regarded suspiciously by some industrialized nations as well. At several points in the preparatory process, it appeared as if the initiative was in danger of being rejected entirely. It required a considerable amount of negotiating skill and effort on the part of the Austrian delegation to finally get the support of most OECD countries for a compromise version that preserved the essential ideas. The negotiators were able to forge an alliance that allowed them to overcome the initial resistance and have the compromise text included in both Agenda 21 and the Rio Declaration.

Protection of the Atmosphere

The Austrian positions at UNCED on atmospheric issues were strongly influenced by the simultaneous negotiations to develop a framework convention on climate change. Austria played a very active but controversial role on these issues; the environmental ministry took the lead in defining the national position. Austria was among the countries that maintained a rather radical approach to targets and timetables for the reduction of greenhouse gas emissions and a change in the patterns of energy consumption and production. These were among the most controversial details debated and negotiated at Rio. Austria remained rather isolated in its position, even among the OECD countries that favored more moderate approaches or, like the United States, were completely opposed to any strict control measures. Given this situation, Austrian delegates could only influence the outcome by intensive lobbying and participation in the drafting of specific points. The fact that many details of concern to Austria can be found in the final text of the Agenda 21 chapter on the protection of the atmosphere is due in large part to the hard work of these negotiators.

Forests

Austria has one of the largest forest covers in Europe, combined with a high degree of dependence on forests for economic and ecological benefits. The forestry issue was doubly of interest because of its linkage to the climate change issue. At an early stage, there were attempts to define a clear and broadly based national position involving several ministries, notably the ministries of environment, and agriculture and forestry. The OECD countries were less divided on the forestry issue than on many other issues, which contributed to Austria's constructive role in helping to build a coalition that included such countries as Germany, France, Finland, Canada, and the United States. As part of the mainstream, Austria was able to include several points that it found of major importance into the final text of the Forest Declaration.

It is interesting to note how Austrian positions on these issues were pursued through different negotiation means and different negotiation roles. In the first case, Austria pursued its own initiative and tried to involve other countries. In the second case, Austria's position led to its isolation. In the third case, it played along with the mainstream. In all cases, the way negotiations were conducted, positions defined, and alliances developed, were strongly influenced by the fact that Austria was not a member of some natural and standing coalition. Instead, Austria was forced to search for and persuade possible allies to take common cause with it on an issue-by-issue basis.

COMPARISON WITH OTHER OECD COUNTRIES

How generalizable are these experiences of the Austrian preparatory process to other industrialized countries? There are likely to be many similarities, but some important differences too. The structure of most delegations of industrialized countries, as well as the structure of their national reports, suggest that their national preparations and intragovernmental coordination followed a logistical pattern similar to the Austrian example. Environment ministries dominated the process in the beginning, but at the end, political forces and foreign offices tended to gain more control over the process. The most important difference is likely to be in the scale of involvement, rather than in its content. Obviously, there are differences in national approach given different traditions and governmental structures. The level of participation at the Rio Conference itself (at head of state level or lower) and national priorities (strong involvement in development aid or environmental concern) tends to shape the response. The manpower capacities of national administrations also play an obvious major role. Another major influence on the level of national preparation is the language factor. Those countries who use one of the UN languages as their mother tongue or working language have a much easier time in analyzing and formulating responses to texts.

One of the most important differences, however, is the fact that most industrialized countries are already integrated into the framework of a supranational coordination process, an important step in managing the complexity of both many parties and many issues. The obvious example is the EC countries, but also the "CANZ group" (Canada, Australia, and New Zealand), and the Nordic Group (Iceland, Finland, Norway, Sweden, and, to some extent, Denmark), which coordinated their positions substantially. Such integration allows smaller countries to make their views and positions known and to have greater influence on certain issues. Existing resources could therefore be allocated more efficiently. Supranational coordination influences greatly the structure of intragovernmental negotiations, because it adds another layer of decision making to be integrated. Coordination among the countries that are members of the Organization for Economic Cooperation and Development (OECD) did not really take place in the UNCED process, although it was active. However, even there, coordination concerned only very specific issues, particularly those on which there were strong differences of opinions among the industrialized countries. For most countries, the involvement in such a supranational coordinating structure offers a decisive difference, enhancing their political weight. For Austria, not belonging to any regional grouping was a real disadvantage as there was no automatic forum for her initiatives.

CONCLUSIONS

The negotiating process stretched the manpower, even of larger nations, to its limits, as the necessity for coordination and integration of responses grew. Future issues dealing with the implementation of Agenda 21 and other results of the Rio Conference will necessitate further intragovernmental coordination, as the process of regime-building continues. The coordinating structures that were created by UNCED should be used for the preparation of that work also, but they need to be enhanced.

Governmental structures were ill equipped to cope with the increased interest of the public, the fragmented negotiation process, the need to coordinate across ministries and agencies dealing in different disciplines, and the dichotomy between proclaimed open "parliamentary" diplomacy and negotiations conducted behind closed doors. Throughout the preparatory process, the odds were heavily in favor of total failure as the talks nearly collapsed several times. Considering the complexity of the negotiation issues, special interest groups and NGOs can play important roles in helping governments coordinate their positions. The impact of NGOs on the style and structure of the talks, not directly on the negotiating results, was considerable. They shaped the responses of the different layers of government involved, as public reaction was intense and had to be taken into account.

In the light of public pressure and increased public interest, the negotiation process that began at UNCED appears to be generating a certain realignment in the definition of "national interest," from self-interest and sovereignty to cooperative interdependence among nations. The big challenge will be how to bridge the divide between the concepts of national resources and global heritage. At UNCED, the traditional nationalist concept largely prevailed in the end despite the more global approach taken by some negotiators. However, the seeds for change have been sown; and the mechanisms for intragovernmental coordination required to produce the change in future negotiations have been given a trial run.

8

The Decision-making Process from a Developing Country Perspective[1]

Oscar A. Avalle

The UNCED negotiation process posed major political challenges to Argentine policy makers. In its substantive aspects, what was at stake was the inclusion of environmental concerns as an independent variable in the design of public policies in Argentina. The inclusion of environmental concerns would allow for a more effective formulation and implementation of the concept of "sustainable development" in the country's growth process. In its formal aspects, UNCED confronted Argentine policy makers with a very complex process of regime-building negotiations to define Agenda 21 and other UNCED-related instruments.

This chapter identifies the key domestic actors in charge of the design and implementation of environmental policies in Argentina, describes the country's policy goals during the UNCED multilateral negotiation process, and analyzes the positions adopted by the Argentine delegation during the negotiations, and the extent to which the country's policy goals made their way into UNCED resolutions. Special attention will be devoted to the major role played by key intergovernmental actors in the articulation of Argentina's position at the negotiation table. The objective is to understand the influence of intragovernmental coordination, as well as supranational coordination within the G-77, on Argentina's capacity to perform effectively in the negotiations.

KEY DOMESTIC ACTORS

UN Resolution 44/228 called for the convening of UNCED to discuss the inclusion of environmental criteria in the design and implementation of economic development policies. For the Argentine government, the process thus initiated entailed the need to define the country's policy goals in terms of the concept of "sustainable development" as well as to identify the relevant domestic actors who would be charged with negotiating Argentina's position at the negotiation table.

[1]Although the author is an official of the Argentine government, the opinions expressed in this chapter are strictly personal, and should not be taken as a reflection of the official Argentine opinion or position in this matter.

Negotiating International Regimes: Lessons Learned from the United Nations Conference on Environment and Development (G. Sjöstedt, *et al.*, eds.; 1-85966-077-0; © IIASA; pub. Graham & Trotman, 1994; printed in Great Britain), pp. 135–147.

Over the years prior to UNCED, the activities of a complex network of national and international NGOs and the impact of environmental problems on the day-to-day life of Argentine society had fueled rising concern over environmental priorities within the definition of growth policies in Argentina. As a result, it was expected that the country's official position at the UNCED meeting should reflect the diversity and aspirations of a pluralist democratic society. Thus, the need arose to define and implement the appropriate ways to identify and represent those domestic conditions as faithfully as possible.

Both the selection of the official representatives to the conference and the negotiation process were a reflection of the country's political and institutional arrangement, especially the level of development of its legal and institutional structure.[2] In accordance with Argentina's federal constitution, the central government shares a host of responsibilities with the provincial authorities. Since environmental issues were not of primary importance at the time the constitution was enacted, they were not treated with either the comprehensiveness or the inter-sectorial approach that they are dealt with at present. Only a few environmental questions were specifically reserved for the central government under the power-sharing arrangement established by the constitution.[3] However, the latter also vested the central government with broad scope to provide for the country's general welfare. As a result of this vaguely defined authority, the central government became entitled, in principle, to address and regulate environmental issues as it deemed necessary.[4]

Although a vast body of legislation has followed since, especially in relation to the usage and exploitation of the country's natural resources, the regulatory framework governing environmental questions in Argentina has suffered, and still suffers, from several shortcomings. Typical of these shortcomings are the existence of numerous regulatory loopholes, overlapping functions at the national and provincial level, and little overall policy coherence. This has resulted in frequent jurisdictional conflicts, weak enforcement, and a generalized lack of efficacy. At least until the 1970s, Argentina lacked a systematic environmental policy. At the institutional level, there was no agency charged with the responsibility of formulating a comprehensive environmental policy at the national, provincial, or municipal levels.

Faced with the need to set u an administrative structure and a cadre of experts for the formulation of environmental policy, the Undersecretary of the Environment was created in 1985. The new agency was given an advisory role in the design of policies relating to environmental conservation. It would report directly to the executive branch, under whose competence the Undersecretary was established. Intense bureaucratic struggles followed the creation of the Undersecretary position, motivated by a poor definition of its areas of competence and extensive functional overla with the Ministry of Economy. As an intrabureaucratic compromise, a new National Commission on Environmental Policy (CONAPA), established in 1988, was given not only an advisory role in policy design (as the former Undersecretary had enjoyed), but also a more comprehensive authority to coordinate the implementation of policies by different agencies within the central bureaucracy.

[2]See the Informe Nacional sobre Problemas Ambientales, Republica Argentina, 1992, for more details.

[3]See Constitucion de la Nacion Argentina, Articulo 26 and Articulo 67 inc. 11 and 16, Buenos Aires, Victor Zavalia.

[4]See Pedro Frias, *Derecho Publico Provincial*, Depalma, Buenos Aires.

Secretariat of Natural Resources and Human Environment

Seeking to fill the legal loopholes and solve intrabureaucratic conflicts, the government created a secretariat of Natural Resources and Human Environment within the competence of the Executive Branch by decree in March 1992. For the first time, a government agency in charge of environmental policies was vested with cabinet-level status as a way to enhance its leverage within the central bureaucracy.

The main role assigned to the new agency involved the provision of all necessary technical assistance to the Executive Branch in the pursuit of activities geared toward the promotion, protection, recovery, and control of the environment and the preservation of renewable natural resources within the Argentine territory. To undertake these activities, the secretariat was entitled to consult other provincial and municipal authorities, national and foreign government agencies, and NGOs in order to promote an optimal interaction and balance of man with the physical and biological milieu.[5]

The granting of so broad a mandate for the new environmental agency was bound to give rise to new jurisdictional conflicts within the central bureaucracy. This time the secretariat's authority was resisted, on the one hand, by a host of agencies within the Ministry of Economy (i.e., the Secretaries of Energy, Mining, and Agriculture, Livestock and Fisheries) and, on the other, by the Ministry of Foreign Affairs, which is solely responsible for conducting, on behalf of the national government, all negotiations taking place in multilateral fora.

Therefore, the authority given to the secretariat of Natural Resources and Human Environment to negotiate on behalf of the national government in multilateral economic fora opened a potential source of jurisdictional conflict with the Ministry of Foreign Affairs. This friction was enhanced by the fact that the officers of the secretariat had never headed an Argentine delegation, nor had the secretariat fully participated in the preliminary stages leading up to UNCED. Lacking sufficient experience and negotiation skills at the outset of the multilateral negotiations, the secretariat was forced to rely on the greater expertise of the diplomatic corps.

THE PROCESS OF DETERMINING ARGENTINA'S POSITION

Experience shows that, in cases where more than one agency has jurisdiction over a certain policy issue, the responsibilities of each participating agency must be clearly defined by the political authority in advance for policy coordination to be effective. Such functional division of labor must be made explicit and translated into a formal power structure, so as to allow each agency to be aware of its respective jurisdiction and role during the subsequent process of negotiation with other parties. This facilitates the coordination of the technical and political staff of the participating agencies to achieve a single policy stance at the negotiation table.

In the case of the UNCED process, early informal meetings were held between the technical staff in charge of environmental policy (i.e., the CONAPA initially, and the secretariat of Natural Resources and Human Environment thereafter), and officials of the Ministry of Foreign Affairs, which would be involved in negotiating the country's position in international fora. Yet, such

[5]Decree No. 534/92, 27 March 1992.

meetings failed to yield a clear definition of functional responsibilities between the agencies involved. Instead, such definition would emerge ad hoc on the basis of the participating agencies' areas of expertise: the secretariat of Natural Resources would provide substantive inputs concerning the technical aspects of the issues under discussion, while Foreign Affairs would be in charge of the political negotiation at the diplomatic level. It was further expected that, in response to changing circumstances, policy coordination through tactical readjustments of the country's position would be facilitated by daily meetings between the upper echelon of Foreign Affairs and of the secretariat, both of whom would be present during the Rio Summit.

In practice, the lack of definition of a formal hierarchical structure, as well as the political responsibilities of the Argentine delegates to the Summit, resulted in a puzzling situation: the ranking of Argentina's senior diplomat in the conference was substantially lower than that of the chief of the technical mission. As will be discussed below, this situation led to frequent misunderstandings, ineffective coordination, and leadership problems within the delegation. In an effort to overcome these deficiencies, the highest-ranking Argentine officials strove to maintain the stability of the country's position throughout the negotiations opted for the continuity of the negotiating team during the whole negotiation process, in spite of the hierarchical problems[6] in order.

The Ministry of Foreign Affairs played a central role in the process of negotiation of Argentina's position during the PrepComs, in which the bulk of the substantive discussions was carried out.[7] The Ministry's influence, which was largely reflected in the composition of the various delegations to the PrepComs, was partly the result of the fact that, unlike other public-sector agencies, the diplomatic corps in most

[6]*La Nacion*, 4 June 1992, Buenos Aires, p. 2.

[7]The Argentine delegation to the PrepComs and UNCED was composed as follows:

PREPCOM I (New York)	
Ministry of Foreign Affairs	4
PREPCOM II (Nairobi)	
Ministry of Foreign Affairs	4
PREPCOM II (Geneva)	
Ministry of Foreign Affairs	6
PREPCOM III (Geneva)	
Ministry of Foreign Affairs	6
PREPCOM IV (New York)	
Ministry of Foreign Affairs	7
CONAPA	3
UNCED (Rio de Janeiro)	
Technical Mission:	
Ministry of Foreign Affairs	12
secretariat of Natural Resources and Human Environment	12
Advisers:	
Legislative branch (federal and provincial), provincial and municipal authorities and NGOs	60
Executive branch:	
Ministry of Foreign Affairs	9
Secretariat of Natural Resources and Human Environment	4
Ministry of Economy:	1
Other executive agencies:	4
Legislative branch:	2

developing countries is composed of a professional core of career personnel,[8] with extensive expertise gained through successive rounds of international negotiations. As a result of this cumulative pool of knowledge, the diplomatic corps usually enjoys a significant comparative advantage *vis-à-vis* other public agencies with formal responsibility over a policy issue. This fact proved to be of particular relevance at the very outset of the negotiation process. Moreover, the presence of diplomatic personnel from the Permanent Missions of Argentina in Geneva and New York made it easier to coordinate a common position with other delegations, both at the bilateral level and within the Group of 77,[9] during the PrepComs as well as in the negotiations.

Foreign Affairs was heavily represented throughout UNCED. An Environment Unit, headed by a senior officer, was set up within the Bureau. It played a coordinating role in the determination of Argentina's negotiation stance, and would become the main spokesman of the Argentine government during the UNCED process. It was specifically in charge of the negotiations involving the Rio Declaration, the financial arrangements of Agenda 21 and the Protection of the Atmosphere, especially the protection of the ozone layer, where the Argentine delegate held the post of vice-president of the International Negotiation Committee on Climatic Change. At the same time, this office within the secretariat of Environment was in charge of contact and communication with the NGOs. The Legal Department of the Foreign Ministry dealt primarily with legal issues, especially those related to fisheries and the oceans, as well as the Rio Declaration.

The Permanent Mission of Argentina to the International Organizations in Geneva participated through a middle-level diplomat, who was mostly involved in the negotiations on waste disposal, but also served as a liaison person within the Argentine delegation. Three officials from the Permanent Mission of Argentina to the United Nations were involved, and two from the economic section (a senior and a junior) and one from the legal section (a senior). They were in charge of the negotiations with the G-77, on economic and trade aspects of Agenda 21 and on the terms of reference for the Commission on Sustainable Development.

IDENTIFICATION OF THE RELEVANT ISSUES[10]

The paucity of human and financial resources made it difficult for the Argentine delegation to follow through on all the relevant issues under discussion in Agenda 21. To overcome this constraint, which affected most developing countries alike, the Argentine delegation opted for a selective approach. Thus, only those policy issues of central concern to the country's interests would be the object of ongoing monitoring and direct participation in the negotiation by one or more Argentine delegates or through other negotiation groups, like the G-77.

[8]See the relevant work on administrative practices in developing countries by Waldino Suarez, *Some Notes on Governmental Rearrangements in Argentina since 1930*, ECR Paper, Freiburg, Germany, 1982.

[9]The G-77 constitutes by far the largest functional negotiation bloc within the UN system. From its inception during the 1964 UNCTAD, the G-77 has served as the main vehicle for the demands of the developing world. It currently represents some 130 developing countries, including Argentina.

[10]For a more detailed discussion of this issue, see Estrada Oyuela, Raül, *Conferencia de las Naciones Unidas sobre Medio Ambiente y Desarrollo: Apuntes para su evaluaciön*, in Revista del Ministerio de Relaciones Exteriores y Culto, ISEN, MREC, Año 1 no. 2, 1992.

The participation in questions deemed of secondary importance was marginal. Negotiation of such questions was left to either the G-77 representative or, where there was no established G-77 position, by another delegation sharing Argentina's policy stance on the issue. This approach prevented the delegation from using up its scarce human resources on questions of marginal importance maximized available manpower.

Most of the developed countries, in particular the United States, Japan, and the European countries, which were represented through the UK as the chairman of the EC, were very well endowed in human and material resources. The huge disparity in resources between developed and developing countries' delegations weakened the latter's negotiation power as a bloc considerably, since the complex technical issues dealt with required that at least one delegate had to be fully dedicated to follow-up and negotiating. This was beyond the means of many delegations from developing countries.[11]

To overcome these constraints and arrive at agreements required the conclusion of alliances among like-minded countries, coalitions, and negotiation groups (like the G-77). Examples of such negotiating blocs are presented below. Several strategic alliances were also formed between developing and developed countries on specific policy issues – for example, on the effects of ozone depletion on agricultural production.

The absence of a clear functional division of roles within the Argentine negotiating team, coupled with the lack of expertise of some delegates in complex multilateral negotiation processes, contributed to the emergence of disparate opinions within the Argentine delegation on certain key issues. Some of these disagreements found their way into the press, as was the case with a request, expressed in a Latin American and Caribbean Group of States (GRULAC) meeting, to mobilize regional support to introduce some changes in the wording of the Rio Declaration. The changes should not have come as a surprise, however, since they had already been announced during the final session of PrepCom IV, as well as at a G-77 meeting in New York in March and April 1992 respectively.[12] At both occasions, Argentina had expressed its disagreement with the final draft of the Rio Declaration, especially its explicit reference to the concept of "equity" contained in Principle 3. This ran counter to a position dear to Argentina, which has traditionally considered that "equality" rather than "equity" should be the main principle governing a country's right to economic development.

Furthermore, the Argentine delegation also resisted, from a philosophic position, the inclusion of a reference to reduce, and ultimately eliminate, unsustainable patterns of consumption linked to the promotion of appropriate demographic policies, contained in Principle 8 of the draft. Such reference would have established a causal link between economic growth and a country's demographic policies, with the risk

[11]Another important weakness common to most developing countries was the lack of logistic support during the Conference itself. For example, while every delegation of developed countries could count on adequate communication and secretariat support, the Argentine delegation, for instance, had at its disposal only a personal lapto computer and two cellular phones at the Rio Center. This lack of means created additional coordination difficulties for the delegation, as well as problems in maintaining a continuous flow of information with the decision makers in Buenos Aires.

[12]See *Ambito Financiero*, 4 June 1992, Buenos Aires, p. 22. Also, *Pagina 12*, 4 June 1992, Buenos Aires, p. 4, and *Cronista Comercial*, 4 June 1992, Buenos Aires, p. 16.

of rendering economic assistance to developing countries contingent upon extra-economic criteria.

Argentina's breaking role toward the wording of Principles 3 and 8 of the Rio Declaration was amplified by the press, which portrayed the country's objections not as an observation to a document under negotiation, but rather as a deliberate attempt to blackmail the whole negotiation process. If successful, Argentina's position would have contributed to improving the substance of the document. At no time was it Argentina's intention to blackmail or break the consensus over the Rio Declaration.[13]

A further element, which was largely neglected at the time, involved the possibility of using Argentina's opposition to the wording of the draft as a bargaining chi to increase the country's leverage on other issues. By threatening to brake the consensus, issue-linkage seemed an appropriate tactical move to enable the delegation to bring more pressure to bear on other points in Agenda 21 (for example, on agriculture).

Nevertheless, this situation forced the secretariat of Natural Resources and the Minister of Foreign Affairs to issue new instructions to the delegates.[14] The strong reaction to the country's position also led to a direct intervention by Maurice Strong, the UNCED Secretary General, and the withdrawal of the objections by the highest-ranking Argentine delegate, under direct instructions of both the secretariat of Natural Resources and the Minister of Foreign Affairs.

Trade and Agricultural Protectionism

Through the G-77, Argentina participated in the negotiations and drafting of the Rio Declaration during PrepCom IV, where it shared the consensus prevailing in the G-77 in all but a few items. Along with other Latin American countries, Argentina pushed for the inclusion in the draft of a strong condemnation of agricultural subsidies and protectionist policies as detrimental to the environment. Another central tenet of the Argentine position was inclusion of a clause foreclosing the imposition of trade restrictions on the basis of environmental arguments.

Both positions were included in the first G-77 draft, despite strong opposition both within and outside the G-77. In the subsequent negotiation process, however, strong resistance from net food-importing countries combined with EC pressure was able to dilute any explicit reference to the unsuitability of agricultural subsidies. As a result, a compromise solution was achieved. It became embodied in Principle 12 of the Rio Declaration, which was intended to cover some of the concerns expressed by Argentina and other exporters of foodstuffs.[15]

As a net exporter of foodstuffs, Argentina is seriously harmed by the agricultural subsidies and protective tariffs imposed by a number of developed countries to shelter inefficient domestic producers. It is widely acknowledged that, from a strictly economic point of view, the preservation of such activities by artificial means is irrational. Argentina has consistently condemned these practices in every international meeting in which the subject has come to the fore. Its goal has been to

[13]*Buenos Aires Herald*, 4 June 1992, Buenos Aires, p. 3, and *Cronista Comercial*, 4 June 1992, Buenos Aires, p. 16.

[14]*Ambito Financiero*, 4 June 1992, Buenos Aires, p.22; *Pagina 12*, 4 June 1992, Buenos Aires, p. 4.

[15] Ing. Maria Julia Alsogaray, in her press comments to *La Nacion*, 9 June 1992, Buenos Aires, p. 3.

mobilize international support to force protectionist countries into adopting more flexible policies.

The adoption of the principle of "sustainable development" afforded Argentina the opportunity to broaden the scope of its opposition to agricultural protectionism, since the artificial protection of agriculture through subsidization threatens to have a deleterious impact on the environment. On the basis of this premise, as reflected in the UN draft resolution A/C.2/46/L.74 on "Protectionism and Sustainable Agricultural Policies," a heated debate took place during the 46th General Assembly. The debate was centered upon the inclusion in the UNCED agenda of the principle of the economic and environmental irrationality of agricultural subsidies, as well as the need to foster an open, predictable, fair, and non-discriminatory multilateral trade system. The main purpose of the Argentine effort was to resist the attempts of some developed countries to manipulate Agenda 21 to allow for the imposition of additional trade restrictions on the basis of environmental criteria. To further its position, the Argentine delegation sought to mobilize the support of other members of the Cairns Group,[16] countries, both developing and developed, that are efficient produers and net exporters of foodstuff.

Two separate blocs, each with clearly defined interests, emerged early in what was to become a lengthy and complicated negotiation process: the EC and the Cairns Group. The EC delegates were strongly committed to delinking environmental and economic questions as two separate sets of issues. Therefore, they adamantly opposed the Cairns Group's proposal to deal with them together, which might open up the possibility of establishing a direct link between protectionism and subsidies on the one hand and environmental damage on the other.

Despite wide differences, the negotiating parties managed to achieve a substantive agreement, during PrepCom IV, not to impose trade restrictions on the basis of environmental considerations.[17] The attempt of EC members to leave economic and trade issues out of Agenda 21, which they wanted to redefine as merely an instrument of environmental policy, was partially neutralized through the ample use of cross-references, particularly in chapters 2 ("International Cooperation to Accelerate Sustainable Development in Developing Countries and Related Domestic Policies"); 14 ("Promoting Sustainable Agricultural and Rural Development"); and 32 ("Strengthening the Role of Farmers").

Protection of the Atmosphere

The progressive depletion of the ozone layer over Antarctica and Argentina's mainland gave Argentine authorities a strong incentive to adopt a defensive role in the agreements leading to the Montreal Protocol and the negotiations of the Convention on Climatic Change. This involvement was mostly carried out by the official in charge of the environmental section of the Ministry of Foreign Affairs, who was appointed vice chairman of the Intergovernmental Negotiation Committee on Climatic Change.

[16]For a more detailed analysis of the Argentine position in the Cairns Group, see Tussie, Diana y Simone,Cristina; El Grupo Cairns: Un nuevo tipo de concertación; en América Latina/Internacional, FLACSO, Buenos Aires, vol. 9, no. 33, July–September 1992.

[17]A/CONF.151/26, Vol. I, especially ch. 2, para. 2.22.

Argentina's concern with this subject was conspicuous in the process of negotiating Agenda 21. The depletion of the ozone layer has a strong negative impact on a food-producing country like Argentina. Besides obvious risks to human health, the core economic activities in the country are harmed as well.[18] Along with other affected countries such as Chile and Uruguay, Argentina introduced a particular program area into this document on preventing stratospheric ozone depletion. The Argentine delegation advocated the introduction of mechanisms aimed at compensating those countries directly affected by ozone depletion. The motion was defeated largely because of the concerted opposition of developed countries and the paucity of hard data on the extent of the damage resulting from ozone depletion. Despite this setback, governments were urged to consider taking appropriate remedial measures in the fields of human health, agriculture, and marine environment, based on the results of research on the effects of additional ultraviolet radiation reaching the Earth's surface. This motion passed with the support of the UN, the NGOs, and the private sector. Along with other delegations, Argentina also took the lead in introducing an explicit reference in Agenda 21 on the need for research to assess the impact of ozone depletion on both the environment and the economic activities of affected countries.[19]

It was further agreed that a concerted effort should be made to monitor the evolution of the ozone layer in the Southern Cone on a permanent basis, to supplement a monitoring program which, with UN Development Program (UNDP) support, is currently being conducted by the governments of Argentina, Brazil, Chile, Paraguay and Uruguay.

The introduction of these elements required the negotiating parties to overcome dissensus in the G-77, stemming from opposition from the Organization of Oil Producing and Exporting Countries (OPEC) to any development policy aimed at limiting hydrocarbon exploitation or otherwise fostering the use of alternative sources of energy.

Oceans, Fisheries and Rivers

Because its extensive coastline, Argentina played a key role in the negotiations on the Law of the Sea. During the UNCED process, the Argentine delegates were also actively involved in discussions centered on chapter 17 of Agenda 21, on the "Protection of the Oceans, All Kinds of Seas, Including Enclosed and Semi-Enclosed Seas, and Coastal Areas, and the Protection, Rational Use and Development of their Living Resources." Argentina's main goal involved the preservation of the country's sovereign rights over a 200-mile exclusive economic zone EEZ from outside interference, especially regarding fishing. In addition, the Argentine delegation played a salient role in the negotiations leading to the decision, announced during the 47th UN General Assembly, to hold an International Conference on Fisheries in 1993.

[18]A/CONF.151/26, Vol. II, ch. 9: Protection of Atmosphere, para. 9.5.
[19]A/CONF.151/26, Vol. II, ch. 14: Program Area (1), and ch. 17: Program Area (e).

Financial Arrangements and Transfer of Technology

The Argentine delegates participated actively in the discussions on financial arrangements and transfer of technology within the G-77. Once a common negotiation position had been determined, Argentina left the substantive negotiations that were carried out by the G-77 itself, then presided over by the Pakistani delegate. Argentina opted for a moderate and realistic approach throughout the negotiations. Although it recognized the disparate responsibility of developing and developed countries in the areas of technology transfer and international finance within the framework of a "new partnershi for development," Argentina sought to avoid the radicalization of demands and the adoption of a confrontational stance by the G-77, which might have endangered the conclusion of a substantive agreement in these two crucial issues.[20] Argentina and Brazil put forth a set of proposals at PrepCom III. This document contained a number of alternative funding proposals to finance Agenda 21.

In the area of technology transfer, Argentina strongly advocated the adoption of new mechanisms of association whereby host countries would benefit from the transfer of environmentally sound technologies while preserving the property rights of patent holders. This position stemmed from an increasing awareness that the bulk of technology transfer in the future is likely to take place through private channels. This requires a basic regulatory framework aimed at safeguarding the intellectual property rights of technology suppliers.

Institutional Arrangements

Through the G-77, Argentina actively participated in the ongoing discussions on the restructuring of the UN's social and economic system.[21] From the outset, Argentine delegates were opposed to the creation of new agencies wherever possible, and the duplication of activities among UN agencies and programs in an effort to enhance overall effectiveness. This position was maintained in the discussions on institutional arrangements in the UNCED process.

A working proposal was initially discussed before PrepCom IV, in a number of meetings between the permanent missions of G-77 countries in New York. The aim of these meetings was to build a consensus on a single negotiating position within the G-77. They resulted in a preliminary agreement to let the ECOSOC coordinate the activities during UNCED, while reserving the substantive negotiation for the General Assembly. If adopted, this arrangement would have made it unnecessary to create a new agency to handle the discussions on behalf of the G-77.

Yet this preliminary agreement forged through lengthy negotiations between the Permanent Missions to the UN was later changed by several G-77 members, following the arrival of new delegations to PrepCom IV. A number of delegations that had previously subscribed to the original G-77 proposal changed their position dramatically, and began to urge the creation of an autonomous organization to follow up the UNCED process. Had this proposal been approved, the mandates of the ECOSOC and the General Assembly would have been subsumed under the terms of reference

[20]For an in-depth analysis of this question, see Carlos, Escude, *Realismo Periferico*, Planeta Política y Sociedad, Buenos Aires, 1992.

[21]UN General Assembly Resolutions 45/264 and 46/235.

of this new organization. During PrepCom IV, moreover, the intense lobbying efforts of NGOs based in developed countries succeeded in persuading a number of developed countries of the need to set up a new organization vested with a specific mandate to follow up the implementation of Agenda 21.

As a result, the previous consensus broke down, stripping the G-77 of a common negotiation stance at both PrepCom IV and the Rio Summit. Faced with this situation, Argentina and other countries tried to mobilize support behind an alternative proposal to place the question of "sustainable development" under the responsibility of a Third Seasonal Committee of the ECOSOC. After lengthy negotiations, it was finally decided that the follow-up of the Rio Conference would be entrusted to an ECOSOC functional committee, called the Commission on Sustainable Development.[22] This arrangement, which retained the ECOSOC's paramount role in dealing with economic issues, blocked the efforts of developed countries to have the economic growth and development agenda subsumed under the environmental agenda within the UN system. The specification of the terms of reference of the Commission on Sustainable Development was left to be determined at the 47th UN General Assembly.

NEGOTIATION BLOCS

In the joint decision-making processes of international negotiation, countries normally seek to enter into tactical alliances to enhance their negotiation power so as to further their own agenda. With the exception of Japan, the United States[23] and the Eastern European nations,[24] the bulk of countries at UNCED expected to increase their leverage at the negotiation table by parking in broad negotiation blocs, rather than articulating their positions independently, Argentina's main negotiation blocs in the UNCED process were the G-77 and smaller regional groups.

The Group of 77 is one of the main negotiation blocs operating within the UN system. A typical feature of the G-77 decision-making process is that every policy issue brought to the Group is decided by consensus after long and cumbersome negotiations among its members. Only those issues on which a substantive agreement is achieved are then expressed formally as the position of the G-77 as a whole. This mechanism, known as the "rule of consensus," is conducive to moderate demands, since the most extreme positions usually lose their edge during the consensus-building process prior to actual negotiations.

However, decision making by consensus represents both a strength and a major weakness of the G-77, since the opposition of a single member suffices to bring the whole decision-making process into disarray and prevents the adoption of a common position in multilateral negotiations. Bereft of consensus, the G-77 abstains from articulating an official position. In such cases, member countries normally

[22]A/CONF.151/26, Vol. III, ch. 38.

[23]Although both the United States and Japan belong to the OECD and other intergovernmental organizations, the latter did not function as a single bargaining bloc within the UN system.

[24]So far, the Eastern European countries have not established any mechanism, whether regional or functional, to articulate their position in international fora. Being "economies in transition," they are faced with a stark dilemma: they are neither "developing" economies, nor do their structural problems allow them to be considered as "developed" countries.

search for alternative alliances to articulate and support their position at the negotiation table.

These constraints notwithstanding, the G-77 played a crucial role during the Rio negotiations. In the first place, the chairman of the G-77 coordinated the positions of key actors during the internal decision-making process prior to the Rio Summit and provided leadership to build a consensus around a common negotiation position. Pakistan's capable leadership during PrepCom IV and UNCED enabled the G-77 to play a central role in key negotiations, such as those involving technology transfer and financial issues.

Secondly, the existence of widespread consensus allowed the G-77 to adopt a common position in most issues under consideration. As a result, the G-77 could mitigate the dearth of human and material resources in numerous developing country delegations. A G-77 member could informally turn over its representation to the Pakistani delegate or a designated spokesman to negotiate on its behalf, whenever there was consensus on an issue or when a direct presence in the negotiations was out of reach. This simple mechanism contributed to a heightened presence of the developing world in the definition of the substance of Agenda 21.

On the other hand, the lack of consensus in the G-77 on a few key issues forced the Argentine delegates to search for alternative channels to articulate the country's position at the negotiation table. Other interest blocs, such as the Cairns Group, offered Argentina a more effective conduit to press for concrete demands in the multilateral negotiations on trade and rural subsidies than was the case with either the G-77 or through direct negotiations.

The GRULAC, the Rio Group,[25] and MERCOSUR[26] were Argentina's three main reference groups at the regional level. Each of them was instrumental at various stages of the negotiations, as the Argentine delegates sought their active support to articulate their position more forcefully, whether within the G-77 or in direct negotiations with developed countries. However, time and resource constraints militated against a strong presence of these groups at the final and decisive stages of the Rio Conference, depriving them of the chance to play a more effective role on behalf of the Latin American countries.

THE ROLE OF NGOS

From the outset of the UNCED process, the Argentine government displayed a genuine commitment to fostering the broadest possible debate on environmental questions in Argentine society. All relevant sectors were strongly encouraged to participate in discussions with public officials of the CONAPA, the secretariat of Natural Resources and Human Environment, as well as the Environment Unit of the Ministry of Foreign Affairs.

Active participation of NGOs in the Argentine delegation was encouraged as well. In fact, numerous NGO spokespersons were invited to serve as advisers in the Argentine official delegation to the UNCED negotiations. As much as 70 per cent of

[25]The Rio Group is a regional policy coordination body among Latin American countries. Its members are: Argentina, Brazil, Bolivia, Colombia, Chile, Ecuador, Honduras, Mexico, Paraguay, Uruguay, and Venezuela. Peru's membershi is suspended.

[26]Regional economic integration process formed by Argentina, Brazil, Paraguay, and Uruguay (Mercado Común del Sur (Common Market of the South).

the Argentine delegation of roughly 200 members was thus accounted for by NGO representatives.

Daily meetings, in which the NGO representatives were briefed by the official delegates about the course of the negotiations, were held every morning during the Rio Conference. These meetings also provided an effective conduit for the exchange of information and suggestions between the official delegation and the NGOs. These initiatives were so successful that several Argentine NGOs would later praise the whole UNCED process as exemplary for the absolute transparency displayed by the Argentine authorities.

CONCLUSION

The Rio Conference opened up a process of multilateral negotiation on a new agenda for development. Following the Rio Summit, the discussions were followed through at the 47th UN General Assembly, the ECOSOC, and the Commission on Sustainable Development.

From the point of view of a developing country, the UNCED process highlighted the willingness of the international community to hold a serious political dialogue on a new development agenda, which takes environmental criteria into account. Rather than limiting the growth prospects of the developing world, the adoption of the concept of "sustainability" offers the potential for a more rational utilization of available resources worldwide. The realization of this potential along the process of sustainable development will translate itself into a higher standard of living for this and future generations.

UNCED and its aftermath point to the consequences of a domestic decision-making process lacking in a clear administrative and political definition of responsibilities within the negotiating team. Such definition must be clearly spelled out in advance, so as to avoid the ambiguities, jurisdictional conflict, and bureaucratic struggles that prevented the Argentine delegation from playing as effective a role as it might have played otherwise. In spite of these problems, the Argentine delegation succeeded in having most of the country's positions included in the UNCED agenda.

Another important lesson of the UNCED process refers to the central role played by intergovernmental and supranational actors in a complex process of international negotiation. For the developing countries as a whole, the G-77 proved to be an efficient vehicle for articulating their demands at the negotiation table. Under Pakistan's capable leadership, the G-77 was able to perform a brilliant task throughout the negotiations, both by coordinating the positions of key member countries and by making u for the paucity of resources in numerous country delegations.

Finally, by opening up new channels of communication between the government and society at large, the UNCED process may have set an important precedent for the future conduct of Argentina's foreign policy, whose consequences may extend well beyond the specific outcomes of UNCED itself.

9

Dynamics of Leadership in UNCED

Lance N. Antrim

In diplomatic terms, UNCED was a substantial success, producing agreement on the principles guiding the balance between environment and development, a 700-page program of global, regional, and national action, a start on a global convention on forests, and the signing of conventions on the global climate and on the conservation of biological diversity. This success grew out of many contributions – substantive contributions from expert groups, support from countries, public pressure, and contributions by diplomats to the text of compromise agreements. Together, however, all of these elements only contributed to the complicity of the process, and each of these was not enough individually to yield success. The complexity had to be managed and the individual components had to be harnessed to work together in a common effort for a common goal; leadership was the linchpin for this success. At UNCED, this leadership was found in three areas: inspiration, substance, and process. Leaders in these three areas, working together in the complex dynamics of conference diplomacy, were instrumental in achieving positive negotiation outcomes.

UNCED was a dynamic activity that progressed through phases in which the focus of the negotiators changed from the definition of issues under debate, through the structuring of agreements, to the negotiation of the details of the final documents. The negotiators constantly evolved their strategies and tactics in response to new events and to information and actions of other parties. Progress through the phases of negotiation was not inevitable, nor was the pace of progress necessarily sufficient to achieve a timely agreement. Good leadership at critical moments served to overcome major obstacles.

The role of leadership in UNCED's success can best be examined in comparison with the conventional role of leadership in diplomatic conferences. This role is illustrated below in the procedures and practices applied in conferences in general, and in the first UN Conference on the Environment and the UN Conference on the Law of the Sea in particular. Within that framework, the adaptation and innovation of leadership roles in UNCED becomes clear, leading to conclusions that may improve the chances of success in other large and complex multilateral negotiations.

Negotiating International Regimes: Lessons Learned from the United Nations Conference on Environment and Development (G. Sjöstedt, *et al.*, eds.; 1-85966-077-0; © IIASA; pub. Graham & Trotman, 1994; printed in Great Britain), pp. 149–163.

CONFERENCE LEADERSHIP IN THEORY AND PRACTICE

Modern multilateral negotiations have been convened since the Congress of Vienna, and over time processes and procedures have been developed to support leaders in these activities. Leadership may be exercised by many parties in a conference: conference officers in both formal and informal settings; conference secretariats in support of the work of the conference; and by governments in explaining positions, putting forward proposals, and making compromises that lead to mutually acceptable agreements. Leadership by officers and by the secretariat can contribute to success, but the commitment of the participating countries is essential. Without a political will on the part of countries, efforts by officers and secretariats cannot succeed. The focus of this chapter, and the following chapter by Ambassador Koh, concerns primarily the leadership of particular key personalities: the Conference chairman, the Secretary General, the working group chairpersons. The leadership of nations and coalitions, the principal actors in negotiation, is referred to here, but is discussed at length in Chapters 5, 7, 8, and 12.

General Nature of Conference Leadership

Leadership in different forms may be exercised by different individuals and groups. There is considerable flexibility in roles, so that strengths in one area may offset weaknesses in another. Key leadership positions include presiding officers, secretariats, heads of national delegations, and representatives of regional and interest groups.

Presiding Officers

Presiding officers are responsible for managing the negotiating processes of a conference. An experienced conference chair, Ambassador W. Lang of Austria, has provided some guidelines for effective leadership by presiding officers of conferences and negotiating groups (Lang, 1989:37–8). The chair of a conference or negotiating group is responsible for the management of the formal procedures: opening the meeting, recognizing speakers and maintaining the speakers list, interpreting the rules, etc. Lang also notes that a chair has an orchestrating role beyond that of managing the formal processes. As the senior officer responsible for the negotiating process, the chair must also manage the informal processes, in order to push the negotiations toward agreement. To this end, a chair should have the following attributes:

(1) creativity and innovativeness, provided that the ideas do not go too far beyond what has been called the permissive consensus of the participants;
(2) constant awareness of the mood prevailing among key actors, seeking the advice of key delegations, particularly with regard to significant procedural and substantive decisions;

(3) exercise of "preventive guidance," that is, be aware of delegations that may impede progress and, if appropriate, include them in the formal or informal circles of decision making;
(4) availability to participants in the negotiations, both in public and private;
(5) capability to separate issues into separate channels, oversee their debate, and recombine the results into a single process;
(6) recognition of critical moments of the negotiations, particularly in terms of submission of chairman's drafts, and in the imposition of time limits and target dates for the group's work.

Secretariat

Secretariats have important roles in multilateral conferences. One role is in providing support to the elected leadership by handling all the details of conference management, such as providing translation services, arranging rooms for meetings, and disseminating documents. In some cases, a secretariat may take on a substantive leadership role by conducting research and preparing conference documents that discuss issues facing the negotiators, and summarizing the current state of understanding and the history of national and international actions on those issues. Sometimes, a secretariat may even be asked to prepare recommendations for debate by national delegations.

Group and National Leaders

Countries, individually and organized in regional and interest groups, are the principal parties in a diplomatic conference. A conference is convened by countries, and it is they that must accept or reject the results of the negotiation. Generally, as the conveners of a conference, a country, or group of countries, is expected to provide the inspiration for a conference that goes beyond national interests to a compromise that reflects the interests of all.

Countries may exert substantive leadership by determining the goals of a negotiation, submitting proposals for debate, accepting or rejecting proposals of the presiding officers and secretariat, and, finally, adopting or rejecting agreements. Countries may lead by clearly defining issues, interests, and proposals for response by other countries.

A country or group may also take on leadership in procedural roles by acting as a mediator, attempting to bridge differences among parties, or supporting the conference leadership in decisions that pressure the recalcitrant parties to move toward agreement.

Forms of Leadership Leadership in diplomatic conferences comes in three forms: inspirational, procedural, and substantive. Inspirational leadership can be expressed as support for the goals of the conference and a commitment to the overall process. Procedural leadership is expressed in the management of the negotiating process. Substantive leadership is expressed in the identification and promotion of responses to the substantive issues assigned to the conference.

All three forms of leadership are found in the UNCED negotiations. The balance among the forms changed over the two and a half years between the passage of the founding resolution and the completion of the conference, reflecting the relationship between the phases of negotiation and the readiness of the countries, the elected leaders, and the secretariat to contribute to the negotiations.

Stockholm, 1972

The 1972 UN Conference on the Human Environment began as an initiative of developed countries: Sweden made a proposal for the conference in the UN General Assembly; and the United States gave strong support, with other countries providing additional support or at least acquiescing to it. The support of the United States and of Sweden provided inspirational leadership and maintained a political will, at least among the industrialized countries, for agreement. The secretariat provided additional inspirational leadership by encouraging the involvement of respected non-governmental organizations and individuals. These NGOs worked directly with governments, and indirectly through the media, to promote the importance of the conference at high levels of national government, contributing to the national political will to reach agreement.

With the political commitment of major industrialized countries, and the behind-the-scenes work of the secretariat to encourage the participation by developing countries and avoid disruptions due to East–West disputes that threatened the conference, the role of the conference officers diminished in importance. Presiding officers maintained the procedural aspects of the negotiation, but governmental proposals and secretariat-sponsored (or secretariat-encouraged) inter-sessional activities provided the substantive leadership that led to the final agreement.

Law of the Sea

In contrast to the Stockholm Conference, the conference officers in the Law of the Sea Conference provided leadership critical to the success of the conference. The Bureau of the Conference (the president of the conference, the vice presidents, and the chairs of the negotiating groups) were responsible for all major procedural decisions, and national delegations (individually and in groups) provided the major substantive leadership through the submission of proposals and contributions of technical experts. The importance of the issues facing the conference ensured a strong political will to reach agreement, at least until the final months when political changes in the United States diminished its commitment to completing the agreement. National political will, assisted by strong procedural leadership by conference officers and substantive leadership by governments, maintained progress over the ten years of negotiation and achieved a final agreement that is largely accepted by all countries as a statement of current customary international law even before it has officially entered into force.

LEADERSHIP IN UNCED

UNCED was the most complex diplomatic conference the UN has yet attempted. With its large participation, multiplicity of issues, numerous interrelationships, and diversity of national interests, there was concern that the negotiators would be able to achieve little beyond rhetoric and photo opportunities. The most significant impediments facing the UNCED negotiations were:

(1) *Too many issues and too little time.* In-depth negotiation of substantive agreements was impossible. There were only 16 weeks formally set aside for negotiation of these issues.
(2) *Political agendas beyond the issues contained in the founding resolution.* Issues of technology transfer and financing of development had long histories of negotiation in other fora of the UN system.
(3) *Competition for attention and resources from other negotiations.* Parallel negotiations on binding conventions on climate change and biological diversity required commitments of skilled diplomats and technical experts, drawing down the personnel resources available to UNCED, particularly in smaller developing countries.
(4) *Limited commitment by major governments.* As laudable as were the goals expressed in Resolution 44/228, national governments were not particularly supportive of UNCED. During the preparations, UNCED was overshadowed by other world events (e.g., the invasion of Kuwait, the coup, and breakup of the Soviet Union, and economic stagnation) that competed for attention in national governments, particularly among the industrialized countries.

There were several points that favored the UNCED negotiations:

(1) *Visibility.* As the 20th anniversary celebration of the Stockholm Conference, UNCED would attract some public attention. The potential for a large number of heads of state and government meant that the negotiations could not be delayed or gutted without adverse public attention on the national leaders.
(2) *Skilled procedural leadership.* Ambassador Koh, with long experience in the UN, had proven his ability to manage a large, complex, multi-issue conference as president of the UN Conference on the Law of the Sea.
(3) *Skilled substantive leadership.* Maurice Strong had demonstrated the capability to organize a global conference and to coordinate substantive contributions from governments, intergovernmental organizations, nongovernmental groups, and individual experts.

In spite of the obvious importance of the issues that were to be discussed, UNCED is notable for a lower national commitment to the negotiations than was the case in either the Stockholm Conference or the Law of the Sea Conference. This limited national commitment can be shown by the decision of the conference to avoid any intersessional sessions and the reliance upon the secretariat for the preparation of most substantive documentation for the conference, particularly in the first half of the preparatory process. The limited national political commitment to the conference required that national leadership be supplemented by procedural leadership from the conference officers and substantive leadership from the secretariat. Most important, however, was the combined efforts of many groups to provide inspirational leadership to promote the development of political will to reach a meaningful agreement.

Inspirational Leadership

The guiding inspiration for UNCED was provided by the World Commission on Environment and Development (known as the "Brundtland Commission"), which promoted the concept of sustainable development as the philosophy for the management of the world's resources. However, the commission, having submitted its report to the UN in 1987, was not available to provide continuing inspirational leadership during the preparations for UNCED. In its place, the Secretary General of UNCED, Maurice Strong, attempted to fill this role. Strong, a former member of the Brundtland Commission, presented the concept of sustainable development to the PrepCom and emphasized the importance of having UNCED implement it in an effective program of action both to the members of the PrepCom and to leaders throughout the world. Strong's role as the principal advocate of UNCED continued through most of the preparatory process. It was only after the fourth and final session of the PrepCom in the spring of 1992 that the role of conference advocate was taken up by many heads of state and by important members of the world media. Even then, Strong remained an important leader in publicly supporting of the success of UNCED.

In the final stage of UNCED, the inspirational role was indeed taken by the heads of state in the summit segment of the conference. Limited to speeches of five minutes, their leadership was not only conveyed in statements, but also through their delegations, which became more determined to gain a substantive rather than a superficial success. Thus, the inspirational leadership of the heads of state added pressure that increased opportunities for the leaders of the negotiation process.

Inspirational leadership may be provided from many sources: the 'champion' among the sponsoring countries, the head of the secretariat or of the conference leadership, the head of a sponsoring agency, or even parties outside the process. While such a leadership role cannot be forced upon any party, it is an important contributor to any negotiation that hopes to go beyond the current state of affairs and create a new order, be it for environment, security, economics, health, or any other area that must be addressed in the international arena.

Procedural Leadership

The UN secretariat provided the initial leadership on the procedural aspects of UNCED. The organizational session of the PrepCom was scheduled for March of 1990. In preparation for this session, the secretariat staff prepared recommendations for the procedural matters that would guide the work of the PrepCom. Among the proposals was one for the structure of the committee, which specified three working groups divided among global, regional, and national issues, plus a group to address legal and institutional matters. The UN Secretary General appointed Maurice Strong as the Secretary General for the conference.

At the opening of the session, the committee elected Ambassador Tommy T.B. Koh as its chairman. Koh and Strong shared the responsibility for procedural leadership during the organizational session, a sharing that was sometimes smooth and sometimes rough. One particular case demonstrated that the responsibility for procedural leadership would be exercised ultimately by the conference officers. As the organizational session came to its final scheduled day, Chairman Koh directed that the committee would work on until it completed its work on the last scheduled day of the meeting. Strong, anticipating that the committee would break and continue its work on the next day, did not arrange for extended hours for interpreters and scheduled meeting facilities and interpretation for the following day. In accordance with his plans, however, Koh kept the committee in session, even after the departure of the interpreters.

Conference Officers and Group Leaders

The principal responsibility for procedural leadership in a diplomatic conference generally rests with the Bureau, which consists of the elected officers of the conference. However, at the organizational session, the PrepCom decided to elect a total of 39 vice chairmen, which would make an extremely unwieldy decision-making body. In order to obtain more effective advice, Koh established his own smaller leadership group. This group, which consisted of the chairmen of the working groups and the leaders of the major regional and interest groups, met frequently to advise Koh on the management of the committee, including such matters as the scheduling of meetings and decisions, creation of special groups, and other procedural matters. In turn, these leaders were responsible for building support within their groups for the decisions made as a result of their advice in the leadership group.

Leadership Structure and Dynamics

As agreed during the organizational session, two working groups were established at the first substantive session in Nairobi. Seven environmental topics were divided among the groups as shown below:

Working Group I	*Working Group II*
Atmosphere and climate	Protection of the Oceans
Desertification, Deforestation and Soil Loss	Hazardous Wastes
Biodiversity	Protection of Freshwater Resources
Biotechnology	

The PrepCom elected Ambassador Bo Kjellen (Sweden) to chair Working Group I and Ambassador Bukar Shaib (Nigeria) as chair of Working Group II.

The activity of the working groups dominated the middle portion of the Nairobi session. The work of each group was structured to begin with a formal session to review the individual issues. After the issues were aired in the formal sessions, the chairmen would draft decisions on each topic for consideration by the group. The groups would then convene in informal session to review the draft decisions. After the decisions were revised and appeared to have consensus support, the groups would convene in formal session to approve the decisions and forward them to the Plenary for adoption.

In practice, there were marked differences between the two working groups. While some of the differences resulted from the subject matter, some important differences resulted directly from the working styles of the chairmen.

Related to the subject matter, the issues assigned to Working Group I were, for the most part, the subjects of years of work in other *fora*. As a result, many participants were knowledgeable regarding the topics and could deal with them with some substantive competence and relate the work of the group to the work of other negotiations on environment and development. However, due to the national positions taken in those other fora, the delegates were limited in their ability to explore alternative approaches or to compromise on their opening positions. By contrast, the issues in Working Group II were collections of national, regional, and global topics that had not been addressed before in a comprehensive fashion. This gave the Working Group II negotiators more flexibility, but it also meant that there was a less solid substantive base for the negotiations. As a result, the Working Group II debates tended to include more political and ideological overtones than did those of Working Group I.

The stylistic differences of the working groups were readily apparent. Ambassador Kjellen (Working Group I) adopted the style of a mediator, while Ambassador Shaib (Working Group II) was a moderator. During the initial formal sessions, Kjellen was more interactive, often questioning a speaker to better understand the stated position. Shaib ran his group more as a sequence of national presentations for which he maintained order and a schedule, but where he kept a low personal profile. This difference in style was a major factor that allowed Working Group II to complete the formal session a day in advance of Working Group I.

After the formal sessions of the working groups were complete, the PrepCom convened in Plenary for a mid-session progress report, while the working group chairs retired to draft decisions based on the results of the formal sessions. The working groups then reconvened in informal session for consultations on the draft decisions. The effects of the stylistic differences of the chairmen became more apparent during this process. Kjellen's drafts drew more specific comments and criticism than did Shaib's, focusing the disagreements more clearly. Kjellen addressed the disagreements through a series of chairman's drafts that combined comments of the working group with his own contributions. The debate during the consultations took the form of delegates attempting to explain their positions to the chairman in order to convince him that their views should be incorporated into the revised text.

In Working Group II, Shaib would listen to opposing views and, if a compromise were not apparent, would incorporate the different positions into the text as alternative bracketed language. Stating a position forcefully and without a move to compromise was sufficient to have a position recorded in a subsequent draft, so that there was little incentive to compromise until late in the session. As the closing date of the Nairobi session loomed, pressure from conference leaders increased, and the working group sessions lasted into the early morning as they worked to complete action on all of its agenda items.

Leadership and the Dynamics of Negotiation

Leaders in negotiation must be aware of the dynamics of a conference and use them to advantage. Two aspects of a case from UNCED illustrate the relationship between conference dynamics and leadership actions.

At the conclusion of the third PrepCom session, Working Group III had conducted serious debate over the content of the Declaration on Environment and Development. The negotiations were making the transition from diagnosis to formula, but many were not prepared to compromise on the details of the declaration. When the PrepCom reconvened in New York, the chairman of Working Group III,

Bedrich Moldan, decided to push the group forward. He prepared a chairman's draft proposal that he viewed as a possible compromise, and that he believed could serve as the basis for negotiation and the development of an agreed text. Unfortunately, neither North nor South were prepared to abandon their positions. Worse, each side, and particularly the South, viewed the proposed draft as leaning too much to the opposing side. In making the proposal, Moldan lost the confidence of some of the parties in his neutrality. As a result, not only did the countries fail to move ahead, but they expressed their discomfort with continuing the negotiations under Moldan's leadership. As a result, Chairman Koh established an informal group to continue the discussions.

The informal group continued debate throughout the session. Although little substantive progress was made, the parties became more aware of each other's interests and concerns. Over the session, it became clear that no party had a chance of winning the others over to its position and that a compromise was needed. In the final week of the session, the co-chairmen of the informal group came to Chairman Koh and asked that he take over the negotiation for the declaration.

Koh recognized that the time was ripe for reaching agreement, but that the concessions that were needed from all parties could not be discussed in an open forum. Nor did he believe that the negotiations could be concluded in the remaining time unless the group was limited in size. With the agreement of the informal group, Koh took on the task of chairing the negotiation of a compromise text. Before starting, he obtained agreement on several points. First, the group would be limited to 16 countries, which would be selected as representatives of regional and interest groups and would be expected to represent the groups' interests and to explain and defend the compromises reached in the negotiations within their groups. Koh began the negotiations based on a negotiating text prepared by the co-chairmen on the evening of 1 April. After meeting until midnight, and reconvening the next morning, Koh was able to produce an agreed text by 6:15 p.m. this same day.

Koh's work was not over with the agreement of the small group. Koh and members of the group had to convince all of the delegations to accept the agreement. At 3 a.m. during the final session, Koh introduced the proposed text of the Declaration on Environment and Development to the Plenary, emphasizing that the text was a package deal that represented the best that could be obtained and that any party that opposed it or tried to modify it would cause it to unravel and would be responsible for the failure of the PrepCom to achieve agreement on this key document. After apologizing to all countries excluded from the small group, and particularly to four countries not part of any of the regional and interest groups represented in it, Koh asked for permission to adopt the Declaration. In spite of a threat of opposition from Israel, Koh ruled the text as adopted and sent it forward to Rio, where it was adopted by UNCED.

The lesson of this case is the importance of timing and trust. Moldan's effort to prepare a compromise text failed, not because of the substance of his proposal, but because the parties did not yet believe that they could not achieve more of their objectives by continuing the negotiations. In contrast, as the deadline loomed in the final week of PrepCom IV, the delegations were unwilling to bear the onus of failing to reach agreement, and to avoid this they were willing to grant Koh unusual authority and trust him to produce an agreement that would equitably share the burden of concessions while satisfying the essential interests of all parties.

Substantive Leadership

There were many sources of substantive information relevant to UNCED. Standing intergovernmental organizations (e.g., UN Environment Programme, the Food and Agriculture Organization, and the World Meteorological Organization) conducted research and printed reports on aspects of the UNCED agenda. Preparations for regional meetings of governments brought UNCED to the attention of national bureaucracies and leaders. The first such meeting, convened by the Economic Commission for Europe, brought UNCED's issues to the attention of the leaders of the industrialized world. However, as the UNCED PrepCom got underway, there was little organization to the complex mass of available information. In response, the conference secretariat moved in to provide leadership in this area.

Governments had little investment in or commitment to the UNCED preparations during the early PrepCom process. The first substantive session (Nairobi, 1990) was devoted almost exclusively to the definition of tasks for the secretariat. These tasks were largely investigatory, and the secretariat was expected to report back to the PrepCom in March 1991, the second session.

The secretariat established a process for responding to the directions of the committee on matters of substance. A number of working parties were convened, each comprised of experts from UN agencies and other organizations. Contributions by the experts were funneled through the working parties before being redrafted by the secretariat for distribution to the PrepCom. Following a process similar to the Stockholm Conference, all reports were submitted through the conference secretariat for distribution as official documents rather than distributed directly by UN agencies.

At the conclusion of the second PrepCom, the secretariat was asked to continue its work in preparing background material. It was also asked to prepare its recommendations for elements of Agenda 21 for consideration at PrepCom III. This marked the high point of secretariat leadership in the substance of the negotiations.

The changes in leadership roles through the course of the preparatory negotiations were, in part, a reflection of the progress made during and between negotiating sessions, as the negotiations progressed from diagnosis, through formula development, and on to the details of the agreement. Although the PrepCom negotiations were restricted to the four substantive sessions, the work of supporting the PrepCom continued between the sessions. The preparations were undertaken in several ways: secretariat information, regional consultation, expert meetings, and national reports.

Secretariat Information

As a result of requests for information that emerged from the first and second substantive sessions of the PrepCom, the UNCED secretariat was charged with the preparation of many reports on a variety of topics. To prepare these reports, the secretariat convened working parties that drew upon the expertise of UN agencies, supplemented by other experts. Drafts were often prepared by the parties, but the secretariat retained the final authority to modify the reports as necessary to meet their interpretation of the PrepCom requests.

The preparation of reports through an interagency committee structure was a time-consuming process. This was exacerbated by the need to provide translation of the reports – almost exclusively in English – into the other five official UN languages. These factors combined to delay the distribution of documents until just before the opening of the second and third sessions of the PrepCom (and, in some cases, documents in the other languages were not available until late in the session – if they were available at all). The effect of these delays on delegations was uneven since the reports were sometimes available to countries that were well connected to the agencies and experts who contributed to their preparation. Thus, while some delegations were able to review the secretariat reports with their governments in advance of PrepComs II and III, others did not even have copies of the translated reports in their hands until late in the sessions. This had a direct impact on the slow pace of the negotiations.

Regional Consultations

Regional meetings on UNCED were organized by the UN regional economic commissions. The first such consultation, conducted by the Economic Commission for Europe (including East and West Europe as well as North America), provided a model for further meetings. Subsequent consultations were held by the Economic Commission for Latin America and the Caribbean, the Economic Commission for Africa, and the Economic and Social Commission for Asia and the Pacific. The results of the meetings were reported to the PrepCom.

Expert Meetings

Meetings of groups of experts on topics related to UNCED were convened under the authority of UN agencies, national governments, and some nongovernmental groups, in coordination with the UNCED secretariat. Meetings of topics included: forest management, protection of freshwater supplies, reduction of land-based sources of pollution, energy and the environment, science and development, sustainable agriculture, and other topics related to the UNCED agenda. The results of these sessions were presented either in official reports of the PrepCom (such as the report on the Halifax meeting on land-based sources of pollution) or in statements and reports provided by the hosts of the meetings.

Other meetings sponsored in coordination with the UNCED secretariat included a symposium on the relationship between the environment and the health and welfare of women and children and the Second World Industry Conference on Environment Management. Secretariat members participated in meetings such as this, both to help direct the conferences toward the issues facing UNCED and to gather information to be incorporated into the secretariat reports and proposals for the PrepCom. In addition, some of the papers presented at these meetings, and at similar meetings on other topics, were reproduced by the secretariat and distributed to delegations as unofficial documents.

National Reports

Following the precedent established by the Stockholm Conference, UNCED's founding resolution invited all states to submit national reports on environment to the PrepCom. The secretariat prepared guidelines for the reports and encouraged governments to submit them before the third session of the committee. A number of reports were submitted at that session, more arrived at the fourth session, and several were submitted at the conference itself.

The national reports had two purposes. First, they were to provide a catalog of national policies and programs related to the environment. Second, the preparation of the reports required internal bureaucratic structures to prepare and approve the reports, which had to be created if they did not already exist. The contribution of the national reports to the PrepCom process varied considerably from country to country. Small countries in particular may have offset the costs of preparing national reports through the allocation of limited personnel and financial resources away from other activities.

Other Sources of Support

Support for the UNCED process also came from other sources that were independent of national governments and international organizations. High-level advisers to the Secretary General, such as the leaders of the Business Council for Sustainable Development, provided advice and contributed information to the secretariat. Among the most effective supporters in the nongovernmental community were the private foundations that donated substantial sums to support the UNCED process. Some funding was funneled to a foundation established specifically to support participation by developing countries. Other funds were given directly to organizations seeking to influence specific environmental and developmental issues. The total sum of funds provided by private foundations is difficult to measure, but it was substantial, and could not help but influence the negotiation process.

National Role in Substantive Leadership

PrepCom III marked the beginning of the shift of leadership from the secretariat to the national delegations. In some areas, such as ocean issues, the leadership role shifted completely, while in others the secretariat remained a principal contributor. By PrepCom IV, however, the government delegations were firmly in control of the substance of the negotiations. During this session the countries took charge and addressed the entire 700-page draft of Agenda 21 paragraph by paragraph, resolving, by one estimate, 85 percent of the content.

ANALYSIS OF LEADERSHIP DYNAMICS

Leadership roles and forms evolved throughout the UNCED process. These changes were related to the progress of the negotiations through the phases of diagnosis, formula, and detail. They were also related to the efforts of the core of the conference leadership to advance the negotiations through the phases in time for the conference in Rio.

Inspirational Leadership

UNCED initially suffered from a lack of inspirational leadership. Most countries did not see the conference as critical to their national interests and did not promote the conference. In some cases, this resulted in assignment of negotiators responsible for general international relations rather than environment and development issues or negotiators with limited experience in conference diplomacy. In lieu of inspirational leadership, the conference Secretary General sought to develop situations that would pressure governments into making serious efforts to reach agreement. One effort was to ensure that the conference would have a high profile. This was accomplished through the promotion of a conference for nongovernmental organizations that would occur in parallel with UNCED, mirroring a similar arrangement in the Stockholm Conference. It was combined with efforts to build interest in the conference by major media outlets. The second effort was to obtain the commitments of heads of state and government to attend UNCED. Both efforts began to show signs of success by the third session of the PrepCom, during which the number of governmental leaders planning on attending began to grow, plans for the parallel conference and participation by NGOs showed significant advances, and the media began to observe and report on the work of the PrepCom.

A special feature of the UNCED negotiations was the anticipation that the full conference would include a segment attended by heads of state and government. This decision was stated in the founding resolution and confirmed in a resolution of the PrepCom at its first substantive session. Anticipation that the senior officials of the participating countries would take part in at least a segment of the conference pressured the participants to engage their senior officials in the preparations for the conference. Engagement of senior officials could slow the preparatory process by complicating domestic preparatory processes for the conference, but it could also raise the level of national commitment to the final outcome of the conference.

Inspirational leadership also had a dynamic nature, but remained throughout less apparent than the substantive and procedural aspects. After the General Assembly convened the PrepCom, there was little attention given to UNCED. Most nongovernmental organizations were focused on the negotiation of binding conventions on climate change and biological diversity. Governments viewed UNCED with caution, considering it likely to get overwhelmed by the North–South differences related to development issues. Intergovernmental leaders had little or no stake in UNCED, other than to be seen as supportive of the process. It fell to the UNCED Secretary General to attempt to provide inspirational leadership in the beginning stages of UNCED. Following the first preparatory session, Mr. Strong traveled around the world, contacting senior governmental officials and leaders of major private and public organizations to build a broad base of support for UNCED. By the third session of the PrepCom, public involvement in the process took on a greater role in inspirational leadership. Major environmental organizations had a substantial presence, and developing country NGOs began to attend in increasing numbers. The effect of these groups, however, was limited because they focused much of their effort on preparations for the activities to be held at the parallel NGO conference rather than the intergovernmental negotiations. Finally, with the preparations complete and the conference underway, the impending attendance of over 100 heads of state provided the inspiration to complete negotiations in time for the summit segment of the conference.

Substantive Leadership

The UN General Assembly adopted the resolution to convene UNCED almost two and a half years before the conference was due to open. It was difficult for national governments to focus their attention on an event that far in the future, so leadership on substantive matters began as the responsibility of the conference secretariat. Acceptance of this charge was confirmed in the first preparatory session, when the countries assigned the responsibility of preparing background reports to the secretariat. It grew in the second session with the request that the secretariat prepare draft recommendations for governments to consider. By the third session, though, the balance began to change as national experts took a greater role in the negotiations and the secretariat was pushed more into a supportive capacity. By the fourth preparatory session, the substantive leadership was clearly in the hands of government delegations.

Procedural Leadership

The dynamics of procedural leadership were somewhat different. In early sessions, leadership was mainly the responsibility of the chairman of the PrepCom, the heads of the two (later three) main working groups, and the leaders of the principal regional and interest groups who acted as friends of the chair, providing advice and helping to implement the decisions of the leadership within their own groups. As the negotiations proceeded to greater degrees of detail, the burden of managing the negotiating process also grew. Leadership was shared as issues were assigned to subsidiary bodies (e.g., contact groups and informal negotiating groups) in order to identify potential compromises for debate and adoption in the full sessions of the working groups and the Plenary.

For the most part, there was little activity between sessions, other than ad hoc personal contacts among delegates. A model that might have provided more continuous involvement is the structure of a major corporation into a board of directors and a chief executive. The board provides the policy leadership to guide the work of the executive. In turn, the executive assesses the resources, goals, and options, provides information to the board, and makes recommendations to the board. The executive provides continuous leadership while the board meets at intervals to provide midcourse corrections. In the conference context, this model would be most relevant when there are long intervals between conference sessions.

RECOMMENDATIONS

UNCED is concluded, but its effects will be felt for decades to come through the agenda set in Agenda 21, through the information gathered and disseminated, and through the awareness created about the interrelationship of environment and development. In its most direct form, the UNCED regime is seen and felt in the institutions established in response to Agenda 21.

The new institutions that take on the task of implementing Agenda 21 will need to continue the intergovernmental processes started in UNCED. The Commission for Sustainable Development, the Intergovernmental Negotiating Committee for a Framework Convention on Drought and Desertification, and other bodies will inherit a negotiating history, procedures, and expectations that will guide their work. An examination of the importance of leadership in UNCED helps identify characteristics needed for strong and effective leadership within these bodies and required for constructive evolution of reform:

(1) Foster inspirational leaders who can maintain commitment to the success of the overall negotiation by keeping common goals in sight of all parties.
(2) Be creative in developing resources for negotiation support by tapping outside sources of funds, fostering technical expertise to serve regional and interest groups, and working with nongovernmental organizations (both profit and non-profit) to expand the information available to the negotiators.
(3) Promote the commitment of national governments to the negotiations. Secretariats may fill leadership gaps, but cannot replace government representatives as conference leaders.
(4) Involve skilled diplomats, particularly from smaller states with limited interests at stake, who can serve as mediators, problem solvers, and chairs of groups. Multilateral negotiation is a special skill that should be respected and nurtured by national governments.
(5) Involve states early on substantive matters, particularly developing countries. Promote leadership by experts in early substantive discussions. Move states into leadership roles early in the negotiation process.
(6) Finally, increase involvement of elected leadership in managing the process between sessions and improve the linkage between elected and appointed officers. The leaders of a diplomatic conference must have leadership themselves. The bureau and friends of the chair provided this type of leadership for UNCED.

10

UNCED Leadership: A Personal Perspective

Tommy Thong-Bee Koh

In 1989, the UN General Assembly decided to convene the Earth Summit in 1992, 20 years after the Stockholm Conference on the Human Environment. The decision to convene the Earth Summit was contained in Resolution 44/228. The text contained in that resolution soon came to be regarded as sacred.

In order to prepare for the Earth Summit, the UN decided to set up a Preparatory Committee (PrepCom). Because of the great interest in the conference, the PrepCom was enormous in size; it consisted of all the member states of the UN as well as non-member states such as Switzerland. The size of the PrepCom made negotiation difficult, and one of my challenges was how to reduce the size of negotiating groups. I will return to this later.

The PrepCom was mandated to hold an organizational session in New York and four substantive sessions in Nairobi, Geneva, Geneva again, and New York in 1991 and 1992. You may wonder why the four substantive sessions were held in three different cities in three continents. Was this an example of the UN diplomats awarding themselves junkets at the expense of their taxpayers? It wasn't. It was an example of the kind of compromises that had to be struck in order to achieve consensus. The New York-based diplomats, who were the most politicized, wanted all the sessions to be held in New York. The Geneva-based diplomats argued that they should be held in Geneva, the home of the UNCED secretariat. The supporters of UNEP, which is based in Nairobi, argued that they should be held in Nairobi.

The organizational session of the PrepCom was two weeks long. It was held in New York from 5–6 March 1990 and had five objectives: to elect its chairman; to decide on the size of the Bureau and the distribution of the number agreed upon among the five regional groups; to decide how many working groups to establish and which regional groups would provide candidates for their chairmanship; to adopt a provisional agenda for the Earth Summit; to adopt its rules of procedure.

Any reasonable person would think that you would need only one or two days, not two weeks, to agree on five such seemingly simple tasks. However, this was not the case, and the two weeks were barely enough to complete our tasks. Of the five tasks, the only simple one was electing me. All the other candidates wisely withdrew when they realized the pain and suffering that the chairman would have to endure for the next two years and three months! The first thing I did on assuming the chair

Negotiating International Regimes: Lessons Learned from the United Nations Conference on Environment and Development (G. Sjöstedt, *et al.*, eds.; 1-85966-077-0; © IIASA; pub. Graham & Trotman, 1994; printed in Great Britain), pp. 165–169.

was to propose that we should refrain from polluting the air in our meeting rooms by prohibiting smoking at all our meetings. Before the nicotine addicts could rally their forces, I asked if there was any objection. Seeing none, I banged the gavel and pronounced that there was a consensus in favor of my proposal. The former Secretary General of the UN, Javier Perez de Cuellar, watched in surprise because no UN chairman had succeeded in defeating the tobacco lobby at the UN before.

The speed with which I used the gavel would give rise later to some unhappiness – and later, I would count to five before banging my gavel. On one occasion, the chairman of the Group of 77, a wonderful man from Pakistan, Ambassador Jamshid Marker, remarked that my counting of 1 to 5 became faster and faster, the longer the meeting lasted!

I failed, however, to persuade my colleagues to accept a relatively small Bureau. For a Bureau to be efficient, it has to be representative but small. Many delegations wanted to be in the Bureau because they thought that it might become a negotiating forum. In the end, I had to accept a Bureau of 42 members, which, in my view, is too large to be useful.

The PrepCom agreed to establish two working groups that would be chaired respectively by a West European and an African. There was, however, no agreement to establish a third working group to deal with questions relating to law and institutions. The third working group was ultimately established at the beginning of the second substantive session in Geneva. The most difficult task was drafting the agenda. Why? Because delegations feared that the wording of an agenda item could tilt the balance in favor of their adversaries.

On the last day of the organizational session, there was still no agreement on the agenda, and I was determined to get one. I instructed the secretariat to arrange for interpreters to be available so that I could work through the night until 6:00 a.m. the next morning. The secretariat did not believe that I meant this, and subsequently I had no interpreters after midnight. Thus I had to persuade the non-Anglophones to work in English. This was by no means an easy task, especially with the Francophone group.

My strategy was to maintain the pressure on the delegates until they agreed to compromise. By 4:30 a.m., the delegates were so exhausted that they asked me to draft a compromise. I called for a short recess and, with the help of about a dozen colleagues representing the various interest groups, succeeded in drafting a compromise. I got my agenda. The meeting adjourned at 6:00 a.m. on St. Patrick's Day. I felt exhausted, but vindicated in my determination not to adjourn the meeting until I secured an agreement. If I had adjourned the meeting, the pressure would have eased and delegations would again dig their heels in. I also wanted to make the point to delegates and the secretariat that when I set a deadline, I meant to keep it. The secretariat never doubted my resolve again. At all subsequent sessions of the PrepCom and the Main Committee, teams of interpreters were ready to serve the meeting through the night and into the morning of the next day on the final day of each session. On two subsequent occasions, we worked through the night: until 4:30 a.m. on the last day of the 4th substantive session in New York, and 6:00 a.m. on the last day of the Main Committee at the Earth Summit in Rio.

Managing a complex negotiating process requires both leadership and team work. I worked closely with the Secretary General of the conference, Maurice Strong, and the various members of the secretariat. Twenty years earlier, he was the Secretary General of the Stockholm Conference on the Human Environment, and I had worked closely with him in preparing for the Stockholm Conference. The fact that our friendship went back 20 years helped us to forge a good working partnership. I kept no secrets from him or his deputy, Mr. Nitin Desai.

I expanded the collective leadership or collegium to include the chairman of Working Group I, Ambassador Bo Kjellen of Sweden; the chairman of Working Group II, Dr. Bukar Shaib of Nigeria; the chairman of Working Group III, Dr. Bedrich Moldan of Czechoslovakia; and the Rapporteur, Mr. Ahmad Djoghlaf of Algeria. I institutionalized the collective management of the negotiating process by holding meetings every morning at 9:00 a.m. with this group and the senior members of the UNCED secretariat. This would be followed by a daily meeting at 9:30 a.m. with the representatives of all the UN agencies. The purpose of the second meeting was to bring all the members of the UN family together and to prevent turf fights and misunderstandings. It was also to tap the expertise and inputs of the various agencies.

The work of the PrepCom was carried out in four principal forums: the Plenary of the PrepCom and the three working groups. The agenda of the Plenary was long and complex. It included the difficult questions of financing sustainable development and the transfer of technology from developed to developing countries. It also included such questions as the relationship between the environment, on the one hand, and, poverty, population, the international economic order, and human settlements, on the other.

A good chairman must avoid the temptation of keeping everything under his wings, and must learn to delegate. He must also be capable of choosing able men and women to whom to delegate responsibility. When it becomes clear that a delegatee is unable to deliver, a chairman must do the very unpleasant job of replacing him with someone else.

At the second substantive session held in Geneva in the spring of 1991, I established a number of open-ended negotiating groups in the Plenary. I appointed Ambassador John Bell of Canada to chair the one on finance; Ambassador Bjorner Utheim of Norway to chair the one on technology; Deputy Foreign Minister John Muliro of Kenya to chair the one on the poverty–population–health cluster; Ambassador Enrique Penalosa of Colombia to chair the one on human settlements; and Mr. Ahmad Djoghlaf of Algeria to chair the one on the international economic order. I coopted the chairmen of the negotiating groups into the collegium.

At the fourth substantive session I replaced Ambassador John Bell with Deputy Foreign Minister Andres Rozental of Mexico, and at the Summit I replaced Rozental with Ambassador Ricupero of Brazil. Also at the Summit, I replaced Utheim with the Dutch Minister of the Environment, Mr. J.G.M. Alders. As one who attaches great value to loyalty and friendship, I have always found it very difficult to abandon a colleague. However, I felt duty-bound to put the best interests of the conference before friendship and loyalty. The fact that both Ricupero and Alders succeeded in their work showed that I was right to make the personnel changes.

The Bureau of a committee or conference is supposed to act as its steering committee, but the Bureau of the PrepCom and the Earth Summit was unable to play this role effectively because of its size: 42 members. It was almost as difficult to reach a consensus among the 42 members of the Bureau as among the 150-plus members of the PrepCom and the 170-plus members of the Summit. I had to invent another body to act as the steering committee.

I convened twice weekly meetings of a group consisting of the chairmen of the five regional groups: the chairman of the Group of 77 (representing the developing countries); the chairman of the EC; the chairman of the Nordic Group; the chairman of CANZ (representing Canada, Australia, and New Zealand); and the three countries that did not belong to any interest group: China, Japan, and the United States. This group of 12 countries and the collegium functioned as the steering committee of the PrepCom and Summit, and it proved to be a very effective body. During critical periods of the PrepCom and Summit, I would convene daily meetings of this group. In order to pacify the members of the Bureau, who quite rightly felt bypassed, I would from time to time convene meetings of the Bureau.

In negotiation, timing is very important. A chairman who acts prematurely risks being rebuffed. A chairman who acts too slowly loses the opportunity to clinch a deal. I have observed that multilateral negotiations often pass through three phases: confrontation, crisis; and resolution. A good chairman must not be unnerved by the phase of confrontation, and must wait for the period of crisis that often follows confrontation. It is at this hour of maximum danger and opportunity that he must strike and bring about a resolution.

Let me illustrate these general observations with the following concrete example. Working Group III, on law and institutions, was established at the beginning of the second substantive session in Geneva. It elected Dr. Bedrich Moldan of Czechoslovakia as its chairman. One of the items on its agenda was the drafting of the Rio Declaration on the Environment and Development, popularly referred to as the Earth Charter. At the beginning of the fourth substantive session, Dr. Moldan offered a compromise draft consisting of ten principles and three prerequisites. However, he moved too soon. Also, his draft was viewed, rightly or wrongly, by the developing countries as favoring the viewpoint of the developed countries. Because of this, the developing countries refused to continue to negotiate under his chairmanship. Instead, an informal contact group was established under the co-chairmanship of Mr. Mukul Sanwal of India and Mr. Ole Holthe of Norway.

On the morning of 31 March 1992, three days before the end of that session, Mr. Sanwal and Mr. Holthe asked for permission to speak to our daily meeting at 9:00 a.m. They reported that they had gone as far as they could and were unable to make any further progress, and requested me to take over the negotiations. The meeting supported their request. I then convened a meeting of the *de facto* steering committee. I said I would be prepared to chair the negotiation provided they agreed to establish a small, closed, representative group of 16: eight to represent the North and eight to represent the South. The meeting agreed to this. The North was represented by the United States; Portugal, the Netherlands, and Germany (EC); Australia (CANZ); Norway (alternating with Sweden); Japan and Russia. The South was represented by Pakistan, India, Iran, Brazil, Mexico, Nigeria, Tanzania, and China.

I then made another request. I requested that Mr. Sanwal and Mr. Holthe produce a negotiating text by 6:30 p.m. on 1 April 1992. They did so, and the group of 16 began its work that same evening; it adjourned before midnight and continued the next morning. A clean text, containing 27 principles, was agreed upon, ad referendum, at 6:15 p.m. on 2 April (A/CONF.151/PC/WGIII/L33/Rev.1). This text would eventually be adopted by the Earth Summit as the Rio Declaration on Environment and Development.

Apart from the clean text of the Rio Declaration, the other documents submitted to Rio contained 350 bracketed statements or instances of disputed words. We had only one week in the Main Committee to remove these brackets and to find acceptable language, and I was not at all sure that the job could be done.

I persuaded the Committee to adopt a number of procedural decisions. First, that the negotiation would focus entirely on the bracketed language – I ruled out of order any delegate who tried to reopen discussion on unbracketed or agreed language. I also rebuffed the attempts by several delegations to insert new brackets on the ground that they had been inadvertently omitted by the secretariat. Fortunately, we had brought along the authoritative documents of the PrepCom. Upon verification, we found no merit in any of the requests. Second, I refused to allow any delegation to make a new proposal if it met with a single objection. The reason for this is that any new proposal must advance the prospect of achieving consensus. Third, I asked the Committee to allow me to establish nine open-ended negotiating groups on the understanding that not more than three would meet concurrently. Fourth, I persuaded the Committee to work from Monday to Saturday and to meet morning, afternoon, and evening. Fifth, I imposed a strict time-limit on the length of statements. Sixth, whenever the negotiation got stuck on a point, I would set up an ad hoc open-ended negotiating group to deal with it and appoint an able colleague to chair the group. In this way, I was able to keep the negotiation moving at a steady pace.

The final meeting of the Main Committee began at 8:00 p.m. on 10 June 1992. It continued through the night and ended at 6:00 a.m. the next morning. I did take one short break, though. At 4:00 a.m., after eight hours in the chair, I was desperate to go to the toilet – I also sensed that there was a lot of tension in the room. I announced that we would recess the meeting for five minutes in order to enable me to make a discharge of non-toxic waste, and I promised to do it in an environmentally safe and sound manner. The delegates broke into laughter and the meeting resumed in a better mood. All bracketed language, excepting those words or statements relating to finance and forests, was resolved. Those two issues were referred to ministerial-level negotiations chaired by Brazil and Germany respectively and consensus was achieved on 12 June. The Summit was therefore able to adopt, on 14 June, the Rio Declaration, Agenda 21, and the Statement of Principles on Forests, by consensus. Thus ended the largest conference the UN has ever held. It was attended by 116 heads of state or government, 172 states, 8000 delegates, 9000 members of the press, and 3000 accredited representatives of nongovernmental organizations.

11

The Role of the Scientific Community in the Preparation of and Follow-Up to UNCED

Julia Marton-Lefèvre

Many of the issues on UNCED's agenda required scientific knowledge and expertise; and, not surprisingly, scientists performed important roles within the system of negotiations that comprised the UNCED process. Scientific organizations, for example, were called upon to provide crucial background information that helped the UNCED secretariat develop the conference's agenda and define the linkages between environmental and developmental issues. However, the UNCED negotiations were very traditional and firmly in the UN's mold: thus it was dominated more by the professional culture of UN administrators and diplomats than by the scientific community. In fact, Agenda 21 can be viewed as an instrument through which scientific knowledge was transformed into a uniquely UN frame of reference. On the other hand, the parallel negotiations to develop a framework agreement on climate change, as embodied in the Intergovernmental Panel on Climate Change (IPCC), were dominated by scientists and a scientific professional culture.

This chapter and the following one portray the differing roles that scientists played, and their relative influence on the UNCED process depending on their direct or indirect levels of participation. In this chapter, the formal role bestowed on the scientific community within the context of UNCED is described. Chapter 12 analyzes the impact of scientists on the climate change negotiations.

PREPARATIONS FOR UNCED

In September 1990, the International Council of Scientific Unions (ICSU) was invited by the Secretary General of UNCED to become the principal scientific adviser to the conference. ICSU immediately took up this challenge and informed its national members of the UNCED process, encouraging them to be involved in the national preparations for the Rio Conference and to ensure the inclusion of a scientific perspective in the national submissions to the conference. While the direct results of this are difficult to measure, it is clear that a number of national papers were prepared that drew upon national scientific expertise, and several delegations

Negotiating International Regimes: Lessons Learned from the United Nations Conference on Environment and Development (G. Sjöstedt, *et al.*, eds.; 1-85966-077-0; © IIASA; pub. Graham & Trotman, 1994; printed in Great Britain), pp. 171–180.

to the Rio Conference itself included scientists. ICSU also provided the UNCED secretariat with the names of independent experts, who either participated in the preparations of key UNCED documents, notably of the chapters in Section II of Agenda 21 on the "Conservation and Management of Resources for Development," or provided comments on the drafts of texts being prepared for Agenda 21.

ICSU was created in 1931 for the principal objective of promoting scientific cooperation for the benefit of humanity. ICSU is international and nongovernmental, and consists of two types of members: 23 disciplinary international Scientific Unions in fields ranging from astronomy to immunology, and bodies from 92 nations that are academies of science or national scientific bodies representing a wide range of scientific disciplines in a given territory. In addition, ICSU has 29 Scientific Associates in fields that are not primarily within the scope of a single union, such as the information sciences, cartography, cell and brain research, and applied systems analysis. Several Associates represent regional bodies, such as the Third World Academy of Sciences (TWAS), and similar organizations in Latin America, Asia, and the Pacific region.

ICSU members set up interdisciplinary bodies on problem areas that none of them can address alone, and presently over 20 of these are in operation. Some of these on oceanic, Antarctic, and space research date from the mid-1950s, while others – in the areas of natural disasters, genetics, and biotechnology – are more recent. Of particular relevance to matters of environment and development are the Scientific Committee on Problems of the Environment, set up in 1969 to assemble, review, and assess the information available on man-made environmental changes and the effects of these on human beings. The International Geosphere-Biosphere Programme: A Study of Global Change (IGBP) was established by ICSU in 1986 to improve our knowledge of the dynamics of the biosphere influencing (and influenced by) global environmental change. An important mission of IGBP is the setting up of a System for Analysis, Research, and Training (START) that will provide for the structure of networks, centers, and sites to address the regional origins and impacts of global change. Other ICSU interdisciplinary bodies deal with training and capacity building in science, and a special Committee deals with the more general questions of Science and Technology in Developing Countries. This Committee (COSTED) has a secretariat in Madras, and was established by ICSU in 1966 to act as an advisory body to ICSU on the range of ICSU activities in developing countries.

ICSU also has numerous joint undertakings with other organizations. The Lectureship Programme in Science and Sustainable Development is in cooperation with TWAS, UNESCO, and the Commonwealth Science Council; the program for a cooperative network for the distribution of scientific literature (INASP) is carried out with TWAS and UNESCO. The International Biosciences Networks, with regional nodes in Africa, Asia, Latin America, and the Arab region, is a joint ICSU – UNESCO undertaking set up over 10 years ago, and the World Climate Research Programme is jointly sponsored by ICSU, the World Meteorological Organization (WMO), and the Intergovernmental Oceanographic Commission (IOC) of UNESCO. The recently established Global Climate Observing System (GCOS) is jointly sponsored by ICSU, WMO, IOC, and UNEP, and the complementary Global Ocean Observing System and Global Terrestrial Observing System are sponsored by ICSU and several UN bodies. A program devoted to the scientific aspects of biologycal diversity, DIVERSITAS, is sposored by the ICSU Union on Biological Sciences (IUBS), the Scientific Committee on Problems of the Environment (SCOPE), and UNESCO.

In May 1990, a conference was held in Bergen, Norway, on "Sustainable Development, Science and Policy." This conference, organized by the Norwegian Research Council for Science and the Humanities and the European Science Foundation, concluded that:

> In order to ensure that the science community is actively and broadly involved in the process leading up to the Brazil Conference, it is strongly recommended that a major science conference be held 6 months in advance. This Conference should take the form of a Global Science Summit. It should underscore the need for a comprehensive, yet focussed scientific approach which is required to face up to the challenges put to the UN Conference in 1992. Beyond Rio '92, the aim is to produce an enduring global research and action agenda in the field of sustainable development.

Following this recommendation and other events bringing the scientific community closer to policy debates and decisions (notably the Second World Climate Conference, held in Geneva in October 1990), the need to bring together the scientific community's position regarding sustainable development became clear and ICSU decided to organize the International Conference on An Agenda of Science for Environment and Development into the 21st Century (ASCEND 21). The conference was held in Vienna in November 1991 with the co-sponsorship of other international nongovernmental bodies (the Third World Academy of Sciences, the International Institute for Applied Systems Analysis (IIASA), the European Science Foundation, the Norwegian Research Council for Science and the Humanities, the Norwegian Academy of Science and Letters, the Stockholm Environment Institute, and the International Social Sciences Council). The purpose of the ASCEND 21 conference was to bring together the understanding and judgment of the world scientific community (encompassing natural, social, engineering, and health scientists) on the issues of highest priority for the future of the environment and development so as to define the agenda of science in these areas for the next 10 to 20 years. The outcome was to provide both a consolidated contribution to the Rio Conference and a perspective for the future of international science in these and other related areas.

The ASCEND conference was attended by nearly 300 people from over 70 countries. Half of the participants came from developing countries, but each person attended strictly on a personal basis. Conference papers were prepared in advance on 16 themes addressing the problems of environment and development, the scientific understanding of the Earth System, and the contribution of science to environment and development strategies. Teams of authors with complementary expertise and experience (in most cases one from a developed country and another from a developing country) prepared the papers, which were thoroughly discussed by working groups in the conference and revised as a result of this review in order to be a part of the final publication of the proceedings by Cambridge University Press which was ready by May 1992, in time for the UN conference.

The themes of the ASCEND conference and the chapters in the publication are:

Problems of Environment and Development:

- Population and Natural Resource Use
- Agriculture, Land Use and Degradation
- Industry and Waste
- Energy
- Health

Scientific Understanding of the Earth System:
- Global Cycles
- Atmosphere and Climate
- Marine and Coastal Systems
- Terrestrial Systems
- Freshwater Resources
- Biodiversity

Responses and Strategies:
- Quality of Life
- Public Awareness, Science, and the Environment
- Capacity Building
- Policies for Technology
- Institutional Arrangements

RESULTS OF THE ASCEND 21 CONFERENCE

The ASCEND 21 conference provided a unique platform for the scientific community to reflect on the issues of environment and development and on the role of science in finding solutions to these problems. The conference stressed a new commitment on the part of the international scientific community as a whole to work together so that improved and expanded scientific research, and the systematic assessment of scientific results, combined with a prediction of impacts, would enable policy options in environment and development to be evaluated on the basis of sound scientific facts. It underlined the classical responsibility of all scholars to undertake research, to publish the results, and to explain the implications for society. It asserted that it is especially important to draw attention to the implications of what is not known: indeed, the precautionary principle advocates that complex, inadequately understood systems should be protected against disturbances until further investigation has provided a scientific understanding of their vulnerability. The conference also provided a model for a future *modus operandi* in which assessment of scientific results serves as a basis for predicting impacts and formulating policy options, leading to authoritative advice on the basis of international consensus among scientists.

The ASCEND conference participants agreed on the nature of the major problems that affect the environment and hinder sustainable development, and identified a number of specific areas through which the scientific community could begin to tackle those problems considered by ASCEND as being of the highest scientific priority: population and *per capita* resource consumption; depletion of agricultural/land resources; inequity and poverty, climate change; loss of biological diversity; industrialization and waste; water scarcity; and energy consumption.

While each of the 16 scientific papers prepared for the ASCEND 21 conference recommended specific action, the overall recommendations of the conference called for:

(1) intensified research into natural and anthropogenic forces and their interrelationships, including the carrying capacity of the Earth and ways to slow population growth and reduce over-consumption;

(2) strengthened support for international global environmental research and observations of the total Earth system;
(3) research and studies at the local and regional scale on: the hydrological cycle; impacts of climate change; coastal zones; loss of biodiversity; vulnerability of fragile ecosystems; impacts of changing land use, of waste, and of human attitudes and behavior;
(4) research on transition to a more efficient energy supply and use of materials and natural resources;
(5) special efforts in education and in building up of scientific institutions as well as the involvement of a wide segment of the population in environment and development problem solving;
(6) regular appraisals of the most urgent problems of environment and development and communication with policy makers, the media, and the public;
(7) establishment of a forum to link scientists and development agencies, along with a strengthened partnership with organizations charged with addressing problems of environment and development;
(8) a wider review of environmental ethics.

Immediately after the ASCEND conference was concluded, the draft Chapter 35 of Agenda 21, entitled "Science for Sustainable Development," was revised and subsequently adopted by UNCED. This chapter, which is in complete harmony with the outcome of the ASCEND conference, has among its objectives the vigorous implementation of the major on-going Earth System Research and Observation programs, as well as the strengthening of interdisciplinary cooperation among the natural, social, engineering, and health sciences. It further calls for periodic objective scientific assessments of global issues and for clearly explaining scientific findings to the general public and to policy makers. Throughout the text of this chapter and the ASCEND proceedings, the total involvement of the scientific communities in the North and the South is stressed.

INVOLVEMENT OF OTHER SCIENTIFIC BODIES IN UNCED

A large number of activities involving a variety of other scientific actors took place before the Rio Conference, and these have been followed up since the conference. No effort has yet been made to account for all of these, but some highlights will suggest their pervasiveness. The joint program involving the World Federation of Engineering Organization (WFEO), the International Federation of Independent Consulting Engineers (FIDIC), and the Consortium for International Earth Science Information Network (CIESIN), entitled "World Partnership for Sustainable Development," was formally launched in Rio during UNCED. This program aims to address the engineers' role in sustainable development through an interdisciplinary partnership to engage in decision-making processes at all levels. The Third World Academy of Sciences (TWAS) and the Third World Network of Scientific Organizations (TWNSO) also began its Program for Sustainable Development, consisting of a network of 20 international centers for science, technology, and the environment to provide a focus for international cooperation based in developing-country institutes. The International Institute for Applied Systems Analysis (IIASA) and the Stockholm Environment Institute supported the secretariat and many working groups preparing UNCED. The World Conservation Union (IUCN) published *Caring for the Earth: A Strategy for Sustainable Living* just before UNCED, and has been particularly active in the biodiversity-related follow-up activities.

The scientific agencies of the UN system also focused on sustainable development during the preparatory years and continue to sharpen their programs in this area. The Intergovernmental Meeting on the World Climate Programme is a follow-up measure, as are the global observing systems that have already been put in place.

OTHER PREPARATORY STEPS TO UNCED

ICSU was selected to represent the scientific community on the International Facilitating Committee for the Independent Sectors input to UNCED. This committee facilitated discussion among nongovernmental organizations in preparation to the UN conference, and organized the Global Forum of NGOs that took place in Rio de Janeiro at the time of the conference. Although science did not have a particular role to play at the Forum, there were a number of science-related symposia organized at the Forum and several of the exhibitors were scientific bodies.

The group of accredited NGOs to the PrepComs, to the Global Forum, and to UNCED was too heterogeneous for most practical purposes, as it included both organizations having objective study as their aim, so as to present a rational basis for policy decisions, as well as those that are pressure groups, and religious organizations that aim to influence decisions in the direction they see as the best one. All have their legitimacy, but scientific organizations lose their credibility if they are seen in the same category as action groups. ICSU, as also numerous other nongovernmental organizations, was present at each of the PrepCom meetings for UNCED and was able to address two of these sessions. In Rio, the president of ICSU, Professor M.G.K. Menon, gave a speech to the UNCED Plenary on behalf of the scientific community, sharing this privilege with 12 out of the 1420 accredited NGOs.

In opening his speech, Professor Menon spoke of the catalytic role of science in the UNCED process and in the future sustainable development regime:

> It is important to stress that it is the scientific community working over several decades on these questions which has brought these aspects to the notice of society. It is this which has led to the increase in public awareness so that people and governments, for the first time in history, are devoting a large part of their time to the global environment and the impact of human activities on it. It is this which has been the basis for the Climate and Biodiversity Conventions which have been placed before the nations of the world to adhere to, as also for the Montreal Protocol on Ozone. ... In the light of this, the scientific community has a responsibility, which it is fulfilling, to provide more precise information on the current status of planet Earth, particularly in respect of the key aspects which define its well-being, and to monitor the changes that are being brought through increased human activities. For all of this we now have available powerful tools of earth observation satellites, oceanographic capabilities, computers for storing accessing and handling vast amounts of data, sophisticated instrumentation and the like. It's not enough only to monitor changes. It is further necessary to model the nature of the change, reduce uncertainties and provide an analysis which will tell humanity where it is going. For all of this scientific work will need to be supported – for only it can provide

an understanding of where we are, in which direction we are going, what are the likely consequences and how we might avoid pathways that can be dangerous.

THE OUTCOME OF UNCED AND ITS IMPLICATIONS FOR THE SCIENTIFIC COMMUNITY

Rio Declaration

While this declaration does not contain a specific reference to the essential role of scientific research of the Earth System in providing a basis for policies for sustainable development, this may be remedied in an Earth Charter based on the Rio Declaration, to be prepared during the coming years.

Agenda 21

Many of its sectoral chapters (9–22), such as those on the atmosphere, land resources, oceans, freshwater resources, biodiversity, biotechnology, and toxic chemicals, are specifically relevant to the scientific community, which would be well advised to take note of these so as to establish its role in the execution of Agenda 21.

Several other chapters are of substantial importance:

Chapter 35 on "Science for Sustainable Development," in harmony with the ASCEND results, encourages the strengthening of partnerships with other NGOs, intergovernmental organizations, and with industry. The need for capacity building in science receives strong emphasis, and of special importance is the proposal for increased interaction between science and decision making: "Strengthen and design appropriate institutional mechanisms at the highest appropriate local, national, subregional and regional levels and within the UN system for developing a stronger scientific basis for the improvement on environmental and developmental policy formulation consistent with long term goals of sustainable development" (quoted from para 35.7.C). The total annual cost for implementing chapter 35 was earlier estimated at $1.8 billion; at UNCED, this estimate was increased to $2.9 billion.

Chapter 31 on the "Scientific and Technology Community" further elaborates the desired collaboration between science, policy making, and public information; it also calls for an examination of the ethical basis for conducting science and technology and the development of codes of practice, where appropriate, in addition to those already in existence.

Chapter 36 on "Promoting Education, Public Awareness and Training" and Chapter 37 on "National Mechanisms and International Cooperation for Capacity Building in Developing Countries" both call for a major strengthening of on-going bilateral as well as multilateral efforts so as to make achievement of sustainable development possible. In this regard, UNDP's recent report on "Human Development" prepared as an input to UNCED is also highly relevant to the scientific community's plans in capacity building.

Chapter 38 on "International Institutional Arrangements," in general, advocates the use of existing mechanisms to ensure implementation of Agenda 21, but there are some significant exceptions: the setting up of a high-level commission on sustainable development to monitor and guide progress on Agenda 21's implementation; strengthening of the Administrative Committee on Coordination (ACC) of the UN organizations and extension of its mandate; a strengthened role of UNEP with respect to scientific research; development of procedures to expand the cooperation between the UN system and NGOs. In addition, the possibility is being opened for setting up a high-level advisory board to advise the Secretary General of the UN on matters of environment and development.

Conventions on Climate Change and on Biodiversity

These each contain clauses that call for appropriate scientific advisory support to the "Conferences of the Parties." It is hoped that, as much as possible, existing mechanisms will be relied upon. An indication to this effect was the recent proposal to the Executive Council of the WMO to involve the IPCC as support to the Framework Convention on Climate Change. Plans for future action on forests and desertification also require adequate scientific support for their further elaboration into conventions or other legal instruments.

In general it can be said that both UNCED and ASCEND call for a stronger role of science in policy making, and better interaction with policy makers and the general public. Of particular significance is the clear demand for independent, nongovernmental scientific advice on global issues and capacity building.

WHAT HAS BEEN LEARNED AND WHAT ARE THE CHALLENGES AHEAD?

For the first time, through the UNCED process, the best available knowledge about the status of the Earth System, its carrying capacity, the changes occurring in it, and its responses to human action has been recognized as an essential ingredient for the design of international policies and strategies for achieving sustainable development. Policy makers need scientists to give them the best available knowledge, and scientists have to carry out systematic world-wide investigations to respond adequately and in a timely manner. Thus, science has received a new mandate and is no longer driven solely by curiosity and the benefits of application in industry, agriculture, defense, and health care. Science is now also looked upon as the provider of policy frameworks, set by the limits and opportunities of the Earth System, for the development and survival of humankind.

Over the past ten years, through the Montreal Protocol (1987), the IPCC (1988), and UNCED (1992), this *demand structure* for best available scientific knowledge has been given shape. The IPCC serves as the "sensor" for the latest scientific information as a basis for decision making in climate change issues, while the international agreements on the ozone layer, on biodiversity, and others that follow each have their own scientific advisory groups to the relevant "Conference of the Parties." The Commission on Sustainable Development of the UN and indeed, the Secretary General himself, will have scientific advisory mechanisms. The Earth Council, a new independent authoritative body, will provide scientific information and assessment in addition to its tasks of following and facilitating the implementation of Agenda 21.

On the *supply side*, the scientific community has the responsibility to generate the required scientific information. Several countries have already stimulated global change research programs and these have been woven together into a coherent international framework. Thus, several major international research programs are now in place that together comprehensively investigate the most urgent global issues. These are the International Geosphere-Biosphere Programme, the World Climate Research Programme, and the Human Dimensions of Environmental Change Programme, along with the two supporting observing systems: the Global Climate Observing System and the Global Ocean Observing System, with a Global Terrestrial Observing System being planned. In order for the Earth System Research Programme to succeed, the participation of scientists from all countries is required. This is not only because reliable measurements, data collection, and field experiments from all parts of the globe are needed, but, especially as called for by UNCED, because every country must be able to rely on its own corps of scientists in taking action on the basis of Earth System Research results, nationally or internationally. This is only possible if an adequate proportion of these scientists have participated in the research in question.

Thus, both on the demand and on the supply side, regrouping is taking place of existing structures that merge with newly set-up bodies so as to arrive at the desired outcome as prescribed by UNCED. It seems clear that UNCED, however governmental a conference it was, would have been very different had it not had such active participation from the various sectors in the independent arena. However, the success was only moderate, and could have been improved with additional time and effort spent – in this case, by the scientific community – on the preparations.

The most important lessons for the scientific community (as for the others) is that it should have started its interactions with the UNCED process even earlier than it did, and it should have thoroughly familiarized itself with the rules of the game so that its interactions with the preparatory machinery would have been easier. While scientists still have some way to go toward achieving a smoother communication with the general public and decision makers, if they want to influence the intergovernmental process, they will also need to learn to communicate in the particular mode of the UN. Learning this language is not always viewed as a pleasant or relevant task, but it is a prerequisite for even moderate success. In addition to learning the language, a constant presence would have been required in the preparatory process, and very few of the large NGOs were willing to devote so much time (or funds) to what they saw as an uncertain investment. It was important to keep the concern of science constantly in front of the governmental participants in the PrepComs, and this was probably not done as systematically as it should have been. Thus, the individual interventions by representatives of scientific bodies were not always heard and, even if the message got through, by the time a document was produced, the message was watered down to an unrecognizable entity.

In order to achieve a more influential role in the UNCED process, the scientific community might have tried to achieve short-term coordination by joining forces with bodies such as ICSU, together with existing partners such as IUCN and IIASA, and with new partners representing engineers and social scientists. This might have given a higher profile to the cause of science, but it is not certain whether the end result would have been so different. The basic problem is that the scientific community is an independent, nongovernmental effort, while UNCED was organized by the UN for governments. Communication and coordination between these very different types of bodies is not easy. Given these basic differences of approach, however, the inputs by scientists can be said to have been moderately successful.

It is probably more important to take the road from Rio and to not lose sight of the commitments made in the preparation to Rio. ICSU, as well as the other bodies referred to earlier, is translating the agenda set by ASCEND 21 in Vienna and by UNCED at Rio into specific actions to be undertaken either by ICSU alone or with its partners. In this, there is a special commitment to work with the scientific communities in developing countries to ensure that sustainable development programs at the national level are based both on sound science and on local needs, and can therefore become a part of larger international programs.

12

Scientific Uncertainty and Power Politics: The Framework Convention on Climate Change and the Role of Scientific Advice[1]

Sonja Boehmer-Christiansen

Although the negotiations concerning global climate change transpired in a different forum, albeit concurrently with the UNCED negotiations, many of the issues, controversies, and debates were common to both. In a sense, the climate change negotiations could be considered the first to fall within the context of the sustainable development regime created by UNCED. After all, the framework convention was signed at Rio and was deemed to be a central outcome of the overall UNCED process. While the impact of the international scientific community at UNCED proper was somewhat vague and problematic (see Chapter 11), its influence on the climate change negotiations was not only catalytic in terms of initially identifying to policy makers the problems, but pivotal in relation to framing the issues, defining likely solutions, and actively encouraging the negotiations themselves. This chapter analyzes the role of scientists and scientific organizations as principal actors in the climate change negotiations.

There is a new scientific universalism in the sense that:

(1) Scientific research is broadening its disciplinary base and interconnectedness as it attempts to understand and model the earth as a unified system; this now includes man as an agent of physical change. The natural science community has long been globally organized and influential. It is strengthening and expanding this influence by both identifying and challenging powerful environmental threat perceptions, especially those of climate change.

(2) Research institutions are making claims that they are able to predict the future "scientifically." While these claims remain suspect - recognized but not always

[1]This chapter is based on a two-year project: "The Formulation and Impact of Scientific Advice on Global Climate Change, " Ref. No. Y320 25 3030, funded by the UK Economic and Social Research Council. The author wishes to thank the UK Department of the Environment and the Hadley Centre for Climate Research at the UK Met Office, and the secretariat of the IPCC Working Group I for their cooperation, as well as many scientists and policy makers in several countries who granted interviews.

Negotiating International Regimes: Lessons Learned from the United Nations Conference on Environment and Development (G. Sjöstedt, *et al.*, eds.; 1-85966-077-0; © IIASA; pub. Graham & Trotman, 1994; printed in Great Britain), pp. 181–198.

admitted by the scientific community itself – such claims become independent international and national actors over which science soon loses control.

(3) Threat perceptions and images of the future, once released into the world of politics and commerce, take on a life of their own and it is how they fare there, rather than scientific knowledge as such, that determines policy responses. Scientific knowledge alone is unable to initiate more than further research agendas.

I hope to support this argument by relating the climate treaty (the outcome) with the activities of the scientific community, explored through the origin, activities, and research networks associated with the Intergovernmental Panel on Climate Change (IPCC). This panel is responsible for making major contributions to the debate that led to the 1992 Framework Convention on Climate Change (FCCC).

THE CLIMATE CONVENTION

The FCCC is described as one of the major achievements of UNCED. The primary purpose of this gathering of people and governments was political: governments that considered themselves "poor" wanted to obtain some commitment to a transfer of resources from the "rich" in the name of sustainable development, a vague concept that everybody had previously accepted as a global "norm." Those considered to be rich tried to weaken this demand or satisfy it within strict limits and on stated conditions. By proving useful to both sides, the institutions of science (having organized themselves around the IPCC) had the opportunity to raise their profile and expand their influence.

The FCCC was agreed upon after only two years of negotiation by an Intergovernmental Negotiating Committee (INC), set up in 1990 and instructed to take into account the scientific consensus developed by the IPCC. The Convention consists of 26 articles and is now open for signature. It will come into force when 50 countries have ratified. The UK, the EC, Japan, and the United States have all ratified – the United States only agreed to comply after the language of the treaty was significantly weakened. It came into force when 50 countries had ratified in March 1994.

The Convention is what it claims to be, a framework agreement that allows common future action if the parties to the Convention desire it, and recommends common but differentiated national action. It does not impose a World Meteorological Order on the community of states. There is no agreement to reduce carbon dioxide emissions by a certain percentage at a certain date, as had been desired by a rather unholy alliance of lobbies and interests during the late 1980s.

Environmentalists and their supporters in the scientific community were disappointed by this outcome and angry with the Bush administration, a reaction that reflects both political naivety and an excessive faith in the power of scientific evidence to compel action. Also disappointed, but for different reasons, were many European countries, including the nuclear industry and the promoters of renewable energy sources. They had hoped for a tougher treaty for reasons of energy and trade policy.

During the negotiations, the United States acted as a defender of Third World interests, a fitting role to the extent that fossil fuel and especially oil price increases would have had a disastrous impact on these economies. The European attempt to have a carbon tax seriously discussed failed, even inside IPCC, as did the attempt to have a protocol on forests linked to the Climate Treaty.

The origin of the FCCC is not straightforward. After initial calls from "independent" scientists in 1985, the UN General Assembly (UNGA) had called for the preparation of a framework convention in 1988 containing appropriate commitments for actions to combat climate change, taking into account the most up-to-date sound scientific knowledge and any existing uncertainties (Churchill and Freestone, 1992: 240–9). The UN Environment Programme (UNEP), headed by Dr. Mostafa Tolba, had hoped that the FCCC, like the Montreal Protocol on ozone depletion, would remain the responsibility of UNEP and the World Meteorological Organizations (WMO).

However, in late 1990 UNGA made the issue its own (Resolution 45/212 on protection of global climate for present and future generations of mankind) by establishing the INC under the auspices of the General Assembly, supported by UNEP and the WMO, and by "taking into account (inter alia) the work of the Intergovernmental Panel on Climate Change." The ad hoc secretariat of the INC was: "to cooperate closely [with the IPCC] to ensure that the panel can respond to the needs and requests for objective scientific and technical advice made during the negotiating process." No such requests were made.

This removed the climate negotiations from UNEP and WMO, probably to the relief of WMO but not UNEP. The influence of UNEP's important nongovernmental allies (globally organized environmental lobbies and research institutes), as well as the impact of the scientific consensus it had helped to negotiate informally inside IPCC, were weakened. Instead, the climate issue was negotiated as part of the wider UNCED bargain, which in turn led to new tactics being adopted by science organizations.

The FCCC was subsequently negotiated. Rather than becoming an agenda for global action, it primarily codified and legitimated the global change research efforts organized by the natural sciences community, with minor inputs from the social sciences.[2] This was surely a major achievement for Global Science, especially the diagnostic disciplines (natural, economic, and demographic).

This global research agenda is now in able hands, although serious funding problems remain.[3] These problems would increase were the climate threat to become too weak to be of concern to politics. While not arguing against the implementation of this agenda, it is arguable (on the basis of previous analyses of international environmental policy responses) that perfection in diagnostics does not lead directly, or easily, to regulation and remedial action (Boehmer-Christiansen, 1992a).

Effective policy responses require a far better understanding of society than is assumed in the linear thinking that underlies international (UNEP/WMO) thinking on environmental policy making. This proceeds from an understanding of the physical problems, to the prediction and economic evaluation of effects, and hence to the

[2]For details, see ICSU/IGBP, *Reducing Uncertainties,* Royal Swedish Academy of Sciences, Stockholm, 1992, which outlines one part of this research program, and WMO/ICSU, *Global Climate Change: A scientific review presented by the World Climate Research Programme,* Geneva, 1990. J. Jager and H.L. Fergusan, *Climate Change: Science, Impacts and Policy: Proceedings of the Second World Climate Conference,* contains an overview of the WCRP by P. Morel: 163–9. Concerning the partial failure of the social sciences to join this effort, and a split in the social sciences over the linkage with the natural sciences, see M.F. Price, "The Evolution of Global Environmental Change: Issues, Research, Programmes,' *Impact of Science on Society,*no. 166, UNESCO, 1992.

[3]As reported in recent issues of *The Globe* (UK newsletter from the Research Councils' Global Change Office), the *Global Change Newsletter* from the IGBP secretariat in Stockholm, and the German newsletter *Global Change Prism.*

technocratic definition of responses options. Actions taken in response are implemented at the national level and below, consequently remaining poorly linked to the global agenda, which has indeed little to offer but the transfer of ever more knowledge and, hopefully, technology.[4]

The above arguments will be supported with evidence from the FCCC itself, and then by a closer analysis of the "IPCC process."

THE IPCC AND ITS ORIGIN: INSTITUTIONS OF SCIENCE AND CLIMATE CHANGE

A Long History

The scientific discussion of climate change brought about by the emission of carbon dioxide and other trace gases emitted by human activities can be traced back to the nineteenth century. It reappeared in the 1930s, the late 1950s, the mid-1960s, the late 1970s, and finally, successfully, in the mid-1980s (Weart, 1992). In 1965, the US President's Science Advisory Council had claimed that supercomputers would be able to make useful predictions down to the regional level within a few years; thirty years later this task had still not been accomplished (McCracken, 1992). During the late 1970s, some scientifically interested diplomats studied the subject and decided that it had the makings of a major task for global diplomacy.[5] The Americans in particular began to invest large amounts of money in related scientific research, much of it financed by the Departments of Defense, Energy, and Commerce, and undertaken in large science research laboratories.[6] In 1980, the Climate Program of the International Federation of Institutes of Advanced Study (IFIAS) and the Aspen Institute (in Germany and the United States) tried to attract attention to the issue.

At the national level, therefore, early expressions of concern can be found – e.g., in the United States, UK and Germany – but these were not effectively communicated to the global policy system, surely not because the scientific community did not have the "agreed" evidence that governments seemed to demand about the sign of a possible climate change. The Aspen workshops raise the question of why this early "warning" was not picked up. This was due to a lack of convergence with global and major national energy policies. Hence the politics of global warming changed significantly when energy prices ceased rising, and the world began facing not an energy "crisis," but an energy glut. The Reagan and Bush administration later

[4]There are welcoming signs that this is slowly being recognized by the experts on climate change, especially those that are beginning to address political, cultural, and behavioral issues rather than science and technology, e.g. G.I. Pearman (ed.), "Limiting Greenhouse Effects: Controlling Carbon Dioxide Emissions," *Dahlem Workshop Reports,* Wiley & Sons, Chichester, 1992.

[5]Here Crispin Tickell proved to be a significant influence and link between the global and national levels, as well as between science and world politics. He persuaded Margaret Thatcher in 1987 that the issue was worthy of her attention, which in turn brought about major policy changes in the UK. See *Climatic Change and World Affairs,* Center for International Affairs, Harvard University Press, 1977, revised in 1986, were he tells how the first effort of science to have climate change research funded was not very successful.

[6]NASA is a large beneficiary of this spending under its Earth Observation System.

decided that the climate threat was being exaggerated for political purposes, and hence stalled negotiations with "science."

The climate threat in support of nuclear power made its public appearance in the UK in 1981, but even earlier in West Germany. By 1983 confidence that oil/energy prices would continue to rise was declining, and energy demand growth was also slowing. In February 1986, oil prices fell sharply.

By 1985, a group of American and European scientists therefore had another go, this time from a more congenial European base (see Villach below). They did so again on the basis of predictions derived from global climate modeling experiments. The environmental research groups and eminent environmental scientists who brought the climate threat to the attention of the world did so with the support of a number of governments, but above all that of UNEP, WMO, and ICSU.[7] The same institutions had been involved in the Aspen workshops, but without the same level of support from environmentalist organizations.

The diffusion of the climate threat perception from the scientific to the political community followed, and was largely the achievement of the Brundtland Report and UNEP. The former was published in 1987, with the US government, not the American environmental research lobby, but weakly represented. In 1988 Margaret Thatcher made her "green" speech to the British Royal Society, and very shortly afterwards the IPCC was formally set up by WMO and UNEP. Many international conferences (e.g., Bergen, Toronto, Hamburg, Tokyo) were then organized by the scientific community, together with a growing number of governmental and non-governmental actors. By 1990, as an outcome of the Second World Climate Conference, governments accepted the need for a climate treaty based on scientific advice. The INC was set up, and the IPCC began preparing its "update" for UNCED.

Villach 1985 – Looking for a Partnership between Thinkers and Doers

In 1985 a coalition of research and energy interests met in a small Austrian village at the invitation of a handful of independent scientists who wanted to provide both the "proof" of the threat and the solution. This group of Anglo-Saxon and Scandinavian scientists came from a range of institutions, several of them deeply involved in environmental advocacy. They were largely self-selected, and uninhibited about telling governments what they ought to be doing. They had made up their mind that "global warming" was an issue demanding immediate policy responses. The Villach meeting was the first gathering to propose the idea of a climate convention.

From the institutional perspective, this meeting is of considerable interest. It was called by the Committee on the Scientific Problems of the Environment (SCOPE), a member of the ICSU, UNEP, (working on climate impacts since 1979) and WMO (researching climate change since 1979). At this meeting the Advisory Group on Greenhouse Gases (AGGG) was set up by some of the participants under the chairmanship of the director of what is now known as the Stockholm Environment Institute (SEI). The AGGG met again, with less publicity and impact in 1987, but then

[7] Important newcomers among the environmental research institutes were the Stockholm Environment (formerly Beijer) Institute, which is strongly supported by the Swedish government, and the American World Resources Defense Council (not popular with Washington because of its aggressive advocacy of energy policy changes). The International Institute for Applied Systems Analysis (IIASA) in Austria remained a loyal supporter, but IFIAS has fallen by the wayside

dissolved itself. It can be considered to be the nongovernmental precursor of the IPCC. The individuals involved came to be major participants in the global publicity and conferencing effort (Toronto, Bergen, Second World Climate Conference) (Paterson, 1992) that followed this meeting and continues until today.[8]

The widely cited SCOPE 29 Report (Bolin, Warrick, Döös, and Jäger, 1986) had been commissioned by the organizers of this 1985 Villach meeting and was to become "the bible" of IPCC's scientific assessment. Although the AGGG itself faded, SCOPE 29 is judged to be the highly influential product of a small number of people carefully selected by a handful of individuals with strong environmental credentials and large needs for research funds. The dominance of Anglo-Saxon environmental science is revealed, a dominance that is carried over to the IPCC and can be traced not only to the ability of government scientists (a purely Anglo-Saxon species) to draft scientific and political documents (in the English language), but also to their close institutional and personal links with government and academic research.

These AGGG scientists were familiar with climate modeling and the scientific understanding of climate, as well as with the needs of UNEP, one of their funding agencies. Very importantly, through ICSU/WMO, and the International Institute for Applied Systems Analysis (IIASA) with its modeling facilities and links to Eastern Europe, this group was able to network with a broad peer group community of natural scientists for support and peer review.[9] There were strong personal links between them, the recently established World Commission on Environment and Development (WCED) and IIASA.[10] As primarily "soft money" organizations relying on governmental and NGO/foundation support, these institutions are necessarily drawn toward policy advocacy by their needs for clients.

The success of the AGGG was largely the result of the ability of nongovernmental institutions to form a coalition with "new" interests, environmental and energy related, that shared the presumption in favor of a serious climate threat and the conviction that emissions from fossil fuel combustion should, and could, be reduced. Through personal commitments and institutional linkages, the nuclear power lobby had joined the debate. Wolf Häfele and R.W. White, major figures in the climate story, were able to link this threat to technology advocacy.

UNEP AND THE WCED

After Villach, between 1985 and 1987, the climate threat and the idea of a treaty was disseminated through the activities and impact of both UNEP and the Brundtland

[8] A recent gathering of climate change experts included many of these activists or their protégés. Their approaches, commitments, and research interests are documented in G.I. Pearman (ed.), "Limiting Greenhouse Effects: Controlling Carbon Dioxide Emissions," *Dahlem Workshop Reports,* Wiley & Sons, Chichester, 1992.

[9] UNEP and WMO have major research programs related to climate change that they could bring to the attention of politics, UNEP having used the climate threat since the mid-1970s to enhance its own role and bring North and South together. WMO began developing its research agenda for climate change in 1979, with major inputs from several scientific unions belonging to ICSU. Its main practical concern, however, was a better understanding of the predictability of climatic variability.

[10] IIASA was very important as a meeting place for scientists from East and West who could "unite" in "value-free" modeling experiments. It had well established global models for energy demand and agricultural patterns that could be linked to climate change data. For IIASA's continuing interest in energy, climate, and environment, see Annual Report, 1991.

Report. The Brundtland Report was the product of five years of consultation and writing by the World Commission on Environment and Development (WCED, 1987). When the WCED picked up the climate threat and advocated changes in energy policy, it did so as part of its proposed North–South negotiations for "sustainable development." In this, UNEP was its major ally. Personal links existed not only between the WCED and the environmental research community, but also with UNEP – for example, Mostafa Tolba was one of the directors of the Beijer Institute (now SEI).

The WCED was chaired by the Norwegian Prime Minister Mrs Brundtland, head of a country very active in selling its natural gas, widely recommended as an environment-friendly, carbon dioxide-reducing fuel.[11] The WCED was attracted to the global warming threat because it seemed to provide the moral issue around which North and South could develop an agenda for sustainability and technology transfer, and thus the energy policies of many countries could be reorganized in a more rational way. The willingness of WCED to "use" the threat of global warming in order to unite mankind against a common threat to its "security" had for some time been given publicity by UNEP (Tolba, 1982).

In his speeches, Mostafa Tolba had mentioned energy and the need for better climate forecasting in 1974 without any reference to global warming. By 1979, however, when addressing the First World Climate Conference, he referred to climate change, the well-documented increase of carbon dioxide, and "the process of carrying out uncontrolled experiments on the earth's atmosphere" (Tolba, 1982: 99). He assured his audience that UNEP was ready to carry out its role in the important area of assessing the environmental impacts of increased levels of carbon dioxide.

This concern was to provide the links with the World Meteorological Organization's climate research program from which IPCC would emerge. ICSU had long collaborated with WMO, and shared with it a concern for developing countries and their ability to contribute to data collection and monitoring. This meant that the research network in which IPCC could embed itself was already taking shape.

A major convergence of environmental threat perceptions, science research agendas, and commercial interest had taken place, and provided the political energy for the climate negotiations. This proved irresistible to many world leaders during the declining days of the Soviet Empire. Soviet scientists still played a major role, albeit a diminishing one, during the next stage, the IPCC process.

THE IPCC AND THE GIVING OF SOUND ADVICE

Its Origin

Once taken up by the nongovernmental AGGG and the WCED, the idea of a climate treaty would need testing and evaluating by more trusted experts. This demand was particularly loudly voiced by developing countries who had no means of independent assessment, and rightly feared the political implications of any attempts to control their economic activities. The world now needed an IPCC; fortunately, a rudimentary body already existed.

[11] While Norway knew of its gas wealth during the 1970s, the need for secure markets became more urgent in the mid-1980s along with the wish to develop expensive new fields.

A Panel on Climate Change had been set up by WMO at its 1987 Congress: "to provide the international assessment that would enable the Directors of National Meteorological Services to advise their governments on the evidence for and nature of, the climate threat and what they might do about it." It is virtually certain that none of those involved in developing the concept of the IPCC foresaw the speed with which it would take off or the depth of the international Pandora's box that it would throw open.[12]

WMO in particular was surprised by the attention paid to the IPCC after it was formally established in 1988 as a joint UNEP/WMO body. WMO had become concerned that UNEP would "run with" the idea of global warming without science.[13] It would bring with it good links with ICSU and governments, especially meteorological offices. ICSU could channel influence through national research bodies, such as the Royal Society and NERC in the UK, the National Science Foundation in the United States, and CSIRO in Australia. WMO's voice therefore proved to be a powerful one, but it belonged primarily to that of the natural science community. UNEP tried to balance this bias by closer links with nongovernmental organizations and research institutes, such as SEI and IIASA (see below), although here too the "number crunchers" and natural scientists dominated.

Tasks and Membership

IPCC is not a research organization, but one through which the institutions of science can present their knowledge claims and agendas to governments. Its job was to gather and evaluate "sound" knowledge and then draw advice from it, two very different tasks. More precisely, IPCC was asked:

(1) to assess available scientific information on climate change (WMO/ICSU expertise);
(2) assess environmental and socio-economic impacts of climate change (UNEP expertise);
(3) formulate response strategies (UNEP/governments' expertise).

IPCC was not asked to inquire about the "socio-economic," or even political/philosophical, causes of climate change, nor about the political obstacles that might have to be overcome during implementation. The institutions behind IPCC could not have handled such questions.

IPCC came to consist of scientists selected by WMO, ICSU, and UNEP in consultation with governments, as well as appointed scientists and government officials, who would meet in four working groups in the relatively open environment that is typical of UN bodies (see Figure 12.1). While the selection of members of two of its working groups was largely, but by no means always, left to the initially selected experts themselves, the third working group became a forum mainly for government people and lobbyists, and hence where politicization became sharpest. This was intensified by the need for collaboration between Working Groups I and III, because Working Group I had been instructed to accept emission data and scenarios

[12]A view from an unpublished paper by W.J. Teggart (Australia's principal delegate to IPCC and vice chairman of Working Group II) and J.W. Zillman (director of the Commonwealth Bureau of Meteorology, WMO delegate, and alternate IPCC delegate).

[13]Interviews.

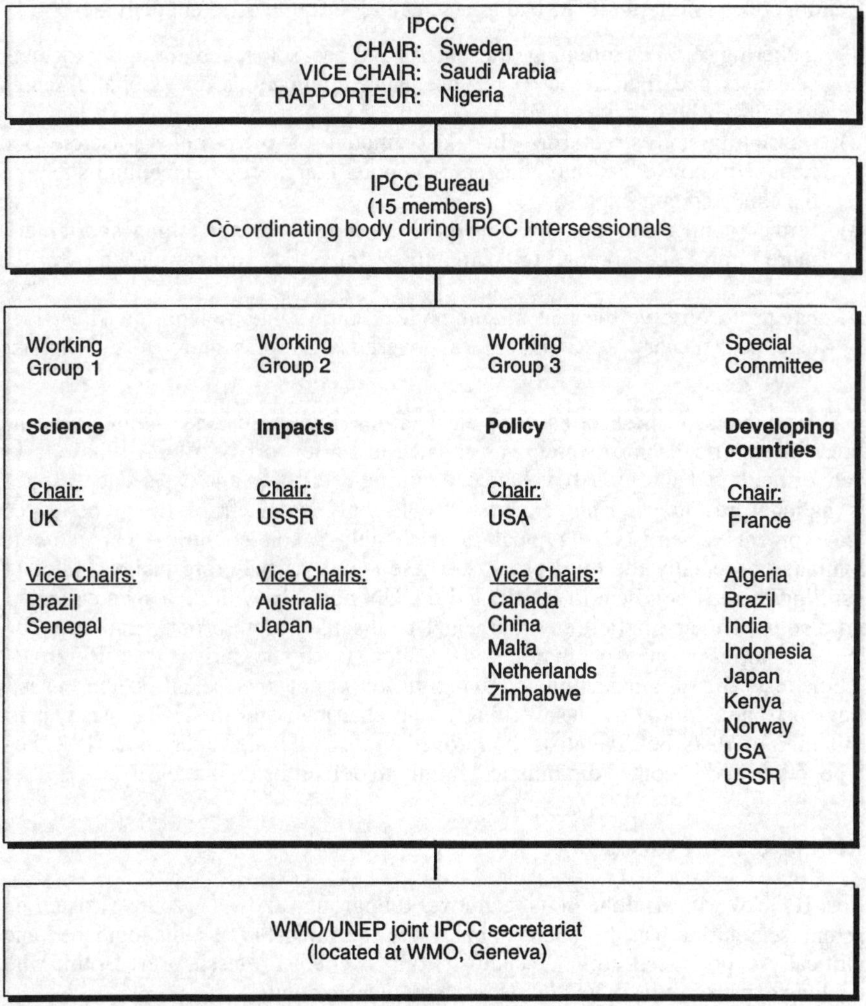

Figure 12.1 Intergovernmental Panel on Climate Change (IPCC, 1988)

from, *de facto,* government sources. This soon proved to be a major issue of irritation, as the needs and values of the two working groups differed considerably, with the emission projections themselves becoming political tools.[14]

[14] From IPCC files and interviews. For a devastating assessment of the weakness of the Working Group III report as a list of platitudes, which also accuses the whole IPCC thinking of being affected by "technological determinism," making socio-economic issues relevant only for impacts (not as causes), and for responses, see Howard Newby (chairman of the UK ESRC), Robbin's lecture presented at the University of Stirling, 4 November 1991.

From observation, the IPCC had to engage in four quite different activities:

(1) gathering (or even initiating) the "latest" and best science, by bringing together scientists and their research results, using publications and global research networks where they existed;
(2) translating and structuring this vast amount of often rather discrete and itemized knowledge, into chapters of reports that were readable and spoke to the educated non-expert;
(3) further condensing this summarized knowledge into something shorter and more simple, i.e., preparing "summaries" for policy makers and the world's media.[15]
(4) having to observe the fate of summarized knowledge, defend, or adjust it in extended plenary sessions before government representatives and diverse lobbyists.

The products of these tasks were an overview, policy makers' summaries, and three full reports, each of which was updated just prior to UNCED. All these tasks were difficult and enormously valuable, requiring dedication and experience, as well as national resources. This expertise could only come from the experienced "government" scientists so typical of the Anglo-Saxon countries that came to dominate, especially the third process. These countries therefore had a chance of instilling the advice given to UNEP and the UN not only with their own concepts, but also with their implicit environmental philosophy, a philosophy that strengthened the emphasis on research rather than action (Boehmer-Christiansen, 1992b).

Scientists and diplomats mingled to legitimate (or not) the "scientific consensus," previously agreed among the working group chairmen and their closest advisers. This initially disturbed scientists, but proved a most valuable experience. IPCC had to negotiate and become "diplomatic," if only to defend its own integrity.

Structure and Process

Most IPCC work was done in its many working groups and sub-groups assisted by a small secretariat, based in Geneva under the chairmanship of a distinguished and politically experienced climate scientist from Sweden, Professor Bert Bolin, who had long experience in WMO/ICSU research management.

The group chairmen, appointed by governments at the suggestion of WMO/UNEP, divided this enormous task according to scientific logic in a rather linear and deterministic (or perhaps rational) way. From scientific theory and available observational evidence to the prediction of the future (Working Group I under a British chairman, Sir John Houghton), the advisory process would lead to predictions of impacts (Working Group II under a Soviet chairman, Yuri Izrael), and hence to strategies or options from which governments could select the most suitable ones (Working Group III under a US chairman, F. Bernthal).

Draft reports written by lead-authors selected from the working groups would be distributed to peers and governments, again discussed on the basis of comments received, and adopted by consensus, if possible, at IPCC Plenary Sessions. The working groups and sub-groups were to receive very different degrees of help from national governments, reflecting not only government policy, but also the ability of

[15]See IPCC Reports of 1990, their executive summaries, and 1992 updates.

the relevant national bodies, with NGO and UN assistance, to relate their expertise to the interests of government departments.

Working Group III became the major forum for prenegotiations and conflicts, but also proved to be of most interest and use to governments, especially those not blessed with an independent domestic supply of "sound" science. Working Group III was always in danger of falling foul of politicians, and hence found consensus formation more difficult than Working Groups I and II. It did not get sufficient support from all governments. Preexisting research networks were often green think tanks and only considered government-friendly if governments wanted their support.[16]

Only Working Groups I and II (chaired by WMO/ICSU scientists with many years' experience both in research and government) could rely on existing international research networks to sustain them and have their work "peer-reviewed" in a way that resembles the methods of an academic community. The less fortunate Working Group III could not rely on a similar network, and probably would have been suspicious had such networks existed. Its primary value was therefore at the national level, especially the extent to which it could bring the relevant governmental bodies together for strategic thinking. One policy question arising from all three working groups is why there was such a concentration on the reduction of carbon dioxide emissions.

Too Much Uncertainty for Policy Making

The perception of the problem and how it would be solved by regulation and technology change thus directly determined the structure of the Panel. Yet the logic of IPCC's tripartite structure was soon causing difficulties as a result of the uncertainties facing scientists and emission experts. Working Group II could not really come to firm conclusions until Working Group I had reported facts sufficiently robust for governments to feel that they had to act, e.g. by reducing emissions, arranging trade-offs between different greenhouse gases or responding by increasing sinks rather than reducing sources. Working Group III in turn was dependent on the assessment of conclusions reached by Working Group II, yet the links between them were weak.

Firm knowledge was not available by 1990, or 1992, although an embattled scientific community held out promises of knowing enough in another decade or so.[17] In 1990, model outputs remained too poor for regional breakdowns of climate change, and by 1992 only slight improvements were reported.

The underlying assumption of UNEP when setting up Working Groups II and III appears to have been the belief that sufficient knowledge was already available, but this would have made the existence of Working Group I rather superfluous! UNEP and WMO had got themselves into a muddle, but common institutional interests prevailed over logic. Uncertainty was, however, built into the substance as well as the structure, and increased as the IPCC process moved along the "straight line" from science to response. It is not surprising, therefore, that a science-based policy perception should produce a treaty that is largely a research agenda.

[16]UNEP probably overstepped its own capacities when it set this group up, or lacked political awareness when it assumed that this group would remain in the hands of its environmental experts.

[17]The Chairman of Working Group I firmly believed that climate predictions would be sufficiently developed to policy by 2005.

With regard to the IPCC process having the capacity to stimulate further research efforts, the potential was enormous and its effectiveness related to the ability of IPCC scientists to link up with national institutions and encourage them. In the countries studied in some detail, national research ministries soon became involved in the IPCC process.[18] Examples are the German BMFT, the British Department of the Environment, the US Department of Energy, and a large array of national laboratories with military connections and academic research organizations (competing for "soft" money in the United States), as well as many ministries concerned with environmental regulation as well as research (US EPA and the German Environment Ministry). The different institutional commitments of these national bodies and their individual philosophies then moved national climate change responses into different directions.

Once the IPCC process was functioning well, scientists, diplomats, administrators and their political masters were increasingly "in communication". The only excluded actor was in fact industry, reduced to lobbying along the sidelines, but this is another, very important, story that is changing.[19]

By late 1991, structure had become a subject of considerable debate within IPCC itself.[20] Should IPCC continue to do its work through three permanent working groups or should it form itself into two groups only, largely devoted to natural science diagnostics, while ad hoc "task forces" were set up for specific, more applied, problems, possibly those relating to implementation? There were still informal, diametrically opposed views within IPCC itself and between governments in autumn 1992.[21] This internal debate extended to whether IPCC should be formally integrated into the climate convention.[22]

In its proposal to the IPCC Plenary in early 1992, the leadership suggested a reduction to two technical working groups, with more complex political issues being "relegated" to ad hoc task forces. A desire to return to a less politicized, i.e., value-free, environment was observed. While technocracy appeared triumphant, science was in fact withdrawing somewhat, lending support to the argument that institutionalized science fares best at the global level if it appears to politics as a value-free service (Proctor, 1991).

In Harare, at its eighth Plenary Session, a new structure was approved. This keeps Working Group I essentially unchanged, while Working Groups II and III are

[18]This happened via direct participation, which was very strong indeed for the UK and the United States on the scientific assessment side, but much less so for Germany, where involvement with impacts was stronger.The leadership of IPCC was very much in the hands of people from the natural sciences.

[19]Industry is catching up by financing it own global research programs, e.g., MECCA (Model Consortium for Climate Assessment) based at the US Electric Power Institute (EPRI), a collaborative effort by utilities from France, Italy, Japan; and the United States, and already using some of the same scientific institutions that have supported IPCC, e.g., NCAR in Boulder, and Maquarie University in Australia. The carrot is a Cray y-MP/2D computer with 16 MW memory, two processors, 128 GB SSD storage.

[20] Interview, IPCC Plenary documents, February 1992.

[21]The IPCC leadership suggested the restructuring of its working groups, including the abolition of Working Group III, and the setting up instead of task forces dealing with specific problems. Governments did not find this an easy decision, with ministries taking different views, for example in Germany. The UK and Australia wanted to keep three groups, but were outvoted in mid-1992.

[22]UNE appeared not to like this at all, while the "hard" science community seemed to be more inclined to play ball, with Bert Bolin reporting in its favor. Governments did not want duplication, i.e., having to support IPCC as a "purer" body assessing science and impacts for UNEP and WMO and this subsidiary group. ICSU wanted IPCC to become the scientific subsidiary body to the FCCC.

merged, and subdivided into four groups (energy, industry, settlement issues; coastal zones and oceans; unmanaged resources and ecosystems; managed ecosystems) (Global Environmental Change Report, 1992). A new Working Group III will deal with "cross-cutting" issues such as the socio-economic impacts of response strategies. The IPCC Bureau has been enlarged. The IPCC may have tried to make itself more attractive to the parties of the FCCC.

Being Diplomatic

Fortunately, the intergovernmental nature of the Panel and the leadership qualities exhibited by most of its senior individuals ensured that "political" problems facing scientists were anticipated and could be forestalled by careful diplomacy.

The problems included the appointment of unwanted people by governments, insufficient resources made available for Third World participants (including identifying suitable persons), insufficient funding for meetings, heated debates in plenaries about carbon taxes and their impact on development, and strong lobbying by the fossil fuel industries as well as by Greenpeace (one group was attacking the "certainties" of science and the other attacking the lack of emphasis on these certainties and possible surprises).

The fossil fuel lobby was probably the most effective nuisance, as it was generally trying to challenge scientific findings in order to weaken the threat perception that could be derived from the Summary. It demanded that the language of the reports should be altered and that emphasis be put on those pollutants – e.g., aerosols – responsible for acid rain and CFCs, which "countered" global warming and for which the IPCC was not responsible.[23]

There were also intensive internal debates about language, i.e., the degree to which it reflected (or did not reflect) the known uncertainties and disagreements between different model predictions and measurements and different methodologies of climate prediction.[24] Trying to be fair to all parties and above all to science itself, the drafters of politically important texts had to put much effort and thought into the skillful use of words.[25]

Scientific uncertainty and political confrontations are therefore reflected in IPCC language as formally transmitted to governments. It is symbolic language, since the precision of mathematics, and lack of data, cannot usually be translated into ordinary language. Ambivalence is also an ancient diplomatic tool that allows various interpretations, wisely permitting the construction of quite different perceptions of danger, especially if quoted out of context. For example, the word "prediction" proved contentious and was therefore used less in 1992 than in 1990. "Scenario" and "hypothesis" became more popular substitutes.

The Policy-makers' Summary of the 1990 Science Report demonstrates some intentional ambiguity. For example, the report is said to state that *from models* "we predict [that under a given emission scenario] ... a rate of increase of global mean

[23]Such lobbying took place at public conferences, in the media, by bombarding IPCC working groups with faxes and attendance at plenaries/attempted attendance at drafting sessions.

[24]From observation of IPCC sessions (both Plenary and working groups), examination of IPCC files and many interviews.

[25]The drafting process was observed by the author thanks to the many copies made available to her by Working Group I.

temperature during the next century of about 0.3 °C per decade [with an *uncertainty range of 0.2 to 0.5 °C per decade*] ... this will result in a *likely* increase in global mean temperature of about 1 °C above the present value by 2025" (Houghton, 1990).

The IPCC had "calculated with confidence" that an immediate reduction of 60 per cent of emissions would have to take place if the *stabilization of concentrations* were to be ensured. This formulation tended to allow the misinterpretation, by environmentalists that included Maurice Strong, that IPCC had allegedly called for the immediate reduction of emission by that amount to prevent global warming.

Climate change may well be in the pipeline; the difficulty for science was, and remains, to predict how, where, and to what extent this complex set of physical phenomena we call climate will alter with the changing composition of the atmosphere. There is therefore much emphasis on "best available" knowledge, when knowledge is admittedly in short supply. This then allows research proposals to become part of policy advice. Both the Summary and the Full Report therefore pay much attention to the research needs of the scientific community and the ways in which they could improve their understanding and ability to predict changes. This could be achieved, for example, through: improved understanding of clouds, oceans, and carbon cycle; systematic observations of climate-related variables on a global basis and of past climates; improved models of the climate system; increased national and international support; and more international exchange of climate data.[26]

Assessment

The IPCC process proved to be a powerful force in the integration of natural science knowledge. It widened the range of actors in an environment that promotes internal consensus agreement, if only for reasons of self-interest. The consensus reached was, however, often little more than symbolic, with the language "papering over" uncertainty and conflicts of interest. The desire to learn more remained the only true commonality. Overall, therefore, global science has done well out of this IPCC process that it carefully initiated and helped to structure. Governments did less well, for science could not, and would not, relieve them of the responsibility of decision making. This may not be entirely reassuring to all those non-scientists who worked so hard to promote the issue, nor to those scientists who joined the debate with strong environmental commitments.

Outside the IPCC, the process of forming a growing network of climate change research continued. Governments and senior politicians, as well as a large array of professional and commercial interests (ranging from international lawyers to professional economists and the managers of the energy industries), soon took up "global warming" as a subject that presented either an opportunity for advancement of growth, or a threat to it – or even survival. In either case, global warming would be a stimulus for change – always provided that other issues would not replace the "salience" of the threat and the opportunities it might offer.

[26]Emphasis was reduced somewhat during the drafting process. The full IPCC research agenda is presented by major ICSU personalities (from a Canadian and a US university) in the *Scientific Assessment Report,* 1990, ch. 11; the other reports have similar sections.

RESEARCH INSTITUTIONS AND THEIR CHANGING INTEREST IN GLOBAL WARMING

Scientific research means finding out the physically knowable that is known to be unknown. Since politicians like to worry about the future (so that they may promise a better one or defend the existing one), future visions of mankind had to enter IPCC predictions and hence advice (Parikh, 1992). For the natural scientists, this occurred because climate models need "predictions" of how emissions will develop in the future. This simple need brought natural science, societal, and applied sciences into direct contact – at times confrontation – with one another. The social sciences and humanities were poorly prepared for this challenge.

To explain the consequent dominance of the natural sciences in the IPCC, a closer look at the institutions involved in the 1985 Villach appeal is necessary, for it allows a more empirical assessment of the political role of science in furthering its own values and interests.

Studying the role of the scientific institutions in the diffusion process of climate change-related knowledge leads not only to the mentioned UN agencies, but also to a variety of national and intergovernmental research bodies.[27] Rather tangentially, this also approaches the question of scientific interest in environmental policy making at both the national and international level, and the linkages between the two. In turn, the considerable power of the scientific, or epistemic, community in the "creation/identification" of environmental threats, and in bringing these to the attention of the international political system, can be assessed, as can its limitation in this process.

The main institutions were the aloof and elitist, but internationally well-organized, ICSU, especially its Scientific Committee on the Problems of the Environment (SCOPE), as well as several "Northern" environmental research institutes and universities, the research sections of several UN agencies with strong environmental commitments, and energy demand modelers. ICSU was later asked to become the "principal scientific adviser" to UNCED (see Chapter 11) (ICSU, 1991).

Between 1985 and 1990, the period between the famous Villach Meeting and the Second World Climate Conference, influential members of the scientific community, together with responsive political bodies, became involved in the dissemination of a powerful "scientific" threat perception. The latter in particular were able to give wide publicity to the issue, using in particular the global network of environmental pressure groups that had grown so vigorously during the 1970s and 1980s, initially in Anglo-Saxon countries (McCormick, 1989; Boehmer-Christiansen, 1991).

After 1990, the strategic behavior of institutional science changed, as emphasis on uncertainties in the predictions of danger came to dominate first the scientific debate, and then also the policy debate. American scientists in particular felt frustrated about demands made upon them to give firm answers. As some "experts" split along lines of political commitment, uncertainties became more fashionable among the natural scientists, who could not but realize that the need for diagnostic knowledge declines as the threat becomes "real" enough to motivate action rather than

[27]The governments of the Netherlands, UK, Canada, and Australia became directly involved on the scientific research side. Behind the scenes, science managers and environmental advocates, like Gordon Goodman and Tom Malone, did valuable diffusion work. While interviews suggested that scientists were becoming worried about the careless use of the climate threat, in some countries this threat was needed to maintain the very funding of the relevant sciences.

more research. Appeals for funding research into "scientific uncertainties" replaces the funding of discovering threats. Research into uncertainties was justified with the argument that it would reduce the costs of emission abatement, a clever tactical response to the claim that emission abatement was too costly.[28]

Alongside the development of the climate change debate one can also document the politics of fuel competition. This successfully challenged the early "scientific consensus" of global warming with the idea of global greening, by collecting evidence to show that more carbon dioxide is good for the planet. Those who saw opportunities for the development of new knowledge (engineering, biotechnology, carbon requestration, energy efficient machines and appliances), on the other hand, continued on the assumption of a real threat to justify their own research and planning. As it needed industrial support, this effort took place primarily at the national level, although even here collaboration was increasing. Soon the "science" of global warming would no longer be needed! By this stage, science and technology policies had already become a part of the environmental policy process and its outcomes.

When international politics, during the late 1980s, turned against the demand for immediate action on economic and feasibility grounds, the scientific community responded by reducing the intensity of the climate "threat" image, discovered scientific explanations for lower observed values, and then turned to industry for further support.

The origin and consequences of both the climate convention and of the IPCC process can therefore be traced both backward and forward to discover linkages with the internationally organized scientific community. The ultimate goal of this community is the full understanding of the physical systems of Planet Earth. To achieve this, the natural sciences are now prepared to enter into the first cautious collaborations with social scientists on diagnostic issues (Price, 1992).

DISCUSSION: THE POWER OF SCIENCE

First, I would argue that the scientific diagnosis of the global environment has created perceptions of both insecurity and opportunities for progress. The institutions searching for new knowledge must protect their own relevance and their (always fragile) global organization, growth, and status. They justify claims to resources by searching for environmental threats, by weakening them, or by promising redress. It is therefore difficult to base policy on science; science is a moving target with few loyalties.

Science-based predictions of possible global warming beyond what is tolerable were quickly taken up by political and commercial lobbies to promote their own agendas using their own interests or values. The transformation of objective knowledge and scientific hypotheses into politically active threat images (or perceptions of risk) is therefore undertaken less by science itself, but, for example, by energy suppliers, environmentalists, and UN agencies, i.e., groups with global ambitions and organizations. Perception of risk, dread, or opportunity attach themselves to

[28]T. Wigley and S. Raper, in a note to policy makers to accompany their review article "Implications for Climate and Sea Level of Revised IPCC Emission Scenarios," *Nature*, vol. 357, 28 May 1992. Scientists who have to fund research are as astute as any other lobbying group about tailoring their arguments (but much less so the facts) to the "needs" of the funding body.

multiple interests, the outcome of which will be decided through their battles with one another. The outcome is unpredictable. Both insecurity and security are served by research. The choice of which perception will prevail is not that of science, but of politics. There is no need to fear science – it is a servant and not a master, and it is the masters we need to watch the most.

Politically, this growth in knowledge may strengthen the dominance of the North by drawing intellectual and material resources away from militarism and consumerism. This societal transformation, if achieved, will require much more than the diagnostic knowledge that the natural sciences can provide. But will this solve the North–South problem?

Secondly, I doubt that "technoscience" will introduce new insecurity. Mankind has lived with technological threats for a very long time and has had to adjust to the consequences of unwise or ignorant actions. A bit more precaution and pre-testing is certainly needed as the scale of impacts increases. Scientific notions that climate change is dangerous for mankind are beginning to have impacts on policy developments in many areas, many of which could be called "technoscience," and would be worthwhile even without climate change – i.e., an environmental threat is used to encourage innovation and investment in the future. Here success depends, surely, on whether individuals, firms, and governments have the foresight and means to do so. This process, if successful, may further strengthen the *Verwissenschaftlichung* of Western society, as well as the potential for technoscience to solve the problems it has created.

Thirdly, I doubt that there will be a World Meteorological Order. Even if humankind were to reorganize itself fundamentally in response to meteorological threats, this could be either democratic or authoritarian, depending on who implements agreed responses. Since the impact of climate change is likely to be harshest on the poorest, I cannot see it becoming a major incentive for a redistribution of power and welfare.

This raises the question of whether it is risky to rely too much on science for policy, a risk that may relate less to environmental damage than to the narrowness of the knowledge base upon which policy responses are based. Technological and political opportunities may be missed if no action is taken until "sufficient" evidence has been collected. The advisory dominance of the natural sciences has become apparent, and may well lead to misconceptions about the powers of this knowledge to direct policy.

Yet the concern of environmentalists remains: before we do understand our planet scientifically, the planet may have rid itself of mankind, or at least of society as we know it. This concern rests on a question that science cannot answer, for it comes from philosophy rather than science. The global science of climate prediction is surely too weak and politically dependent to create an independent perception of serious risk or global insecurity: this is done (or not) by the political actors who use scientific debates for their own purposes.

My own question is which of the two is the greater threat today: that mankind is destroyed by climate change, or that it destroys itself by not learning how to deal with global poverty and violence springing from the lack of fairness in the distribution of resources and welfare. Efforts to make environmental security the basis of global organization may therefore be a mistake. We can approach the environmental threat more safely by ensuring that our societies do not fall apart for non-environmental reasons, though it will not be in the interest of knowledge to say so.

CONCLUSIONS

Science may be needed to reassure and calm (when too much fear or anxiety poses threats to political instability), or to raise concern and dread of the future. It can promise solutions as well as expose dangers. It cannot lose as long as it remains a trusted source of legitimate authority. It must therefore remain flexible and responsive to political needs – and even fashion.

The call for immediate action to reduce greenhouse gases will no longer come from scientists. Having warned us in collusion with the environmentalists, they are now busy for at least another decade. One risk I have identified in the global warming story, therefore, is that of excessive faith in knowledge as an incentive for action. Even if there is no climate change, the increase in knowledge that we are likely to gain will be enormous, but what will we do with it? Who will benefit from it?

International environmental treaties in general face a major difficulty. Because of their potentially major effects on virtually the whole of society (income distribution, commercial competition, and lifestyles), governments will approach them extremely cautiously. They cannot trust science to the extent of making policy fully dependent on it. While strengthening scientific endeavor and enterprise, the dependence of policy on science may make governments hostage to research lobbies and lead to missed opportunities. As the current desire of IPCC to remain a purely "technical body" shows, scientists prefer to be free from commitment and want to return to value-free research, leaving the "use" of knowledge to others.

One of the characteristics of the climate convention, and many other international environmental treaties, is their almost total reliance on scientific evidence and argumentation for the justification of action. More specifically, this involves evidence of harm or damage provided on the basis of knowledge claims made by the natural sciences. Why should this be so? One reason is surely that diagnostic science has so little to say about solutions. It protects the "sovereignty of states," which are then left to draw their own conclusions. The other reason relates to the power of science to protect itself and promote its own growth.

If there is a risk to society arising from the New Scientific Universalism (global modeling), it is that it encourages policy to be based on far too narrow a conception of mankind. If it were adopted as the foundation of policy, it would make precaution and common sense difficult and allow politicians to hand responsibility to a "priesthood" of people primarily interested in finding out more. Too much environmental globalism may become a justification for the powerful to dominate policy and exploit resources for their own benefit. I am not against global science, but against the interested use of science in global politics.

Having studied the climate threat, I have concluded that the main environmental problem facing the world today is not potential environmental change, but the use of such threats to further strengthen the North, and the institutions of science as clients of power and wealth. The poor now have the power to destroy the planet faster than climate change, beginning with our fragile political systems. Can technoscience help here? Perhaps because it cannot help, political and scientific elites find environmental threats so useful in instilling feelings of insecurity and, hopefully from this, of common purpose, and the willingness to sacrifice. The interests of politics and science do not always coincide.

13

The Role of Nongovernmental Organizations in UNCED

Ann Doherty

Nongovernmental organization (NGO) is a sterile term for a vibrant entity, and NGOs were involved in UNCED to an unprecedented degree.[1] Nearly 1500 organizations were accredited to the UNCED process, and they represented a vast array of sectoral and interest groups, including agriculture, environment, development, health, human rights, indigenous peoples, peace, population, religion, trade, youth, and women. In degrees that varied by country and stage of the negotiations, many of these NGOs were permitted to assist in the preparation of their national report, submit written statements, and make oral interventions in Preparatory Committee (PrepCom) meetings, and in some cases were invited to join their national delegations to UNCED. They were also instrumental in providing the secretariat and national delegations with background documents and information used in the drafting of Agenda 21.

However, despite this unusual access, many NGOs appeared frustrated by their lack of substantive input into the UNCED negotiations. During the two-year preparation process, NGOs attending PrepComs were disappointed by the increasing number of informal negotiations to which they were barred access, as it was in these closed sessions that many of the most important decisions were made. In the end, a great number of NGOs seemed disillusioned and frustrated by the outcomes of UNCED, since few of their goals for concrete change in the realms of environment and development were achieved. Many attributed this perception of inefficacy to the

[1]At the conception of the UN system, the term "NGO" was used as an umbrella to describe all of the independent actors that had some interest in international affairs. Traditionally, NGOs have been limited to not-for-profit groups, thus excluding business and industry. An alternative term, "independent sector," was popularized during UNCED, due to the aversion of some NGOs to being lumped together in the same category as business. For the purposes of this chapter, the term NGO will be used to describe not-for-profit pressure groups that have expanded across national boundaries, and have to some degree become involved with the operation of the UN system. To avoid confusion, business and industry will be considered an independent sector, but not members of the traditional NGO community. This distinction is necessary, as one of the many unique features of UNCED was that it assembled all of these disparate actors in an often awkward embrace.

Negotiating International Regimes: Lessons Learned from the United Nations Conference on Environment and Development (G. Sjöstedt, *et al.*, eds.; 1-85966-077-0; © IIASA; pub. Graham & Trotman, 1994; printed in Great Britain), pp. 199–218.

privileged role played by business and industry in the negotiations, as victories won by this sector often meant defeat for NGOs seeking reform of the global system.

Taking into account the massive amounts of time, energy, and expense devoted to the process by numerous NGOs, was their participation in UNCED a worthwhile pursuit? Could more effective NGO participation have resulted in greater successes (e.g., binding conventions) at UNCED? Or does the international negotiation system by its very nature discourage the participation of outside groups? Can NGOs contribute fruitfully to a negotiation process of the UNCED type or are they primarily an impediment to progress? Are certain types of NGOs better suited to the UN fora than others? Finally, did NGOs benefit from participating in UNCED in ways other than influencing the official process? These questions are important, since the role of NGOs in future negotiations will most likely continue to increase.

NGOs will be examined in two ways. First, it is instructive to directly juxtapose NGOs with their opposites: governments. The characteristics of governments are well defined. They are powerful, sovereign, economically motivated, experienced, financially secure, well resourced, and often bureaucratically inflexible. Generally, those governments with the strongest combination of these traits are most successful in achieving their goals within the system. By extension, those NGOs with goals and tactics most like those of governments will be most comfortable and effective working within the system. Nongovernmental actors that possess fewer governmental traits are more likely to be frustrated, and may choose other means of attaining their goals.

The tension created between NGOs that are more effective working within the process and those that are more productive outside creates a second level for analysis. To some extent, this tension is a reflection of the divisions between governments throughout UNCED: between Northern and Southern objectives and principally between environment and development. Differences of goals between the more established environmental groups from Northern countries and the grassroots, development-oriented NGOs from the South were partially resolved within the NGO community, with many strong coalitions bridging the hemispheric and environment/development gaps. What was more difficult to resolve were differences in tactics between "inside" and "outside" NGOs. This dynamic was an important factor during UNCED, and may be the force that will impel the NGO movement into the next era of international cooperation.

In an attempt to illuminate some of the questions raised within the proposed framework, the historical roles of NGOs both outside and within the UN system are traced, focusing first upon the precursor to UNCED: the 1972 Stockholm Conference on the Human Environment. Next, UNCED itself is explored: the process, the problems, the products, and the tensions between actors. Many of the observations and analyses are based upon primary data collected from NGOs accredited to UNCED via a detailed questionnaire (see Appendix 13.1 on p. 215 for the basic results). Finally, some conclusions about the impact of NGOs on the negotiations, on their movement, and on future post-UNCED regime governance are discussed.

ROLES OF NGOs AT THE UN

The UN officially sanctions nongovernmental participation for the following purposes: mobilization of popular support for and publicizing of UN activities, providing expertise to the secretariat and member states, and monitoring the implementation of UN conventions (ECOSOC Resolution 1296, 1968). However, two essential functions of NGOs – educating public opinion and offering alternative perspectives and solutions to governments – are far more controversial within the UN and its member states.

It is not uncommon for NGOs to possess greater scientific, technical, and statistical expertise than governments and the secretariat. NGOs often have a more interconnected and holistic view of the issues that are tackled within the UN and they can be helpful in illuminating these linkages to delegates. For example, NGOs have been instrumental in emphasizing the interactive nature of the global economic system, environmental degradation, development strategies, poverty, and the military. In addition, NGOs may be particularly helpful to delegates from small or less wealthy nations, who are often responsible for handling several issue areas concurrently and may need concrete comprehensive information. (Such assistance, of course, is not without benefit to the NGO, who has the chance to convince the open-minded delegate that the negotiating strategies offered are superior to all others.)

One of the most valuable roles played by NGOs within the UN system is that of enforcing compliance with treaties and conventions. Accredited NGOs have an advantage over the media and the rest of the public in that they can be present in consultative meetings, where they can acquire intimate knowledge about the activities of states in areas such as human rights, environment, and disarmament. Some delegates refer to the process of careful note-taking and conferring by the NGOs present at meetings as "silent lobbying" – a powerful mechanism in encouraging the accountability of governments to the public. And in addition to pressuring transgressive governments, many NGOs are also active in the field – monitoring the implementation of and compliance with agreements, assessing environmental, health, and other impacts, and publicizing violations, a politically sensitive task that governments may be reluctant to perform.

In the past decade, many NGOs have enhanced their reputations as providers of credible scientific information, accurate facts and statistics, and sound policy options. Some choose to utilize this information within the UN, but the majority focus their educational capacities upon the rest of the nongovernmental community. NGOs are practiced in disseminating critical information to the public through publications and the media, and thereby forcing issues on to the political agendas of decision makers. Through these activities, NGOs can build a large domestic constituency that makes it difficult for a government to deviate from a position in the interest of expediency or under pressure from commercial lobbies (Burke, in Willetts, 1982: 114). This role of public educator, which often involves working outside the UN system and taking critical perspectives on UN programs and policies, is not overly popular among governments and secretariat officials.

Yet, NGOs within the UN offer what governments and the secretariat cannot or choose not to provide – innovation, flexibility, objectivity, and independence. They are not constrained in the same way as governments to satisfy constituencies or preserve sovereignty. Unlike governments, they often enjoy broad grassroots support that instills legitimacy to their work. Moreover, NGOs are often not pressured to reach an internal consensus as in large governmental bureaucracies, which can suppress differing ideas, criticism, and dissent (Chiang, 1981: 6). As instruments of democratic representation, NGOs can be considered as the "main social countervailing power to the state" (Lador-Lederer, 1963: 60).

However, NGOs that have the ability to glide smoothly between their grassroots supporters and international politicians are rare entities. Many NGOs are either unfamiliar or impatient with the stately paced, nitpicking and politicking lobbying process. They often become frustrated and experiment with other methods of influencing the proceedings with varying degrees of success. As these alternative mechanisms tend to further complicate an already complex procedure, these NGOs become unpopular within the secretariat, with delegates, and with their more professional lobbying counterparts. As a result, few NGOs have mastered the art of transferring a grassroots sense of urgency and responsibility into the formal arena of the UN.

THE 1972 STOCKHOLM UN CONFERENCE ON THE HUMAN ENVIRONMENT

The environment became an item on the global agenda for the first time in 1972, at the UN Conference on the Human Environment (UNCHE) held in Stockholm. When the Swedish government first proposed the idea of holding an environmental conference, it met with lukewarm endorsements by both governments and NGOs, neither of which were particularly anxious about the state of the environment. Developing countries, in particular, were frankly disinterested in conservation efforts, preferring to concentrate their efforts on the quickest possible rate of development. However, once the preparatory process for the conference was initiated, over 100 nations and in excess of 400 NGOs became intimately involved in the formulation of a Declaration with 26 Principles, and an Action Plan with five resolutions and 109 recommendations.

It is believed that there were more NGOs present in Stockholm than at any previous UN conference. They undertook a panoply of tasks during the preparatory period, which included assisting government delegations in the preparation of their national reports, providing information to governments and the secretariat, lobbying on specific issues, and publishing a daily newspaper for both NGOs and governments. However, during the actual two-week conference period, NGOs were relegated to a separate "Miljöforum" (environmental forum), which was physically distant and emotionally removed from official proceedings. In the parallel conference, NGOs had daily briefings on the progress of the official meeting, heard visiting speakers, and organized demonstrations.

The efficacy and equitableness of having a separate forum for NGOs was disputed during Stockholm and continues to be a matter of controversy among NGOs. As the number of organizations seeking to participate increases with every global conference, universal accommodation of every interested NGO in the official event has become logistically impossible. Yet many NGOs feel alienated from the actual decision-making process when confined to a separate area, particularly for those who were not involved in the preparatory process. In Stockholm, it was clear to most in the government delegations that the NGO activities had little discernible effect on "the real action." There has since been real disillusionment on the part of many NGOs as they have come to realize how little a role they actually played (McCormick, 1989: 101). However, many nongovernmental actors support the parallel meeting structure as an opportunity to criticize the official process unhindered, and to offer alternative views, capture the attention of the media, and thus the general public, and to communicate with NGOs from different areas of the world on issues of common concern.

In the two decades between Stockholm and Rio, NGOs zealously exchanged information and coordinated campaigns in what has become a powerful movement and a major force in international politics. In the early 1980s, there were an estimated 13 000 environmental NGOs in the industrialized nations and close to 2500 in developing countries. The growth rate was, and continues to be, phenomenal, particularly in developing countries over the past decade. Cooperation between these Northern and Southern NGOs has been impressive for the most part, and in many ways has surpassed that between governments from the different hemispheres.

As communications between citizens' groups in different parts of the world grew in scope and complexity, so did the nature of environmental problems during the 20 years between UNCHE and UNCED. First, they became more explicitly interconnected, as environmental problems including climate change, biodiversity destruction, and deforestation began to elicit global concern. Second, the connections between the environment and other areas – including development, demilitarization, trade, debt, and women's issues – became more prominent. NGOs were paramount in the process of bringing these interconnections to the attention of governments and the public, and have become progressively more integral in this capacity. Thus, when the UN General Assembly called for a world conference on environment and development in Resolution 44/228 in 1989, the global NGO community rallied to the cause.

THE RIO CONFERENCE

Participation and Accreditation

UNCED was groundbreaking for the NGO community in several respects. It was the first time that environmental issues were examined formally in conjunction with developmental problems in international negotiations. Moreover, it involved a massive mobilization of the NGO community, which allowed practically universal access, at least in principle, to official negotiations.

There were several prominent NGO networks that coordinated and facilitated NGO access to UNCED. The most influential of these were the International Facilitating Committee (IFC), which was created specifically to assist NGO work within UNCED, and was a co-coordinator of the NGO Global Forum in Rio; the Environmental Liaison Centre International, created after Stockholm to facilitate communication between NGOs; and the Forum of Brazilian NGOs for UNCED, the other coordinator of the Global Forum. There were also several active national networks that were created specifically for UNCED, including the US Citizen's Network and the Canadian Participatory Committee for UNCED. It is important to keep in mind that although these official networks were the most visible, NGO participation was also catalyzed in nonofficial and less observable ways. Thousands of communities, grassroots groups, and schoolchildren from all over the globe were involved in UNCED for a different purpose: their goal was not to lobby governments nor to directly influence negotiations, but rather to vocalize their concerns on environment, development, poverty, and other related issues. Even after UNCED, these international, national, and subnational groups continue to unite in what is becoming an increasingly dynamic and powerful movement.

At the outset, the UNCED secretariat supported NGO participation in all aspects of the conference. General Assembly Resolution 44/228 specified that NGOs with consultative status to ECOSOC be permitted to participate in UNCED and the secretariat interpreted this to include their participation in the PrepCom meetings. The negative emotional reaction by some national delegates to this expansion of eligibility was not anticipated, nor was the prolonged battle between the secretariat, governments, and NGOs that was launched at the first PrepCom. But most of all, no one was prepared for the voluminous influx of NGOs seeking accreditation over the two-year preparatory process.

Although there were no more than one dozen NGOs in Nairobi at the inception of the UNCED process in August 1990, their role, as well as the future role of NGOs in UNCED, immediately became a matter of heated debate that obstructed all substantive discussions for nearly the entire first week of negotiations. The majority of governments present openly and vociferously encouraged NGO participation for various reasons: the Brazilian Ambassador, for example, cited their creativity and imagination; the head of the Canadian delegation spoke of the need to ensure that "NGO networks ... be regarded as systems that, because of their effective functioning, ensure a wide involvement of concerned citizens in many countries" (Goree, 1990: posted on en.unced.general); and Secretary General Maurice Strong lauded the abilities of NGOs to provide substantial contributions to the process, including papers, reports, and statistics. A few delegations, however, were reluctant to so readily sanction the participation of NGOs. Mauritania and Tunisia, in particular, preferred to avoid the entire question of nongovernmental participation until the next meeting of the General Assembly: as a result of previous experience, they may have been suspicious of the pro-environmental protection and anti-development postures of many Northern NGOs. After much debate and pressure from the anti-NGO delegations, the question of general NGO participation at UNCED was deferred to the December 1990 General Assembly session. The Plenary voted to allow NGO participation for the remaining two weeks of the first PrepCom meeting, but a poor precedent had already been set in the realm of cooperation between NGOs and governments.

Nonetheless, recommendations for NGO participation were drafted by the pro-NGO coalition, with the basic proposals that NGOs accredited to the UNCED process be permitted to submit papers and presentations to the PrepCom, and to make oral statements on matters within their special competence at meetings when approved by the PrepCom chairman. The recommendations further specified that all participation by NGOs manifest equitable regional distribution, a balance between environment and development organizations, and include grassroots as well as more established groups. Secretariat assistance for NGO participation was also stressed – in particular, the need for support of NGOs in their information dissemination and communication efforts in preparation for the conference.

The official participation process was further complicated by discord within the NGO community. The perennial problem of the definition of an NGO was resurrected: many were disturbed that, for UNCED purposes, the International Chamber of Commerce and other business coalitions were grouped together with the predominantly not-for-profit NGO community. Furthermore, the Environmental Liaison

Centre International (ELCI) publicly withdrew its membership in the International Facilitating Committee (IFC) due to concerns about the IFC's representativeness and mandate. The rifts in the nongovernmental community were deemed by many as poorly timed, since the struggle for opportunities to participate would be aided by a unified NGO front. However, crisis was avoided, and consensus was eventually, although temporarily, achieved.

The General Assembly approved NGO participation at its meeting in December 1990 and NGOs arrived in Geneva in March 1991 for the second PrepCom under the impression that their troubles were over. However, the delegate from Tunisia immediately resuscitated the qualifications issue, claiming that his recollection of the resolution was that only coalitions of organizations would be allowed to speak. PrepCom Chairman Tommy Koh clarified the meaning of the resolution, which provided for NGOs speaking individually unless their numbers became unmanageable. Furthermore, problems with accreditation began almost instantaneously. The process was designed to work as follows: prior to the beginning of any PrepCom, an NGO interested in participating in PrepCom meetings could present to the secretariat its credentials and a written statement of its relevance and competence within the UNCED framework. The secretariat would consider these applications, and submit both positive and negative accreditation recommendations to the PrepCom. The PrepCom then had a 24-hour period in which to accept or reject these advised applications; if unable to meet during this period, these NGOs under consideration would be temporarily accredited during the interim. Finally, any accredited NGO would remain eligible for all succeeding PrepComs and the official event in Rio de Janeiro. Notwithstanding the clarification of the accreditation process, however, the secretariat was unable to process the influx of NGO applications received at the start, preventing the recommendations from being passed on to the PrepCom, and during the first few days of the negotiations, NGOs were forced to remain silent in the Plenary and working groups. Many of the NGOs in Geneva were disillusioned by this involuntary exile from the proceedings:

> Despite official "lip-service" by many countries to NGO involvement, there are several countries who are openly hostile and many more we suspect that are using front countries to delay and block NGO participation. There is a growing sense of frustration from many NGOs who believe that the process wants our nominal participation but that a commitment to real involvement has not materialized in time to allow input during critical periods. To date, everything regarding NGO involvement has happened too late in the process to allow anyone to claim that NGOs have been involved throughout the PrepCom process (Goree, 1991, posted on en.unced.general).

However, once the hitches were finally worked out in the accreditation process and the number of secretariat staff devoted to this task was increased, nearly all of the NGOs that applied for accreditation were accepted by both the secretariat and the PrepCom. Further positive developments in Geneva were the appearance of many of the provisions promised to NGOs at the first PrepCom, including an NGO lounge and offices with copy and fax machines. Briefing sessions for new NGOs were provided by the International Facilitating Committee (IFC), and more information became available for distribution. NGO concerns regarding the need to facilitate developing country participation through funding mechanisms were partially alleviated by the establishment of a Southern participation fund by the Canadians.

The extent to which NGOs were allowed to participate in official proceedings depended upon the designation of a negotiation session as formal, informal, or informal–informal. NGOs could present oral interventions only in formal sessions. In informal sessions, they were permitted to observe only with the permission of the chairperson. And in informal–informal sessions, where most of the real nuts and bolts negotiations took place, NGOs were entirely prohibited. During the first three PrepCom meetings, NGOs had virtually unlimited access to sessions, which were for the most part formal and informal. However, as time pressures increased and patience decreased, more sessions were informal–informal, and only accessible by NGOs on official delegations. At the final PrepCom in New York, there were very few formal sessions. This, unfortunately, coincided with a major increase in the number of accredited and participating NGOs, as well as the gradually enhanced ability of some NGOs to contribute more effectively as they learned how to work within the UN system.

During the third PrepCom, NGOs had several struggles with the secretariat and governments over access to informal working group sessions. The official regulations were that the chairperson's permission was needed in order for NGOs to observe. However, decisions about the level of formality in meetings seemed to be made on a capricious basis, and the degree of openness varied not only from working group to working group, but also from day to day within the different groups. NGO frustrations gradually built up, and came to a climax on the final evening of PrepCom III, during a formal discussion concerning many aspects of the next PrepCom in New York. The chairman of Working Group I made a unilateral decision, based on the lateness of the meeting and the general fatigued condition of delegates, to close this session to NGOs, many of whom were already seated in the room. Many of them were reluctant to leave and had to be escorted from the room by conference security guards. Among all of the governments generally supportive of NGO participation, the US government was alone in openly objecting to this forced removal, but only briefly, as the general mood among delegates was one of impatience to end this phase of the negotiations. At several points during the third PrepCom, various NGOs considered completely discontinuing their participation in UNCED, due to the inability of the secretariat and delegates to decide what role would be played by NGOs, and the lack of accountability and transparency shown at these closed sessions.

Although the accreditation mechanics were operating more smoothly at the final PrepCom in New York, problems with NGO access to negotiations continued. The proportion of informal meetings had increased since Geneva and NGO access to most meetings was still decided on a case-by-case basis. During the first week of the fourth PrepCom, NGOs were allowed to sit only in the gallery above the conference room, making it nearly impossible to make contact with delegates or the chairperson, or to obtain official documents. By the second week, the secretariat had implemented a ticketing system, which would allow 35 NGOs on the floor at any given time during formal and informal sessions that were open to NGOs. The tickets were distributed to the earliest arrivals, which was rarely a problem except at occasional meetings of strong interest to all NGOs. Another frustration for NGOs was the insistence by the PrepCom chairman that NGOs focus on sectoral rather than individual interventions in the interests of time and simplicity. An editorial from *Crosscurrents*, an independent NGO publication, observed that:

> NGOs have spent a lot of money and time in following the UNCED process only to find that the U.N. is not ready to incorporate them in its workings and accept them as partners. The U.N. seems to feel that by allowing the NGOs into the corridors, it has created a Frankenstein, and that the monster is out of control As the U.N. has already found, NGOs do not form into neat little groups behind a single spokesperson with a simple message that can be read out in two minutes (*Crosscurrents* editorial, 6–9 March 1992).

In Rio, the issue of sectoral interventions resurfaced. The secretariat had taken the initiative to allocate separate periods of speaking time to 12 sectors, which angered many NGOs. Some disliked the artificiality of the division in a community with an inherent ability to work holistically and seek common goals, whereas others were frustrated that certain "elite" NGOs were chosen to represent their entire sector. A coalition of NGOs accredited to the UN drafted a letter to the Secretary General:

> In our view, it is not meaningful to call for "monolithic" positions to be established by any "sector". It can even be an asset if divergent views and different approaches are heard. Nobody can claim to single-handedly represent one particular constituency, for example "youth" or "women". It is our hope that your affirmation and its active follow up by the secretariat will help to dispel the impression that some initiatives are actively promoted at the expense and exclusion of others (*Crosscurrents*, NGO Plenary Protest, 11 June 1992).

In Rio, the final number of NGOs accredited to UNCED rose to 1420. The secretariat estimated that ad hoc UNCED NGOs were organized in 90 percent of the involved nations, and 70 percent of governments cited "full and close participation from the nongovernmental citizens' affinity groups" (*Earth Summit Times*, June 1992). The majority of accredited NGOs were from Northern industrialized countries, but the number of Southern country NGOs was increased by nearly 100 through the Developing Country NGO Participation Fund and numerous initiatives by wealthier NGOs to sponsor the participation of poorer groups. Another important trend in UNCED participation was the unprecedented number of NGOs on official delegations. During PrepCom IV, approximately 15 delegations included NGOs either as full participants or as official observers. This number rose to approximately 150 NGOs on official delegations by the Earth Summit.

How did NGOs view their overall access to UNCED? Our questionnaire endeavored to ascertain the level of satisfaction among accredited NGOs concerning various aspects of access to official negotiations. Concerning access to negotiating sessions, the great majority (76 percent) were dissatisfied, and a few pointed out that this access became progressively worse from PrepCom to PrepCom and was dismal by Rio. (Predictably, those NGOs that were members of delegations were significantly more likely to be pleased than those not on delegations.) Regarding the amount of speaking time allotted to NGOs, the proportion of NGOs dissatisfied was even stronger: a mere 12 percent found this amount of time to be adequate. Although the immediate implication of these figures is that the process was inadequate in providing for NGO access and speaking needs, one should also take into account the possibility that NGOs did not make full use of the opportunities given to them due to their unfamiliarity with the process. However, a third measure of access, which asked NGOs to estimate the number of written statements that they submitted to delegates, indicated that NGOs were indeed well organized and functioning knowledgeably within the system. The average number of written interventions per NGO hovered between 5 and 6 in a broad range from 0 to 50. Of course, the quality of these interventions is undetermined, but given the fact that many of them were laboriously discussed and drafted by coalitions of NGOs, it can be assumed that this level of input is fairly reliable. A final measure was the level of access that should be allowed for NGOs at future negotiations – universal, the same as at UNCED, or restricted. The majority (62 percent) were in favor of universal access, 38 percent preferred the same level, and not a single NGO responded that access should be restricted. This is in contrast to the opinions of some governments, who have stated that NGOs could be more "effective" if they were more carefully screened and were present in reduced numbers.

An analysis of when NGOs became involved in the UNCED negotiations yields further insight into perceived access and efficacy of NGOs. Only the most extreme cases were included – those NGOs involved as early as the first PrepCom in Nairobi, and those who became involved only at Rio. The resulting statistics confirmed the hypothesis that the later the involvement in the process, the higher the level of frustration and feelings of inefficacy among NGOs. Whereas the earliest involved NGOs met with both their own and with other delegates several times per week, the NGOs that were not accredited until Rio met with other delegates as seldom as bi-weekly, and with their own delegates less than once a week. These latecomers were also less satisfied with the frequency with which their concerns and ideas were incorporated into official documents.

Structures and Processes

NGOs created their own organization structures and implemented unique processes throughout the two-year preparation period for UNCED. They formed a sub-system that mimicked the structures and processes of governments and the UN and facilitated NGO participation within the official system. The NGO system sponsored various daily meetings and briefings, sectoral conferences, and national, regional, and international conferences, forums, and networks. There were also a number of NGO publications, including several newspapers (*Earth Summit Times, Crosscurrents, Terraviva*), and a detailed daily summary of official negotiations (*Earth Summit Bulletin*). Communications between NGOs were essential in spurring the mass mobilization of pressure groups that occurred around UNCED; this was facilitated by several NGO electronic networking systems. In contrast to governments, which generally prefer official arenas for communication, NGOs used these alternative communications networks to exchange information and formulate strategies. In fact, it was observed that "the planning for this Earth Summit has involved the most massive communications exercise ever undertaken in the name of sustainable development" (Hanson and Regallet, 1992: 36).

For many NGOs accredited to UNCED, lobbying was their primary activity. Lobbying at UNCED was manifested in many forms, including education of delegates, dissemination of information, and advocacy of particular causes. Some NGOs were very issue-focused, and came prepared to work within their area of expertise to have specific changes made in documents. These NGOs met daily with other like-minded lobbyists, prepared interventions, and tracked delegates. Many of these specific-issue lobby groups were either regional or sectoral in character: for example, the NGOs most involved in the desertification negotiations were predominantly African, and many indigenous peoples became active in the forest, oceans, and biodiversity debates. Other NGOs concentrated on issues that were only superficially covered on the agenda. These issues – e.g., trade, militarism, debt – were broader and less open for discussion, thus making concrete victories practically nonexistent.

Contact with delegates took place at various times and in different manners. Some NGOs preferred to pass notes to delegates during official sessions; others attempted to corner governmental representatives in the hallways or at coffee breaks; and still others found that the best lobbying was conducted away from the negotiations. In addition, those NGOs chosen to participate on official delegations had unusually prolonged and intimate relations with delegates from many countries, and were able to become fully enmeshed in the process. An important part of their work involved transferring their privileged knowledge to the general NGO community.

Lobbying, when performed well, is a complex procedure. NGOs must judge not only where and when their input is most appropriate, but must ensure that their interventions are clear, well documented, and relevant to the phase of negotiations. Those who devoted the majority of their time and energy to effecting change in official documents were occasionally rewarded, and there are numerous examples in Agenda 21 of text that was suggested by NGOs. Nonetheless, a common NGO complaint was that governments adopted their text solely for the sake of appeasement, and after much struggle. Some NGOs regarded these scattered rewards with frustration, as "fragments of the text without the spirit of the whole recommendation are meaningless" (*Crosscurrents* editorial, 30 March 1991).

When asked how often governments incorporated NGO decisions, our questionnaire provoked a broad range of answers. Those who said that their views were "often" incorporated into documents were few, and tended to have been on delegations or had some other special status in relation to the official process. The most common response was "sometimes," and the remaining answers were evenly divided between "seldom" and "never." A representative comment from this question was "They took some formulations, but never the intentions." Another section of the questionnaire asked NGOs to "describe the most effective way to lobby delegations." The answers were quite simple: maintaining direct, personal contact in order to create a good working relationship as early in the process as possible, preferably beginning in the home country; providing specific deletions and alternatives in the language and documents that delegates are familiar with rather than general statements of principle; being diplomatic, not falling asleep in meetings, and thanking delegates when they do something right.

Another question that provided illuminating responses was which sectors or interest groups were the most effective lobbyists during the UNCED process. Whereas coalitions between different types of groups were common, there were several sectors and interest groups that were particularly visible. Women were deemed the most effective, with business coming a close second, and environmental groups third. Youth, indigenous, and development groups each got honorable mentions.

The Women's Caucus, which was active at PrepComs and further strengthened during the 1990 World Women's Congress for a Healthy Planet, was generally considered the most organized group at PrepComs, and their success was evident by an impressive number of significant interventions and textual changes. For example, when the Group of 77 moved to strike out all references to family planning and population in response to the US threat to delete any mention of over-consumption in Agenda 21, women effectively channeled their outrage and managed to have the original language restored. The success of women in having their concerns reflected in official documents was attributed in questionnaire responses to the coordination by a strong leader in Bella Abzug of the Women's Environment and Development Organization (WEDO); the development of coherent lobbying strategies at the Miami conference; the success of the group in learning how the process worked; and the establishment of good coalitions with government delegates and the secretariat.

As previously mentioned, business has not traditionally been considered an NGO, but the UNCED accreditation process was set up so that not-for-profit business coalitions were allowed to participate in the same capacity as other nonprofit groups. Thus, the International Chamber of Commerce was accredited, as was the Association for Chemical Manufacturers. The Business Council for Sustainable Development (BCSD), a coalition of 50 corporate leaders including Chevron, Dow Chemical, Dupont and Royal Dutch Shell, was created specifically for UNCED, and was chaired by Stephen Schmidheiny, a personal friend and the "chief adviser on industry and business" to Secretary General Maurice Strong. Furthermore, business leaders involved in these so-called NGOs participated on some delegations as governmental advisers. Such preferential treatment for business allowed this sector to have overwhelming influence upon the process, including a paragraph in Agenda 21 about the importance of the free market economy. Questionnaire respondees had much to say about the success of business as an NGO: Business "has been favored by the UNCED secretariat," "succeeded in escaping all regulations," and "reduced the scope of the Conference." Furthermore, "Corporate interests ruled the agenda and entrenched themselves further as economic dictators," "Business has money and their point of view is often the same as the leaders." Few NGOs seemed to have used this unusual contact with business as an opportunity to forge new coalitions.

The success of the environmental sector at UNCED is self-explanatory. This sector primarily encompasses large, well-established and well-funded organizations such as the World Wildlife Fund, the International Union for the Conservation of Nature (IUCN), and the Sierra Club, as well as some smaller grassroots groups. These organizations are generally from industrialized countries and are often focused on conservation issues such as forests, biodiversity and oceans. They are generally well financed, well prepared, and experienced in lobbying. The environmental NGOs appeared to have reaped the most rewards from UNCED: not only were their contributions incorporated into official documents, but they profited from the opportunity to build coalitions with development groups and other NGOs.

Youth had a unique role in the UNCED process. Many did not have the experience or issue-specific backgrounds necessary for in-depth lobbying of delegations. Moreover, most of them were disillusioned with the efficacy of lobbying alone to effect change and felt that the exclusion of several vital issues from the agenda was a crucial omission. Thus, they focused a good portion of their time publicizing the fact that they considered UNCED a failure: planning actions and demonstrations, issuing critical press releases, and making occasional disparaging statements to the Plenary concerning the sluggish progress of negotiations and the lack of political will on the part of many governments. They were praised by questionnaire respondees for their "refusal to compromise" and for "succeeding in stretching the envelope of the range of debate." On the other hand, those committed to working inside the process were quite critical of the role of youth – for example, pointing out that "they lost patience and developed an outside strategy that undermined the work of those who were working hard to change from within."

The role of indigenous peoples in UNCED is difficult to categorize, as most of the indigenous peoples participating in UNCED considered themselves sovereign nations rather than NGOs. As Oren Lyons, chief of the Onondaga nation, explained: "UNCED accredits organizations and NGOs. But we will certainly not subject our nations to an NGO status. That disenfranchises us from the discussion because there is not a specific place for us. We are requesting special accreditation for indigenous nations and peoples" (Lerner, 1992). In fact, many of the indigenous peoples did not consider themselves part of the NGO community present at PrepComs and in Rio, and often conducted their business independently without forming cross-sectoral coalitions. This was reflected in the section of the questionnaire that asked NGOs to identify sectors or organizations with which they felt they had inadequate contact: indigenous peoples groups were the most frequent response.

A significant number of accredited NGOs avoided lobbying altogether during UNCED preparations or supplemented their lobbying with other tactics, including alternative conferences, workshops, and demonstrations. These groups were generally cynical about official participation, and felt that their strengths and skills could be better used working outside the process in some form. Youth were common outsiders, as well as more radical NGOs from the Northern countries and many developing country NGOs. Those working inside the process and those on the outside frequently regarded each other with suspicion and distrust. Insiders feared that their hard-won positions within the official process would be jeopardized by the more independent and critical tactics of a subset of NGOs; and those NGOs who eschewed lobbying in favor of direct action, or other outside events, were critical of inside NGOs, many of whom they considered as being coopted by the UNCED process. The authors of *EcoCurrents* were critical of this trend:

> The UNCED process has divided, coopted and weakened the green movement.... On the one hand UNCED brought every possible NGO into the system of lobbying governments, while on the other hand it quietly promoted business to take over the solutions. NGOs are now trapped in a farce by which they have lent support to governments in return for some small concessions on language and thus legitimized the process of increased industrial development.... After decades of battle the UN discovered the truth of the old adage, if you can't beat someone, join them...by making them believe they [NGOs] were winning ground inch by inch, they failed to notice that they were now becoming part of the system (Finger and Chatterjee, 1992: 4).

North versus South

Environment and development issues define the North–South separation perhaps more precisely than any other set of problems. From the outset, differences of perspectives and goals between the Group of 77 developing nations and the industrialized countries colored the UNCED negotiations. These differences were also visible within the NGO community, although many barriers were overcome by the end of the two-year process, and new coalitions between Northern and Southern countries will probably sustain this partnership. As Vandana Shiva from the Third World Network pointed out: "Those of us deeply involved have found our partners are crossing the North–South divide much more effectively than governments" (NGLS, E&D File No. 25).

One section of our questionnaire asked NGOs to comment on whether or not they observed a difference in the goals and/or tactics of Northern and Southern NGOs. Some 80 percent of those polled answered in the affirmative and provided brief descriptions of these differences. According to their responses, Northern NGOs focused much more on "cosmetic" environmental conservation problems, whereas Southerners were more inclined to work on debt, poverty, development, or economic systems. This coincided with their respective tactics, with Northern NGOs working more incrementally on sectoral issues, and Southerners focusing on broader, more cross-sectoral goals and more fundamental systemic change. Terms that were frequently mentioned in reference to Northern strategies were "experienced," "specialized," "pragmatic," "technical," "domineering," and "aggressive." Southerners were categorized as "radical," "analytical," "practical," "ideological," "theoretical," and "subtle." Northern NGOs had superior resources and information and were more organized lobbyists. However, some NGOs pointed out that Southern NGOs had a great deal of patience and lobbied hard for more interconnection between issues. Some felt that Northern NGOs compromised too much in the process, whereas Southern groups held fast to their hard-line positions. As one respondent put it, "Northerners lobbied governments, while Southerners built an international NGO movement."

Further analysis of the responses revealed some interesting results. First, when Northern and Southern groups were compared, there was a significant difference ($p < .007$) in the level of negotiations at which each became involved. The average Northern NGO became involved in the UNCED process during PrepCom III, whereas the average Southern NGO did not participate fully until the final PrepCom seven months later. This delayed involvement in the process, in large part due to lack of information and funding, greatly reduced the chance of Southern NGOs becoming integrated into the complex negotiating process. Indeed, Southern NGOs met less frequently with either their own national or other government delegates on average than did Northern NGOs (every second week rather than every week), and found this level of access to governmental representatives less useful ($p < .043$). Another interesting difference between Northern and Southern NGOs was their rating of the effectiveness of gathering information on issues discussed at UNCED ($p < .008$). It can be hypothesized that the frustration with information collection on the part of Southern NGOs stems at least in part from the availability of most information being in English only.

Outcomes: NGO Global Forum, Agenda 21, and Alternative Treaties

The Global Forum has been described as a circus, as Woodstock II, and as a colossal mess. The estimated number of nongovernmental participants was 30 000 and they traveled from 166 countries. The extent of the activities was vast: from intense sectoral negotiating sessions that resulted in 30 "alternative treaties" to a protest against the World Bank; from theater and dance to celebrity appearances; and from workshops on a panoply of issues to a backward march to Rio Centro to symbolize NGO opinion of the progress made at UNCED. The excitement was heightened by the near-bankruptcy of the event: with a debt totaling US $2 million, the electricity, translation, and meeting areas were saved at the last minute only by an emotional fund-raising drive. Many NGOs were enthusiastic about the opportunities to meet other like - minded people; others were disgusted by the "non - serious" tone of the event.

The Forum was completely separate from the official UNCED conference. The events were held 45 kilometers apart and travel between them was difficult and expensive. Attempts to minimize the physical distance (regarded by some as an intentional tactic to distract meddlesome NGOs) were made with tele-conferences and visits by some delegates to the Forum. However, many were not assuaged, including Forum organizer Chip Lindner: "You got the feeling, if you were an NGO, that there was a sense of tokenism, you were somehow a lesser citizen, a lesser human being. What was lost was this great facility for human interaction with Heads [of State]" (E&D File No. 25).

Many of the NGOs who had been lobbying at the PrepComs over the previous two years focused their energies on the official process at Rio Centro; each accredited NGO was permitted two observers in the official negotiations. However, due to the fact that there was little left to lobby by the Earth Summit, and the problem that Rio Centro was as full of delegates, secretariat staff, security, and media as the Global Forum was packed with NGOs, led many to comment that they felt even less influential than they had during the PrepComs.

One substantial product of NGO participation in UNCED was a chapter in Agenda 21 called "Strengthening the Role of Major Groups." The chapter discusses the creation of a "real social partnership" between governments and NGOs, and discusses the need to provide "mechanisms for the substantive involvement of NGOs at all levels from policy and decision-making to implementation" (A/Conf.151/PC/100/Add.13). A large percentage of this chapter was drafted by coalitions of NGOs, and discussed at length in official sessions. Indeed, its very existence is rather impressive, when one considers that NGOs were such a source of controversy at the first PrepCom.

An alternative treaties process was first proposed during the third PrepCom as a way to supplement and react to the official negotiating process. In Rio, over 3000 NGOs collaborated on the drafting of more than 30 alternative treaties at the Global Forum, and an elaborate structure was created for follow-up and implementation. Each treaty had both a Southern and a Northern coordinator, and regional meetings to discuss treaty implementation were scheduled for the next year. The alternative treaties process was in many respects a reaction to the general failure of governments to produce strong commitments to action at UNCED, and a desire to produce results that were more democratic than those coming from the official side. The NGO treaties cover a broader range of issues than does Agenda 21 and are more detailed and strongly phrased. They are an attempt to be proactive rather than critical of governments, and to achieve solutions that can be implemented independently of governments. On the other hand, some NGOs found the alternative process overly bureaucratic and analogous to the official process in its procedural hang-ups and squabbles over phrasing. Some NGOs called the alternate treaty process "dogmatic," as "stifling creativity," "lopsided," and failing in crucial linkages (UNCED NGO Press Release no. 253, posted on en.unced.general).

Post-Rio NGO Activities

Post-UNCED work among NGOs began almost immediately after the Summit ended. The treaties are still being reviewed and signed, and UNCED evaluation meetings have taken place in many countries. Most of the UNCED-related monitoring and implementation of Agenda 21 work will take place on local and national levels, but future global collaboration is also in the works, with an international UNCED follow-up and future planning meeting slated for 1993 in the United Kingdom. In Rio, NGO networks discussed future participation in a number of different UN conferences, including the 1992 General Assembly meeting, the 1993 Conference on Human Rights, the 1994 Population Conference, the 50th Anniversary of the United Nations, and the 1995 Conference on Women. In the questionnaire, virtually all (99 percent) of the responding NGOs planned to continue networking on a regional or international level, and the majority (93 percent) planned to be involved in UNCED follow-up, e.g., implementing Agenda 21.

One issue that will doubtless be debated in the post-Rio period is the idea of "institutionalizing" NGO input with some sort of advisory mechanism from a select number of NGOs. The benefits of such a mechanism are simplicity and the assurance that NGO input would be considered. The drawbacks are that the selection process for such a body could be highly controversial and it would be difficult to ensure that the voices of all sectors of society were being taken into account. Response to the issue of institutionalization for NGOs in the questionnaire produced an even split between those in favor of such a device and those opposed. Those supporting institutionalization cited the UNCED proposal for a Sustainable Development Commission, which would incorporate NGO input as a suitable mechanism. Many qualified their support with the requirement that such a body be open and accountable and not dominated by larger, more established NGOs. Interestingly, the reactions of those opposed to institutionalization were among the most vehement responses in the entire questionnaire. These anti-institutionalists feared the "bureaucratization," "sterilization," "homogeneity," "cooptation," "power struggles," the transformation of NGOs into "a rubber stamp," and adoption of general government-like behavior. Fears surfaced that "the voices of small and poor NGOs would be lost among big, rich, and powerful NGOs," that "the global relationship of NGOs is in formation and must evolve unconstrained by artificial and premature bureaucracy," and "the NGO community does not sympathize with the idea of creating a UN-style NGO bureaucracy to 'represent' such a vast and diverse movement."

CONCLUSIONS

As it is premature to make final declarations about the implications of UNCED, it is difficult to assess whether NGO participation was worthwhile. If only the NGO perspective is considered, participation was at least valuable in terms of developing new networks, acquisition of information, and heightened public awareness. As far as the success of the conference itself, although few expectations were met in terms of binding agreements, those that were hammered out can only be implemented through the active intervention and monitoring by NGOs. When asked to evaluate their participation in UNCED in retrospect, and whether the time, money, and energy devoted to the process was worthwhile, a surprising majority of NGOs replied in the affirmative. Most qualified their answers though, as the majority of NGOs did not feel that they had a real impact on the official UNCED process. However, NGOs generally appreciated the value of the process in other ways. For example, Patricia Carney, a US NGO, commented: "While we may not have gotten exactly what we wanted or needed from the Earth Summit, an enormous amount of positive action has begun. We left with the strong message that – even if governments won't take leadership – individual citizens, organizations and businesses will take significant actions, and that the mechanisms are in place for this to happen" (Hussain, 1992: 5).

One of the major impediments affecting the outcome of UNCED was that the agenda was set without NGO input, thus excluding some issues deemed crucial by the NGO community. Furthermore, the earlier that connections were made between governments and NGOs, the more influence NGOs had on national positions, which otherwise tended to become inflexible early in the negotiations. Providing education and orientation for NGOs about working within the UN system and with government delegations could also reduce frustration levels for both parties.

How could NGO participation have been more effective in attaining their goals for UNCED? Much revolved around the concept of support: more financial and human resources for NGOs, prior distribution of draft treaties, better meeting facilities and translation services, an information clearinghouse for NGOs, greater access to governments, more support for groups working outside the process, and more support from NGO movements in home countries would have likely yielded improved effectiveness. One of the most important lessons learned in the UNCED process was that in order to have any effect whatsoever on the official "inside" negotiations, NGOs must become fully involved and at the earliest phase of the process.

It would be a mistake to conclude that only "inside" NGOs have any chance of being effective in negotiations of the UNCED genre, or that "outside" groups should completely abandon all official activities. On the contrary, lobbying is most effective when complemented by the generally more creative proposals and statements generated outside the process. NGOs should capitalize on the fact that they are not governments and do not have to work within the narrow confines of bureaucracy. Whereas governments were unable to bridge the gaps effectively between environment–development and North–South in UNCED, NGOs proved that diverse sectors and hemispheres can cooperate productively and overcome traditional divisions. Through the UNCED experience, NGOs have been transformed into a diverse but cohesive and communicating movement: one that has learned from its unchartered path through the UNCED negotiations, and can play a major role in the future governance of international environmental regimes.

APPENDIX 13.1 QUESTIONNAIRE FOR UNCED NGOS

The total number of completed questionnaires received and tabulated was 79. Out of a pool of 1420 accredited NGOs, this is a response rate of over 5%. The North/South balance was roughly equivalent to the ratio of accredited NGOs from these hemispheres: 59 from Northern countries responded, and 20 from the South. All sectors were well represented, except business. The questionnaire was sent only to NGOs that were accredited to the official process; thus, it is important to keep in mind that this grouping represents only a small (less than 5%) percentage of the total number of NGOs that participated in the Global Forum and other UNCED-related events.

1 – Please circle the negotiations that you or another representative of your organization have attended:
PrepCom 1 PrepCom 2 PrepCom 3 PrepCom 4 Rio Conference

On average, the NGOs who responded became involved in the UNCED process during the fourth PrepCom.

2 – Were you or your organization part of an official delegation? Yes 33% No 66%

3 – Please circle the level that you (or your organization) work on:
Local National Regional International

Most organizations worked on most or all of these levels; only 4 worked only on the local level .

4 – If you associate yourself (or your organization) with any particular sector(s) and/or issues(s), please circle:
Youth Women Indigenous Religious Labor Agriculture Business Development Environment Health Trade Human Rights Peace/Military Other

There were representatives of all of the above sectors; most considered themselves members of two or more of the categories.

5 – How often did you meet with other NGOs on issues of common interest during PrepComs/ at Rio?
every day several times per week once weekly bi-weekly never
50% of the respondees met with other NGOs every day, and most of the rest several times per week.

6 – How often did you attend the following NGO events?
NGO Strategy Meetings:
every day 25% several times per week 47% once weekly 8% bi-weekly 8% never 12%

NGO-Government Dialogues:
every day 10% several times per week 39% once weekly 15% bi-weekly 18% never 13%

NGO Plenaries:
every day 20% several times per week 49% once weekly 9.5% bi-weekly 12% never 9.5%

Sectoral Meetings (e.g. Women):
every day 25% several times per week 44% once weekly 10% bi-weekly 4% never 17%

Interest Group Meetings (e.g. Trade):
every day 18% several times per week 44% once weekly 17% bi-weekly 7% never 14%

7 – Did you observe a difference in the goals and/or tactics of "Northern" and "Southern" NGOs?
Yes 80% No 20%

8 – Did you network/build coalitions with organizations from countries besides your own?
Yes 91% No 9%
If so, were these networks/coalitions on a regional basis?
Yes 51% No 49%

9 – Were there NGO sectors/organizations that you felt you did not make enough contact with?
Yes 79% No 21%
Lack of time was the main reason for not having enough contact

10 – Please circle the sector(s) and/or interest group(s) that have, in your opinion, been the most effective lobbyists during the UNCED process:
Youth 17 Women 44 Indigenous 18 Religious 5 Labor 0 Agriculture Business 37 Development 16 Environment 27 Health 0 Trade 6 Human Rights 1 Peace/Military 2
* numbers are out of a total pool of 79 questionnaires

11 – How often did you met with delegates from other governments?
every day 21% several times per week 23% once weekly 12% bi-weekly 17% never 27%

12 – How often did you meet with delegates from your own government?
every day 28% several times per week 17% once weekly 14% bi-weekly 24% never 17%
Was this sufficient? Yes 42% No 58%

13 – Was the level of access you had to official negotiations (PrepComs and Rio) adequate?
Yes 76% No 24%

14 – Was the amount of speaking time you had in official negotiations adequate?
Yes 12% No 88%

15 – Please approximate the number of written statements you submitted to delegates:
The average number of written interventions per NGO hovered between 5 and 6 in a broad range from 0 to 50.

16 – How often did delegations incorporate your ideas and concerns into their decisions?
Often 12% Sometimes 44% Seldom 22% Never 22%

SECTION II - GOALS

NGOs had various goals that they hoped to achieve during the UNCED process. By circling the provided responses, please rate HOW IMPORTANT the following goals were to yourself and/or your organization and measure HOW EFFECTIVE you think you were in attaining these goals.

1 – Lobbying on specific issues on the UNCED agenda (i.e. biodiversity, climate)

How important?	Very 62%	Somewhat 31%	Not at all 7%
How effective?	Very 58%	Somewhat 26%	Not at all 16%

2 – Lobbying on specific issues NOT on the UNCED agenda (i.e. trade, militarism)

How important?	Very 58%	Somewhat 26%	Not at all 16%
How effective?	Very 5%	Somewhat 39%	Not at all 56%

3 – Coalition building/networking with other NGOs

How important?	Very 85%	Somewhat 12%	Not at all 3%
How effective?	Very 33%	Somewhat 63%	Not at all 4%

*ranked 1st in importance, 2nd in effectiveness

4 – Coalition building/networking with government delegations

How important?	Very 42%	Somewhat 48%	Not at all 10%
How effective?	Very 8%	Somewhat 58%	Not at all 34%

•ranked 9th in importance, 9th in effectiveness

5 – Facilitating dialogue between governments

How important?	Very 28%	Somewhat 37%	Not at all 35%
How effective?	Very 2%	Somewhat 52%	Not at all 46%

*ranked 11th in importance, 12th in effectiveness

6 – Obtaining information on issues discussed at UNCED

How important?	Very 76%	Somewhat 23%	Not at all 1%
How effective?	Very 44%	Somewhat 52%	Not at all 4%

*ranked 3rd in importance, 1st in effectiveness

7 – Providing information to delegates on particular issues

How important?	Very 62%	Somewhat 28%	Not at all 10%
How effective?	Very 12%	Somewhat 68%	Not at all 20%

*ranked 6th in importance, 8th in effectiveness

8 – Education of public about issues through media (e.g. press conferences and releases)

How important?	Very 83%	Somewhat 16%	Not at all 1%

How effective? Very 28% Somewhat 59% Not at all 13%
*ranked 2nd in importance, 3rd in effectiveness

9 – Supporting projects of your organization
How important? Very 47% Somewhat 40% Not at all 13%
How effective? Very 17% Somewhat 58% Not at all 25%
*ranked 8th in importance, 7th in effectiveness

10 – Working "outside" the process (e.g. demonstrations and protests)
How important? Very 36% Somewhat 38% Not at all 26%
How effective? Very 19% Somewhat 53% Not at all 28%
*ranked 10th in importance, 6th in effectiveness

11 – Facilitating future NGO access to international negotiations
How important? Very 66% Somewhat 24% Not at all 10%
How effective? Very 20% Somewhat 63% Not at all 17%
*ranked 5th in importance, 5th in effectiveness

12 – Monitoring implementation of UNCED commitments in your country post-Rio
How important? Very 73% Somewhat 21% Not at all 6%
How effective? Very 22% Somewhat 56% Not at all 22%
*ranked 4th in importance, 4th in effectiveness

13 – What degree of future access should NGOs be allowed in international negotiations like UNCED?
Universal access 62% Same level of access 38% Restricted access 0%

14 – Should NGO input be institutionalized? (e.g. with an intergovernmental advisory mechanism)
Yes 52% No 48%

15 – Do you plan to be involved in UNCED follow-up? (implementation of Agenda 21/ conventions)
Yes 93% No 7%

16 – Do you plan to continue networking on a regional/international level?
Yes 99% No 1%

17 – In retrospect, was the time/money/energy devoted to the UNCED process worthwhile?
Yes 81% No 19%

Part IV

The Outcome and Lessons Learned for Future Regime-building Negotiations

14

What Will It Take to Ensure Effective Global Environmental Management? A Reassessment of Regime-building Accomplishments

Lawrence E. Susskind

UNCED, or the Earth Summit as it was more popularly known, fell short of the goals that the UN General Assembly had set for it,[1] only two of the seven projected treaties were signed. Worse still, the most important cross-cutting questions of how best to strengthen the UN-sponsored global environmental management system to ensure sustainable development were not addressed. Two non-specific agreements –the Rio Declaration and Agenda 21, spelling out general principles and a comprehensive list of problems requiring attention – were signed, though, along with conventions calling for further monitoring of climate change and technology sharing to protect biodiversity. However, neither of these two treaties set deadlines nor did they require signatory countries to adopt less environmentally destructive resource management practices.

Much has been made of the fact that more heads of state met at UNCED to discuss global environmental issues than had ever gathered previously. However, neither rules, regulations, nor relationships were altered in any significant way. While consciousness was raised, expectations were heightened, and environmental issues were raised to a higher level on the world policy agenda, at least for several months, these do not constitute success. The most important measure of regime-building success in the environmental field is the extent to which institutional capacity to ensure sustainability (both domestic and international) is enhanced. By this measure, UNCED was only modestly successful.

There were, though, two important institution-building accomplishments at UNCED: the decision to continue (and increase funding for) the Global Environ-

[1] In the fall of 1989, when the UN General Assembly called for the Conference on Environment and Development, there was some hope that treaties dealing with climate change, transboundary air pollution, deforestation, soil loss, desert expansion and drought, conservation of biological diversity, protection of the oceans and seas, protection of freshwater resources, and strategies for financing all these improvements, could all be signed in Rio.

Negotiating International Regimes: Lessons Learned from the United Nations Conference on Environment and Development (G. Sjöstedt, *et al.*, eds.; 1-85966-077-0; © IIASA; pub. Graham & Trotman, 1994; printed in Great Britain), pp. 221–232.

ment Facility (GEF) and the decision to create a new UN Commission on Sustainable Development (CSD). Each of these efforts has proceeded haltingly, and neither is supported by the kind of broad-based North–South coalition needed to ensure long-term success. Without unified support, the GEF will not be able to generate sufficient funds to support implementation of existing treaties (let alone more meaningful accords aimed at reaching specific goals by pre-set dates); nor will the CSD be able to fulfill the coordination role that is so sorely lacking within the UN system.

Four obstacles to more effective global environmental management blocked the path at Rio. Effective management of common pool resources requires all states to accept certain constraints on the ways in which they pursue economic development; yet, most nations continue to resist collective efforts to ensure wise management of shared resources – claiming infringement of their sovereignty. Second, the nations of the South (i.e., G-77) do not have the resources necessary to reverse the destructive forces of overpopulation and poverty that have decimated many of their most valuable natural assets; yet the nations of the North are not inclined to provide the technical and financial aid needed to help the South implement more sustainable development practices. Third, the nations of the North refuse to alter the historic consumption patterns that have generated enormous amounts of global pollution and depleted vast stocks of natural resources – far in excess of the North's "fair share" of the world's resources. Fourth, most elected leaders are unwilling to incur political and economic costs now so that future generations may benefit; yet, this is what is required to reverse the ecological destruction that current development patterns are causing.

In the face of such obstacles, it is not surprising that the results of most global environmental negotiations, and Rio was no exception, have been "lowest common denominator" agreements that only apply to some countries and contain weak or nonexistent enforcement mechanisms (Susskind, 1994). Indeed, the UN-sponsored treaty-making system that has emerged in recent years accommodates the political needs of both developed and developing nations, but yields global agreements that fall far short of what is needed to ensure global sustainability. The current system permits heads of state, such as those who gathered at the Earth Summit, to sign vague agreements while avoiding the risk of political reprisals (at home and abroad). Our political leaders have been able to claim symbolic victories regarding their attempts to protect the environment while avoiding almost any constraints on investment and development practices. They do this by signing conventions that require nothing more than a willingness to submit reports and meet again (although, even the submittal of reports is sometimes controversial). Moreover, they are not obliged to adopt subsequent protocols that emerge from future meetings of treaty signatories.

To go beyond the treaties that have been adopted thus far, and to achieve real regime building success in the environmental management field, at least four changes in the U.N.-sponsored treaty-making system will be required:

1. Non-governmental interests will have to be guaranteed a more formal continuing role (independent of national governments) at all stages of international treaty negotiation. This will enhance their capacity to influence domestic decision-making and, ultimately, to fight for global convergence of environmental regulations as well as more effective enforcement.

2. A much tighter link will have to be made between the harmonization of global environmental protection and resource management efforts and the economic well-

being of nations. Even though such linkages will make negotiations more complicated, tougher environmental treaties will be resisted until they are coupled with sufficient development assistance to ensure that political and economic benefits are generated *in the short run.* To accomplish this, environmental treaty-making will need to be linked directly to global trade and debt management policies.

3. There must be a dramatic increase in the level of financial support for collaborative scientific research to pinpoint the ways in which various regional ecosystems respond to global insults. Unless global policies can be targeted in ways that are sensitive to variations in ecosystem carrying capacity and institutional management capabilities, we will not be able to craft cost-effective treaties. Until it is possible to make the case that the costs imposed on participating nations and regions are fair and appropriate, environmental diplomacy will fail.

4. There will need to be a dramatic increase in financial and political support for global environmental monitoring. Unless and until independent and reliable monitoring reports are regularly available to groups within every country, it will not be possible to force compliance with global environmental protection and resource management standards, even if they are spelled out in detailed treaty protocols. Such standards cannot be effectively enforced by a centralized "command-and-control" system; rather, grassroots community efforts – along the lines of the human rights monitoring process that has evolved over the past few decades – will be required (Susskind, 1994).

THE OUTCOMES AT RIO CONFIRM THE WEAKNESSES OF THE EXISTING CONVENTION – PROTOCOL APPROACH TO TREATY-MAKING

Most of the attention at the Earth Summit was focused on the Climate Change and Biodiversity Treaty negotiations. Yet, neither of these negotiations produced particularly noteworthy treaties. Indeed, the rush to meet the artificially imposed June 1992 deadline may well have produced inferior agreements than would otherwise have evolved. Historically, it has taken anywhere from eight to ten years to generate sufficient scientific and political consensus to trigger collective action: that is, to ensure ratification of accords on complex global environmental issues (Spector and Korula, 1993). The imposition of the June 1992 negotiating deadline did nothing to remove the obstacles that have caused environmental treaty-making to move so slowly or have produced weak treaties that, at best, slow the rate of environmental deterioration, but never repair the damage that has already been done.

The Climate Change Treaty

The parties to the Climate Change Convention promised to:

(1) develop national inventories of anthropogenic emissions;
(2) implement and publish national programs aimed at mitigating climate change;
(4) promote sustainable management of sinks and reservoirs of greenhouse gases;
(5) cooperate in preparing for adaptation to the impacts of climate change;

(6) take climate change into account in developing social, economic, and environmental policies;
(7) promote scientific cooperation and data collection;
(8) share information related to climate change;
(9) promote and cooperate in public education related to climate change.

No emission targets were specified; no deadlines were set. No attempt was made to set out the kinds of activities that each country should undertake to reduce the risks associated with climate change.

The treaty also states that the extent to which developing countries are expected to implement their obligations depends on the developed countries fulfilling their commitments, particularly the promise to provide financial resources and transfer technology. The treaty points out that economic development and poverty eradication remain the overriding priorities of developing countries, implying that environmental protection must take a "back seat." The section of the Climate Change Treaty outlining financial obligation says only that "provision should be made for the appropriation of financial resources on a grant or concessional basis under the guidance of all the parties." No specific funding requirements were specified.

The treaty assigns the usual responsibilities to the Conference of the Parties and a secretariat. It calls for a "subsidiary body for scientific and technological advice" to be created along with a subsidiary body for implementation (open to all parties) to be comprised of government representatives "expert on matters related to climate change." No specific performance milestones are listed. No enforcement powers are granted to any institution.

In the end, the Climate Change Convention achieved the absolute lowest common denominator outcome – a statement of concern about the possible dangers of climate change and a promise to work together to collect additional information. The parties have agreed to meet again to review the reports that each may provide. This rather inconsequential outcome was clearly a function of the South's unwillingness to accept any responsibility for mitigating adverse effects of the build-up of greenhouse gases caused by development in the North, unless the North is willing to increase substantially the development assistance given to the South. The North, however, unwilling to admit responsibility for the build-up of greenhouse gases, not only refused to promise additional aid, but was adamant in its view that it would not be necessary to alter its development patterns in response to the dangers of climate change. The stated goal of environmental advocates, which was ultimately rejected, was that all nations of the world should agree to cut back their emission of greenhouse gases to 1990 levels by the year 2000. Note, though, that 1990 levels were the initial trigger that raised international concern in the first place! Nevertheless, the developed nations, particularly the United States, were unwilling to endorse even this non-remedial goal (although the Clinton administration seems to have reversed the Bush administration on this point).

Gareth Porter and Janet Brown, in their excellent book *Global Environmental Politics,* suggest that global environmental negotiations involve four political processes – issue definition, factfinding, bargaining, and regime strengthening. Issue definition brings problems to the attention of the international community and suggests the type of international action required. Once issues are identified, factfinding brings parties together in an attempt to establish agreement and to clarify the scope of differences in the understanding of the problem and of possible policy options.

Bargaining, they suggest, hinges on the leverage and cohesion of veto coalitions – groups of states that can block international cooperation (Porter and Brown, 1991). Regime strengthening presumably occurs after a first round agreement has been reached and improved understanding of the environmental problem(s) is achieved. Thus, scientific evidence, especially the product of joint monitoring or collaborative research, is meant to be given increasing weight over time. In the case of the Climate Change Convention, however, it is far from certain that this will happen; not only because there will always be a great deal of uncertainty surrounding the sources and impacts of greenhouse gases, but also because the South has decided that it will not "give" on environmental issues until the North agrees to a massive reallocation of resources.[2]

Perhaps the Climate Change Convention will lead to some regime strengthening over time, but this will not be because scientific results dictate the next steps in international bargaining. Regime strengthening could occur if independent environmental interests in a sufficient number of countries gain enough strength to push their national governments to take unilateral steps to reduce the emission of greenhouse gases. At that point, countries that have been forced to take action will band together to argue for harmonization of international efforts so that none is disadvantaged economically. In short, there is no inevitability about the process of regime strengthening, especially if it depends on the building of scientific consensus and the dominance of scientific evidence over national self-interest.

If we look closely at the institutional arrangements and assignment of responsibilities specified by the Climate Change Treaty, we can see why they are not likely to lead to regime strengthening. Signatory states face no penalty if they fail to file complete or accurate reports. In fact, there is no mechanism to determine whether national reports are at all accurate. Under the circumstances, there are sure to be gaps in the information provided. Protocols to standardize national reporting have yet to be written and, when they are, there is a good chance that the South will resist any effort to impose Northern data-gathering requirements or a centralized authority with the power to review or revise what nations submit. Thus, even if independent groups of scientists reach agreement on why and how greenhouse gases cause climate change, it will not be easy to estimate what remedial actions will work or what their regional implications are likely to be, since we are unlikely to acquire adequate information to permit that level of detailed modeling. My hunch is that we are not likely to know much more about the dynamics of climate change after the next round of national reports is received than we do now. As long as a significant number of countries see monitoring as a threat rather than as an opportunity for global learning, it is not obvious how or why regime strengthening will occur.

The Biodiversity Treaty

The signatories to the Convention on Biological Diversity pledged to cooperate in efforts to conserve and promote the sustainable use of biological diversity. They promised to:

[2]Adil Najam, "A Strategy for the South," in Lawrence Susskind, William Moomaw, and Adil Najam, International Environmental Negotiation, vol. 3. (Program on Negotiation at Harvard Law School, Cambridge, Massachusetts), 1993.

(1) develop national and cross-sectoral plans for the conservation and sustainable use of biological diversity;
(2) monitor, through sampling and other techniques, the components of biological diversity;
(3) establish a system of protected areas where special measures will be taken to conserve biological diversity;
(4) regulate or manage biological resources important to the conservation of biological diversity whether within or outside protected areas;
(5) rehabilitate and restore degraded ecosystems and promote the recovery of threatened species;
(6) establish means to control the risks associated with the use and release of living modified organisms resulting from biotechnology;
(7 adopt measures for the ex-situ conservation of components of biological diversity, preferably in their place of origin;
(8) facilitate access to genetic resources for environmentally sound uses by other countries and not impose restrictions that run counter to the objectives of the Convention;
(9) facilitate access and transfer to the other states of technologies that are relevant to the conservation and sustainable use of biological diversity, on concessional and preferential terms where mutually agreed.

The developed countries are supposed to provide new and additional financial resources to enable developing countries to meet the incremental costs of implementing the Biodiversity Treaty. However, it is left to subsequent meetings to decide how much this will cost, where the money will come from, and how responsibility for meeting these financial obligations will be assured.

Even after signing the Biodiversity Treaty, states still retain the option of saying when and how (or even whether) they will provide access to biological resources within their borders. There are no penalties for failing to achieve the goals of the treaty. There are no deadlines by which targets must be met. There is no grant of authority to supersede national sovereignty; indeed, efforts to ensure that national sovereignty is in no way compromised (which remains paradoxical given that almost all global resource management measures require participating countries to accept some limitations on the exploitation of resources in exchange for the co-operation of other nations) explain why so few requirements are actually included in the treaty. As was the case with the Climate Change Treaty, and indeed with almost all international environmental negotiations, the North was not willing to promise the South the resources it needs to implement more sustainable development practices. Moreover, the North is unwilling to alter its historic consumption patterns in exchange for concessions by the South. And, finally, most elected leaders in both developed and developing countries are unwilling to incur political and economic costs so that future generations might retain the same choices that we now have. The result is weak treaties and a hope that irrefutable scientific evidence will emerge, leading to regime strengthening. The leaders who signed the most recent treaties are congratulating themselves for having taken important first steps, even though no results are guaranteed. And, why should they do any more than that? There will always be experts, assigned by their national governments, to point out that scientific uncertainty surrounding the current state of affairs should lead to caution, that the weaknesses of the theoretical basis for forecasting future impacts call for modest proposals, and the relative merits of taking no action while more data are gathered should be carefully considered. This provides cover for leaders who prefer to take no action.

The GEF and the CSD

In spite of these difficulties, the UNCED negotiators did make two important institutional commitments. First, they agreed to retain the GEF; and second, they created the CSD. The UNCED representatives agreed that developed countries should reaffirm a commitment to reaching the longstanding UN target of 0.7 percent of GNP for Official Development Assistance (ODA). Those who signed Agenda 21 urged that developed nations augment their aid programs until the 0.7 percent goal is met. The UNCED secretariat initially estimated that the full cost of implementing Agenda 21 would be $600 billion per year, of which about $125 billion annually would come from the North and the balance from developing country resources. By any stretch of the imagination, this was an untenable goal. At most, UNCED generated additional aid commitments of less than $10 billion.

Faced with these financial constraints, the Earth Summit negotiators sought ways of financing the implementation of Agenda 21. They decided to build on the GEF, although the South demanded certain changes in its organization and operation before it would agree. The GEF is administered by the World Bank, along with UNDP and UNEP. The GEF was created in 1990 as a three-year pilot program and given a mandate to allocate $1.3 billion for projects related to global warming, biodiversity, international waters, and ozone depletion. The South's distrust of the World Bank (which it perceives as intrusive in domestic policy making and dominated by developed countries) led to the adoption of a new GEF voting system for allocating aid funds that does not mimic the World Bank's reliance on a system weighted according to the size of each country's contribution. Instead of scraping the GEF (which the parties could have demanded), UNCED reaffirmed an earlier April agreement on restructuring it.

GEF decision-making procedures will now be more transparent to member countries and aid recipients. The reforms further called for involvement of NGOs in GEF project development and administration. So, in exchange for the North's willingness to modify the GEF's administrative structure, the South accepted (at least temporarily) a North-dominated system for allocating aid. While the GEF will still receive funds pursuant to the terms of each individual treaty for which it has financial responsibility, the overall "pot" of money will continue to grow and, from the standpoint of the South, it may be possible to argue later on that "fair shares" of the total GEF budget should be allocated to specific countries or regions, regardless of the project proposals they have been able to generate.

While the money provided through the GEF will still be project specific, it can now be construed as something more closely akin to compensation. While grants are supposed to cover the costs that developing countries will face in meeting their obligations under the Montreal Protocol, Climate Change Convention, and other treaties – and take account of the scientific merit of each project proposal – by putting all the funds under one auspice, it will be much easier for developing nations to keep track of the overall allocation of treaty-related monies. The South is likely to look askance at an overall pattern of allocations that favors one continent or one country over others. In the final analysis, GEF allocations may be judged less on their technical merit, and more in terms of the extent to which basic needs in different parts of the world are being met.

At PrepCom III in Geneva in August 1991, Bangladesh, supported by Norway and France, proposed the creation of an Earth Commission or a Commission on Sustainable Development (CSD) as an intergovernmental body, elected from ECOSOC, but open to all member states and agencies of the UN. This body would receive reports and recommendations from a committee of experts, which would, in turn, receive national reports from each member state describing its success in meeting treaty commitments. The committee would then make recommendations to the CSD, which could investigate them and report to the General Assembly. The Commission would be open to the participation of NGOs accredited by ECOSOC. It would have a small secretariat based in Geneva (Roddick, 1993). This version of the CSD was based on the UN Commission on Human Rights.

Some countries, like the United States, initially argued against creating any new institutions, or allocating any additional aid for sustainable development. Rather, they advocated strengthening UNEP (Roddick, 1993). Sweden proposed a Commission on Global Governance, aimed at streamlining the role of the UN's specialized agencies and strengthening the position of the Secretary General. While other delegates to the PrepCom saw no need for anything more than an annual session of a revitalized ECOSOC, which ostensibly coordinates all UN institutions; this was not, in the eyes of most countries, sufficient to ensure the integration of desperate environmental protection and economic development activities.

At PrepCom IV in New York, Venezuela once again proposed the Commission. Backed by Mexico and Colombia, Venezuela called for a commission of ECOSOC, on a par with the Commission on Human Rights (Roddick, 1993). The CSD as it finally emerged from Rio and the subsequent General Assembly session is a "high level" functional Commission of ECOSOC, consisting of 53 government representatives, reporting through ECOSOC to the General Assembly. Its primary role is to review progress in implementing Agenda 21, as well as the overall integration of environment and development within the UN system. Initially, it will meet annually for two to three weeks, before the regular ECOSOC session. It will review progress on finance, transfer of technology, and government successes and failures in integrating environment and development. In spite of the refusal of Brazil, India, and China to allow the CSD to review national reports formally, the Commission can receive information sent to it by any nation or organization.

The General Assembly formally gave the CSD the following assignments:

(1) monitor UN progress in implementing Agenda 21;
(2) consider information on the implementation of environmental treaties which the signatories agree to provide;
(3) consider information from governments such as "periodic communications or national reports" on the activities they undertake to implement Agenda 21, the problems they face, and the issues they consider important;
(4) review progress on technology transfer and on governments' financial commitments under Agenda 21;
(5) receive and analyze input from NGOs.

There were, as I have hinted, numerous points of contention regarding the design and operation of the CSD. At the General Assembly session and at subsequent meetings of the CSD, the mandate of the commission, its membership and the frequency of its meetings, the location of its meetings and its secretariat, its position within the UN bureaucracy, the endowment of its secretariat, the procedures by which it would operate, and its relationship to and the role of NGOs in its operation, were all debated (Wolz, 1992; Sessions, 1992). While most of these have been temporarily resolved, the structure of the CSD is sure to evolve. The same North–South conflicts that plagued the GEF simmer just below the surface of the current CSD agreement. Those who want the CSD to play an aggressive watchdog role are countered by those who view any second-guessing of national reports as an abridgement of sovereignty. Those who feel that the internal operations of disparate UN agencies can be coordinated from within or on high (even with the strong support of the Secretary General) are sure to be disappointed.

FURTHER INSTITUTIONAL REFORMS ARE REQUIRED

Most recent international environmental negotiations have followed a two-step approach. An initial series of meetings is held to review scientific evidence and draft a framework convention. Then, subsequent meetings of the signatories focus on the preparation of detailed protocols. The convention–protocol approach has produced a number of first-step agreements – the Climate Change Convention and the Biodiversity Treaty being the most recent examples. The Montreal Protocol is the best-known example of what the second step in the two-step process is supposed to generate. It is inevitable, however, that the two-step convention–protocol approach to treaty negotiation will take a long time and reinforce the tendency to seek lowest common denominator agreements. Unless the treaty-making system is substantially reformed, international environmental treaties will continue to take decades to adopt and impose the same requirements on all signatories, often neglecting available scientific and technical information that argues for regional or even sub-regional variations in standards and timetables for implementation.[3]

The convention–protocol approach has, for the most part, been dominated by the most powerful states. They have taken the initiative on issues of environmental protection. Now, however, the South is demanding a greater role and insisting on the transfer of financial resources before further treaties are considered. The ad hoc nature of the convention–protocol approach is partly to blame for the current gridlock. In the absence of a formal negotiating system spelling out the rights of each country to help set the agenda and the obligations of secretariats to ensure that certain minimum thresholds of support from UN members will be met, the North and the South feel compelled to hold out for "everything" they want, each time a new treaty is up for negotiation. Most global environmental treaties signed thus far (and there are dozens of them dating back to the turn of the century) have not been ratified by most nations. The environmental problems to which the treaties were addressed have not been resolved (Susskind, 1994). Further improvement will require at least four kinds of institutional reforms.

[3]For a list of these reforms, see *The Salzburg Initiative,* prepared by the International Environmental Negotiation Network.

STRENGTHENING THE ROLE OF NON-GOVERNMENTAL INTERESTS

Unofficial actors can play several important roles in the process of global environmental treaty-making, but they have not been given a clear mandate to do so. They can serve as scientific advisers or information gatherers at the point at which risks are being defined or problems are being diagnosed. They can play the role of advocates, mobilizing public opinion within each country as well as on a worldwide basis, pressing heads of state to advance an issue higher up the political agenda. They can also make negotiations more democratic – ensuring that the concerns of segments of the population that may not be important to certain national leaders are nevertheless addressed by international assemblies. They may assume the role of change agents – promoting new and different policy approaches that have not yet won support in international bureaucratic ranks. Unofficials, in addition, can serve as monitors, providing a key independent check on the information provided by official sources or gathering data when countries fail to meet their reporting requirements. Finally, unofficials can serve as intermediaries or facilitators, suggesting and helping to implement action on stop-gap measures when countries are too slow to act or there is no time to move collectively when formal treaties have clearly failed.

Given this multiplicity of roles and functions, it is not surprising that unofficials want a guarantee that their involvement will not be blocked by the UN and its member institutions. Nongovernmental interests want the UN to acknowledge formally their right to participate. At present, at the outset of each treaty-making effort, unofficials must invest substantial organizational resources to plead for the right to be at the negotiation table. Often, as was the case at the Rio Earth Summit, they are forced to settle for parallel conferences or restricted observer status. They are, though, seeking something closer to a fully fledged partnership with the governmental members of the UN.

The exact form this partnership should take is not clear, but several principles that might guide its design are: first, the various segments of the unofficial community should be recognized as separate and distinct. Second, nongovernmental interests need to be "at the table" at all stages of the treaty-making process. While some nongovernmental interests will serve as members of national delegations, others should be present as independent actors, even if somewhat similar interests are represented on both national delegations and at-large. Since only countries vote, there need be no fear that nongovernmental interests will be given undue advantage if they are represented in several ways. The final principle should be an emphasis on informality. Too much of the dialogue at the UN-sponsored conferences has become stilted, leading to half-hearted initiatives that value caution far more than imagination. While the language of diplomacy and the rules of official etiquette will undoubtedly be preserved, more informal give-and-take during working sessions and other portions of official conferences should be encouraged.

Retaining the status quo regarding the role of unofficials is unacceptable. They have too much to offer, and they have the potential to fill the gaps in what governments have alone been unable to do. One such area is in representing the interests of future generations.

STRIVING TOWARD WORKABLE LINKAGE

Issue linkage can facilitate international environmental negotiations in three ways. First, by adding an issue, one party can offer others additional advantages, and thus a reason to agree. Second, adding an issue, and thereby bringing other parties to the bargaining table, makes it possible to counteract the power of a blocking coalition (by increasing the size of the coalition that favors agreement). Finally, adding an issue makes it possible to shift the institutional locus of a negotiation to a new venue in which implementation may be easier. Each of these linkages involves building or modifying coalitions.

A crucial element in the success of multilateral negotiation is the ability to add – very judiciously – issues and parties for purposes of expanding the zone of agreement. The appropriate scale and scope of a negotiation, and thus the use of issue linkage, depend on the size of the coalition required to respond to efforts to block consensus. Changes in the agenda must be made with the consent of all interested stakeholders. When there is unanimity, any linkage is acceptable. When doubts are raised, linkages must be argued on their merits – that is, proponents must show either a functional or a causal connection between issues or a past precedent legitimizing such a connection. Failing this, linkage is likely to be rejected. The key test of the acceptability of a proposed linkage is the impact it has on the long-term relationships among the parties.

I have described elsewhere a new approach to environmental treaty-making that could systematize environmental treaty negotiations and synchronize global expectations (Susskind, 1994). More specifically, all countries would be able to rely on the fact that certain global environmental treaties would move through a predictable multi-state process with explicit time limits and voting requirements. This would permit linkage between and among multiple treaty negotiations.

PINPOINTING REGIONAL SOLUTIONS WITHIN A GLOBAL MANAGEMENT CONTEXT

There will always be uncertainty hovering over global environmental treaty negotiations. One way of handling uncertainty is to invest more money in basic environmental research that might produce the scientific equivalent of a "smoking gun." As a result of ongoing British efforts to monitor meteorological change at the South Pole, for example, the hole in the ozone layer was confirmed, and directly linked to CFCs. That "smoking gun" certainly spurred action on the Montreal Protocol. There is no guarantee, though, that expanding basic environmental research will yield the evidence that will reduce uncertainty on other global issues in a timely way.

An alternative strategy would be to organize critical experiments (on a small scale) and work to ensure that the results are shared regionally and globally. Such small-scale demonstrations might establish beyond doubt that environmental threats exist, that they are caused in a certain way, or that a particular response to such threats is likely to be effective. In the absence of a central environmental planning authority, regional experimentation, networking among adjacent nations, and regional capacity building would be most helpful.

I am particularly convinced that groups of countries organized on a bio-regional basis can and should seek to take collective action in the face of environmental threats even before there is sufficient agreement to justify or propel a global response. New regional capacity building centers could well be the locus of the small-scale experiments that lead to global action.

PUSHING FOR COMPLIANCE THROUGH LOCAL MONITORING

Oran Young argues that the prospect of "shaming" – exposing treaty violations to the public – may be a source of even greater fear among national leaders than the application of sanctions. "Policy-makers," he writes, "like private individuals are sensitive to the social opprobrium that accompanies violations of widely accepted behavioral prescriptions" (Young, 1992). These feelings, Chayes and Chayes (1991) point out, are intensified by having to confront colleagues demanding explanations for violations. This, of course explains the resistance that countries sometimes display toward reporting requirements, independent reviews of national reports, or other mechanisms designed to inform the public of their behavior. Monitoring is effective, then, because it increases "transparency," although because anything other than pure self-reporting typically runs afoul of claims of sovereignty, this is not easy to achieve.

While countries insist that no one outside their borders ought to be empowered to second-guess them, the sovereignty argument does not apply to people and organizations within their own borders. Thus, one way around the sovereignty problem is to create groups within each country to take responsibility for monitoring compliance with global environmental treaties. These groups, especially when they join forces on a worldwide basis, may be able to shame noncomplying nations into changing their behavior. By working together, highly motivated local activists can achieve the competence and credibility they need to bring the full weight of international opinion to bear on noncompliers. This is the approach that Amnesty International has used in pursuing noncompliers with the UN's human rights provisions. It may well be appropriate to build a parallel local monitoring and enforcement system in the environmental field (Susskind, 1994).

CONCLUDING OBSERVATIONS

The essence of regime strengthening is institutional reform. Unfortunately, the Earth Summit hardly dealt at all with questions of institutional redesign – save for the discussions of the GEF and the CSD. While these represent moves in the right direction, they do not address the inherent weaknesses in the convention–protocol approach to treaty-making or the flaws in a UN system that has for decades accorded only minor emphasis to environmental issues. We need to bring the nations of the world together to focus on the broader problem of redesigning our multilateral institutions to deal with the problems of sustainability that were not apparent when the UN was created almost 50 years ago. Regime strengthening on a treaty-by-treaty basis without overall reform of the multilateral institutions arrangements that currently exist will never lead to global action of the sort needed to remedy the environmental damage we already face or to respond to the future environmental threats that are sure to arise.

15

Looking Ahead

Gunnar Sjöstedt, Bertram I. Spector, and I. William Zartman

LESSONS FOR NEGOTIATING FUTURE REGIMES

There is general agreement that concrete results of the UNCED process in the areas of environment and development were relatively meager. Susskind elaborated on this theme in Chapter 14, and pointed out that the commitments made in the two treaties signed in Rio (on climate change and biodiversity) were conspicuously weak. The institution that was set up with some difficulty to deal with the implementation of the UNCED outcome (the Commission for Sustainable Development) was endowed with an organizational structure and position within the UN system such that it is not likely to survive very long as a meaningful mechanism for real coordination and supervision.

These rather harsh judgments of the value of the UNCED process and its accomplishments are seemingly founded on the view that international regimes have an impact on the performance of states and other international actors only through their *rule component,* which is typically defined in terms of an international treaty. For instance, in the case of environmental treaties preceding the UNCED process, say, in the case of acid rain or ozone depletion, the rules of the new regime stipulate what industrial emissions of pollutants should be restricted and by how much in each particular signatory country. This outlook presupposes a strong link between *regime operation,* pertaining to the systemic level of analysis, and *compliance*, representing state responsibilities and action necessary to secure the implementation of an international regime at the national level.

According to this view, the function and significance of other regime elements cannot be fully understood and fairly evaluated except in terms of their supportive relationship to the rule component of the regime. For instance, *procedures* typically relate to organizational structures or collective working methods that have been created with the specific purpose of assisting rule compliance in a very practical way. In contrast, norms and principles are background factors that, in interaction with one another, give legitimacy and authority to the *rule component* of the regime. *Norms* define the general or long-term objectives motivating the regime and the way its rules are constructed. *Principles* represent the basic epistemic component of the regime. For instance, in the European regime on acidification, the epistemic

Negotiating International Regimes: Lessons Learned from the United Nations Conference on Environment and Development (G. Sjöstedt, *et al.*, eds.; 1-85966-077-0; © IIASA; pub. Graham & Trotman, 1994; printed in Great Britain), pp. 233–249.

component explains how the phenomenon of acid rain is produced by long-range transboundary air pollution. The norm that "the polluter pays" influences how cost-sharing is undertaken between signatory powers. According to the traditional way of thinking, the nations that are parties to the regime feel the impact of norms and principles through the medium of the rules of the regime; specific articles of the agreement manifest the regime by laying out the obligations of signatories. State action is not directly linked to the dynamics of norms and principles as such.

However, a broad regime building process like UNCED may have an impact beyond compliance with a few concrete rules. Presumably, norms, as well as principles, may under certain conditions have a direct impact on state interaction or societal economic processes within nations. In fact, several chapters have indicated the significance of norm-building processes during the work of the PrepCom and the Rio Conference. The complex problems of environment and development were highlighted to an unprecedented degree through the media around the world. Thousands of journalists covered the Rio Conference as well as a multitude of NGOs; in fact, Doherty reports that hundreds of NGOs were active in the process (Chapter 13). As a result, decision makers, as well as the general public, in many countries were updated about the many environmental and development issues on the UNCED agenda. Even if this impact on opinion-building is assumed to have been a temporary phenomenon, it has left traces in the collective memory of at least some nations.

UNCED also strengthened particular norms in the area of environmental politics. It may be claimed that one of the main functions of UNCED was to make the norm-loaded notion of sustainable development more acceptable and credible as an operational concept in regime-building processes. You will recall that several of the so-called cross-sectoral issues on the UNCED agenda expressed, or referred to, the notion of sustainable development. Other norms, unfolding in the environmental area, notably the "polluter-pays-principle," moved somewhat further toward the status of formal international law by inclusion in the Rio Declaration.

Several of the chapters highlight the importance of information-gathering and collective learning in the UNCED process. The work of the PrepCom included a massive general build-up of knowledge and scientific information concerning environment, development, and the couplings between these two vast problem areas; recall, for example, the large-scale network of study groups organized by the UNCED secretariat to support issue clarification in the PrepCom (Chapter 4). The two case studies of how individual countries, Argentina and Austria, worked out their policy and strategy for UNCED give further testimony about the importance of collective learning in the process (Chapters 7 and 8). These two cases also illustrate how collective learning affected policy planning at the national level. First, organized information-gathering in UNCED produced a pool of knowledge that actors in the process could draw from. Secondly, UNCED catalyzed domestic activities leading to a reinforced cumulation of knowledge/information about the environment as well as development issues. At the international level, the working groups organized by the UNCED secretariat not only cumulated information in the UNCED context itself, but also redistributed knowledge between the many international agencies that were involved.

Collective learning in UNCED did not pertain exclusively to the substance of issues; it related to organizational structures and working methods employed for policy making and negotiation as well. Interestingly, the authorities in Argentina as well as in Austria had similar experiences when they became seriously engaged in the UNCED process in early spring 1990. In both countries, existing institutions and practices were insufficient to cope with the requirements of the UNCED agenda, especially the cross-sectoral issues and the general relationship between the environment and development. New routines had to be established. The procedures for policy coordination were especially cumbersome and provoked inter-agency rivalry, all the way up to the ministerial level.

At the international level, the preparatory work for UNCED evoked problems of coordination and leadership. Chapter 4 argued that Agenda 21 represented an effective instrument to deal with these challenges during the UNCED process. The intention was that Agenda 21 should have the same function in the post-UNCED world as well. However, in Chapter 14, Susskind expressed well-founded doubts that the body set up to monitor and direct the implementation of Agenda 21 – the Commission for Sustainable Development – is likely to become a rather toothless mechanism or may disappear altogether. Without the support of a competent and effective Commission, Agenda 21 will not be able to serve as the same guiding frame of reference in future regime-building processes as it did in UNCED.

Concrete agreements concerning future undertakings and new institutions produced in the UNCED process represent building blocks for continued regime-building related to environment and development. For instance, a framework agreement may become more fully developed and specified, and institutions may be employed either to monitor the implementation of earlier deals among states or to catalyze new initiatives. Thus, *lessons for the future* represent another type of result from the UNCED process. Lessons typically pertain to "how things should be done" – how negotiations and other forms of state interaction that are part of the regime-building process should best be conducted. Sometimes, the lessons drawn represent favorable experiences at the present time that may be replicated in the future. However, on other occasions, negative lessons may be equally or even more important to register – for instance, to understand what procedures and process rules should be avoided in the future.

As in most multilateral negotiations with global participation, the large number of participants represented a problem in its own right. This predicament was further enhanced by the extraordinarily large number of NGOs that took part in the preparatory process or were present in Rio de Janeiro during UNCED (Chapter 13). Many interesting lessons can be categorized into two dimensions of regime-building: *actor strategies* and *process*.

Lessons Concerning Actor Strategies

The interaction of competing actor strategies constitutes the engine of regime-building processes. The correlation of actor interests determines the contents and form of the agenda and provides leadership for probing into possible negotiation solutions, including the search for formulas and the accommodation of detailed objectives. However, there are several indications that leadership at UNCED was performed in a distinct way as compared to other multilateral negotiations. In Chapter 4, Sjöstedt argues that the UNCED secretariat performed more of an assertive and constructive leadership role than seems to have been common in other multilateral negotiations, at least until PrepCom IV in March 1992. In Chapter 9, Antrim credits the Bureau leadership for the successful unfolding of the process, and particularly singles out the decisive chairmanship of Ambassador Koh of Singapore. From Koh's own account (Chapter 10), it seems clear that his leadership role was particularly important toward the end of the UNCED process when the essence of the collective decision process was *choice* rather than *search*. Hence, the mounting importance of the chairmanship temporarily coincided with a rapidly waning leadership role of the UNCED secretariat. One explanation for this development is that the leadership functions of the secretariat pertained especially to issue clarification and interconnected activities, whereas that of the Bureau and the chairman of the PrepCom was particularly related to the exchange of concessions and the end game. This distribution of work can be expected to emerge in any multi-party negotiation dealing with a multitude of complex issues, but was unusually pronounced in the case of UNCED. The analysis conducted in Chapter 4 indicates that one major cause for this state of affairs was the self-constrained role of some of the actors – specifically nations and coalitions – that had a potential, but unrealized, capacity to lead.

The performance of the Great Powers in UNCED can largely be explained in terms of *interests.* Although most industrialized countries certainly wanted to bring the UNCED process to a successful end, no leading nation belonging to this group wanted to make far-reaching commitments with regard to specific issues such as climate change, biodiversity, or additional financial or technological assistance to developing countries (Chapter 5). It seems clear that particularly during the later stages of the UNCED process, the leading OECD members, particularly the coalition of EC nations and the United States, made an effort to control the UNCED process to pave the way for a Meeting of Heads of State or Government, as well as a decent final declaration. Their strategy was to hold back "extremist" demands with regard to both environmental and development issues. Thus, the leading industrialized nations did not combine their efforts to attain process control with assertive and promotive tactics linked to particular issues. They were satisfied instead to muddle through the PrepCom process and the Rio Meeting without having to underwrite excessively costly commitments.

In some respects, developing more than industrialized countries were the most assertive actors in the UNCED process, particularly with regard to the so-called cross-sectoral issues, such as additional financial resources and the transfer of environmentally sound technology. With regard to these issues, negotiations developed along familiar lines where offers and claims tabled by some nations were met with defensive as well as offensive countermoves by other countries. The main problem was that the countries making the principal requests, and hence playing the offense in the negotiation game, were considerably weaker than the nations to which these claims were directed. Developing countries could not claim concessions from industrialized countries; they could only ask for them with reference made to generally accepted norms of fairness and justice. Otherwise, the power base of the Southern nations was generally very weak. Most developing countries had little to trade, except for their own acceptance of agreements worked out in the negotiation. Moreover, these governments were information-poor as well, and were strongly dependent for information and assessments from UN agencies or other countries.

The lack of important knowledge and information severely constrained many countries, not only in the Third World, to work out independent national strategies that could be pursued in UNCED. The information constraints were especially strong with regard to the environmental problems on the UNCED agenda. The reason is that development issues, like financial assistance and technology transfer, were leftovers from many years of debate and negotiation in most UN agencies about a New Economic Order and related topics. Furthermore, it was relatively easy to take a position on development issues as they are typical "more-or-less" questions. The knowledge problems confronting actors involved in UNCED are illustrated in the case study about Argentina, one of the advanced developing countries (Chapter 8). It is clearly stated that the Argentines were in no position to deal with all the issues on the UNCED agenda. A narrow selection of a few issues was chosen for policy making and direct continuous monitoring of the work of PrepCom. The two basic criteria for this selection are noteworthy. First, an issue solidly on the UNCED agenda, like the depletion of the ozone layer, was singled out. The reason was that Argentina is one of the few countries that are directly victimized by the growing ozone hole in the stratosphere. Second, the government of Argentina gave priority to an issue that was not formally on the UNCED agenda, namely the elimination of trade barriers for agricultural products. Argentine negotiators were instructed to link the agricultural issue to any other issue on the agenda, so that an opportunity would be generated to argue for trade liberalization. In this particular case, the UNCED process functioned as a "garbage can" decision model. In other words, UNCED represented a negotiation context in which all sorts of issues could be inserted to promote important national objectives. It seems reasonable to suspect that Argentina was not the only nation that used UNCED as a garbage can. Another example was the intervention of a group of Arab oil producers during the Rio Conference with the purpose of blocking the final framework agreement on climate change. In this case, the Arab interests were quite obvious: to delay a regime-building process that would ultimately contribute to a scaled-down demand for petroleum products.

If many countries throw a variety of issues into the garbage can, a complex hidden agenda will emerge. If this happens, as seems to have been the case with UNCED, actor strategies will be partly targeted against the garbage can rather than the official agenda. Consequently, comprehensive national strategies in a large conference context like that of UNCED will become very difficult to detect and understand unless the garbage can – the hidden agenda – is taken into consideration.

Lessons Concerning Process

As in other multilateral negotiations, a major task related to *process management* in UNCED was to find ways to cope with the great number of actors and the multitude of issues. The methods employed in UNCED need to be carefully assessed as they represent positive as well as negative lessons. There are two topics especially that should be considered in this connection: the role of NGOs and developing countries in the process.

According to the account given by Doherty in Chapter 13, NGOs have rarely had such free access to an interstate bargaining process as they had in the case of UNCED. However, this open-door policy was far from uncontroversial. The decision taken by the Plenary Committee of the PrepCom to permit NGO representatives to take part in all formal, as well as some informal, sessions of PrepCom bodies was preceded by an intensive and protracted debate during the meeting in Nairobi. The experiences from UNCED indicate that in a regime-building process of this type, extensive participation of NGOs may produce noteworthy benefits, for example, related to implementation effectiveness. The other side of the coin is, however, that a large NGO participation in a regime-building process also entails considerable costs. During the meetings of the PrepCom where NGOs had the right to participate actively in the deliberations, the list of speakers became unreasonably long. Often the prepared speeches of NGO representatives introduced new or different ideas that were largely irrelevant within the context of the current dialogue between national governments. As a consequence, the time left for constructive debate between nations with differing interests often became seriously curtailed.

One lesson for the future is that although a greater participation of NGOs in regime-building processes in the areas of environment and development should be welcomed and encouraged, the terms of access for NGOs need to be carefully assessed. It is necessary to consider that the character of a multilateral negotiation usually changes drastically from its initiation to the conclusion of a final agreement that terminates the process. For example, the demand for new knowledge and information is much more limited at the end of the negotiation, when concessions are exchanged and deals are made, than when the agenda is set and issues are clarified in the earlier stages of the process. Some NGOs may be capable of performing a constructive role from the beginning to the end of the process. However, it may be more reasonable to constrain or circumscribe the activities of certain NGOs in the regime-building process or negotiation. For instance, some scientific organizations that are in a position to supply significant information during the process stage of issue clarification may have little to contribute when hard bargaining and the exchange of concessions prevail. In contrast, other NGOs may have but a layman's knowledge about the technical issues, but can be in a position to communicate the agreements reached in the negotiation to the general public or to certain social strata. Maybe distinctions such as these should be taken into consideration when access rules are formulated for NGOs. Selection is obviously very sensitive for political reasons. However, it is, no doubt, an important mission to elaborate such selection criteria to facilitate future negotiations. A reasonable tradeoff has to be found between two basic considerations. One is that if hundreds of NGOs are given free access to the negotiations, there is a risk that the process may become overloaded. The other is that increased participation of competent private organizations in international regime-building processes is not only desirable, but *necessary,* due to the continually reinforced relationships of complex interdependence in the global system.

One of the basic objectives of UNCED was to persuade Third World nations to undertake more far-reaching commitments in the environmental area. A major concern, therefore, was to secure the participation of developing countries to the highest degree possible. Procedural rules were established to attain that objective. One such rule was to use texts prepared by the Group of 77 as a point of departure for discussions and negotiations in the PrepCom. Another example was the rule that only two meetings could be held simultaneously to give nations with small delegations a chance to follow the proceedings properly. Chapter 8 demonstrates that for a relatively developed Third World nation like Argentina, the Group of 77 was of immense importance. This coalition helped Argentina to monitor general developments in the UNCED process so that it could concentrate its own analytical and diplomatic resources on a few issues that were of primary importance. These and other measures facilitated the access of developing countries to UNCED, as well as their active participation in the negotiations. They were, hence, beneficial for the process.

The benefits accrued were, however, not free of charge. They impeded process effectiveness in different ways. One negative effect was that the pace of the process was slowed down. Another major repercussion was that the overall problem-solving capacity of the UNCED process was hampered. In spite of its gigantic agenda, the work of the PrepCom was only distributed formally between four different negotiation bodies, including the Plenary Meeting. Each working group therefore had to cope with an agenda much too broad to permit in-depth analysis and discussion. For some time, this problem could be managed with the help of Agenda 21, which represented an administrative framework, rather than truly analytical or conceptual framework. However, in the end (during PrepCom IV in New York) a different and much more differentiated distribution of work was established. In future negotiations on the environment and development, a facilitating strategy on the basis of something akin to Agenda 21 is unlikely to represent a viable solution; a much more penetrating problem analysis is likely to become necessary. Then, quite new formulas will have to be elaborated, accommodating a constructive tradeoff between the two important requirements of easy process access for developing countries and effective process dynamics.

In several respects, *issue linkages* represented a characteristic feature of the UNCED process with regard to goal structure as well as to the development of its agenda. First, a highly visible manifestation of interlinked issues was the presence of the evident cobweb of physical interdependence between many of the topics on the agenda – for instance, between climate change, the ozone layer, deforestation, and desertification. Secondly, one of the main political objectives of UNCED was to highlight the couplings between *environment* and *development* and design long-term operational strategies to cope with them. Thirdly, another overarching aim of the UNCED process was to develop a holistic international long-term plan of action for sustainable development, and for the whole range of issues subordinated to this concept. This approach required that topics be sufficiently focused – narrow and clearcut – to permit the actors to come to an agreement on concrete programs of action. On the other hand, the holistic ambition also required that the interdependence – the structure of linkages – between these specified themes be noted when UNCED's long-term plan of action was designed and carried out.

As one of the leading objectives of UNCED was to consider and cope with issue linkages, it is reasonable to ask if this ambition was, in fact, realized. Evoking this question, it has first to be acknowledged that the question of issue linkages was far from ignored; it was manifestly at the forefront throughout the process. This may be cited as an accomplishment in its own right, as it was part of UNCED's mission to point out and stress the need for a holistic approach to the treatment of environmental and development questions at the global level. It is quite clear that UNCED succeeded in further consolidating the notion of sustainable development, which had become a solid international catchword as a result of the Brundtland Report. UNCED transformed this normative, indeed ideological, notion into a set of operational concepts.

In the UNCED process, issue linkages were handled most effectively at the administrative level. The concrete measures proposed and decided upon in the UNCED process that were related to issue linkages mostly concerned the distribution of work and cooperation between many UN institutions with responsibilities in the areas of environment and development. Thus, from one point of view, Agenda 21 may be regarded as a design for a coordinated long-term plan of action. This was one of the most important and tangible results of the whole UNCED process. The leadership of the various UN agencies concerned became better informed about, first, the work programs of other institutions and, secondly, of the prospects and problems of interagency coordination. The high-level Commission on Sustainable Development was created under the auspices of the UN Economic and Social Council (ECOSOC) with the objective of supervising, guiding, and coordinating this work.

The administrative approach to issue linkages had obvious advantages. Notably, it was a feasible and controllable approach. At some stages in the process, it was widely doubted that UNCED could be brought to an end with even a minimum degree of success. However, all things considered, the UNCED process was managed remarkably smoothly, especially with regard to the established time schedule. The difference is striking in comparison to the developments of the Uruguay Round of GATT negotiations, the end stage of which took place at about the same time as the UNCED process was launched. Their closing ministerial session in Brussels scheduled for late 1990 ended in complete failure in spite of at least five years of intensive negotiation.

Thus, the management of issue linkages and other forms of complexity seem to have been easier and more effective in the UNCED process than in the GATT Round. This observation is somewhat intriguing as there were evidently numerous issues on the UNCED agenda that were more technically difficult and complex than the average item within the Uruguay Round. One explanation is that the UNCED process was characterized to a considerable degree by complexity and uncertainty avoidance. Notably, neither negotiating parties nor the UNCED secretariat had the motivation to penetrate and analyze the truly complex environmental issues on the agenda. They left the tough issues for subsequent negotiations within the sustainable development regime they had created.

CONSENSUS BUILDING AND INSTITUTIONALIZATION

Large multilateral negotiations, such as UNCED, are inherently unwieldy events. Zartman (1994) has characterized the process of multilateral negotiations as a series of valiant maneuvers to manage complexity within a diverse supraorganizational setting. For mutually beneficial outcomes to be achieved, the process of negotiation among over 150 sovereign national entities must somehow be organized and managed effectively; muddling through with no real plan to manage complexity, *and* achieving success, can be an accidental occurrence.

Various mechanisms to manage complexity were used with some degree of success in the UNCED negotiations. In Chapter 4, Sjöstedt describes the steps taken to reach consensual knowledge on particular issues under negotiation. Spector, in Chapter 5, analyzes the process by which countries with differing national interests adjusted their preferences over the course of the negotiation to reach mutually compatible compromises on the sensitive issue of financial resources. Schally (Chapter 7) and Avalle (Chapter 8) both describe approaches to intragovernmental coordination by which the internal stakeholders bargain among themselves to arrive at a single national position and bargaining posture. Discussing the multifaceted roles of leadership at UNCED, Antrim (Chapter 9) points to different types of leaders using specific procedures to help parties reach consensus. NGOs also helped in defusing the complexity of negotiation. Some in the scientific community nurtured transnational epistemic groupings and conducted meetings to influence and coalesce diverging policy directions (see Marton-Lefèvre and Boehmer-Christiansen in Chapters 11 and 12). Others served as objective third parties, facilitating the process of finding common ground among competing coalitions.

Unfortunately, the problems of managing complexity do not end when multilateral negotiations are concluded. The prospect of building an international regime to administer the agreed solutions requires the design and activation of additional creative mechanisms to manage a new set of complex relationships and situations. The post-negotiation period involves not only implementation of provisions agreed at the bargaining table, but a continual process of management, monitoring, adjustment, and continued negotiation as the effects of the negotiated provisions are fed back to enhance policy learning. Spector and Korula (1993) have called this a *post-agreement negotiation process:* agreements must be implemented and enforced, but often this occurs within the context of an international regime that employs sustained negotiation as its main vehicle of operation. This continued negotiation serves to resolve disputes that may arise, fill in details, augment partial agreements, and adjust regimes that must be modernized to reflect new scientific information. Post-agreement negotiation provides a stable mechanism to implement and expand regimes peacefully, thus reducing complexity.

If regime management is conducted as a negotiation process, one important element of managing this process is consensus building. Formalized voting procedures to govern decision making by all of the signatory members within a regime can have a polarizing effect. It can easily cause parties to become inflexible in their approach to sensitive issues. Forcing issues to a vote causes parties to commit themselves to particular positions rather than submit it to further discussion and debate; activity takes the form of a rigid pledge rather than an adaptable tradeoff. It cuts off the road to further discussion and possibly the finding of some common ground. Thus, it is preferable to build consensus within a regime than to resort to voting.

Rule by consensus is certainly accepted as a valuable mechanism of decision making in multilateral negotiations and of governance within international regimes. However, much is left to chance. If consensus emerges from a debate, it helps to move things forward; if it does not, maneuvering toward building consensus can assume an ad hoc process. Then, leadership style, personality, and organizational culture are often the driving forces motivating consensus formation. For example, Dr. Mustafa Tolba of the UN Environment Programme (UNEP) actively pursued a consensus-building role during the ozone depletion negotiations by conducting informal consultations (Szell, 1993). Secretary General Maurice Strong played a similar role in the prenegotiations leading up to the 1972 Stockholm Conference on marine pollution, helping to motivate the delegations and identify areas of agreement and gaps in understanding. Ambassador Tommy Koh served a consensus-building role in the Law of the Sea negotiations and stimulated the formation of helpful coalitions (Herter, 1991; Antrim and Sebenius, 1992). At an organizational level, the secretariat of the International Atomic Energy Agency played a major consensus-building role in the nuclear pollution talks in 1986 by drafting the agenda and a proposed text (Sjöstedt, 1993). UNEP served a similar function in drafting the 1974 Mediterranean Action Plan. Finally, the scientific community was called upon to mediate in the Mediterranean pollution talks by providing independent factfinding, diagnosing the problem, and recommending the range of scientifically viable solutions (Thacher, 1993).

Mediation and Consensus-building Mechanisms

Rather than leaving this critical function of consensus building to chance, international regimes would be wise, in their formative stages, to institutionalize procedures that facilitate the development of consensus among large numbers of signatory parties. As in many of the examples cited above, a third party mediator, in the form of a secretariat, a chairperson, or some such function, can be assigned the catalytic task of developing consensus among diverging positions. Mediation can be used to help settle disputes, uncover common interests, and cobble together agreements. However, to be effective, mediators must be sensitive to variations – for instance, in the situation and context, the types of actors, the divergence in their positions, and the intensity of dispute, and adjust and temper their strategic and interpersonal tools and approaches appropriately. Spector and Korula (1992) have gathered a *propositional inventory* drawn from substantiated experimental findings that suggests the likely effectiveness of mediational approaches under differing circumstances. Practitioners can be guided by the inventory to a proposed repertoire of tactics and strategies.

Specifically, the Spector and Korula study targeted the literature on facilitative mediation. Mediational strategies that are particularly relevant to consensus-building tasks typically involve the opening and supporting of communication channels and the facilitation of interaction between parties. The role of communicator/facilitator is at the most passive end of the mediational continuum (Touval and Zartman, 1985) and is typified in the international context by the provision of "good offices." Table 15.1 summarizes the study's results in a series of prescriptive "homilies" for the practical mediator. While these findings may appear to be very simple and obvious, they are supported by empirical evidence from a large number of laboratory experiments and field studies. Based upon the more fully elaborated propositional inventory, four facilitative mediation roles were deduced. While the roles are distinct, they can be, and often are, implemented simultaneously in practice.

The Go-between

Go-betweens serve as the conduit for information between disputing parties. They take on the responsibility of making contacts and keeping channels of communication open. They serve as delivery mechanisms for proposals, demands, and concessions.

The Fact-finder

Fact-finding is among the most common roles assumed by facilitative mediators. Fact-Finders serve as objective information collectors about the dispute; they gather the facts on an impartial basis and investigate allegations put forth by the parties. Their goal is to readjust misperceptions that result from inaccurate information or a misreading of the facts.

Table 15.1 Research Findings on Effective Mechanisms for Facilitative Mediators[1]

The go-between
- Associate communication with authoritativeness
- Encourage "staying in touch"
- Educate parties in constructive communications
- Encourage "complete" messages

The fact-finder
- Gather information
- Provide objective data
- Quote law and legal precedent
- Provide accurate information on each party's position
- Provide information on each party

The counselor
- Have each party state their own point of view
- State other's point of view
- Be non-evaluative
- Recommend role playing
- Cite dependencies
- Cite superordinate goals faced by disputing parties
- Indicate costs to third party
- Call for empathy
- Praise parties
- Maintain momentum
- Encourage friendly attitudes
- Limit the scope of issues
- Seek early agreement on easier issues
- Reduce public position-taking and posturing
- Encourage "fair" proposals
- Educate on cultural differences
- Educate parties on bargaining dynamics
- Encourage reflective statements
- Suggest cooling-off period
- Avert and convert intangible issues
- Promise gains for cooperation
- Fractionate issues

The sponsor
- Establish mediator's presence
- Establish and control agenda
- Avoid audiences
- Select neutral sites
- Maintain secrecy
- Encourage face-to-face talks
- Create deadlines

[1] The experimental social psychological research literature on negotiation and conflict resolution was reviewed to identify implementation mechanisms that have been shown to be effective in achieving successful outcomes – improved communication or agreement – among disputing parties. The mechanisms identified in this literature *have been substantiated* as being effective in systematic research findings – either in field or laboratory tests. Together, the results represent a *propositional inventory* that describes a set of authoritative prescriptions for mediators that have been verified through controlled experimental channels. This assessment benefited greatly from several major reviews of the experimental research literature on negotiation and mediation: Druckman (1973); Rubin and Brown (1975); Wall (1981); Pruitt (1981); Carnevale and Pruitt (1992); and Kressel and Pruitt (1989).

Source: Spector and Korula (1992).

The Counselor

The counselor serves the role of educator and adviser to the disputing parties. Such supportive activities can range from very passive assistance – just providing a presence – to consultations with the parties, but stops short of offering proposals for solution. Counselors also function as sounding boards for the disputants, and sometimes as confidants, as they assume more of a trusted role.

The Sponsor

The Sponsor organizes and/or hosts fora in which the disputants can talk directly or through the mediator. Again, playing a facilitative role, the sponsor can provide the venue, send out invitations, arrange for or exclude media coverage, and chair sessions.

Within the regime context, facilitative mediators that follow these prescribed roles and paths can serve the important function of promoting consensus among the parties. Formalizing such a mediational function institutionalizes a vital feature of regime governance, while making it more efficient by reducing its inherent complexity.

Developing Consensus-building Procedures at the Global Environment Facility – An Example

Several of the prescriptive mediational approaches mentioned in Table 15.1 were recommended and incorporated into the governing principles of an important regime element emerging from UNCED – the Global Environment Facility (GEF). A common demand of countries represented at UNCED was that negotiated agreements be implemented by existing institutions. The GEF, an agency jointly administered by the UN Development and Environment Programs and the World Bank was selected at UNCED to be the interim funding mechanism for the climate change and biodiversity conventions. An important condition guiding this choice was that the GEF make serious adjustments to the decision-making rules by which it is governed – how it develops policy, how it selects projects for funding, and how it administers funds. Governed largely by World Bank procedures, the GEF was viewed suspiciously by developing nations as a vehicle for donor countries, and particularly the United States, to exercise influence over the developing world through granting projects that placed extensive economic conditions and restrictions on the grantee. UNCED instructed the GEF to reform its governance procedures to provide a more equitable framework that would be acceptable to all countries – both donors and grantees.

Proposals were prepared by the GEF Administrator for its first post-UNCED meeting of participants in December 1992 in Abidjan (GEF, 1992). These proposals largely addressed the GEF's legal status, as well as reformed decision-making procedures, attempting to balance the interests of all parties in a restructured GEF. One of the stated goals in these proposals was to avert deadlock in the Participants' Assembly, its decision-making body, by encouraging consensus among the parties, thereby bypassing the need for voting. In line with this objective, some mediation mechanisms that were identified in the previous section were offered as proposals to the Assembly to be included as explicit *consensus-building activities* in the GEF's decision-making procedures. These functions would be carried out by the GEF secretariat not as ad hoc activities, but as prescribed tasks. These proposals are presented below as examples of how the facilitation of consensus building can be incorporated formally into the management of international regimes to reduce complexity.

The GEF secretariat was called upon to conduct *early preparatory activities* to ensure that consensus is forthcoming at the Assembly meetings. In the event that consensus is not easily achieved, *alternative dispute resolution (ADR) methods* could be used during the Assembly meetings, again aided by the GEF secretariat, to actively seek consensus. Only as a last resort were voting methods to be invoked to deal with deadlocked issues. The following ADR mechanisms were recommended:

For Early Facilitation Prior to Meetings:

(1) The GEF secretariat, as the source of background papers and proposals, can *integrate the various party points of view* to design specific proposals that account for different constituency positions. The secretariat can do this by polling the constituencies and conducting role-playing exercises, for example.
(2) The secretariat can play an important role in early consensus building by actively *supporting constructive communications* among the parties. Such constructive communications seek to transmit accurate accounts of the positions of each party and the principles of fairness held by the various constituencies, rather than emphasizing differences. This is likely to yield greater understanding and trust among parties.

For Dispute Resolution Methods During Meetings:

(1) The chairman of the Participants' Assembly can be empowered to *form a small ad hoc problem-solving committee* comprised of three to five constituencies to address deadlocked issues, seeking to identify novel ideas that will overcome the impasse. Creative tradeoffs or solutions would be reported back to the full Assembly for final decision.
(2) Such an ad hoc problem-solving committee can sometimes operate more effectively with the help of *trained facilitators* who either know the substance of the deadlocked issue very well or are skilled in special problem-solving techniques, such as creativity methods. These facilitators can be supplied by the GEF secretariat.
(3) The secretariat and the chairman of the Participants' Assembly can encourage consensus by *fractionating contentious issues* into more manageable pieces. If certain elements of the problem area can be solved quickly as a result, it will increase trust among the parties and improve the chances for finding agreement on the more difficult issues.
(4) If the differences among constituencies are extreme, *active mediation* supported by the secretariat or the chairman can be useful in seeking a convergence of interests and agreement.

The redesign of the GEF's decision-making structure in response to the North–South debates at UNCED was just a small step toward institutionalizing mediation-based consensus-building mechanisms into the operation of an important international environmental regime. It can be seen as a natural outgrowth of the desire to manage complexity and generate a more effective regime, one capable of achieving agreement despite extensive interest divergence.

Such approaches are central features of regime governance. The agreement among parties to formalize these mechanisms as standard operating procedures to achieve their objectives in the regime is a negotiating achievement in itself. This achievement indicates a degree of maturity and stability in the regime based on a common political will to avoid impasse and realize the overarching objectives for which the regime was established. The facilitative mediational techniques described in this chapter offer straightforward post-agreement support toward these goals.

REGIME EVOLUTION AND FUTURE CHALLENGES

The sets of rules, principles, expectations, and routines established in the multiple practices and agreements emanating from more than two years of UNCED experience are not fixed, nor are its final commandments writ in stone. To stay alive, they need to evolve to meet changing situations and unfolding knowledge. Innately, they are also bound to evolve under the internal dynamics of their own successes and failures, as they face consequences of their measures and reactions to their regulations. Thus, external and internal challenges shape the course of the regime as it navigates through time and – unlike the image – these challenges shape the very nature of the regime itself.

Although much of this evolution is unforeseeable, the nature, even if not the specifics, of the challenges can be anticipated, even in the area of external surprises. Anticipation, in turn, provides the basis for action and the lessening of surprises, and therefore of some further policy-relevant analysis. It should not be forgotten, however, that challenges are not merely the product of neutral events, natural winds that knock down any object in their path; they also come from the intentional effects of policy makers seeking to deflect or accelerate the evolution of the regime and therefore looking for policy-relevant analysis for their own purposes.

UNCED is at least a triple regime, as Chasek's chapter has graphically illustrated. Northern countries have a clear focus on its efforts to set up new norms, principles, expectations, and (more loosely) regulations in the area of environment. However, it also was the latest attempt to create a similar context for thinking and action in the area of development. Southern countries, in turn, have looked on it as the beginning of a new regime that links the two, focusing on the environmental impact on development as well as the developmental impact on environment. Not all these three overlapping regimes can be expected to evolve through time at the same speed or in the same form, and part of the policy dynamic will involve conscious efforts to foster one in relation to the other two.

In all three areas, the basic movement of the regime is like a sea wave, not in its common image of an inexorable surface movement, but in its kinetic reality, where movement on the top is propelled by energy at the base. In its public, diplomatic phase, UNCED registered the formal progress analyzed in the previous chapters of this book. That phase completed, its work now returns to the individual states' domestic arenas, at both the governmental and the nongovernmental (NGO) level. The meeting at Rio was designed to create institutions and momentum in both arenas. As the Schally and Avalle chapters indicate (Chapters 7 and 8), the need to prepare for Rio brought about the creation of new environmental ministries in some countries and the coordination of environmental activities among established ministries in the rest. These ministries now live under the organizational imperative to defend their existence, by hiring staff, making budgetary claims, and showing justifying activity. This does not mean that they thereby will win the day in policy debates, but it does mean that they are an element among others in determining new national policy directions. Even a basically unfriendly government, such as the Bush administration in Washington, was able only to deflect, not deter, the pressures that resulted in the Rio preparations and documents, and the US Environmental Protection Agency was a body with a mind of its own, often difficult to control.

On the other side, UNCED was the largest fair for NGOs that the world has ever seen, and, as Chapter 13 records, they came home from Rio invigorated and frustrated. The combination makes for a very active array of pressure groups, some of them operating for the very first time in Third World country politics, and others well established in a competitive context in developed democracies, as emphasized in Chapter 14. Momentum on the environmental, development, and joint fronts depends on the dynamism of the NGOs, defined in the UNCED sense as not just public interest groups, but also business. Only the alliance of scientists, public advocates, and business will provide the discourse, finance, and electoral clout to keep governments focused on fulfilling the UNCED goals (Zartman, 1993).

None of these three groups, nor their cooperation together, guarantees the implementation and expansion of the UNCED norms, principles, expectations, and regulations. However, they do practically guarantee an equal and opposite reaction, the mobilization of efforts by opponents to regain in domestic application what was lost in diplomatic negotiation. Business and labor groups and various competing interests join efforts with ministries devoted to conflicting concerns to limit the effects of the plan of action and associated agreements. Many of these groups might not be specifically "anti-UNCED," but simply efforts competing for scarce resources or conflicting in their own orientations. Nothing can indicate what the outcome of these domestic confrontations will be, since it depends on many external variables, but repeated reactions as well as actions are to be expected.

These confrontations bear on the course of the regime at two pressure points, in conflicts over agenda and conflicts over action (Bachrach and Baratz, 1962). Contending forces vie over the place of UNCED-related issues on various agendas, from that of public attention to that of legislative consideration; once they reach the point where action is required, the contention among forces renews over two aspects of action-specific measures and their financing. While these confrontations are self-supporting, given the contending forces involved, they also benefit from one major source of external pressure, the foreseen accident. Indeed, most environmental negotiations have been triggered by a catastrophe that scientists and interest groups have warned against, falling in the midst of a debate on a plausible solution like a piece of dust into a supersaturated solution (Zartman, 1993). Such catastrophes can literally be accidents or they can be further startling and confirming scientific evidence, demanding public attention and official action. Inland seas, deserts, atmosphere, and wastes, as well as population growth, health, and nourishment, all contain catastrophes waiting to happen. They will trigger attempts to lock the stable door after the horse has bolted and debates affecting the course of the UNCED regime.

Despite the return to the base as the arena of regime dynamics, there are continuing manifestations of the regime dynamic at the level of public diplomacy. As Chapter 14 details, Agenda 21 is replete with calls for further action on the global and regional levels, as well as national ones, to contribute to the development of further norms, principles, expectations and regulations. These actions take three forms: extension, implementation, and consolidation. The global debate passed to the UN General Assembly at the 47th session in 1992, where, despite widely dissipated attentions and implementation efforts that have to compete for a place on the world agenda crowded with noisier security issues, plans were made and institutions created to move the regime forward (III *ENB*1-3).

The first result was the Intergovernmental Negotiating Committee to elaborate a convention on Desertification (INC-D), which met throughout 1993 and 1994 to extend UNCED concerns into a new area. Prepcom meetings for an International Conference on Population and Development (ICPD) began before UNCED, in May 1991, and continued thereafter two years later, in preparation for the actual conference in September 1994 to extend and consolidate the UNCED regime into a large area of activity. Two other diplomatic activities linked the UNCED regime to the regime on the seas as revised by the Law of the Sea Conference that ended a decade earlier; the UN Conference on Fish Stocks met in July 1993 and projected further sessions for 1994 to resolve strong differences over the appropriate degree of international controls, and a conference on national guidelines for the integrated management of coastal zones was to be held in 1994 to set standards for national implementation. A conference on the sustainable development of small island states was also scheduled for 1994, after preparatory committee work in 1993. All of these activities planned at Rio keep parts of the momentum alive, extending coverage into new areas by elaborated new norms and regulations and consolidating established efforts by closing loopholes. The accent on tightening specific aspects of the regime has shifted the role of driver or conductor from the global to the specific level. As chairs, Swedish Ambassador Bo Kjellén and Fijian diplomat Satya Nandan have been the conductors of the Desertification and Fish Stocks Conferences, for example.

The most important institutionalized effort to monitor the implementation of the UNCED regime is the Commission on Sustainable Development (CSD) of ECOSOC, which met in its first annual session in June 1993 in Rio. Its contribution to the furtherance of the regime depends on its ability to give policy direction and monitor and generate information on the implementation of Agenda 21, which in turn requires both solid capabilities and innovative artifices to insure cooperation and transparency. Typical of the latter were such plans from the first session as the scheduling of country-hosted intersessional meetings on focused topics (nine were volunteered for 1994), the arrangement of ministerial sessions about a round table to encourage dialogue, and the inclusion of other than environmental ministers in CSD work (V *ENB*.12; 12)

Efforts to extend, implement, and consolidate the UNCED regime have also been pitched at the regional level, between global and national activities. Agenda 21 specifically targets regions in regard to transportation and environment, transboundary air pollution, and movement of hazardous wastes, marine environment, and sustainable development of small islands, among others. Regional activities have the obvious strengths and weaknesses, allowing for ready regions to move ahead and slower regions to lag behind, but the result is a pressure that moves with the direction of the momentum and thus generally favors regime progress.

All of these activities and actions tend to focus on the extension, implementation, and consolidation of the regulatory aspect of regimes, whether in their binding or nonbinding form. Behind this lies a softer area of norms, principles, and expectations, general notions on which specific provisions lie. It is not clear how firm a normative foundation UNCED had laid for itself. Like the UN Conference on the Law of the Sea a decade earlier, UNCED was built on a basic tradeoff between environmental concerns for the North and developmental concerns for the South. However, there is no evidence or assurance that either the equality or the tradeoff itself has taken root in the popular mind or in policy makers' calculations.

Appendix A

Resolution Adopted by the UN General Assembly: Resolution No. 44/228

New York, 22 December 1989
United Nations Conference on Environment and Development

THE GENERAL ASSEMBLY,

RECALLING its resolution 43/196 of 20 December 1988 on a United Nations conference on environment and development,

TAKING NOTE of decision 15/3 of 25 May 1989 of the Governing Council of the United Nations Environment Programme[1] on a United Nations conference on environment and development,

TAKING NOTE also of Economic and Social Council resolution 1989/87 of 26 July 1989 on the convening of a United Nations conference on environment and development,

TAKING NOTE further of Economic and Social Council resolution 1989/101 of 27 July 1989 on strengthening international co-operation on environment through the provision of additional financial resources to developing countries,

RECALLING its resolutions 42/186 of 11 December 1987 on the Environmental Perspective to the Year 2000 and Beyond and resolution 42/187 of 11 December 1987 on the report of the World Commission on Environment and Development,[2]

TAKING NOTE of the report of the Secretary-General on the question of the convening of a United Nations conference on environment and development,[3]

MINDFUL of the views expressed by Governments in the debate held at its forty-fourth session on the convening of a United Nations conference on environment and development,

RECALLING the Declaration of the United Nations Conference on the Human Environment,[4]

[1]See Official Records of the General Assembly, Forty-fourth Session, Supplement No. 25 (A/44/25), annex I.

[2]See A/42/427, annex.

[3]A/44/256-E/1989/66 and Corr.1 and Add.1 and 2.

[4]Report of the UN Conference on the Human Environment, Stockholm, 5–6 June 1972, and corrigendum (UN publication, Sales No. E.73.II.A.14), chapter I.

Negotiating International Regimes: Lessons Learned from the United Nations Conference on Environment and Development (G. Sjöstedt, *et al.*, eds.; 1-85966-077-0; © IIASA; pub. Graham & Trotman, 1994; printed in Great Britain), pp. 251–258.

Deeply CONCERNED by the continuing deterioration of the state of the environment and the serious degradation of the global life-support systems, as well as by trends that, if allowed to continue, could disrupt the global ecological balance, jeopardize the life-sustaining qualities of the Earth and lead to an ecological catastrophe, and recognizing that decisive, urgent and global action is vital to protecting the ecological balance of the Earth,

RECOGNIZING the importance for all countries of the protection and enhancement of the environment,

RECOGNIZING also that the global character of environmental problems, including climate change, depletion of the ozone layer, transboundary air and water pollution, the contamination of the oceans and seas and degradation of land resources, including drought and desertification, necessitates action at all levels, including the global, regional and national levels, and the commitment and participation of all countries,

Gravely CONCERNED that the major cause of the continuing deterioration of the global environment is the unsustainable pattern of production and consumption, particularly in industrialized countries,

STRESSING that poverty and environmental degradation are closely interrelated and that environmental protection in developing countries must, in this context, be viewed as an integral part of the development process and cannot be considered in isolation from it,

RECOGNIZING that measures to be undertaken at the international level for the protection and enhancement of the environment must take fully into account the current imbalances in global patterns of production and consumption,

AFFIRMING that the responsibility for containing, reducing and eliminating global environmental damage must be borne by the countries causing such damage, must be in relation to the damage caused and must be in accordance with their respective capabilities and responsibilities,

RECOGNIZING the environmental impact of material remnants of war and the need for further international co-operation for their removal,

STRESSING the importance for all countries of taking effective measures for the protection, restoration and enhancement of the environment in accordance, inter alia, with their respective capabilities, while at the same time acknowledging the efforts being made in all countries in this regard, including international co-operation between developed and developing countries,

STRESSES the need for effective international co-operation in the areas of research, development and application of environmentally sound technologies,

CONSCIOUS of the crucial role of science and technology in the field of environmental protection and of the need of developing countries, in particular, for favourable access to environmentally sound technologies, processes, equipment and related research and expertise through international co-operation designed to further global efforts for environmental protection, including the use of innovative and effective means,

RECOGNIZING that new and additional financial resources will have to be channelled to developing countries in order to ensure their full participation in global efforts for environmental protection,

PART I

1. DECIDES to convene the United Nations Conference on Environment and Development, which shall be of two weeks' duration and shall have the highest possible level of participation, to coincide with World Environment Day, on 5 June 1992;

2. ACCEPTS with deep appreciation the generous offer of the Government of Brazil to act as host to the Conference;

3. AFFIRMS that the Conference should elaborate strategies and measures to halt and reverse the effects of environmental degradation in the context of increased national and international efforts to promote sustainable and environmentally sound development in all countries;

4. AFFIRMS also that the protection and enhancement of the environment are major issues that affect the well-being of peoples and economic development throughout the world;

5. AFFIRMS further that the promotion of economic growth in developing countries is essential to address problems of environmental degradation;

6. AFFIRMS the importance of a supportive international economic climate conducive to sustained economic growth and development in all countries for the protection and sound management of the environment;

7. REAFFIRMS that, in accordance with the Charter of the United Nations and the applicable principles of international law, States have the sovereign right to exploit their own resources pursuant to their environmental policies, and also reaffirms their responsibility to ensure that activities within their jurisdiction or control do not cause damage to the environment of other States or of areas beyond the limits of national jurisdiction and to play their due role in preserving and protecting the global and regional environment in accordance with their capacities and specific responsibilities;

8. AFFIRMS the responsibility of States, in accordance with national legislation and applicable international law, for the damage to the environment and natural resources caused by activities within their jurisdiction or control through transboundary interference;

9. NOTES that the largest part of the current emission of pollutants into the environment, including toxic and hazardous wastes, originates in developed countries, and therefore recognizes that those countries have the main responsibility for combating such pollution;

10. STRESSES that large industrial enterprises, including transnational corporations, are frequently the repositories of scarce technical skills for the preservation and enhancement of the environment, that they conduct activities in sectors that have an impact on the environment and, to that extent, have specific responsibilities and that, in this context, efforts need to be encouraged and mobilized to protect and enhance the environment in all countries;

11. REAFFIRMS that the serious external indebtedness of developing countries and other countries with serious debt-servicing problems has to be addressed in an efficient and urgent manner in order to enable those countries to contribute fully and

in accordance with their capacities and responsibilities to global efforts to protect and enhance the environment;

12. AFFIRMS that, in the light of the foregoing, the following environmental issues, which are not listed in any particular order of priority, are among those of major concern in maintaining the quality of the Earth's environment and especially in achieving environmentally sound and sustainable development in all countries:

(a) Protection of the atmosphere by combating climate change, depletion of the ozone layer and transboundary air pollution;
(b) Protection of the quality and supply of freshwater resources;
(c) Protection of the oceans and all kinds of seas, including enclosed and semi-enclosed seas, and coastal areas and the protection, rational use and development of their living resources;
(d) Protection and management of land resources by, inter alia, combating deforestation, desertification and drought;
(e) Conservation of biological diversity;
(f) Environmentally sound management of biotechnology;
(g) Environmentally sound management of wastes, particularly hazardous wastes, and of toxic chemicals, as well as prevention of illegal international traffic in toxic and dangerous products and wastes;
(h) Improvement of the living and working environment of the poor in urban slums and rural areas, through the eradication of poverty by, inter alia, implementing integrated rural and urban development programmes, as well as taking other appropriate measures at all levels necessary to stem the degradation of the environment;
(i) Protection of human health conditions and improvement of the quality of life;

13. EMPHASIZES the need to strengthen international co-operation for the management of the environment to ensure its protection and enhancement and the need to explore the issue of benefits derived from activities, including research and development, related to the protection and development of biological diversity;

14. REAFFIRMS the need to strengthen international co-operation, particularly between developed and developing countries, in research and development and the utilization of environmentally sound technologies;

15. DECIDES that the Conference, in addressing environmental issues in the developmental context, should have the following objectives:

(a) To examine the state of the environment and changes that have occurred since the United Nations Conference on the Human Environment, held in 1972, and since the adoption of such international agreements as the Plan of Action to Combat Desertification, the Vienna Convention for the Protection of the Ozone Layer, adopted on 22 March 1985, and the Montreal Protocol on Substances that Deplete the Ozone Layer, adopted on 16 September 1987, taking into account the actions taken by all countries and intergovernmental organizations to protect and enhance the environment;
(b) To identify strategies to be co-ordinated regionally and globally, as appropriate, for concerted action to deal with major environmental issues in the socio-economic development processes of all countries within a particular time-frame;

(c) To recommend measures to be taken at the national and international levels to protect and enhance the environment, taking into account the specific needs of developing countries, through the development and implementation of policies for sustainable and environmentally sound development with special emphasis on incorporating environmental concerns in the economic and social development process and of various sectoral policies and through, inter alia, preventive action at the sources of environmental degradation, clearly identifying the sources of such degradation and appropriate remedial measures, in all countries;

(d) To promote the further development of international environmental law, taking into account the Declaration of the United Nations Conference on the Human Environment,[5] as well as the special needs and concerns of the developing countries, and to examine in this context the feasibility of elaborating general rights and obligations of States, as appropriate, in the field of the environment, and taking into account relevant existing international legal instruments;

(e) To examine ways and means further to improve co-operation in the field of protection and enhancement of the environment between neighbouring countries, with a view to eliminating adverse environmental effects;

(f) To examine strategies for national and international action with a view to arriving at specific agreements and commitments by Governments for defined activities to deal with major environmental issues in order to restore the global ecological balance and to prevent further deterioration of the environment, taking into account the fact that the largest part of the current emission of pollutants into the environment, including toxic and hazardous wastes, originates in developed countries, and therefore recognizing that those countries have the main responsibility for combating such pollution;

(g) To accord high priority to drought and desertification control and to consider all means necessary, including financial, scientific and technological resources, to halt and reverse the process of desertification with a view to preserving the ecological balance of the planet;

(h) To examine the relationship between environmental degradation and the international economic environment, with a view to ensuring a more integrated approach to problems of environment and development in relevant international forums without introducing new forms of conditionality;

(i) To examine strategies for national and international action with a view to arriving at specific agreements and commitments by Governments and by intergovernmental organizations for defined activities to promote a supportive international economic climate conducive to sustained and environmentally sound development in all countries, with a view to combating poverty and improving the quality of life, and bearing in mind that the incorporation of environmental concerns and considerations in development planning and policies should not be used to introduce new forms of conditionality in aid or in development financing and should not serve as a pretext for creating unjustified barriers to trade;

(j) To identify ways and means of providing new and additional financial resources, particularly to developing countries, for environmentally sound

[5] Report of the UN Conference on the Human Environment, Stockholm, 5–16 June 1972, and corrigendum (UN publication, Sales No. E.73.II.A.14), chapter I.

development programmes and projects in accordance with national development objectives, priorities and plans and to consider ways of effectively monitoring the provision of such new and additional financial resources, particularly to developing countries, so as to enable the international community to take further appropriate action on the basis of accurate and reliable data;

(k) To identify ways and means of providing additional financial resources for measures directed towards solving major environmental problems of global concern and especially of supporting those countries, in particular developing countries, for which the implementation of such measures would entail a special or abnormal burden, owing, in particular, to their lack of financial resources, expertise or technical capacity;

(l) To consider various funding mechanisms, including voluntary ones, and to examine the possibility of a special international fund and other innovative approaches, with a view to ensuring, on a favourable basis, the most effective and expeditious transfer of environmentally sound technologies to developing countries;

(m) To examine, with a view to making recommendations on effective modalities for favourable access to, and transfer of, environmentally sound technologies, in particular to the developing countries, including on concessional and preferential terms, and on modalities for supporting all countries in their efforts to create and develop their endogenous technological capacities in the field of scientific research and development, as well as in the acquisition of relevant information, and, in this context, to explore the concept of assured access for developing countries to environmentally sound technologies, in its relation to proprietary rights, with a view to developing effective responses to the needs of developing countries in this area;

(n) To promote the development of human resources, particularly in developing countries, for the protection and enhancement of the environment;

(o) To recommend measures to Governments and the relevant bodies of the United Nations system, with a view to strengthening technical co-operation with the developing countries to enable them to develop and strengthen their capacity for identifying, analysing, monitoring, managing or preventing environmental problems in accordance with their national development plans, objectives and priorities;

(p) To promote open and timely exchange of information on national environmental policies, situations and accidents;

(q) To review and examine the role of the United Nations system in dealing with the environment and possible ways of improving it;

(r) To promote the development or strengthening of appropriate institutions at the national, regional and global levels to deal with environmental matters in the context of the socio-economic development processes of all countries;

(s) To promote environmental education, especially of the younger generation, as well as other measures to increase awareness of the value of the environment;

(t) To promote international co-operation within the United Nations system in monitoring, assessing and anticipating environmental threats and in rendering assistance in cases of environmental emergency;

(u) To specify the respective responsibilities of and support to be given by the organs, organizations and programmes of the United Nations system for the implementation of the recommendations of the Conference;

(v) To quantify the financial requirements for the successful implementation of Conference decisions and recommendations and to identify possible sources, including innovative ones, of additional resources;

(w) To assess the capacity of the United Nations system to assist in the prevention and settlement of disputes in the environmental sphere and to recommend measures in this field, while respecting existing bilateral and international agreements that provide for the settlement of such disputes;

PART II

1. DECIDES to establish the Preparatory Committee for the United Nations Conference on Environment and Development, which shall be open to all States Members of the United Nations or members of the specialized agencies, with the participation of observers, in accordance with the established practice of the General Assembly;

2. DECIDES that the Preparatory Committee shall hold an organizational session of two weeks' duration in March 1990 and a final session, both at United Nations Headquarters, as well as three additional substantive sessions, the first at Nairobi and the following two at Geneva, the timing and duration of which shall be determined by the Preparatory Committee at its organizational session;

3. DECIDES that the Preparatory Committee, at its organizational session, shall elect, with due regard to equitable geographic representation, a chairman and other members of its Bureau, comprising a substantial number of vice-chairmen and a rapporteur;

4. DECIDES that the host country of the Conference, Brazil, shall be ex officio a member of the Bureau;

5. REQUESTS the Secretary-General, following the organizational session of the Preparatory Committee, to establish an appropriate ad hoc secretariat at the United Nations Office at Geneva, with a unit in New York and another unit in Nairobi, taking into account the decisions to be made by the Preparatory Committee regarding the preparatory process for the Conference and based on the principle of equitable geographic distribution;

6. DECIDES that the ad hoc secretariat will be headed by the Secretary-General of the United Nations Conference on Environment and Development, who will be appointed by the Secretary-General of the United Nations;

7. REQUESTS the Secretary-General of the United Nations to prepare a report for the organizational session of the Preparatory Committee containing recommendations on an adequate preparatory process, taking into account the provisions of the present resolution and the views expressed by Governments in the debate at the forty-fourth session of the General Assembly;

8. DECIDES that the Preparatory Committee shall:

(a) Draft the provisional agenda of the Conference, in accordance with the provisions of the present resolution;

(b) Adopt guidelines to enable States to take a harmonized approach in their preparations and reporting;

(c) Prepare draft decisions for the Conference and submit them to the Conference for consideration and adoption;

9. REQUESTS the United Nations Environment Programme, as the main organ dealing with environmental issues, and other organs, organizations and programmes of the United Nations system, as well as other relevant intergovernmental organizations, to contribute fully to the preparations for the Conference on the basis of guidelines and requirements to be established by the Preparatory Committee;

10. REQUESTS the Secretary-General to ensure the co-ordination of contributions from the United Nations system through the Administrative Committee on Co-ordination;

11. INVITES all States to take an active part in the preparations for the Conference, to prepare national reports, as appropriate, to be submitted to the Preparatory Committee in a timely manner, and to promote international co-operation and broad-based national preparatory processes involving the scientific community, industry, trade unions and concerned non-governmental organizations;

12. REQUESTS relevant non-governmental organizations in consultative status with the Economic and Social Council to contribute to the Conference, as appropriate;

13. STRESSES the importance of holding regional conferences on environment and development with the full co-operation of the regional commissions, and recommends that the results of such regional conferences be introduced into the preparatory process for the Conference, bearing in mind that regional conferences should make important substantive contributions to the Conference;

14. DECIDES that the preparatory process and the Conference itself should be funded through the regular budget of the United Nations without adversely affecting other ongoing activities and without prejudice to the provision of sources of extrabudgetary resources;

15. DECIDES to establish a voluntary fund for the purpose of assisting developing countries, in particular the least developed among them, to participate fully and effectively in the Conference and in its preparatory process, and invites Governments to contribute to the fund;

16. REQUESTS the Chairman of the Preparatory Committee to report to the General Assembly at its forty-fifth and forty-sixth sessions on the progress of work of the Committee;

17. DECIDES to include in the provisional agenda of its forty-fifth and forty-sixth sessions an item entitled "United Nations Conference on Environment and Development".

85th Plenary Meeting
United Nations General Assembly
New York

22 December 1989

Appendix B

The Rio Declaration on Environment and Development

Preamble

The United Nations Conference on Environment and Development,

Having met at Rio de Janeiro from 3 to 14 June 1992,

Reaffirming the Declaration of the United Nations Conference on the Human Environment, adopted at Stockholm on 16 June 1972, and seeking to build upon it,

With the goal of establishing a new and equitable global partnership through the creation of new levels of cooperation among States, key sectors of societies and people,

Working towards international agreements which respect the interests of all and protect the integrity of the global environmental and developmental system,

Recognizing the integral and interdependent nature of the Earth, our home,

Proclaims that:

Principle 1

Human beings are at the centre of concerns for sustainable development. They are entitled to a healthy and productive life in harmony with nature.

Principle 2

States have, in accordance with the Charter of the United Nations and the principles of international law, the sovereign right to exploit their own resources pursuant to their own environmental and developmental policies, and the responsibility to ensure that activities within their jurisdiction or control do not cause damage to the environment of other States or of areas beyond the limits of national jurisdiction.

Principle 3

The right to development must be fulfilled so as to equitably meet developmental and environmental needs of present and future generations.

Negotiating International Regimes: Lessons Learned from the United Nations Conference on Environment and Development (G. Sjöstedt, *et al.*, eds.; 1-85966-077-0; © IIASA; pub. Graham & Trotman, 1994; printed in Great Britain), pp. 259–263.

Principle 4

In order to achieve sustainable development, environmental protection shall constitute an integral part of the development process and cannot be considered in isolation from it.

Principle 5

All States and all people shall cooperate in the essential task of eradicating poverty as an indispensable requirement for sustainable development, in order to decrease the disparities in standards of living and better meet the needs of the majority of the people of the world.

Principle 6

The special situation and needs of developing countries, particularly the least developed and those most environmentally vulnerable, shall be given special priority. International actions in the field of environment and development should also address the interests and needs of all countries.

Principle 7

States shall cooperate in a spirit of global partnership to conserve, protect and restore the health and integrity of the Earth's ecosystem. In view of the different contributions to global environmental degradation, States have common but differentiated responsibilities. The developed countries acknowledge the responsibility that they bear in the international pursuit of sustainable development in view of the pressures their societies place on the global environment and of the technologies and financial resources they command.

Principle 8

To achieve sustainable development and a higher quality of life for all people, States should reduce and eliminate unsustainable patterns of production and consumption and promote appropriate demographic policies.

Principle 9

States should cooperate to strengthen endogenous capacity-building for sustainable development by improving scientific understanding through exchanges of scientific and technological knowledge, and by enhancing the development, adaptation, diffusion and transfer of technologies, including new and innovative technologies.

Principle 10

Environmental issues are best handled with the participation of all concerned citizens, at the relevant level. At the national level, each individual shall have appropriate access to information concerning the environment that is held by public authorities, including information on hazardous materials and activities in their communities, and the opportunity to participate in decision-making processes.

States shall facilitate and encourage public awareness and participation by making information widely available. Effective access to judicial and administrative proceedings, including redress and remedy, shall be provided.

Principle 11

States shall enact effective environmental legislation. Environmental standards, management objectives and priorities should reflect the environmental and developmental context to which they apply. Standards applied by some countries may be inappropriate and of unwarranted economic and social cost to other countries, in particular developing countries.

Principle 12

States should cooperate to promote a supportive and open international economic system that would lead to economic growth and sustainable development in all countries, to better address the problems of environmental degradation. Trade policy measures for environmental purposes should not constitute a means of arbitrary or unjustifiable discrimination or a disguised restriction on international trade. Unilateral actions to deal with environmental challenges outside the jurisdiction of the importing country should be avoided. Environmental measures addressing transboundary or global environmental problems should, as far as possible, be based on an international consensus.

Principle 13

States shall develop national law regarding liability and compensation for the victims of pollution and other environmental damage. States shall also cooperate in an expeditious and more determined manner to develop further international law regarding liability and compensation for adverse effects of environmental damage caused by activities within their jurisdiction or control to areas beyond their jurisdiction.

Principle 14

States should effectively cooperate to discourage or prevent the relocation and transfer to other States of any activities and substances that cause severe environmental degradation or are found to be harmful to human health.

Principle 15

In order to protect the environment, the precautionary approach shall be widely applied by States according to their capabilities. Where there are threats of serious or irreversible damage, lack of full scientific certainty shall not be used as a reason for postponing cost-effective measures to prevent environmental degradation.

Principle 16

National authorities should endeavour to promote the internalization of environmental costs and the use of economic instruments, taking into account the approach that the polluter should, in principle, bear the cost of pollution, with due regard to the public interest and without distorting international trade and investment.

Principle 17

Environmental impact assessment, as a national instrument, shall be undertaken for proposed activities that are likely to have a significant adverse impact on the environment and are subject to a decision of a competent national authority.

Principle 18

States shall immediately notify other States of any natural disasters or other emergencies that are likely to produce sudden harmful effects on the environment of those States. Every effort shall be made by the international community to help States so afflicted.

Principle 19

States shall provide prior and timely notification and relevant information to potentially affected States on activities that may have a significant adverse transboundary environmental effect and shall consult with those States at an early stage and in good faith.

Principle 20

Women have a vital role in environmental management and development. Their full participation is therefore essential to achieve sustainable development.

Principle 21

The creativity, ideals and courage of the youth of the world should be mobilized to forge a global partnership in order to achieve sustainable development and ensure a better future for all.

Principle 22

Indigenous people and their communities, and other local communities, have a vital role in environmental management and development because of their knowledge and traditional practices. States should recognize and duly support their identity, culture and interests and enable their effective participation in the achievement of sustainable development.

Principle 23

The environment and natural resources of people under oppression, domination and occupation shall be protected.

Principle 24

Warfare is inherently destructive of sustainable development. States shall therefore respect international law providing protection for the environment in times of armed conflict and cooperate in its further development, as necessary.

Principle 25

Peace, development and environmental protection are interdependent and indivisible.

Principle 26

States shall resolve all their environmental disputes peacefully and by appropriate means in accordance with the Charter of the United Nations.

Principle 27

States and people shall cooperate in good faith and in a spirit of partnership in the fulfillment of the principles embodied in this Declaration and in the further development of international law in the field of sustainable development.

Appendix C

Agenda 21: Programme of Action for Sustainable Development – Table of Contents

1. Preamble

SECTION 1: SOCIAL AND ECONOMIC DIMENSIONS

2. International cooperation to accelerate sustainable development in developing countries and related domestic policies
3. Combating poverty
4. Changing consumption patterns
5. Demographic dynamics and sustainability
6. Protecting and promoting human health
7. Promoting sustainable human settlement development
8. Integrating environment and development in decision-making

SECTION 2: CONSERVATION AND MANAGEMENT OF RESOURCES FOR DEVELOPMENT

9. Protection of the atmosphere
10. Integrated approach to the planning and management of land resources
11. Combating deforestation
12. Managing fragile ecosystems:
    Combating desertification and drought
13. Managing fragile ecosystems:
    Sustainable mountain development
14. Promoting sustainable agriculture and rural development
15. Conservation of biological diversity
16. Environmentally sound management of biotechnology
17. Protection of the oceans, all kinds of seas, including enclosed and semi-enclosed seas, and coastal areas and the protection, rational use and development of their living resources
18. Protection of the quality and supply of freshwater resources:

Negotiating International Regimes: Lessons Learned from the United Nations Conference on Environment and Development (G. Sjöstedt, *et al.*, eds.; 1-85966-077-0; © IIASA; pub. Graham & Trotman, 1994; printed in Great Britain), pp. 265–266.

Application of integrated approaches to the development, management and use of water resources
19. Environmentally sound management of toxic chemicals, including prevention of illegal international traffic in toxic and dangerous products
20. Environmentally sound management of hazardous wastes, including prevention of illegal international traffic in hazardous wastes
21. Environmentally sound management of solid wastes and sewage-related issues
22. Safe and environmentally sound management of radioactive wastes

SECTION 3: STRENGTHENING THE ROLE OF MAJOR GROUPS

23. Preamble
24. Global action for women towards sustainable and equitable development
25. Children and youth in sustainable development
26. Recognizing and strengthening the role of indigenous people and their communities
27. Strengthening the role of non-governmental organizations: Partners for sustainable development
28. Local authorities' initiatives in support of Agenda 21
29. Strengthening the role of workers and their trade unions
30. Strengthening the role of business and industry
31. Scientific and technological community
32. Strengthening the role of farmers

SECTION 4: MEANS OF IMPLEMENTATION

33. Financial resources and mechanisms
34. Transfer of environmentally sound technology, cooperation and capacity-building
35. Science for sustainable development
36. Promoting education, public awareness and training
37. National mechanisms and international cooperation for capacity-building in developing countries
38. International institutional arrangements
39. International legal instruments and mechanisms
40. Information for decision-making

Bibliography

A/CONF.151/PC/24 (Document for UNCED PrepCom II), "Protection of Land Resources: An Integrated Approach," 24 January 1991.

A/CONF.151/PC/35 (Document for UNCED PrepCom II), "Environmentally Sound Management of Toxic Chemicals: Progress Report of the Secretary-General of the Conference," 31 January 1991.

A/CONF.151/PC/26 (Document for UNCED PrepCom II), "Progress report on the preparations for the FAO/Netherlands Conference on Agriculture and Environment," 24 January 1991.

A/CONF.151/PC/29 (Document for UNCED PrepCom II), "Environmentally Sound Management of Biotechnology," 31 January 1991.

A/CONF.151/PC/27 (Document for UNCED PrepCom II), "Conservation and Development of Forests: Progress Report by the Secretary-General of the Conference," 5 February 1991.

A/CONF.151/PC/28 (Document for UNCED PrepCom II), "Conservation of Biological Diversity," 5 February 1991.

A/CONF.151/PC/52 (Document for UNCED PrepCom III), "Science for Sustainable Development," 28 June 1991.

A/CONF.151/PC/42/Add.2 (Document for UNCED PrepCom III), "Protection and Management of Land Resources: Options for Agenda 21," 2 July 1991.

A/CONF.151/PC/43 (Document for UNCED PrepCom III), "Human Settlements," 4 July 1991.

A/CONF.151/PC/69 (Document for UNCED PrepCom III), "Protection of Oceans, All Kinds of Seas including Enclosed and Semi-Enclosed Seas, Coastal Areas and the Protection, Rational Use and Development of their Living Resources: Background Paper,"4 July 1991.

A/CONF.151/PC/51 (Document for UNCED PrepCom III), "Progress Report on Financial Resources," 5 July 1991.

A/CONF.151/PC/55 (Document for UNCED PrepCom III), "Education, Training, and Awareness for Sustainable Development," 9 July 1991.

A/CONF.151/PC/66 (Document for UNCED PrepCom III), "Conservation of Biological Diversity: Background and Issues," 9 July 1991.

A/CONF.151/PC/53 (Document for UNCED PrepCom III), "Report on Transfer of Technology," 10 July 1991.

A/CONF.151/PC/64 (Document for UNCED PrepCom III), "Conservation and Development of Forests," 10 July 1991.

A/CONF.151/PC/54 (Document for UNCED PrepCom III), "Environmental Health Aspects of Development," 11 July 1991.

A/CONF.151/PC/45 (Document for UNCED PrepCom III), "Poverty and Environmental Degradation," 19 July 1991.

A/CONF.151/PC/73 (Document for UNCED PrepCom III), "Protection of the Quality and Supply of Freshwater Resources: Application of Integrated Approaches to the Development, Management and Use of Water Resources," 25 July 1991.

A/CONF.151/PC/60 (Document for UNCED PrepCom III), "Protection of the Atmosphere: Sectoral Issues," 29 July 1991.

A/CONF.151/PC/76 (Document for UNCED PrepCom III), "Environmentally Sound Management of Solid Wastes and Sewage-Related Issues: Background," 29 July 1991.

A/CONF.151/PC/62 (Document for UNCED PrepCom III), "Protection and Management of Land Resources: Combatting Desertification and Drought," July 1991.

A/CONF.151/PC/47 (Document for UNCED PrepCom III), "The International Economy and Environment and Development," 2 August 1991.

A/CONF.151/PC/59 (Document for UNCED PrepCom III), "Protection of the Atmosphere: Transboundary Air Pollution," 3 August 1991.

A/CONF.151/PC/88 (Document for UNCED PrepCom III), "Prevention of Illegal International Traffic in Toxic and Dangerous Products and Wastes," 16 August 1991.

A/CONF.151/PC/100/Add.24/Annex I (Document for UNCED PrepCom IV), "Recommendations on International Strategy and Action Programme Including Technical Guidelines for the Environmentally Sound Management of Hazardous Wastes of the Ad Hoc Meeting of Government-Designated Experts Convened by UNEP, December 1991, Nairobi."

A/CONF.151/PC/103 (Document for UNCED PrepCom IV), "Survey of Existing Agreements and Instruments and its Follow-up," 20 January 1992.

AA/CONF.151/PC/100/Add.4 (Document for PrepCom IV), "Safe and Environmentally Sound Management of Radioactive Wastes," 12 December 1992.

A/CONF.151/PC/100/Add.18 (Document for PrepCom IV), "Managing Fragile Ecosystems: Sustainable Mountain Development," 12 December 1992.

Adams, Richard H., Jr. 1983. "The role of research in policy development: The creation of the IMF Cereal Import Facility." *World Development*. 11:7, pp. 549–563.

Advisory Panel on Food Security, Agriculture, Forestry and Environment to the World Commission on Environment and Development. (1987) *Food 2000: Global Policies for Sustainable Agriculture*. London: Zed Books.

Albin, Cecilia (1992) "Fairness Issues in Negotiation: Structure, Process, Procedures and Outcome." Working Paper WP-92-88, Laxenburg, Austria: International Institute for Applied Systems Analysis (December).

Alcamo, J. & Hordijk, L. & Shaw, R. (eds) (1990) *The RAINS Model of Acidification: Science and Strategies in Europe*, Dordrecht (Netherlands): Kluwer Academic Publishers.

Antrim, L. (1991) "Report on the Processes of Negotiation at the Preparatory Committee of the UN Conference on Environment and Development," Occasional Paper, Washington, DC: Project on Multilateral Negotiations (American Academy of Diplomacy and the Paul H. Nitze School of Advanced International Studies, April.

Antrim, L. and Chasek, P. (1992) "The UNCED Negotiating Process," *Ocean and Coastal Management*, Volume 18, number 1, pp. 79–99.

Antrim, Lance and James K. Sebenius (1992) "Formal Individual Mediation and the Negotiators' Dilemma: Tommy Koh and the Law of the Sea," in J. Bercovitch and J.Z. Rubin, eds.,

Mediation in International Relations: Multiple Approaches to Conflict Management. St. Martin's Press.

Assuncao, L. (1990) "Summary of the current state of preparations for the United Nations Conference on Environment and Development to be held in Brazil in 1992." (unofficial UN Document posted on Econet in conference en.unced.documents).

Austria (1992) *National Report*, UNCED.

Bachrach, Peter and Morton S. Baratz (1962) "Two Faces of Power," *American Political Science Review* 56, 4:947–952 (December).

Barratt-Brown, Elizabeth P. (1991) "Building a Monitoring and Compliance Regime Under the Montreal Protocol." *Yale Journal of International Law*. 2, pp. 519–70.

Bernstein, J., Chasek, P., and Goree, L. (1991) "PrepCom III: A Compilation of the Four Weekly Synopses," (document posted on Econet in conference en.unced.news), 9 September .

Bernstein, J., Chasek, P., and Goree, L. (1992a) "PrepCom IV: The Final Stop on the Road to Rio," *Earth Summit Bulletin*, Vol. 1, No. 27, 20 April.

Bernstein, J., Chasek, P., and Goree, L. (1992b) "A Summary of the Proceedings of the Fourth Session of the UNCED Preparatory Committee" *Earth Summit Bulletin*, Vol. 1, No. 27, 20 April.

Bernstein, J., Chasek, P., and Goree, L. (1992c) "Post-PrepCom Highlights," *Earth Summit Bulletin*, Vol. 2, No. 1, 1 June.

Bernstein, J., Chasek, P., and Goree, L. (1992d) "UNCED Highlights, 12 June 1992," *Earth Summit Bulletin*, Vol. 2, No. 11, 13 June.

Bernstein, J., Chasek, P., and Goree, L. (1992e) "A Summary of the Proceedings of the United Nations Conference on Environment and Development," *Earth Summit Bulletin*, Vol. 2, No. 13, 16 June.

Bhagwati, J.N. (ed) (1997) *The New International Economic Order: The North-South Debate*, Cambridge (Mass.): MIT Press.

Boehmer-Christiansen, S.A. (1991) *Acid Politics: Energy and Environmental Policies in Germany and Britain*. London: Belhaven.

Boehmer-Christiansen, S.A. (1992a) "How Much Science Does Environmental Performance Really Need?" in E. Lykke, ed., Achieving Environmental Goals. London: Belhaven.

Boehmer-Christiansen, S.A. (1992b) "Environmental Policy-Making: Science or Technology-Led?" International Environmental Affairs (Autumn).

Bolin, Bert, R.A., Warrick, Bo *Döös*, and J. Jäger, eds (1986) *SCOPE 29: The Greenhouse Effect – Climatic Change and Ecosystems*. Chichester: Wiley and Sons.

Bread for the World. (1987) *Policy Statement on U.S. Agriculture*. Washington, DC: Bread for the World, May.

Bread for the World. (1989) *Agriculture Advisory Statement*. Washington, DC: Bread for the World, August.

Brown, Lester, et al. (1984) *State of the World 1984*. New York: W.W. Norton.

Brundtland Bulletin. (1990) Issue 9/10.

Burton, John (1990) *Conflict: Resolution and Provention*. New York: St. Martin's Press.

Carnevale, Peter and Dean Pruitt (1992) "Negotiation and Mediation." *Annual Review of Psychology* 43:531–82.

Centre for Applied Studies in International Negotiations (1992) *Issues and Non Governmental Organizations Programs*. Report on NGO Activities at UNCED and the Global Forum. Geneva: CASIN.

Chayes, Abram and Antonia Chayes (1991) "Compliance Without Enforcement: State Behavior Under Regulatory Treaties," *Negotiation Journal*, July.

Chiang, Pei-heng. (1981) *Non-Governmental Organizations at the United Nations*. New York: Praeger Publishers.

Churchill, R. and D. Freestone, eds. (1992) *International Law and Climate Change*. London: Graham and Trotman/Nijhoff.

CONGO Planning Committee (1991–1992) *Crosscurrents, An Independent Newspaper for UNCED*.

Cross, John (1978) "Negotiation as a Learning Process," in I. William Zartman, ed., *The Negotiation Process, Theories and Applications*. Beverly Hills, CA: Sage Publications.

Cross, J. G. (1983) *A Theory of Adaptive Economic Behaviour*, Cambridge (England): Cambridge University Press.

Desai, N. (1991) "Second preparatory meeting to bring issues into sharper focus," *Earth Summit News*, Vol.1 No.1, UNCED, Conches, Geneva, Switzerland.

Dooge J., et al. (1992) *An Agenda of Science for Environment and Development into the 21st Century*, Cambridge University Press.

Drèze, Jean and Amartya Sen, eds. (1990) *The Political Economy of Hunger, Vol 1, Entitlements and Well-Being*. Oxford: Clarendon Press.

Druckman, Daniel (1973) *Human Factors in International Negotiations: Social Psychological Aspects of International Conflicts*. Beverly Hills, CA: Sage Publications.

Druckman, D. (ed.) (1977) *Negotiations: Social-Psychological Perspectives*, Beverly Hills: Sage.

Druckman, Daniel (1986) "Stages, Turning Points and Crises: Negotiating Military Base Rights, Spain and the United States," *Journal of Conflict Resolution* 30: 327–360.

Druckman, Daniel (1993) "Situational Levers of Negotiation Flexibility, *Journal of Conflict Resolution*, (May).

Druckman, Daniel, Jo Husbands, and K. Johnston (1991) "Turning Points in the INF Negotiations," *Negotiation Journal* 6: 55–67.

Dubash, Navroz and Michael Oppenheimer. (1992) "Modifying the Mandate of Existing Institutions: NGOs." In Irving M. Mintzer, ed. *Confronting Climate Change: Risks, Implications and Responses*. Great Britain: Cambridge University Press.

Earth Summit Bulletin (1991–1992) as published during the PrepCom and UNCED.

Earth Negotiation Bulletin (ENB) (1992–1993) various issues.

ECOSOC. (1968) United Nations ECOSOC Resolution 1296. "Arrangements for Consultation with NGOs."

Environment Canada (1990/1991) *The International Environment: A Reference Book*, Vol I and II.

Ezekiel, Hannan. (1989) *Food Aid, Food Imports and the Food Consumption of the Poor.* Mimeo. Washington, DC: International Food Policy Research Institute. December 27.

Falk, Richard. (1971) *This Endangered Planet: Prospects and Proposals for Human Survival.* New York: Vintage Books.

Finger, Matthias and Pratap Chatterjee. (1992) *EcoCurrents.* Geneva: Ecogreen.

Fisher, Roger, William Ury, and Bruce Patton (1991) *Getting to Yes, Second Edition.* New York: Penguin Books.

Food and Agriculture Organization. (1987) *Evaluation of the Food Security Assistance Scheme.* Rome: FAO, November.

Garcia, Jorge Garcia. (1981) "The nature of food insecurity in Colombia," in Alberto Valdes, (ed.) *Food Security for Developing Countries.* Boulder, CO: Westview Press.

Global Environment Facility (1992) *Report by the Chairman to the December 1992 Participants' Meeting, Part 1: Main Report.* Washington, DC: Global Environment Facility.

Global Environmental Change Report (1992) Vol. IV, No. 22: 6 (20 November).

Goodwin, Neva R. (1991) "Lessons for the world from U.S. agriculture: Unbundling technology." *World Development.* 19:1, pp. 85–102.

Goree, L. (1990) "PrepCom I Chronicles." Posted on ECONET in conference en.unced.-general.

Goree, L. (1991) "PrepCom II Chronicles." (document posted on Econet in conference en.unced.general), March–April.

Haas, P.M. (1991) "Obtaining International Environmental Protection through Epistemic Consensus" in Rowlands, I. H. & Greene, M. (eds) *Global Environmental Change and International Relations,* London: Macmillan Academic and Professional Ltd.

Hanson, Arthur J. and Gabriel Regallet. (1992) "Communicating for Sustainable Development." *Nature and Resources.* 28:1.

Hathaway, Dale. (1981) *Testimony before the United States House of Representatives Committee on Agriculture,* July 22.

Herter, Christian Jr. and Jill Binder (1993) *The Role of the Secretariat in Multilateral Negotiation: The Case of Maurice Strong and the 1972 U.N. Conference on the Human Environment.* From the Case Study Series of the Project on Multilateral Negotiation. Washington: American Academy of Diplomacy and the Paul H. Nitze School of Advanced International Studies, Johns Hopkins University.

Homans, George (1961) *Social Behavior.* NY: Harcourt Brace Jovanovich.

Houghton, J.T., et al., eds. (1990) *Climate Change, The IPCC Scientific Assessment.* Cambridge: Cambridge University Press.

Huddleston, Barbara, D. Gale Johnson, Shlomo Reutlinger, Alberto Valdes. (1984) *International Finance for Food Security.* Baltimore: Johns Hopkins Press for World Bank.

Human Development Report (1990) United Nations Development Programme

Hurrell, Andrew and Benedict Kingsbury, eds (1992) *The International Politics of the Environment.* Oxford: Clarendon Press.

Hussain, Saneeya. (1992) "Reflections on Rio". *Concordare.* Cambridge: Harvard Law School.

ICSU (1991) *Science International* (September).

Iklé, Frederick and Nathan Leites (1962) "Political Negotiation as a Process of Modifying Utilities," *Journal of Conflict Resolution* 6: 19–28.

Independant Sector Network. Multiple issues.

Intergovernmental Panel on Climate Change (IPCC). Martin L. Parry, lead author. (1990) *The Potential Impact of Climate Change on Agriculture and Forestry*. Draft report, April.

International Institute for Applied Systems Analysis, Environment and Development Project. (1991) *Systems Analysis, Conceptual Models, and Their Role in UNCED*. Mimeo. Laxenburg, Austria: IIASA, revised July.

Katheryn Sessions (1992) "Institutionalizing the Earth Summit: The UN Commission on Sustainable Development, United Nations Association, Occasional Paper No. 2, October.

Khan, S.A. (1989) "Global Development Challenges – The Potential of Third World Non-Governmental Organizations." *Bulletin of Peace Proposals*. 18:2, pp. 105–108.

Koester, Ulrich and Alberto Valdes. (1984) "The EC's potential role for food security for LDCs: Adjustments in its STABEX and stock policies." *European Review of Agricultural Economics*. 11: 415–437.

Koh, Tommy T.B. and Shanmugam Jayakumar (1985) "The Negotiating Process of the Third United Nations Conference on the Law of the Sea," in Myron Nordquist, ed., *United Nations Convention on the Law of the Sea, 1982: A Commentary*, volume 1. Dordrecht: Martinus Nijhoff.

Koh, Tommy T.B. (1992) "The Earth Summit's Negotiating Process: Some Reflections on the Art and Science of Negotiation," *The Seventh Singapore Law Review Lecture*, Faculty of Law, National University of Singapore, December 15, 1992.

Krasner, S., ed. (1983) *International Regimes*. Ithaca, NY: Cornell University Press.

Kremenyuk, Victor, editor (1991) *International Negotiation: Analysis, Approaches, Issues*. San Francisco: Jossey-Bass Publishers.

Kremenyuk, Victor A. "The Emerging System of International Negotiation," in Victor A. Kremenyuk, ed., *International Negotiation*. San Francisco: Jossey-Bass, 1991. pp. 22–39.

Kressel, Kenneth, Dean Pruitt, and Associates (1989) *Mediation Research: The Process and Effectiveness of Third-Party Intervention*. San Francisco, CA: Jossey-Bass.

Lador-Lederer, J. Joseph. (1963) *International Non-Governmental Organizations and Economic Entities: A Study in Autonomous Organizations and Ius Gentium*. Leyden: A.W. Sythoff.

Lang, Winfried (1989) "Multilateral Negotiations: The Role of Presiding Officers," in F. Mautner-Markhof, ed., *Processes of International Negotiations*. Boulder: Westview Press.

Lappé, Frances Moore and Joseph Collins. (1978) *Food First*. New York: Ballantine.

Lele, Uma and Winfred Chandler. (1981) "Food security: Some East African considerations," in Alberto Valdes, ed. *Food Security for Developing Countries*. Boulder, CO: Westview Press.

Lerner, Steven. (1992) *Beyond the Earth Summit*. Washington: Commonweal.

Livezey, L.W. (1984) "Human Rights and the NGOs." *Center Magazine*. 17:3.

Luce, R.D. & Raiffa, D. (1957) *Games and Decisions*, New York: Wiley.

May, Elizabeth. (1990) "News From Nairobi." Posted on ECONET in conference en.unced.general.

McCormick, J. (1989) *The Global Environmental Movement*. London: Belhaven.

McCormick, John. (1989) *Reclaiming Paradise: The Global Environmental Movement*. Bloomington: Indiana University Press.

McCracken, Michael (1992) *The Scientist*, 4 May: 30.

McDonald, John W. (1990) *Global Environmental Negotiations: The 1972 Stockholm Conference and Lessons for the Future*. American Academy of Diplomacy Occasional Paper #2, January.

Najam, Adil (1993) "A Strategy for the South", to appear in Lawrence Susskind, William Moomaw, and Adil Najam, *International Environmental Negotiation*, Vol. 3 (Program on Negotiation at Harvard Law School, Cambridge, Massachusetts).

Nash, J.F. (1950) "The Bargaining Problem", *Econometrica* 18: 155–162.

NGO Press Releases. Posted on ECONET on en.unced.general.

Palme, T. (1992) "Rio-konferensen. FN:s konferens om miljö och utvecking i Rio de Janeiro i juni 1992.", *UD informerar, 1992:5*, Utrikesdepartementet: Stockholm.

Parikh, Jyoti K. (1992) "IPCC Response Strategies: Unfair to Poor?" *Nature* (December).

Parikh, Kirit S. (1990) "Chronic hunger in the world: Impact of international policies." In Jean Drèze and Amartya Sen, eds. *The Political Economy of Hunger, Vol 1, Entitlements and Well-Being*. Oxford: Clarendon Press, pp. 114–145.

Paterson, Matthew (1992) in Caroline Thomas, ed., *The Environment in Industrial Relations*. London: RIIA. pp. 155–195.

Porter, Gareth and Janet Brown (1991) *Global Environmental Politics*. Boulder: Westview Press.

Price, F. (1992) "The Evolution of Global Environmental Change: Issues, Research, Programmes," in *Impact of Science on Society*, No. 166. Paris: UNESCO.

Proceedings of *Bergen Conference on Sustainable Development, Science and Policy* (1990) Bergen, Norway, May.

Proctor, R.N. (1991) *Value-Free Science? Purity and Power in Modern Knowledge*. Cambridge, MA: Harvard University Press.

Pruitt, Dean (1981) *Negotiation Behavior*. New York: Academic Press.

Raiffa, Howard (1982) *The Art and Science of Negotiation*. Cambridge, MA: Belknap Press/ Harvard University Press.

Rapoport, A. (1964) *Two-Person Games*, Ann Arbor: University of Michigan Press.

Rittberger, Volker. (1983) "Global Conference Diplomacy and International Policy-Making: The Case of UN-Sponsored World Conferences." *European Journal of Political Research* 11 pp. 167–182.

Roddick, Jacqueline (1993) "UNCED, its Stakeholders, and Post-UNCED Process: The Commission on Sustainability," to be published in the *Journal of Global Environmental Change* Draft.

Rothman, Jay (1992) *From Confrontation to Cooperation: Resolving Ethnic and Regional Conflict*. Newbury Park, CA: Sage Publications.

Rubin, Jeffrey and Bert Brown (1975) *The Social Psychology of Bargaining and Negotiation*. New York: Academic Press.

Sand, Peter H. (1990) *Lessons Learned in Global Environmental Governance*, Washington: World Resources Institute.

Sen, Amartya. (1990) "Food, economics, and entitlements." In Jean Drèze and Amartya Sen, eds. *The Political Economy of Hunger, Vol 1, Entitlements and Well-Being*. Oxford: Clarendon Press, pp. 34–52.

Shaw, Roderick. (1991) *Environment and development: Agricultural land requirements in 2025*. Mimeo. Laxenburg, Austria: International Institute for Applied Systems Analysis. April 26.

Shaw, Roderick, G. Gallopin, P. Weaver, and S. Öberg (1991) "Sustainable Development: A Systems Approach." Final Report. Laxenburg, Austria: International Institute for Applied Systems Analysis (December).

Sjöstedt, Gunnar. (1991) *The Issue Analysis: A Summary Research Outline*. Mimeo. International Institute for Applied Systems Analysis and the Swedish Institute of International Affairs, June.

Sjöstedt, Gunnar, editor (1993) *International Environmental Negotiations*. Newbury Park, CA: Sage Publications.

Sjöstedt, G. (1994) "The Story of the Uruguay Round" in Zartman, I.W., ed., *International Multilateral Negotiations*, San Francisco, CA: Jossey-Bass Publishers.

Sjöstedt, Gunnar (1993) "Negotiations on Nuclear Pollution: The Vienna Conventions on Notification and Assistance in Case of a Nuclear Accident," in Gunnar Sjöstedt, editor, *International Environmental Negotiation*. Newbury Park, CA: Sage Publications.

Sjöstedt, Gunnar and Bertram I. Spector (1993) "Conclusions" in G. Sjöstedt, ed., *International Environmental Negotiation*. Newbury Park, CA: Sage Publications.

Sohn, Louis B. (1973) "The Stockholm Declaration on the Human Environment," *Harvard International Law Journal*, Vol. 14, 3:423–515.

Spector, Bertram I. (1983) "A Social-Psychological Model of Position Modification: Aswan," in I. William Zartman, ed., *The 50% Solution*. New Haven: Yale University Press.

Spector, Bertram (1991) "The Development of Agenda 21: Generating a Viable Formula." Laxenburg, Austria: International Institute for Applied Systems Analysis. Working Paper WP-91-14,. (May).

Spector, Bertram I. (1992) *International Environmental Negotiation, Insight for Practice*, Executive Report, Laxenburg: IIASA.

Spector, Bertram (1993a) "Decision Analysis: Evaluating Multilateral Negotiation Processes," in I. William Zartman, editor, *International Multilateral Negotiation*. San Francisco, CA: Jossey-Bass.

Spector, Bertram (1993b) "Decision Analysis for Practical Negotiation Application," *Theory and Decision*, 34,3 (May).

Spector, Bertram, guest editor (1993c) "International Negotiation: Theory, Methods, and Support Systems," special issue of *Theory and Decision*, 34, 3 (May).

Spector, Bertram I. and Anna R. Korula (1992) "Facilitative Mediation in International Disputes: From Research to Practical Application." Laxenburg, Austria: IIASA Working Paper WP-92-16 (February).

Spector, Bertram I. and Anna R. Korula (1993) "Problems of Ratifying International Environmental Agreements: Overcoming Initial Obstacles in the Post-Agreement Negotiation Process." *Global Environmental Change* 17, 4:369–381 (December).

Starke, Linda (1992) *Signs of Hope*, The Center for our Common Future.

Stein, J. (ed.) (1989) *Getting to the Table*, Baltimore (Md): Johns Hopkins University Press.

Susskind, Lawrence (1994) *Environmental Diplomacy: Negotiating More Effective Global Agreements*, Oxford University Press, New York.

Swedish UNCED Delegation (1992) Telefax 1992–06–08: "UNCED – rapport från första veckan (Report from the first week)."

Szell, Patrick (1993) "Negotiations on the Ozone Layer," in Gunnar Sjöstedt, editor, *International Environmental Negotiation*. Newbury Park, CA: Sage Publications.

Thacher, Peter (1993) "The Mediterranean: A New Approach to Marine Pollution," in Gunnar Sjöstedt, editor, *International Environmental Negotiation*. Newbury Park, CA: Sage Publications.

Tolba, Mustafa (1982) *Development without Destruction*. Dublin: Tycool.

Tolba, Mostafa. (1988) *Evolving Environmental Perceptions from Stockholm to Nairobi*. Nairobi: United Nations Environment Program.

Touraine, Alain. (1985) "Social Movements and Social Change." *Social Research*. 52:4.

Touval, Saadia and I. W. Zartman (1985) "Introduction: Mediation in Theory," in S. Touval and I. W. Zartman, editors, *International Mediation in Theory and Practice*. Boulder, CO: Westview Press.

Towards Sustainability, A European Community Programme of Policy and Action in relation to the Environment and Sustainable Development (1992). Brussels: European Community.

Ulvila, Jacob (1990) "Turning Points: An Analysis." in J. McDonald Jr. and D. Bendahmane, editors, *U.S. Bases Overseas*. Boulder, CO: Westview Press.

Ulvila, Jacob and Warren Snider (1980) "Negotiation of International Oil Tanker Standards: An Application of Multiattribute Value Theory." *Operations Research* 28 (81–96).

UNCED (1992) Decisions 1/25; 1/28; 1/29.

UNCED (1991) "Second Prepcom identifies areas for action," *Earth Summit News*, Vol. 1 No. 2, UNCED, Conches, Geneva, Switzerland.

UNCED (1991) *Newsletter*, March 11.

J.W.M. la Rivière and J. Marton-Lefèvre (1992) *UNCED and its Implications for ICSU's Future Work, Science International*, December.

Underdal, A. (1992) "The Concept of Regime "Effectiveness", *Cooperation and Conflict*, volume 27, number 3.

UNDPI (1992) "Atop the Summit: World Leaders Meet to Push for Sustainable Development," UN Department of Public Information Earth Summit Press Release.

United Nations, Economic Commission for Europe (1979) *Convention on Long-Range Transboundary Air Pollution*.

United Nations. (1989) "United Nations Conference on Environment and Development," General Assembly Resolution 44/228, 22 December.

United Nations. (1992) *Agenda 21*. New York: United Nations, August.

United Nations Economic Commission for Europe (ECE). (1990) *Bergen Ministerial Declaration on Sustainable Development in the ECE Region*. A/CONF.151/PC/10.

United Nations Economic and Social Commission for Asia and the Pacific (ESCAP). (1991) *Report of the Meeting of Senior Officials on Environment and Development in Asia and the Pacific*. IHE/SOED/Rep and Annex. March 19.

United Nations Economic and Social Commission for Asia and the Pacific (ESCAP). (1990) *Report of the Ministerial Level Conference on Environment and Development in Asia and the Pacific*. IHE/MCED/Rep., November 19.

United Nations Development Program (UNDP). (1991) *Human Development Report 1991*. press release, May 22.

United Nations Conference on Environment and Development, Preparatory Committee (UNCED PrepCom) Secretariat Reports. (1990–1991) A/CONF.151/various reports.

United Nations Economic Commission for Latin America and the Caribbean (ECLAC). *(1991) Sustainable Development: Changing Production Patterns, Social Equity and the Environment*. Santiago, Chile. LC/G.1648 (CONF.80/2)Rev. 1. February 12.

United Nations Economic Commission for Europe (ECE) (1991) *ECE Synthesis Paper Based on the National Reports Submitted by the ECE Member Governments*. April. GE.90–21329.

United Nations Non-Governmental Organizations Liaison Service. 1992. "NGOs at PrepCom IV." E&D File Number 25.

Valdes, Alberto and Panos Konandreas. (1981) "Assessing food insecurity based on national aggregates in developing countries", in Alberto Valdes, ed. *Food Security for Developing Countries*. Boulder, CO: Westview Press.

von Braun, Joachim. (1988) "Effects of technological change in agriculture on food consumption and nutrition: Rice in a West African setting." *World Development*. 16:9 pp. 1083–1098.

Wall, Jr., James (1981) "Mediation: An Analysis, Review, and Proposed Research," *Journal of Conflict Resolution* 25: 157–80.

Weart, Spencer (1992) "From the Nuclear Frying Pan into the Global Fire," *Bulletin of Atomic Scientists* (June): 19–27.

Willets, Peter, ed. (1982) *Pressure Groups in the Global System*. London: Frances Pinter Publishers Limited.

Winham, G.R. (1986) *International Trade and the Tokyo Round Negotiations*, Princeton, N.J.: Princeton University Press.

Winham, Gilbert and Karin Kizer (1993) "The Uruguay Round Midterm Review" Washington, DC: Foreign Policy Institute, Johns Hopkins University, School of Advanced International Studies.

Wolf, Amanda. (1990) *Food Security in Relation to a Major Employment-Oriented Development Effort: Policies for Ensuring Reliability of Food Supply in the Context of Increasing Demand*. Mimeo. Washington, DC: International Food Policy Research Institute, May.

Wolz, Brigit (1992) "The Commission on Sustainability," paper submitted December, 1992 to the Seminar on International Environmental Negotiations at the Massachusetts Institute of Technology.

*World Development Report (*1990).Washington DC: World Bank.

World Resources Institute (1992–1993) *Towards Sustainable Development, A Guide to the Global Environment, 1992*. Washington, DC: WRI.

World Commission on Environment and Development (WCED). (1987) *Our Common Future*. Oxford: Oxford University Press.

World Bank. (1986) *Poverty and Hunger: Issues and Options for Food Security in Developing Countries*. Washington, DC: World Bank.

Young, Oran (1989) *International Cooperation: Building Regimes for Natural Resources and the Environment*. Ithaca, NY: Cornell University Press.

Young, Oran (1992) "The Effectiveness of International Institutions: Hard Cases and Critical Variables," in James N. Rosenau and Ernst-Otto Czempiel (Editors), *Governance Without Government: Order and Change in the World of Politics*, (Cambridge University Press, Cambridge, Massachusetts) pp. 160–192.

Zartman, I. William (1987) *Positive Sum: Improving North-South Negotiation*. New Brunswick, NJ: Transaction.

Zartman, I. William and Maureen R. Berman (1982) *The Practical Negotiator*. Yale University Press.

Zartman, I. William (1993) "Lessons for Analysis and Practice," in Gunnar Sjöstedt, editor, *International Environmental Negotiation*. Newbury Park, CA: Sage Publications.

Zartman, I. William (1994) ed., *International Multilateral Negotiations*. San Francisco, CA: Jossey-Bass Publishers.

Index